NORFOLK
IN THE
SECOND WORLD WAR

A PICTORIAL HISTORY 1939-1945

NEIL R. STOREY

HALSGROVE

British Library Cataloguing-in-Publication Data
A CIP record for this title is available from the British Library

ISBN 978 1 84114 990 5

HALSGROVE
Halsgrove House,
Ryelands Industrial Estate,
Bagley Road, Wellington, Somerset TA21 9PZ
Tel: 01823 653777   Fax: 01823 216796
email: sales@halsgrove.com

Part of the Halsgrove group of companies
Information on all Halsgrove titles is available at: www.halsgrove.com

Printed and bound in Great Britain by SRP Ltd., Exeter

Contents

DANGER of INVASION

Last year all who could be spared from this town were asked to leave, not only for their own safety, but so as to ease the work of the Armed Forces in repelling an invasion.

The danger of invasion has increased and the Government requests all who can be spared, and have somewhere to go, to leave without delay.

This applies particularly to :—

SCHOOL CHILDREN
MOTHERS WITH YOUNG CHILDREN
AGED AND INFIRM PERSONS
PERSONS LIVING ON PENSIONS
PERSONS WITHOUT OCCUPATION
**   OR IN RETIREMENT**

If you are one of these, you should arrange to go to some other part of the country. You should not go to the coastal area of East Anglia, Kent or Sussex.

School children can be registered to join school parties in the reception areas, and billets will be found for them.

If you are in need of help you can have your railway fare paid and a billeting allowance paid to any relative or friend with whom you stay.

If you are going, go quickly.

Take your
NATIONAL REGISTRATION IDENTITY CARD
RATION BOOK
GAS MASK

ALSO any bank book, pensions payment order book, insurance cards, unemployment book, military registration documents, passport, insurance policies, securities and any ready money.

If your house will be left unoccupied, turn off gas, electricity and water supplies and make provision for animals and birds. Lock your house securely. Blinds should be left up, and if there is a telephone line, ask the telephone exchange to disconnect it.

Apply at the Local Council Offices for further information.

Private Car and Motor Cycle owners who have not licensed their vehicles and have no petrol coupons may be allowed to use their cars unlicensed for one journey only and may apply to the Police for petrol coupons to enable them to secure sufficient petrol to journey to their destination.

ESSENTIAL WORKERS MUST STAY
particularly the following classes :—

Members of the Home Guard
Observer Corps
Coastguards, Coast Watchers and Lifeboat Crews
Police and Special Constabulary
Fire Brigade and Auxiliary Fire Service
A.R.P. and Casualty Services
Members of Local Authorities and their officials and employees
Workers on the land
Persons engaged on war work, and other essential services
Persons employed by contractors on defence work
Employees of water, sewerage, gas & electricity undertakings
Persons engaged in the supply and distribution of food
Workers on export trades
Doctors, Nurses and Chemists
Ministers of Religion
Government Employees
Employees of banks
Employees of transport undertakings,
**   namely railways, docks, canals, ferries,**
**   and road transport (both passenger and goods).**

When invasion is upon us it may be necessary to evacuate the remaining population of this and certain other towns. Evacuation would then be compulsory at short notice, in crowded trains, with scanty luggage, to destinations chosen by the Government. If you are not among the essential workers mentioned above, it is better to go now while the going is good.

Invasion danger notice displayed in coastal towns and villages in Norfolk, 1941

Introduction

The Second World War had a profound and unprecedented effect on the people of Norfolk. During that conflict thousands of local men and women 'did their bit' in the armed forces while so many others they left behind were part of a most remarkable effort, many of them facing extreme danger, on the home front in a host of occupations, volunteer and auxiliary forces. This book is an overview of their stories, much of it in the words of documents, books, newspapers and periodicals written or published during the war or in the immediate aftermath. I do not claim to be encyclopaedic but I sincerely hope this volume will prove to be a useful starting point or reference work for researchers over the years to come and some small tribute to all those from our county who gave so much during the conflict.

By way of an introduction to this book I am drawn to the thoughts of those who were present on the eve of the Second World War; especially the bright young men who stood on the brink of manhood in 1939; sons of those who had returned from the 'War to end all Wars,' too young to personally recall that conflict but witness to the world crisis unfurling before them, epitomised in the editorial of *The Gresham*, the school magazine for Gresham's School, Holt, published in the February of that fateful year:

> *'The future of the world rests in the hands of the younger generation.' How many times have we heard this? It may surely be said that wherever there is a concentration of youth, be it at a meeting of the Hitler Jugend or an English School (Speech Day) this remark will appear in one form or another. A little reflection will reveal the kind of responsibility which older generations have bestowed upon us. Strife, turmoil and distress characterise the world to-day. At home, for example we find two million unemployed and abroad, terrorism and persecution.*
>
> *How we, the younger generation, respond to the demands which will have to be made of us, if the affairs of the world are to be straightened out, depends upon the way in which we are being launched into this world. It will be evident that a Hitler Youth and a member of an educational institution in this country will act very differently under the responsibility of the future. For the young German, from his earliest days, will have been fostered with propaganda. His ideas have been formed for him, and he is given little chance of rational thought. In this country, however, our education claims – and the claim is just – to promote reason and protect the young mind against the floods of propaganda and the storms of national emotion. Its object is to teach us to be responsible citizens (how often also have we heard this!). Because it is our privilege, or perhaps our fate, to be educated in this way, responsibility of the future rests all the more heavily upon our shoulders; it is important we should realise that.*
>
> *In a school like ours, which is situated 'away from the madding crowd' we are sheltered from the world, and we tend to forget the importance of the things that are happening around us. But the very fact that we are thus protected makes our training all the easier and all the more effective. While we are here, nurtured with enlightenment (and boiled milk) we must avail ourselves to the fullest extent, of the facilities laid before us. Only by so doing can we be fully prepared for what the future has in store for us. For there is much to be done in the world to-day. Somebody must do it and we cannot always leave it to someone else.'*

Neil R. Storey
2010

The Gresham's School OTC shooting team on the eve of the Second World War. (GSA)

Acknowledgements

The author would like to express his gratitude to all those individuals, families, museums and organisations that have so generously shared their memories, archives, collections and research with the him over the last twenty five years. There are too many to mention all by name but he would like to extend his personal thanks to the following:

Stewart P. Evans, Bob Collis, Bruce Hogg, Mike Osborne, Peter Brooks, Peter Stibbons, John Warwicker, John Lincoln, Mary Blathwayt, Ivor Self, Pamela Austin, Merv Hambling, Alex Noel-Todd, Adrian Hoare, Judy Ball, Joan Banger, Geoff Caulton, John Gilbert, Jim Baldwin, Mick Jennings, the late John Slaughter, Major John Raybould, Theo Fanthorpe, Robert Skinner, Michael Bean, Roy Scott, Kate Thaxton, Curator of The Royal Norfolk Regimental Museum, The late Colonel John Boag and Major Gary Walker, The Suffolk and Norfolk Yeomanry, Norfolk Local Studies Library, The Second Air Division Memorial Library, King's Lynn Library, Great Yarmouth Library, University of East Anglia Library, Norfolk Record Office, The British Resistance Organisation Museum, Parham, Maggie Secker, BBC Radio Norfolk, The Norfolk & Suffolk Aviation Museum, Flixton, The Imperial War Museum, The Royal Naval Museum, Portsmouth, The National Archives, Megan Dennis, Gressenhall Farm and Workhouse Museum of Norfolk Life, The Norfolk Federation of Women's Institutes, The Norfolk St John Ambulance Archive, Mundesley Maritime Museum, The Griffon Area Partnership, The Commonwealth War Graves Commission. Thanks must be extended to my wonderful students and lecture audiences for their interest and input and last but by no means least to my dear son Lawrence and beloved Molly for all their love and support.

Picture Credits

(GC) Geoff Caulton

(GSA) Gresham's School Archive

(GFWM) Gressenhall Farm and Workhouse Museum of Norfolk Life

(IWM) Imperial War Museum

(JG) John Gilbert

(RC) Bob Collis

(MMM) Mundesley Maritime Museum

The funeral cortège of Pilot Oberfw. Wilhelm Stolle and Observer Hellmut Krüger from the Dornier Do.17Z-3 that crashed off Scolt Head. Pictured by the wall of the churchyard at Old Catton, August 1940. (RC)

1 The Road to War

On 19 January 1915 the first bombs dropped by Zeppelins on English soil fell on a number of locations along the Norfolk coast. Four were killed and many were injured. Over the next few years of the war Zeppelins droned over the landscape to bomb London and other locations across the country. Even after the Armistice in 1918 the spectre of aerial bombardment remained in the minds of many. As early as 1921 a War Office and Air Ministry joint committee was set up to consider the defence of South East England, south of a line drawn from Portland Bill to The Wash. The committee found 'a highly organised system is essential for the rapid collection and distribution of information and intelligence regarding the movements of hostile and friendly aircraft throughout the whole area of possible air operations.' From these findings the first air observation posts were set up around London.

Officers of the No.3 Acceptance Park RAF Mousehold Heath, Norwich, November 1918

By the 1930s aircraft technology had grown apace. In 1933 H.G. Wells published *The Shape of Things to Come* in which he, albeit fictionally, explored the potential changes wrought in the nature of warfare and included harrowing descriptions of cities destroyed by bombing.

Wells had, in fact, articulated a wider ground swell of public concern about air attacks. In October 1933 the Air Defence Intelligence System was extended to include the counties of Dorset, Norfolk and Suffolk. The inaugural meeting for the formation and recruitment of the Norfolk Observer Corps was held at The Norwich Lad's Club early 1934 but the planned recruitment talk was found to be unnecessary because Mr John Dain the Chief Constable of Norwich had already spoken to a number of likely local contacts and had mustered all the volunteers initially required for the new OC unit entirely from the offices of Norwich Union. In those early days, because of the military sensitive nature of their duties, all OC volunteers were sworn in as Special Constables. In effect the OC volunteers served two masters: the police who maintained them and the military authorities for Air Defence. Soon after joining the volunteers would receive a certificate of membership, OC lapel badge and arm band. This latter item looked like a police 'on duty' arm band but had the title Observer Corps picked out in red letters over the stripes.

The location of OC Posts was always dependant on their proximity to centres of habitation and telephone lines for their reports to the plotting centre. Most observers provided their own binoculars; the main instrument they were trained upon and issued. One observer would sight along a piece of wood while another worked a 'height' bar and read off height and direction – a rather Heath Robinson arrangement by all accounts but it was cheap to produce and simple to operate. The first posts were established at Mundesley and Wymondham with more rapidly following until by the end of November 1934 there were 34 OC Posts across the county and a Centre or Operations Room in a semi-basement under the Norwich Telephone Exchange at the corner of Dove Street and Guildhall Hill. The area to be known as 16 Group (Southern Area) was ready and became operational on 1 March 1935 with S. C. 'Nobby' Spalding as the first Group Controller.

Dr Otto Lund reporting in from the Mundesley Observer Corps Post

In September 1935 Prime Minister Stanley Baldwin issued a circular entitled Air Raid Precautions (ARP) that invited local authorities to set up working committees and undertake measures, such as the construction of public shelters to protect the populace. In Norfolk the County Council sent delegates to a regional conference organised by the Home Office at Cambridge to consider precautions to be taken in the event of air raids. Norfolk and most of the County Councils across the country did take on board the need to establish ARP committees and did so, the Norfolk County Air Raid Precautions Committee held their first meeting in February 1936, but very few went so far as to construct any shelters. Many of the local emergency services also registered their interest with their local committees and asked for emergency plans to be drawn up.

It took events on the world stage during the Spanish Civil War and the international horror and revulsion at the bombing of Madrid in November 1936 to galvanise the active development of air raid precautions in Britain.

St John Ambulance County Officer William Balls demonstrates the Service Gas Mask at the M&GN Railway Station, Cromer, March 1936 (GFWM)

The same month the British Government took direct action and created an Air Raid Wardens Service and emergency services were beginning to hold ARP courses. At the Norfolk Ambulance conference at Attleborough in January 1937 it was reported by St John Ambulance County Officer William H. Balls that some ARP courses had been held but they had been having great difficulty procuring lecturers so he hoped it would soon be possible to train members from the county to become qualified instructors in their own right. Mr H.O. Brown, Deputy Clerk to Norfolk County Council stated, on behalf of the council, that they were 'looking to the St John Ambulance and to their sister organisation, the Red Cross to staff the dressing stations and first aid aspects of ARP in Norfolk.' These were to be under the general supervision of Dr Ruddock West. It was intended there would be 'base hospitals' in the Poor Law Institutions and 'casualty clearing hospitals' in the general and cottage hospitals of the county. These would be staffed by local GPs and trained nursing staff from hospitals and institutions and district nurses. The voluntary aid societies would be responsible for first aid posts based in schools and similar public buildings, mobile first aid parties and casualty transport.

Norfolk Constabulary had recently been issued with a gas van and had appointed an Inspector who commenced training with volunteers from Norwich City Council. The van was equipped with a 'chamber' to pass through wearing a gas mask to enable people to experience exposure to gas wearing a gas mask in an attempt to familiarise people with such events if a gas bomb was dropped primarily to try to avoid panic and to teach the public how important it was that the mask fitted properly and should be kept in a good state of repair. This was no joke and many men were still alive who had served in the First World War who were still suffering from or had seen the horrors of poison gas first hand and feared gas bombs really could be dropped on the civilian population. It was mentioned The Air Raid Precautions Handbook was soon to be published and that the local authorities would ask The St John and Red Cross to help by going about in their local town or village to explain the dangers of poison gas and air raids in general and to suggest how simply those dangers could be avoided. All this was well and good in principle but there was a lack of detailed planning and cohesion; this was blamed on the lack of official information and guidelines. The feelings of many concerned people in February 1937 were summed up at the meeting of the Wayland Rural District Council the Chairman, Mr G W Webster stated:

'...with regard to setting up a system of air raid precautions the whole position is chaotic. Nobody seems to know anything.'

The Rev. H. Anderson added: '*We are absolutely in a fog as to the provision of things that would be necessary if an air raid took place. I am told there must be building materials, any amount of surgical articles, and other things, but we are not told where to get them or who is to pay for them. The County Council ought to have a scheme covering all the necessary points before the District Council can formulate a scheme for its own area.*'

Similar concerns were voiced by Mr W. G. Carpenter who had been told to provide a stock of water mains to take the place of any that might be damaged as well as corrugated iron sheeting, independent heating and lighting apparatus. Lord Bury pointed out that even the St John Ambulance and Red Cross who were so keen to help could not get on because no information could be obtained as to what age the classes of men would be exempt from the fighting forces or other services.

More horrors from the Spanish Civil War with the bombing of Guernica in April 1937 drove on the development of Britain's air raid precautions. Britain felt vulnerable, our mass population areas were centred around industrial areas and suggestions based on the events in Spain saw warnings of 'knock out blows' whereby some nine million people could be exposed to air attack the moment war broke out. Estimates spoke of if bombing continued over 60 days as many as 600,000 would be killed and 1,200,000 injured and mass panic would ensue. Another estimate propounded that 100,000 tons of bombs would be dropped on London alone in the first 14 days, a figure that was to prove to exceed the entire quantity of explosives dropped on the city during the entire war but over the years 1937-39 it was taken very seriously, thousands of compressed cardboard coffins for air raid casualties were produced for City and County Council Casualty Clearing Services; members of the police, St. John Ambulance and Red Cross trained as instructors and the first public ARP lectures were staged across the county. Both the St John Ambulance and British Red Cross Society embraced ARP training with enthusiasm and Anti-Gas challenges were included in their County Competitions. The first Air Raid Precautions Bill was brought before parliament in late 1937 and by the end of the year the ARP organisation had recruited over 200,000 volunteers nationally, Chief Wardens had been appointed, the initial national structure of the ARP organization was in place and a number of local areas had produced their initial ARP schemes.

At the meeting of Depwade Rural District Council in December 1937 the District Chief Air Raid Warden, Mr A T M Berney-Ficklin of Tasburgh, presented his initial report for their local scheme of air raid precautions; it was adopted and remains a typical example of the type employed in the rural areas across Norfolk. The report began by identifying The Pulham Market Public Assistance Institution as a suitable area headquarters that could also serve as base hospital and casualty clearing hospital.

The Institution was proposed as the designated place where any warnings or impending air raids would be received. The responsible officers were to be Mr G S Scarlett the Clerk to the RDC and his deputy Mr R Ingham. They in turn would warn: the police at Harleston, the Fire Brigades and decontamination squads at Dickleburgh, Harleston, Long Stratton and Scole; the District Transport Officer (Mr F H Easton of Bunwell); the District Chief Air Raid Warden (Mr A T M Berney-Ficklin); Mrs Young and the Rev. H S Bally who were in charge of the first aid centres at Harleston and Pulham Institution; Mrs Sargent and the Rev. F W Glass who were in charge of the Long Stratton First Aid Centre. It was noted 'The method of giving a general warning to the civil population has not yet been decided as the ARP Committee are awaiting a report on a Home Office investigation of warning apparatus.' Air Raid Wardens were to be responsible for giving warnings in each village and it was considered that some 155 of them would be required in the Depwade district.

Casualty Clearance exercise in Service Gas Masks, North Walsham 1937

The Sanitary Inspector was asked to investigate and compile a report on the suitability of Harleston, Long Stratton and Pulham Institution for first aid stations and propose the necessary adaptations to the buildings, for emergency supplies of water and light and for gas and splinter proofing of windows and doorways.

An ambulance was to be stationed at each first aid centre, the British Red Cross had been asked to provisionally arrange a minimum staff of 38 for each centre, which would include a reserve to form a mobile first aid party.

For transport and communications a census of all owners of motor vehicles in the district had been obtained and a form of enrolment was to be sent to the 965 owners already identified. The committee was confident there was enough water within the area for the four fire brigades in the area at Dickle-

Assembling Civilian Gas Masks for the people of Wells, 1939

Left and Right: Gas Mask Drill on Fakenham School field, September 1939 (GFWM)

Air Raids Precautions

A PUBLIC

MEETING

TO WHICH ALL ARE WELCOME

will be held on

Friday, April 29th, 1938

At 7.45 p.m., in

DRAYTON VILLAGE HALL

Lecturer   -   DR. MARRIOTT

Chairman   -   REV. WENHAM, M.A.

ADMISSION FREE

Organised by Drayton Women's Institute.

Don't Forget !   Don't Forget ! !   Don't Forget ! ! !

APRIL 29th, at 7.45 p.m.

burgh, Harleston, Scole and Long Stratton. It was recommended volunteer fire parties were raised in every parish. The fire brigades were asked to recruit the personnel (a leader and five men) for each of the decontamination squads. It was considered that demolition and rescue work could best be carried out by arrangements with local builders.

In 1938 Stella Isaacs, the Dowager Marchioness of Reading was asked by the government to form The Women's Voluntary Services for Air Raid Precautions which was to act as a support unit for the ARP. By May 1938 with the objectives of " the enrolment of women for Air Raid Precaution Services of Local Authorities, to help to bring home to every household what air attack may mean, and to make known to every household in the country what it can do to protect itself and the community." The organisation was designed so that no woman held a rank at a local level, the appointment of 'group leader' being assigned to the most able and appropriate women for the duration of a particular task or project. There was no compulsory uniform, members of the WVS could perform their duties wearing their lapel badge but many chose to buy the approved uniform.

By the end of the Munich Crisis in September 1938 everyone in Britain had been issued a gas mask, a booklet advising how to protect your home against air raids had been delivered to every household, a million feet of air raid shelter trenches had been dug, the Observer Corps had had its first general call out, the emergency services had been placed on stand by and the first pilot for the government's evacuation scheme was staged. Under the planned evacuation scheme Britain was divided into three categories. There were those denoted 'Evacuation Areas,' the main areas being: Metropolitan London, The Medway Ports of Chatham, Rochester and Gillingham; Southampton, Portsmouth and Gosport on the South Coast and the industrial areas of the Midlands such as Coventry, Derby, Birmingham and Merseyside and the North like Bradford, Grimsby, Leeds and Newcastle. In Scotland the great ports such as Clydebank, Dundee, Dunfermline, Edinburgh, Glasgow and Rosyth were all 'Evacuation Areas.' Areas around large military installations delineated 'Danger Zones' were also placed in the 'Evacuation Area' category. The second classification were the 'Neutral Areas;' places where it was considered there was a risk of bombing but children would neither be evacuated from or to these locations. The third class were 'Reception Areas' assayed to be 'safe from bombing.' In Norfolk only Norwich and Yarmouth were classified as 'Neutral' areas, the rest of the county was designated a Reception Area, despite the concerns voiced by some local councils about their area not being safe enough to become a place suitable to receive evacuees.

London County Council drafted plans for the evacuation of 637,000 children from London with other measures in draft for Britain's industrial cities such as Birmingham and Manchester. In the event about 5,000 children were evacuated under this scheme. By early 1939 all the children from the pilot evacuation had returned home. In January and February 1939 Local Authorities in Reception Areas began the search for potential foster homes for evacuees. Volunteers described as 'Visitors' interviewed householders and filled in census forms. These returns were to help decide how many evacuees could be billeted in each area.

Coxswain Henry Blogg shakes the hand of Captain Argüelles of the Cantabria *outside the Red Lion, Cromer, November 1938. Many of the other men are members of the Lifeboat* H.F. Bailey. *The woman and child are the Captain's wife Trinidad and their daughter Veyona.*

The widening threat of war was brought all too close to Norfolk shortly after 3pm on 2 November 1938 when gunfire was heard off our coast in the direction of the Cromer Knoll Light Vessel. A report was received by the coastguard from a British Steamer that an armed cruiser had been firing on a Spanish vessel and had inflicted severe damage upon it. Cromer No. 1 Lifeboat *H.F. Bailey* attended the SS *Cantabria* 12 miles offshore and found her heeling to starboard after being fired upon and strafed by machine gun fire. Fire had broken out and number of the crew had fled in two lifeboats. Some crew had been picked up by the attacking ship, others had managed to reach the British merchant vessel *Pattersonian* that had responded to the *Cantabria*'s SOS signal. Captain Blackmore of the *Pattersonian* then manoeuvred his vessel between the Spanish ships and the lifeboat to stop any further attack. The Cromer Lifeboat found and rescued five still aboard the stricken ship namely, Captain Argüelles, his wife Trinidad their son Ramon, aged six, their daughter Veyona, aged eight and the second steward, Joaquin Vallego. The Captain had preferred to stay on board and face death rather than run the risk of capture by his enemies and he implored Coxswain Henry Blogg that they be taken to shore pointing out the attacking vessel was 'a fascist ship' which proved to be the Spanish Nationalist Auxiliary cruiser *Nadir*, part of General Franco's navy.

This incident attracted national media attention and received international press coverage, it provoked questions in Parliament about the protection of merchant shipping in the North Sea and a statement was given by the Parliamentary Secretary to the Admiralty playing down any need for an increase in naval patrols. The Captain of the *Cantabria* was photographed with his family and steward thanking his rescuers in front of the Red Lion Hotel at Cromer but those who had been rescued by the *Pattersonian* that were landed at Great Yarmouth were initially far more reticent to face the cameras fearing reprisals from Franco if their faces appeared in the international press. Taken to the Yarmouth sailor's home they got over their fears and were even filmed for a Pathé News feature.

The Fascist movement had been known across Britain in the form of The British Union of Fascists (BUF) formed in 1932 by a former Labour government Minister and former Conservative MP, Sir Oswald Mosley. Commonly known as 'Blackshirts' at one point the BUF party claimed 50,000 members but following their increasing anti-Semitism and a number of high profile violent exchanges such as the Battle of Cable Street in 1936 the membership fell to about 8,000 and the Public Order Act (1936) was passed banning political uniforms and required police consent for political marches. Moseley did carry on and even enjoyed brief success on the back of the 'Peace Campaign' to prevent conflict with Germany. Many towns across the country were visited by Moseley, Norfolk was no exception. Attended by his lieutenants and local activists Moseley gave many of his addresses from on top of a wooden box; most of those who attended did so more through curiosity than political beliefs. When Moseley came to Norwich he gave his address in the Market Place one Sunday afternoon. He had no amplification equipment so he summoned up his best voice projection to deliver his speech. A local wireless and radio dealer, known for his left wing allegiances, was not keen on Moseley and drove his van equipped with megaphone speakers to a position nearby and played music to drown out the BUF leader. In May 1940, the BUF was banned outright by the government, and Mosley, along with 740 other fascists, was interned for most of the war years. Pockets of blackshirt supporters were believed to exist across the country, curiously a special investigation was conducted by government authorities into the blackshirt supporters and sympathisers in Sheringham. Rumours spread, perhaps there was a leak about the investigation, but one of the strangest tales that spread was that William Joyce's aunt lived in Sheringham and she had been caught signalling to enemy aircraft with a torch! Those who had been blackshirts were often teased for their beliefs, one old soldier who had been a Japanese prisoner of war wore his BUF lapel badge in the years after the war – on parade one day I heard the ribbing he got as one of his old comrades said – 'You never would fight against Hitler.'

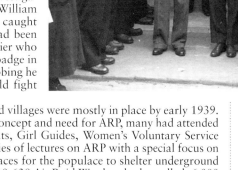

'Blackshirt' Leader Sir Oswald Moseley (centre left) and his supporters photographed on their tour of East Anglia

The ARP schemes and organisation for most towns and villages were mostly in place by early 1939. Members of the public were becoming familiar with the concept and need for ARP, many had attended lectures given at such diverse organisations as Boy Scouts, Girl Guides, Women's Voluntary Service and the Women's Institute; even teachers were given a series of lectures on ARP with a special focus on the treatment of children in case of an emergency and places for the populace to shelter underground had been identified across the county. By February 1939 10,630 Air Raid Wardens had enrolled, 6,000 of whom were already fully trained and in March Norwich City Council took over one of the most modern factories in the city on Sussex Street to create and ARP headquarters, training school and central store from which it established a network of 80 warden's posts.

The military forces of Norfolk, as always, were made up of high quality officers and men but the preparations and recruitment they were allowed to make had been restricted by the War Office and when the expansions of the forces were finally permitted in 1939, many officers and men felt such things really had been left to 'the eleventh hour' when preparations could have been made so much earlier. The decision had been taken to expand the Royal Air Force back in 1935 and work had begun on the re-activation and development of some of the First World War airfields in the county such as RAF Marham where reconstruction commenced in 1935, the airfield became active again in April 1937 and the first squadron, No 38, arrived the following month with their Fairey Hendon bombers. In 1936 Bircham Newton was assigned to Coastal Command and a major re-building programme was undertaken. There were also new-build airfields such as Scottow Aerodrome (later known as RAF Coltishall) begun in February 1939. Sadly the major recruitment drive for RAF and RAFVR personnel to fly, crew and maintain the planes did not occur until 1939 and it was only in July 1939 that it was announced that a RAFVR recruitment and training centre was to open in Norwich. The centre, that was to be associated with No. 40 Elementary and Reserve Flying Training School at Norwich Aerodrome, appealed for applications from volunteers in the area for pilots, air observers and wireless operator air gunners.

RAF Bircham Newton in the mid-1930s

The two Regular Army battalions of The Royal Norfolk Regiment had, like so many of their county regiment counterparts, enjoyed the years of peace and had been able to take the time to promote the smartness, drill, regimental sports and training the pressures of war had restricted. Both battalions predominantly served alternately in the UK and on the North West Frontier of India throughout the 1930s. There was no major recruitment drive nor compulsion to join, the posters at the recruiting offices simply emphasised the old peace-time legend 'Join the Army and see the World.' Joining up, however, was simple. If you were a fit young man of reasonable intelligence you would probably be accepted. The experience of two young men – Jack Forrest and Verdun Storey from Worstead is typical. In 1935 Jack wanted to join up with The Royal Norfolk Regiment and Verdun went along to keep his

B Company, 2ⁿᵈ Battalion,
The Royal Norfolk Regiment,
Aldershot 1936

mate company and they bicycled up to Britannia Barracks in Norwich together. Both ended up in The Regiment. Both ended up as well respected senior NCOs and both went to war.

The Territorial Force that had been stood down at the end of the First World War had been reconstituted and re-named the Territorial Army in 1920 and had slowly grown in membership through the 1920s and 30s. As the recruiting booklet *The Defence of Britain* (1934) put it 'So far are we from Universal conscription that the Peace Establishment of the Territorial Army asks for only 175,000 men out of a male population of over 3,000,000 men between the age of 20 and 30. It definitely is not a case of 'Every young man should be in the Territorial Army; it is rather none but the best are wanted in the Territorial Army' – admirable sentiments but not good enough for a military force facing the growing menace of Nazi Germany.

Full expansion of the TA was only ordered on 2 March 1939 when it was announced that the size of the TA was to be doubled. The total strength of the TA was to be 440,000: the field force of the Territorial Army was to rise from 130,000 to 340,000 with an additional 100,000 all ranks required to form the anti-aircraft section. In Norfolk the 4th and 5th Battalions, Royal Norfolk Regiment (TA) were increased by another two made up of new recruits and trained men and NCOs from the 4th and 5th Battalions. For many TA Officers this late expansion was deplorable and really should have been addressed in the mid 1930s when the Nazis began to militate the German people and rebuild their armed forces on an ever growing scale. Many saw the chance to expand when the TA began training units in Anti-Aircraft gunnery and searchlight defence, but rather than expand the TA to accommodate this, extant units were converted over to AA. The hasty measures the TA had to adopt in training the men in 1939 left many officers with the feeling that when the war was declared, as Major Monty Smyth of the 6th Battalion, The Royal Norfolk Regiment succinctly put it, 'we were caught with our pants down!'

On 26 May The Military Training Act 1939 (often referred to as 'The Militia Act') was passed by Parliament. It was our country's first peacetime act of conscription. It applied to all males aged between 20 and 21 years old and required the 35,000 men in this age bracket from across the country to answer a compulsory called up to serve for six months full-time military training after which it was stated they would be transferred to the Reserve for three and a half years during which time they 'might be recalled in an emergency for full time duty.' In reality most of these lads commonly known as 'Militiamen' were still in uniform when war broke out and they were in 'for the duration.' The first party of Militia men for The Royal Norfolk Regiment arrived at Britannia Barracks during the summer of 1939. The Regular army recruits were moved into a tented camp to allow space for the militiamen to be accommodated in the barracks. By August there were 200 of these recruits at the barracks but facilities were limited; there had to be two

'Militia' Recruits for The
Royal Norfolk Regiment,
Britannia Barracks, Norwich
1939

sittings in the dining hall and there was a perpetual jigsaw puzzle to solve in fitting all the squads into the limited space available. The new gymnasium was still under construction and the number of rifle ranges really should have been doubled. It is to their credit 'M' Company, as the militia intake were called, made excellent progress during their training, the *Regimental History* commenting: 'the keenness shown by all concerned was a good augury for the troubles which lay so close ahead.' Shortly after war was declared the large number of volunteers wishing to join up swamped the recruiting offices and a combined Navy, Army and RAF recruiting centre was opened at the Norwich Agricultural Hall.

The summer of 1939 saw the emergency services of Norfolk gear up for war. Training was essential; the British Red Cross Society alone staged 289 First Aid and 102 Home Nursing courses across the county. Smartness, efficiency and regular practice of their skills was also an important part of training for all voluntary emergency services so training nights and parades became a weekly feature, the new recruits made distinctive on their public appearances by their civilian clothes and arm bands

as they marched with their longer serving fully uniformed comrades. The last major county parade before the outbreak of war was that of Norfolk St John Ambulance who held a service at Norwich Cathedral followed by a march past with over 700 personnel on parade at Eaton Park on Sunday 11 June.

Some units such as the Air Raid Precautions personnel only had arm bands, silver lapel badges and tin helmets so wearing work clothes, privately purchased overalls or the issue decontamination suits these new ARP units undertook their first major public exercises. The various emergency services and ARP volunteers were put through their paces with staged incidents using fireworks to simulate explosive bombs, smoke canisters for poison gas bombs and small fires representing incendiaries. One such exercise took place at Sheringham on the evening of Tuesday 4 July. The scenario was an aeroplane had circled the town and dropped a High Explosive (HE) bomb near Alexandra Road causing extensive damage to water and sewage mains and drew on the ARP workers, rescue and shoring-up parties. Incendiary bombs that 'fell' on Beeston Common were dealt with swiftly by the fire brigade and auxiliaries and the decontamination squads were called to the War Memorial where there was a persistent gas bomb and to Hastings Lane to deal with a non-persistent gas bomb. The Control Officer and Message Officer was Major G S Rogers, assisted by Mr Jordan. Police and Specials were also in attendance to block passage through damaged roads and to direct traffic around obstructions. There were a number of realistic casualties dealt with under the supervision of Mrs Kilgour Baker and Supt. Sidney Day of Sheringham St John Ambulance Brigade. The umpires were Mr Bown, Major H. Tru May (ARP Officer for Northern Area of Norfolk), Mr F Hall Smith, Mr B T F Carrick (Divisional Warden) and Mr C. Gurney. After the exercise Major J. Wormald (Chief Warden for the Northern Area of Norfolk) and Major Rogers. It was noted at the debrief that some of the locals took the exercise less seriously and comment was recorded in the UDC minutes: 'Wardens and Special Constables are asked to ensure a more rigid discipline among the civil population.'

At Wells an imaginary 'state of emergency' was declared by HM Government for their scenario. Early on the evening of Monday 10 July 1939 a preliminary caution was received at the Report Centre and Head Warden (Mr H. Farrow) promptly ordered all wardens to man their posts. Later an action warning was received ordering the siren to be sounded. The wardens took up the warning by sounding short, sharp blasts upon their whistles. At 7pm a flight of aeroplanes supposedly appeared from over the sea and passed over the town dropping a number of HE and incendiary bombs as they did so. One HE had a direct hit upon a large building, demolishing it and blocking the road junction of Mill Road and Clubbs Lane causing four casualties.

In Church Street two incendiary bombs were dropped and fire began to spread rapidly causing three casualties. Two people were 'killed' and two 'injured' when one HE and an incendiary bomb dropped behind the Post Office. Another HE bomb dropped on Polka Road damaging electric cables and water mains. The railway bridge on the Fakenham Dry Road was 'destroyed' and the road blocked by an HE bomb. A challenging exercise indeed for all the organisations involved, with realistic casualties made by the liberal use of paint, treated under the observance of Dr Stewart (Medical Officer for ARP), Dr E W Hicks and Miss Rungary (first aid Commandant). After the exercise all concerned retired to the Primary School for a debrief by the area officers.

Between the hours of 12 midnight on the night of 13 July until 4am on 14 July 1939 the first test blackout was conducted for the entire county of Norfolk. The announcement, made by Bartle Frere, Chairman of Norfolk County Council Air Raid Precautions Committee was made in the local press and posters headed 'Important Notice – Air Raid Precautions' were displayed on prominent notice boards stating: 'Householders and all other occupiers of premises are accordingly asked to assist by ensuring that lights in the premises are extinguished, or screened by dark curtains or dark blinds... It is

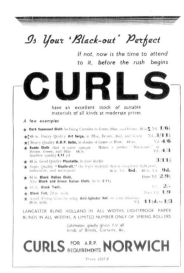
particularly desirable that external lights and other lights directly visible from the sky should be extinguished or screened. As lighting in streets will be restricted, vehicles should, so far as possible, keep off the roads during the darkened period.'

The posters took pains to answer a popular concern and point out 'It is emphasised that there is no intention, in connection with the black-out of cutting off lighting or power supplies at the mains.' Overall it was recorded as a great success but there were some failures such as the Fakenham tradesman whose usual practice was to leave his shop windows on all night did not return to his business and extinguish the light. However the worst offenders were found to be villagers who kept the lights on all night and made no attempt to screen their windows.

Norwich ARP and emergency services took the opportunity to stage a practice drill dealing with the effects of an imaginary air raid. Firms such as Caleys, Reckitt & Colman and Boulton & Paul suspended their night shifts in order to co-operate while others worked through the night with minimum light. The whole scene was surveyed by Mr W. Riley (Chairman of the ARP Committee), the city's Chief Constable Mr J H Dain and his Deputy, Supt. H W Ball from the top of City Hall. At Cromer their ARP services, Special Constables and Observer Corps staged an exercise and even the motorists complied with the request to use side lights only and were guided through the town by a series of red oil lamps. Holt's street lamps were extinguished and during the 'zero' hours 'not a glimpse of light could be seen' the same was achieved along the North Norfolk coast from at Bacton to the Burnhams. Towns and villages had their 'Specials' on the beat and many could simply return the report that they appeared as if they had been 'blacked off the map.' At North Walsham, however, there were reports of lights in various sectors. Wardens were told not to take action but to report the infringements to Special Constables. This was done and by 1am every light was extinguished and the black-out was very efficient. A car that was thought to have lights that were too bright was spotted, was soon stopped and found to be a police car patrolling the district!

Senior Officers and NCO Instructors with Bofors Guns, Royal Artillery Anti-Aircraft Training Camp, Stiffkey, August 1939.

The summer of 1939 was glorious and many people did make an extra effort to have a little holiday, even if it was just a day trip to the seaside. The August Bank Holiday saw the LNER arrange 1,800 extra trains across their system but the visitor numbers were dramatically down on previous years, many Londoners cancelled their holidays and the coastal resorts of Norfolk suffered badly, to the degree local councils, hoteliers and shopkeepers from the coastal resorts sent deputations and appeals to parliament for financial assistance. Hunstanton was off to a bad start after the pier pavilion theatre suffered a severe fire on Saturday 10 June. Two women, Miss Doris Bassford of Leicester and Miss Winifred Taylor of Wembley, were trapped at the end of the pier by the flames and had to jump into the sea to escape. In July Cromer, Sheringham and a number of areas around were set upon by a plague of Greenflies 'as thick as a fog' at times, so dense they caused traffic to slow down and cyclists to dismount. And to be honest, although very necessary, as the military presence and activities in coastal areas increased and the gunfire from the Weybourne AA Camp thundered over the North Norfolk beaches, holiday-makers were presented with an unwelcome reminder of the impending war instead of the welcome escape they desired. But that said, across the country people entered into preparations for war with good cheer and all the same vigour as preparing a family trip to the seaside. Indeed, sand and spades were to the fore as council workmen were joined by male and female volunteers, some of them boys and girls, filling the sandbags and building up blast walls for public buildings from town halls and police stations to hospitals, wardens posts and homes. At the end of July Norwich Education Committee authorised the expenditure of £37,000 to pay for the construction of trench shelters for its schools and further works were carried out digging out the trenches for public shelters, factories and businesses at many locations across the county. Some folks even improvised their own outdoor trench shelters in their back gardens.

The school authorities of Gresham's School at Holt provided tools, emergency lights and materials to enable the digging of shelter trenches at short notice from the time of the Munich Crisis. Experimental digging had been carried out by the school's Manual Labour Party and the OTC. In the last fortnight of July, with little or no disturbance of School periods were constructed shelters for each house. They adopted the official ARP shelter with modifications to enable mass construction using 8" x 2" wall plates; joists 4" x 2" and galvanised sheet-roofing with brushwood at the end of the joists to keep open contact with the earth and reduce condensation, faggots spread over metal sheets for drainage, a six inch layer of stones over 2ft of soft earth to prevent the penetration of shrapnel, earth and turf or grass-seed completed the arched roof. Each shelter was also fitted with duckboards and electric light. The Houses undertook their work in a spirit of enthusiasm and friendly rivalry. Five shelters were constructed: Howson's – close to the tall hedge between the Old Sana-torium and the Tennis Courts; Farfield – next to the hedge behind the music rooms; Woodlands – sited between the Gymnasium and the woods; Old School House – between the trees at the end of Mr. Gamble's garden and the Tennis Courts and Kenwyn – on 'the Beach' near the wooden fence.

The first batch of 300 Anderson shelters reached Norwich in late August. These shelters were supplied free to all homes with an income that did not exceed £250 a year with a suitable garden. Made from pre-formed corrugated sheet-steel the Anderson was supplied in 21 pieces with a bag of nuts and bolts. The householder (and helpful neighbours) would join together to dig out the ground, assemble the shelter and pile a good lot of earth back on top. In Norwich the trench shelters were supplemented by sixty surface shelters. Quicker and easier to build than the underground type these public shelters cold hold up to 50 people and were constructed with 14-inch brickwork and were claimed to be blast and splinter proof. The first of these shelters in the city were constructed around the Cattle Market and on terraced streets where there were concreted and paved back yards rather than gardens.

The golden sands of our coastline were darkened, at least on occasions, between May and August by the sinister cigar-shaped shadow cast by the *Graf Zeppelin II* (LZ 130) moving slowly along the coast. Most of those who saw it or heard about it were firmly of the opinion that its intentions were malevolent and their suspicions were later to be confirmed. The *Graf Zeppelin* was reconnoitring the tall radio towers that had been erected along the North Sea Coast from Portsmouth to Scapa Flow. The sites were photographed and the experts on board conducted a series of radiometric tests which suggested the radio towers were involved with some form of radar. The radio towers were indeed signif-icant as they formed the then top secret Chain Home Radio Direction Finding (RDF) system of coastal radar stations. The system otherwise known as AMES Type 1 (Air Ministry Experimental Station) provided long-range detection of aircraft. Two of the original 15 sites planned in 1937 were in Norfolk, at West Beckham and Stoke Holy Cross.

Through the summer of 1939 The Observer Corps had expanded across the country, new areas were formed and 16 Group became part of the Midland Area under Group Captain V. O. Rees as overall Commandant at Hucknall in Nottinghamshire. The OC itself had all its administration, recruit-ment and payments transferred from the already burdened police to the Air Ministry. Although they lost their Special Constable status the OC spotters became entitled to a payment of 1s 3d an hour with a maximum of £3 a week for their long hours of duty (a decision made after it was clear a 24 hour watch could not be maintained without many OC members receiving some recompense for loss of wages). The OC were also put to the test as the RAF conducted a major national air defence exercise from 9 -11 August. It was the first full practice for the modern air defence system including fighter and bomber squadrons, anti-aircraft divi-sions, air raid warning organisations and OC. Certain bomber squadrons represented hostile raiders and flew in to 'attack' from across the North Sea. The wave of aerial intruders that flew over Norfolk came in over Sheringham on its way to Norwich and were successfully 'intercepted' but in general the low cloud hampered the exercise, there was no clear outcome but many really felt a shiver as they contemplated 'the shape of things to come.' The county and indeed the country were gearing up for war and for many in those latter days of that sunny August of 1939 it was not a matter of if but when hostilities would be declared.

On 24 August schoolteachers were recalled from their summer holidays and were thrown in at the deep end making the preparations ready for the 'go' signal for Operation Pied Piper. On 27 August notifications were received by Billeting Officers in Norfolk stating the numbers of children that would be

Left: Digging out the Norfolk Chronicle *air raid shelter trench at Fakenham, August 1939 (GFWM)*

Right: Family dugout in their garden at Walsingham, August 1939 (GFWM)

Sandbag walls and a wooden cover protects the stained glass window of Norwich Guildhall, 1939.

Evacuees from London arrive at King's Lynn, 1 September 1939

Evacuees from London arrive at King's Lynn, 1 September 1939

sent to be re-homed in their area and on 31 August 1939 the dreaded order was sent out by the Ministry of Health: 'Evacuate Forthwith.' The order had been expected. The following day, although not the day war was declared, Friday 1 September is significant for two reasons, one is that on this day the Territorial Army was sent orders to mobilize and the second was the greatest human evacuation in the history of the British Isles took place. The total numbers evacuated are truly remarkable: 827,000 school children; 524,000 mothers with children under school age, 103,000 School Teachers and helpers; 13,000 expectant mothers and 7,000 people with disabilities. Hospitals were also cleared for emergency use. The Norfolk and Norwich Hospital cleared 284 beds for under the scheme.

From as early as 6.30 am on 1 September children began to gather in their school playgrounds ready to depart. None of them knew where they were going, who they would be staying with or when they would return.

Operation Pied Piper went like clockwork but it is true to say the journey of evacuees from across the country varied in duration, incidents, experiences and emotions felt at the time; every evacuee I have ever met has their own memories but often share common touchstones of the experience so, to get a flavour of the day, I shall relate a 'typical' evacuee child's journey from London to Norfolk.

After gathering in the school playground, one of the 1,589 assembly points in London, each child clutching a suitcase, pillowslip or brown parcel of their prescribed items to take with them a luggage label would be affixed to the child usually bearing their name, school, current home address and number allotted to their evacuation party (usually their school). They may well have been joined there by Evacuation Officers wearing 'L.C.C. EVAC.' marked arm bands; their job was to ensure the safe passage and suitable paperwork regarding numbers was maintained and exchanged; mostly it fell to the council education officers and teachers to take on this role but there were also volunteers.

The children were then moved out – some marching behind the banner or placard of their school all the way to their local station, singing as they went; others piled onto transport usually buses, coaches local trains or the underground to one of the capital's 168 'Entraining Stations' – mostly main line stations or suburban stations in outer London such as New Cross, Richmond or Ealing Broadway and there they would depart for the countryside. The main detraining centres in Norfolk were at King's Lynn, Norwich, Thetford, Diss, Downham Market, New Hunstanton and Swaffham. Thousands of London children were also brought to the eastern counties on steamers from the Thames disembarking at Felixstowe, Claremont Pier in Lowestoft and at the Fish Wharf in Great Yarmouth. Some parents managed to follow the children to the departure points and tearfully waved them off. For most children it was a long journey, some had never ridden on a train before and in carriages without corridors the excitement and or distress led to 'little wet accidents' or those on boats, many of whom had never even seen the sea before, suffered sea sickness. Despite this being the greatest and most concentrated mass movement of people in the history of Great Britain no serious accidents were recorded.

Ahead of the children the towns and villages across the county had been involved in what the local press hailed as 'perhaps the biggest co-operative effort ever made by the government, the local authorities, and the public of Norfolk' the provisions that had been sent for the children that had arrived for the children were stated to have included 976 cases of tinned milk, 21,000lb of biscuits, 73,000 cases of chocolate and 21,000 carrier bags. There had also been an appeal for at least 12,000 blankets and rugs for children being housed temporarily at Yarmouth before being sent to rural areas. The following were the Norfolk Women's Voluntary Service for Civil Defence centres and contacts established in 1939:

County Organiser: Viscountess Bury, Eccles Hall, Norwich
Blofield & Flegg: Mrs Harry Cator, Ranworth Hall
Depwade: Mrs Paulin, Thorpe Abbotts Place, Diss
Dereham (East): Mrs Gordon Aldiss, Fairbourne, Norwich Road, East Dereham
Diss Urban District: Miss Paulin, Thorpe Abbotts Place, Diss
Downham Market: (a) Mrs Gibb, Sandfield House, Downham Market
                 (b) Mrs Buchanan, Clackclose, Downham Market

Docking: Mrs Reed, Hole House, Holme-next-Sea
Downham: Mrs Swann, Beck House, Feltwell
Erpingham: (a) Lady Sanderson, Hill House, Northrepps
         (b) Miss Gilbert, Admiralty Cottage, Mundesley
Forehoe & Henstead: Mrs Busutill, Old Rector Swardeston
Freebridge Lynn: Viscountess Downe, Uphall, Hillingdon (Temporarily The Paddocks, Grimston)
Great Yarmouth: Mrs Carr, 11, Wellesley Road, Great Yarmouth
Hunstanton, Mrs Bull, Waverley House, Greengate Road, Hunstanton
King's Lynn: Miss Appleby, 46, Queen Street, King's Lynn
Loddon: Mrs Cadge, Farthing Green House, Loddon
Marshland: Mrs J. Cannon, High House, Terrington St. Clements
Mitford & Launditch: Mrs Bullard, Hill Farm, Gressenhall
Norwich: Miss Burton, Harford Manor, Ipswich Road, Norwich
Swaffham Urban District: Mrs Townend, The Hollies, Swaffham
Swaffham Area: Miss I. Montomery, Great Cressingham Rectory
Thetford: Mrs Law, Redcastle Furse, Brandon Road, Thetford
Walsingham: Miss Nancy Jones, Cranmer Hall, Fakenham
Wayland: Mrs Lubbock, Warren House, Old Buckenham
Wymondham, Mrs Gooch, Rydal Mount, Wymondham

Some children arrived at their destinations in daylight, others in darkness, only upon arrival did they find out where they were. Met by the local Billeting Officer a further bus or char-a-banc journey or a walk took them to the reception centre, often a town, church or school hall. Before they were taken inside a nit inspection would have been carried out, children with sore throats were given a gargle, some children were even given a wash and brush up, whole groups of toddlers were bathed in enamel bowls by the waiting volunteers from such organizations as St John Ambulance, British Red Cross Society, Women's Voluntary Service or Women's Institute. Some children had no such luxury and remember thanking goodness that someone picked them despite their having wet knickers or pants.

The children were then brought into the hall and lined up; the prospective foster parents would then choose the child they wanted. Although attempts were made to keep brother and sister siblings together this was not always possible. The feelings of who will pick me, I wonder what they will be like, I hope I am not last to be chose are just a few of the gamut of thoughts that ran through their minds. The pretty little girls and the boys who could be useful around the home or farm were usually chosen first but there was usually a residue and so they would be taken house to house among the known likely houses to find them a home. Rates for payment for those giving homes to evacuees were 8s. 6d per week for an unaccompanied child, if you took in a family the rate was 5s. for each adult and 3s. for each child. The first party of about a thousand children that arrived in Norwich on the morning of 1 September were

Evacuees and local school children, Fakenham, September 1939 (GFWM)

found homes by the afternoon but as the day wore on and children arrived at later and later hours places did become a little more difficult to find, particularly when more children arrived than expected. Some children ended up having to spend an uncomfortable night sleeping in the church hall but great efforts were made by the local people and the adults that accompanied the children to make the best of the situation and morale and behaviour remained at a good standard.

Billeting Officers did have legal powers to compel those with suitable space in their homes to take in evacuees, a small number of prosecutions for refusal are known but this really was a last resort, no Billeting Officer would want to force children upon a household that objected so strongly against taking them in. Once found a home the evacuee would then write on the pre-paid official card to send their new address to their parents.

Most evacuee children saw it as a great adventure; many had not considered the ramifications of their separation from their family. Mums tried hard to put a brave face on the situation, busying themselves with the preparations, ensuring all was packed, shoes properly polished and children presentable but inside, to be parted from her children to an unknown location and family is a stress that could only truly be understood by one who had to live through it. In retrospect, despite the bombing and horrors they saw numerous mothers would record the day my children were taken for evacuation was the worst day of the war. But in fact war was not declared until two days later; by the end of that month statistics show a quarter of the population had changed their address.

The mournful tones of Prime Minister Neville Chamberlain announcing 'this country is at war with Germany' on 3 September 1939 came as no surprise but unlike the First World War this news was not greeted with the throwing of streamers and singing in the streets. The bloody lessons of The First World War were well remembered and remained all too real for many; what had been claimed to be 'the war to end all wars' caused many who had lived through it to shake their heads and say, with some bitterness, 'never again.' But they also knew the danger Hitler posed and they would never want to see Britain or her Empire under the jackboot of the Nazis and great confidence was placed in our British Expeditionary Force to go out and deal a knock-out blow to 'this upstart Hitler.' The declaration of war was greeted in the county with the unique stoicism and even humour that we Norfolk folk often find in the face of adversity. This is epitomised in the Depot Notes for *The Britannia*, The Regimental Journal of The Royal Norfolk Regiment. Written a few days before the declaration of war is the comment:

'War is, as these notes go to press, most likely and so we can but wish all in the IX of Foot, God Speed, God's Blessing and Good Luck, if there's no means of keeping the peace.'

And so the county of Norfolk marched, with its head up and eyes fixed to the horizon, across our freshly harvested fields, to war.

Building a hay stack, North Norfolk, Harvest 1939 (GFWM)

2 Front Line Norfolk

The county of Norfolk with its miles of seaboard and natural harbours has proved to be an attractive landing ground for any potential invaders of our sceptre isle for centuries, indeed an ancient couplet relates:

'He who old England hopes to win
Must at Weybourne Hope begin'

During the First World War trenches, emplacements and some of the first purpose built concrete pillboxes were erected as part of the county's defences. During the inter-war years little consideration had been given to the coastal defences of Great Britain.

From the outbreak of war in 1939 the defence of Norfolk was entrusted to the 18th (Eastern) Division. The division was composed of all Territorial battalions, most of them with East Anglian connections viz:

The guns of Weybourne Anti-Aircraft Gunnery Practice Camp blaze away c1939

18th Division H.Q.
    135th (Hertfordshire Yeomanry)Field Regt, Royal Artillery
    198th Field Ambulance, Royal Army Medical Corps
    118th Field Regiment, Royal Artillery
    287th Field Company, Royal Engineers
    125th Anti Tank Regiment, Royal Artillery
    148th Field Regt, Royal Artillery
    288th Field Coy, Royal Engineers
    560th Field Coy, Royal Engineers
    251st Battalion, The Recce Regt (5th Battalion, The Loyal Regiment (North Lancashire))
    9th Battalion, The Royal Northumberland Fusiliers

53rd Infantry Brigade
    2nd Battalion, The Cambridgeshire Regiment
    5th Battalion, The Royal Norfolk Regiment
    6th Battalion, The Royal Norfolk Regiment

54th Infantry Brigade
    4th Battalion, The Royal Norfolk Regiment
    4th Battalion, The Suffolk Regiment
    5th Battalion, The Suffolk Regiment

55th Infantry Brigade
    1st Battalion, The Cambridgeshire Regiment
    5th Battalion, The Bedfordshire and Hertfordshire Regiment
    1st/5th Battalion, The Sherwood Foresters

Pictured during his tour of East Coast defences, Winston Churchill inspects Officers and men of 2nd Battalion, The Cambridgeshire Regiment at Holt, 7 August 1940. (IWM)

The immediate defence of the Norfolk Coast was entrusted to the 53rd and 54th Brigades including the 4th, 5th and 6th battalions of The Royal Norfolk Regiment which, naturally, contained many local men. The winter of 1939-40 that they weathered patrolling and guarding our coast proved to be one of the coldest and bitterest winters on record, so cold that the sea froze in places as did all but one of the toilets in the barrack huts of the 5th Battalion at Weybourne Camp. The men of the 4th Battalion fared little better in their requisitioned holiday camp barracks at Gorleston.

The 6th Battalion were far more fortunate being quartered in hotels and private houses in Sheringham. The battalion took up defensive positions along the coast from Cromer to Weybourne with specific orders to prevent seaborne landings between Beach Road and the Old Hythe with company alarm posts in Augusta Street, Waterbank Road, Montague Road and Holway Road. Three vital points to be held were the sea wall from Beach Road to the Burlington Hotel, the stretch of beach from the lifeboat house to the Old Hythe and the area around Dead Man's Hill and the northern side of Oak Wood. Reserves were held in readiness south of Golf Course Hill (Skelding Hill) with Battalion HQ at the Golf Clubhouse. Each soldier was issued with 120 rounds of ammunition and 2000 rounds allocated to every Bren gun.

The pillboxes of the Great War still looked out with unblinking eyes through the 'Phoney War' months of 1939 and into early 1940 but it was only as things took a turn for the worse for the BEF in France that consideration was given again to the construction of fixed defences and anti-invasion works. The now de-classified 'Secret' files of the War Office provide the 'chapter and verse' of the considered dangers of invasion, potential enemy landing areas and defences of Norfolk. Firstly, the coast had to be surveyed to ascertain which beaches were suitable for the disembarkation of troops, landing of armoured fighting vehicles (AFVs), tanks or landing craft. Each section commenced with a description of the shore, general nature of foreshore, slope, floor, rise and fall of tide etc and concludes with comments for each location were sent in three reports from Naval Officer in Charge Yarmouth to Commander in Chief, The Nore and Flag Officer in Charge Harwich between 30 May and 2 June 1940. What follows is a transcript of the original documents edited to the key points and comments pertinent to invasion vulnerability:

SECRET REPORT ON EAST COAST OF ENGLAND

Reconnaissance report for right half of
18 Division 54 Infantry Brigade Sector: Kessingland to Winterton Ness

LOWESTOFT (SUFFOLK) TO GORLESTON CLIFFS (NORFOLK)

Extent: 5 miles

Approach from seawards: clear

Facilities for landing various arms: suitable for infantry and light vehicles. NOT suitable for tanks owing to flat nature of beach.

Possibility of landing aircraft on beach: Narrow stretch of firm sand between H.W. and L.W. marks. Soft sand above H.W. mark. Unsuitable for landing aircraft.

The Hinterland
(A) Exits: Good road exits in urban areas. Lateral road follows coast about 1 mile inland – one road exit at Corton
(B) Assembly positions: No definite localities. Flat and featureless country.
(C) Objectives for first flight: Top of cliffs provide suitable objective for infantry.
(D) Landing grounds for aircraft: Suitable areas- the immediate hinterland

Tank Conditions: Exit from beach definitely barred along full extent of sub-section except at 991183 [map ref.] and the tunnel at Gorleston cliffs. Immediate hinterland provides suitable tank country to a depth of some 7 or 8 miles, when marsh system is a semi-circular formation is met.

GREAT YARMOUTH
SHORE

Extent: 2 miles

Approach from seawards:

The Scroby Bank Shoal, at about 1 mile offshore, covers the approaches on the northern side of the town and as far North as Beach House Golf Links approximately. This bank is dry along whole extent at all states of tide.

Approaches from the South of this Bank, while shoaling and confused, provide no obstruction to the navigation of small craft.

The harbour approaches are easy. Harbour has 14 feet of water and strong tides.

Facilities for landing various arms: Beach very suitable for infantry. Unsuitable for disembarkation of AFVs. Pleasure piers and harbour offer many facilities for landing stores and personnel. Scroby Bank shoal, just off shore, would however prove a very strong deterrent.

Harbour: Facilities for small commercial port in regard to quayage, lifting appliances etc. Vulnerable – fixed defences weak. Blocking and mining difficult owing to strong tidal condition. Possibility of landing aircraft on beach: Unsuitable

The Hinterland
(A) Exits: Three main road exits – from southern end of town, from centre due west and from northern end of the town
(B) Assembly Positions: ———
(C) Objectives for first flight: ———
(D) Landing grounds for aircraft: Nil for land aircraft. Ample facilities for sea-planes

Tank Conditions: Free exit from beach into town but disembarkation from landing craft would present considerable difficulty.

Breydon Water, River Bure and marshy country lying immediately in rear of town would restrict vehicles entirely to the roads.

GREAT YARMOUTH TO WINTERTON NESS
SHORE

Extent: 9 miles approx.

Approach from seawards: From north side of Scroby Bank shoal approaches are clear for shallow draft vessel. A sand bank extends off shore from California to Winterton. This bank has not more than 4 feet of water at H.W. springs.

Facilities for landing arms: Very suitable for infantry. Somewhat doubtful whether slope of beach is sufficiently steep to allow disembarkation of AFVs.

Possibility of landing aircraft on beach: Doubtful. Sand too soft above H.W.

The Hinterland
(A) Exits: In the sand dune area free exit along full extent. In cliffs area only exits are at Caister, California, Hemsby and Winterton.
(B) Assembly Positions: flat featureless country
(C) Objectives for first flight: Dunes and cliffs provide good objectives.
(D) Landing grounds for aircraft: No areas suitable for landing aircraft. Ample facilities for sea planes on Broads – back areas.

Tank Conditions: It is very improbable that tanks should be disembarked along this stretch of coast. The country inland is however suitable for tanks until the line of the Rivers Bure and Thurne, is met at a depth of some 6 or 7 miles.

Summary
Assuming that steep-to conditions are essential requirement for disembarkation of tanks, the whole of this coast section, from Kessingland to Winterton Ness may be considered unsuitable.

It is however vulnerable to Infantry and probably to motor bicycle motorised troops. Light vehicles also could probably be disembarked at almost any point except where a few offshore obstructions exist. It is also vulnerable to Infantry landing by seaplane of float plane on inland lakes.

Reconnaissance report for the left half of 18 Division,
54 Infantry Brigade Sector from Winterton Ness to Weybourne

HAISBOROUGH SAND

Lying about 8½ miles off shore, having least depth of ½ fathom at L S Springs provide a dangerous approach covering the full length of this sub-section and beyond. It would be dangerous for even shallow draft boats to attempt crossing at any state of tide. Usually rough water on Bank except dead calm weather. Approach to beach would, therefore have to be made by deep water channels to North of South of Bank.

Shore
Facilities for landing various arms suitable for infantry and light vehicles. Some form of beach roadway would probably be necessary to run normal wheeled vehicles over soft sand. Owing to inshore sand bar and generally flat nature of beach generally unsuitable for AFVs. It is just possible that craft drawing 4'6" might beach on ridge at H.W.M [high water mark].

Possibility of landing aircraft on beach.

Firm level sand at low water 5 to 700' in width would provide quite possible landing ground. Patches of 'lows' (shallow lakes) would provide some obstacles.

The Hinterland
(A) Exits: Free exit in sand dunes area for inf. or tracked vehicles in cliff area, exit restricted to gaps of which there are 6. Bacton Green provides one exit suitable also for wheeled vehicles. Lateral road communications along coast or within 2 miles of coast.
(B) Assembly positions: Flat featureless country
(C) Objectives for first flight: Line of sand dunes or cliffs provide suitable objectives.
(D) Landing ground for aircraft: No particularly obvious areas. Broads district in back areas

provide suitable landing grounds for sea or float planes.

(E) Tank Conditions: Assuming tanks could be disembarked (which is very doubtful) immediate hinterland provides reasonable country. Line of North Walsham – Dilham Canal about 5 miles inland provides a tank obstruction except for road crossings.

BACTON GREEN TO OVERSTRAND
SHORE

Extent: 8 miles

Approach from seawards: Northern limit of Haisborough Sand lies approximately abreast of Bacton Green, direct approach to this coast sub-section therefore is open from seawards.

Facilities for landing various arms: Suitable for inf. and light vehicles. Unsuitable for AFVs even at H.W.

Possibility of landing aircraft on beach: possible at low water.

The Hinterland
(A) Exits: The only exits for vehicles, either tracked or wheeled, along this sub-section is at Mundesley.
(B) Assembly position: Flat country gives way to undulating grassy country [sic]. Open partly wooded.
(C) Objectives for first flight: Top of cliffs and few exits – very difficult to scale.
(D) Landing grounds for aircraft: 250 acre field at Paston (7852). (This field is in process of being blocked).

Tank Conditions: Generally good tank conditions. Line of Norfolk and Suffolk Joint Railway provides some obstacles in cuttings and embankments.

OVERSTRAND TO CROMER
SHORE

Extent: 2½ miles

Approach from seawards: similar to those in preceding sub-section.

Overstrand is a small seaside resort standing on 50' high vertical cliffs. It had numerous pedestrian accesses to the beach but no access for vehicles.

Cromer is a moderate sized resort and longshore fishing centre, no harbour. Small pier exposed to easterly weather conditions. Highest point reached about 120 to 130 feet. It has numerous exits from the beach suitable for vehicles or pedestrians.

Hinterland
Undulating fairly close country with large wooded area.

CROMER TO SHERINGHAM
No change in the general character along this sub-section either on the coast or in the hinterland. There are two exits from the beach suitable for tracked or wheeled vehicles.

SHERINGHAM TO WEYBOURNE HOPE
SHORE

Extent: 6½ miles

Approach from seaward: clear

Facilities for landing various arms: suitable for infantry. Feasible for AFVs along this sub-section is unlikely to be attempted

Possibility of landing aircraft on beach: Quite unsuitable

The Hinterland
(A) Exits:
(B) Assembly positions:
First class tactical country in immediate hinterland. Hilly, wooded and grassy.
(C) Objectives for first flight: Top of high cliffs. Difficult to scale. Few exits.
(D) Landing grounds for aircraft: Difficult in immediate hinterland. Suitable landing grounds in back areas.

Tank Conditions: Exit from beach only. Suitable tank country in immediate hinterland and particularly in the back areas which is undulating, partly wooded country.

Summary
Again assuming that steep-to conditions are an essential requirement for the disembarkation of tanks there are only two possible sectors e.g. Winterton Ness to Bacton Green and Sheringham

to Weybourne Hope. Of these the former would require accurate timing to arrive at the top of H.W. and would also require calm weather. The latter while providing the essential steep-to beach, would be possible only at ¾ to ½ tides and above and would be impossible in anything but dead calm weather.

The coast, generally, is vulnerable to infantry and some stretches of the beach might possibly be used by aircraft at L.W.

There are suitable areas of hinterland for landing both aircraft and sea planes.

Reconnaissance report for right half of 18 Division, 53 Infantry Brigade Sector From Weybourne Hope to King's Lynn

FROM WEYBOURNE HOPE TO THE HOOD
SHORE

Extent: 9,000 yards

Approach from seawards: Clear for shallow draft craft.

Facilities for landing various arms: Feasible for all arms at all stages of tide. Beaching of heavy landing craft would be dependent upon finding dead calm weather. In swell or surf conditions, while not perhaps impossible, the operation would be risky.

Possibility of landing aircraft on beach: Not possible.

The Hinterland
Exits: Several road exits. Free exit across country except in local water crossed areas.
Assembly positions: No definite locality.

Objectives for first flight: Excellent position top of shingle ridge.

Landing grounds for aircraft: Ample facilities in back areas of hinterland.

Tank Conditions: Slow going over flats line new cut (5362) provides probable tank obstacle restricting movement to roads.

FROM THE HOOD (EXCL.) TO BRANCASTER HARBOUR MOUTH
SHORE

Extent: 11,000 yards

Approach from seawards: Confused shoal water, Blakeney Overfalls from off Blakeney to off Wells provide an additional navigational hazard. The harbours and creeks while navigable at top of spring tides craft drawing up to 9 feet are difficult of approach and without intimate local knowledge would be difficult to locate; in dark impossible. 5 to 6 knot tide at ebb and flood would make the handling of lighters or landing craft very difficult. Finally the channels are continually altering and in some cases have quite changed within the last two or three months.

Facilities for landing various arms: Quite impractical for AFVs, possible for infantry but penetration inland would be more difficult.

Possibility of landing aircraft on beach: Possible for aircraft along large extent.

BRANCASTER HARBOUR TO HUNSTANTON

This sub-section, some 12,000 yards in length, provides several areas with free exits from the beaches. The beach is sand along full extent, generally firm and quite flat. At L.W. it has a width of at least 1,000 yards. Water is uniformly shallow. It is subject to rapid variation in weather conditions, a heavy swell, surf getting up from dead calm in slight changes of wind. A complete change can occur in under an hour, without warning, even in summer months.

It is quite impracticable for disembarkation of AFVs. Infantry in light vehicles could be landed if weather risks were accepted.

HUNSTANTON TO STUBBORN SANDS
The general conditions of the proceeding sub-section apply equally as far as Stubborn Sands where the general character changes somewhat. Stubborn Sands contains a small bay of some 4,000 yards length. It is less subject to variations in weather being sheltered to some extent and having at H.W. deeper water inshore.

The foreshore is moderately steep-to, mixed sand and shingle ebbing off to flat sand. It has an average width at L.W. of about 1500 yards.

The shore above H.W.M is shingle giving on to low dyke-intersected flat open country in the immediate hinterland. It contains two narrow road exits.

The disembarkation of AFVs would be possible at about ½ tide and above. The beach would however be difficult to locate except in daylight.

Lynn Channel, navigable for ships up to 17 feet is definitely vulnerable. Quays have 18' alongside. Banks of river at steep-to hard mud. There are no lifting appliances other than a small crane for lifting moorings. (Note: Navigation marks have been removed)

Summary
There are three areas in this coast section where AFVs might be disembarked e.g.
> Weybourne Hope to the Hood
> Stubborn Sands
> King's Lynn

Taking all factors into consideration the first two of these might be classed as possible but not probable. King's Lynn is, however vulnerable.

The entire section is vulnerable to aircraft landing.'

Seasoned officer Admiral Frederic Charles Dreyer, one of the GOC-in-C's advisors on anti-invasion measures was despatched to the East Coast and made his observations from Kessingland in Suffolk to King's Lynn and transmitted his findings in a memorandum giving his recommendations for the defences along the East Coast of England from the Headquarters of the 18th Division in Norwich to GOC-in-C Home Forces, Kneller Hall, Twickenham on 3 June 1940:

> *Passing North of Great Yarmouth. The beach of which is wired, there is a gap opposite to Ormesby St Margaret and there is another opposite Hemsby and a third opposite Winterton. These must be blocked with concrete obstacles and mined.*
> *Passing North towards Cromer there are a large number of gaps in the sand dunes which should be completely blocked with concrete obstacles, dannert wire and mines. These gaps exist between the Hundred Stream and Mundesley.*
> *Inland the road crossings of the North Walsham and Dilham Canal about 5 miles inland should be prepared for instant demolition.*
> *Passing north of Bacton Green the beach itself is suitable for the landing of infantry and light vehicles but the cliffs vary in height from 20 to 100 feet and it would appear that thoroughly filling the gaps therein will meet the situation, particularly in view of the large number of German mines laid out to seaward in the Would and the Haisborough Gat.*
> *There is also a gap in Overstrand which must be filled in.*
> *The small pier at Cromer should have a large section removed and the exits from the beach for vehicles or pedestrians should be blocked with concrete and dannert wire.*
> *Between Cromer and Sheringham there are two gaps in the cliffs which must be filled in as above.*
> *Between Sheringham and Cley which includes Weybourne Hope there are 7 gaps in the cliffs or dunes. These must be completely blocked as above.*
> *Major Crofton-Diggins who had taken part with Col. Spicer R.M. in the very valuable reconnaissance of the coast between Lowestoft and King's Lynn and whose advice I have had the great advantage of having, informs me that during their reconnaissance they consulted local opinion. A retired Major living at Stiffkey who has spent years in small craft off this coast and in wild fowling, stated that the weather could change on this coast from a flat calm to a very nasty sea inside an hour with practically no warning.*
> *Other local opinion obtained entirely corroborated this. All also agreed that the marshy hinterland would necessitate the use of light bridging equipment by any invader as the channels are numerous, steep sides and deep.*
> *The sands of north of Wells-next-the-Sea would at low water provide very good landing grounds for aircraft.*
> *With regard to landing of tanks on the beach between Weybourne Hope and King's Lynn the reconnaissance has shown that there are 3 areas where this could be done.*
> *1. Weybourne Hope to the Hood. The blocking of gaps would greatly impede this.*
> *2. Stubborn Sand off Heacham. The blocking of the two roads to Heacham must be very completely carried out with concrete and mine and dannert wire*
> *3. King's Lynn is vulnerable to attack. The navigational marks in the channels have been removed but local information is to the effect that up to September 1939 a Dutch company ran small steamers to King's Lynn on a regular service. The officers were changed frequently and thus a large number must know the channels.*
> *The Harbourmaster was of opinion, however, that even the local pilots would not attempt to enter at night as the lights are extinguished. In this connection it is also of interest to note that a German cable ship was observed before the war to be cruising inside the Sheringham Bank off Weybourne. This calls attention to the fact that the Norwich Command (18 Div) must close all gaps and roads mentioned in this memo and at the same time be prepared for an infantry attack on any portion of the coast.'*

The value and respect for well informed local knowledge is well demonstrated by the reaction of Nore Command immediately following the initial reconnaissance when Commander Burton RN, Resident Naval Officer, King's Lynn was sent a letter by Capt. W. Croucher D.S.C., the Lynn Dock Master on 2 June 1940 with reference to his recent interview regarding the possibility of landing enemy troops at King's Lynn in which he stated:

> *'I have had a good opportunity of studying the various types of Dutch built vessels... The vessels are shallow draught with an average speed of 10 knots and fitted with every modern*

device for accurate navigation and the masters know every little channel from Cromer to King's Lynn and Boston. With this knowledge I do not think any attempt would be made to land troops on the River front until they had taken the town by surprise, by landing troops along the coast line from Cromer to Hunstanton and whence to King's Lynn...'

The concerns over the expertise of German steamer captains and their knowledge of the Norfolk coast was also voiced in a letter from another man who had been interviewed during the reconnaissance, Mr A. Palmer of the ship brokers Garland and Flexman of King's Lynn.

Commander Burton passed the letters directly to Flag Officer in Command, Harwich who took the comment very seriously and wasted no time and arranged the extension of the Auxiliary Patrol to the Wash using Lowestoft Auxiliary Patrol vessels based in King's Lynn, minuting the decision on 8 June 1940.

Admiral Dreyer returned to the East Coast defences on 13 June and was met at King's Lynn by Major Crofton-Diggins and they undertook a further inspection from the Wash to Bacton. His return was further examine the feasibility of the Wash as an invasion route and was further prompted by contact from experienced military officers who suggested he inspect the beach between Sheringham and Cley from the point of view of tank landings. He also wanted to reconsider the findings of the East Coast reconnaissance that was:

'made on wrong premises, for in fact tanks can be landed on a very gently sloping beach on which the modern landing craft drawing some 3 feet having grounded, the door can then be let down and the tank, which can operate for a short time in 4 feet of water, then proceeds down the door and up onto the beach.'

Dreyer asked an experiment be conducted to see if a tank could be landed on the west shore of The Wash between Boston and Gibraltar Point. If this was possible, he concluded, tanks be certainly be able to land at Heacham and New Hunstanton for a period on either side of High Water. The beaches from Brancaster to Cley could stand a tank landing but the marshy background to the beaches would certainly scupper any chances of a major tank advance, indeed large areas of these marshes between the coast road and the sea had been allowed to flood as an anti-invasion measure shortly before his visit. Dreyer commented:

'The defence of the beach between Cley and Sheringham is of importance and no doubt every obstacle to tanks will be put up as soon as possible.'

Moving on to Cromer he was frustrated to see the pier was still intact but he was assured there would soon be 'a very large gap made in it.' Dreyer went further to formally note his recommendation that in all commands piers should at least have charges and detonators placed upon them with a sentry so in the event of invasion they could have gaps blown in them to foil the enemy.

On 14 June Dreyer called on Major General L. H. K. Finch DSO GOC 18(East Anglian) Division at his headquarters in Norwich and updated him with the findings of the latest reconnaissance and had a lengthy discussion about beach landings and defence measures. Later that day Dreyer discussed local conditions in the Wash near King's Lynn with Lieut. Commander A.H.M. Burton the R.N.O. King's Lynn. He was informed that two 6" guns had been mounted at Greenlands Farm covering the channel to the town but being on old mounting the guns were only able to fire up to about 6000 yards. Ships were no longer allowed to move at night in this sector.

Dreyer spoke to the Harbour Master regarding questions of pilotage and was concerned to learn that it was possible to get ships up drawing 16 feet and 6 inches and at H.W. neaps drawing 13 feet. Across the Wash at H.W. Springs the maximum draughts for ships was 10 feet. Dreyer noted his concerns in his report:

'This must be borne in mind when considering what difficulties an enemy ship would encounter when entering the Wash at night. Very useful ships can be designed to draw not more than 10 feet when carrying a good load. The large number of German fast motor craft each carrying 50 to 100 men must be borne in mind.'

Admiral Dreyer concluded with his possible invasion scenario and his suggested methods to counter such a threat:

'The Wash is in my opinion a dangerous area which we must be prepared to deny the enemy. Without indulging in 'the painting of pictures' it is not unreasonable to consider the case of the enemy landing on the beach North of Skegness and simultaneously on the Southwold reaches and rushing the Wash with large bodies of Troops in fast motor boats landing at King's Lynn and Boston and opening the Boston sluices to flooded the country in a southerly direction this impeding lateral movement of the defenders. The situation to be still further complicated by a diversionary landing well to the northward.
I strongly recommend that the Admiralty may be asked to consider the taking of immediate action to remove all navigational mark buoys and Lightships in the Wash and the laying of a minefield and also 'Table Cloth Nets' (latter to impede fast Motor Boats). I understand that at present the use of the Wash by shipping is practically nil.'

A minefield was laid and a boom placed across the wide Lynn Deeps channel that leads into the Wash on 5 July 1940. This left only the narrower 'Boston Deeps' where from that time all traffic would enter and leave the Wash and a pilot became necessary. In September 1940 the G.H.Q. Reconnaissance Unit undertook a study to determine the feasibility of an enemy landing in The Wash. The numerous sandbanks and beaches, especially those between King's Lynn and New Hunstanton were considered 'suitable for landing troops, M.T., A.F.Vs or aircraft' and comment was made how 'the coastline gener-

Soldiers from 6th Battalion, The Royal Norfolk Regiment assembling the anti-invasion road block defences at Sheringham, 1940. (IWM)

ally is remarkably similar to the northern German seaboard.'

The report stated 'Tides run at speeds of up to five knots. The rise and fall of the water is only about 25ft. The rise and fall on the North German seaboard is only 4ft which could be a serious difference if practicing landings in the Wash while still in Germany.' But after pointing out both Boston and particularly King's Lynn were ports of consequence and although the tides were complicated the enemy were thought to possess charts 'just as good as our own' and that trade routes between the continent and King's Lynn would be well known the reports' conclusion was simple:

'An enemy landing in the wash would be a difficult operation but it is feasible. It is more probable that the operation would be a raid or a diversion, than the Wash area would be the main objective of an expedition.'

It must be mentioned that many of the units along the coast had not waited to early June to act on the invasion threat. Most had already improvised some anti-invasion works since May 1940.

The 6 Royal Norfolk at Sheringham were directed to send a platoon to guard Cromer Pier on 10 May. On 11 May II Corps HQ ordered the immediate fortification of Great Yarmouth, Gorleston, Weybourne and Lowestoft. All companies of the 4th and 5th Battalions, The Royal Norfolk Regiment were ordered to battle stations on a front from High Kelling to Overstrand and serious works were carried out installing road blocks, digging weapons pits, sandbagging and reinforcing defensive emplacements at vulnerable points across the area and on the main roads. Orders stipulated 'Special watch is to be maintained for enemy parachutists.'

The men of 4 Royal Norfolk constructed roadblocks consisting of herring barrels filled with sand and lashed with timber all around the perimeter of Great Yarmouth and Gorleston, an anti-tank ditch was excavated around the Great Yarmouth golf course and a gap was blown in Britannia Pier to prevent its use as an enemy landing stage. Torpedo warheads were also installed in the seaward end of the pier with an electrical firing connection so if the enemy landed they would literally be blown sky high. The idea was undoubtedly good, but the switch for making the necessary connection was installed beside the side of the switch that operated the beach floodlights. It was always a tense moment when orders were received to test the floodlights in case the NCO in charge of the post closed the wrong switch!

Great ingenuity was also shown by young officers, NCOs and men of 4 Royal Norfolk as they installed cunningly prepared trip wires, claxon horns and bell alarms in the vicinity of their section posts; these, however, caused inconvenience to senior officers unaware of their existence when visiting the posts at night.

A sentry from 2/5th West Yorkshire Regiment keeps a watchful eye over the public who were allowed access to restricted areas of the beach defences at Sheringham, July 1941. (IWM)

With all of the improvisation and rush to set up these defences sometimes men with little experience were charged with tasks normally performed by those of more experience and some tragic accidents did occur. The first casualties of the 4th Battalion were incurred during this period when two men from 'A' Company were killed whilst laying mines in front of the racecourse.

The initiatives of the infantry battalions along our coast could only do so much. Once the reconnaissance reports were received Field Marshal Ironside, the GOC Home Forces and his staff were quick to see as many of the defences suggested in the reports from the regions were vigorously implemented. Ironside's strategy was to construct a coastal 'crust' consisting of miles of scaffolding designed to tear the bottoms out of landing barges along the beaches and coils of barbed wire defences stretching across the dunes, interspersed with concrete pillboxes and gun emplacements at strategic positions. Soon 50,000 anti-tank mines had been issued and orders for a further 200,000 were in place.

Emergency Gun Batteries were to provide the most formidable component of these defences. The first batteries in Norfolk appeared in June 1940 and were sited at King's Lynn, Hunstanton, Brancaster, High Cape covering Wells harbour and Holkham Bay, Cley Eye, Sheringham, Cromer, and Happisburgh. Each of these consisted of twin batteries armed with 6-inch naval guns. A further 4-inch gun battery was sited at Winterton and at Great Yarmouth three batteries were established – twin batteries with the 6-inch naval guns on both the North and South Denes and a battery on Gorleston Pier armed with two 12-pounder Q.F. (quick-firing) guns to cover the harbour entrance.

Admiral Dreyer visited the batteries shortly after their creation and emphasised their best location is among sand dunes where they could be 'completely and carefully camouflaged from aircraft and surface vessels. But he was, however, concerned about the lack of fire control apparatus for the gun emplacements on the beaches. Dreyer also expressed his opinion that the batteries did not offer enough protection to the gun crew and that there should be overhead as well as all round vertical protection against the splinters from bombs. This situation was soon rectified with covered casemates erected such as those that still survive at the Happisburgh Battery. All guns were mounted by Royal Navy personnel. The weaponry deployed at the batteries was often far from up to date, for example the No 1 Gun at Cromer had first been issued in 1906 when it was mounted upon HMS *Africa*,

Men of 325ᵗʰ Coastal Battery, 514ᵗʰ Coast Regiment (Anti-Aircraft), 2ⁿᵈ Corps at the North Denes, Great Yarmouth run to their positions on the alarm 'Enemy raiders approaching,' August 1941. (IWM)

while the No.2 had been issued in 192 and had served upon on HMS *Dublin* until 1925 and both of the gun mountings were dated 1905. From August 1940 the Norfolk coastal batteries were manned by the 565ᵗʰ, 546ᵗʰ and 514ᵗʰ Coastal Artillery Regiments RA of II Corps. The battery Headquarters for East and North Norfolk was at the Cliff Hotel Gorleston with 384 Battery at Winterton, 325 on the North Denes at Great Yarmouth, 427 Battery were on South Denes and Gorleston Pier, 277 Battery were on Gorleston Golf Links, 191 Battery at Hopton, 324 Battery at Cromer and 197 Battery at Mundesley.

Around the batteries a series of infantry defences, barbed wire, weapons pits, slit trenches and pillboxes were constructed. By October 1940 1,697 miles of wire, 440 miles of anti-tank obstacles and 73 miles of anti-tank mines had been built, excavated and set up across the Eastern Command Area.

Further coastal fire power would also have been provided from Anti-Tank gun emplacements at Holme and Heacham and the AA Camp at Weybourne who had installed some 5.25-inch dual purpose guns. There were usually secondary armaments and emplacements around the batteries ready for local defence including spigot mortars mounts and light machine guns turrets and further firepower available from mobile artillery units based a little further inland. Construction work for the coastal batteries was completed by December 1940.

The Civilian Population

The civilian population of Norfolk were all too aware that there was a clear and present danger of invasion in May 1940. Of course, like the rest of the country, they had seen the state of the war on Movietone news and read all about it in the papers but the inhabitants of the coast had seen the invasion defences being built first hand. There were already restrictions on where you could go and travel became limited as road blocks were set up and sentries from both the army and the Home Guard would ask for identity cards and enquire 'Is your journey really necessary?' On 31 May orders were given for all signposts to be taken down, milestones uprooted and all names of streets, railway stations and villages to be obliterated. Lord Haw-Haw commented on one of his German radio broadcasts received in Britain that the removal of signage was nothing more than a callous attempt by the British government to enforce their 'stay put' policy by making it difficult for the population to remove themselves to a place of safety if the invader came.

One group who were moved en masse at this time were the children who had been evacuated to the coast and locations immediately inland in September 1939. The government ordered the removal of all such children who were within 10 miles of the coast of Suffolk, Essex, Kent and part of Norfolk namely the Urban Districts of Cromer, North Walsham, Sheringham, Blofield and Flegg, Erpingham, Loddon and Smallburgh and Great Yarmouth. The children, said to number a total of about 8,000, were removed to the Midlands and South Wales.

Citizens who were not in the armed forces or working in Air Raid Precautions wanted to do something proactive to help defend their country from invasion. In May there was a massive response to an appeal for Local Defence Volunteers (see Chapter 4) and local invasion committees established to co-ordinate the local forces and prepare the defence of their town or village in the event of invasion. The population were advised to immobilise vehicles be they bicycles or motors when left unattended, hide food supplies and destroy or bury maps or similar materials which may help the enemy. Railway companies issued emergency orders marked 'Secret' which dictated the evacuation of locomotive and rolling stock away from the invasion area and its destruction if it could not be moved. Selected Observer Corps posts in the invasion area were issued with two rifles and ammunition. On 10 May 1940 the Norwich OC Centre sent out the signal:

> 'In the event of landing of enemy by parachute or boat posts will hang out as long as possible. If forced to retire posts will cut wires and try to take instruments with them. Failing this the instruments are to be destroyed.
> NOTE: This message is strictly secret and on no account to be mentioned outside the post.'

It was a time of popular fears, rumours and even black propaganda. On 13 June 1940 a ban on the ringing of church bells was announced; henceforth they would only be rung by the military or the police to give warning of invasion to the civilian population. Fears of enemy paratroops being dropped were very real, indeed the LDV were created in direct response to this concern and such units were often referred to in the press as 'Parashots.' There had been were fears over the 'Fifth Column' since 1939. These enemy agents and sympathisers were believed, very much in the spirit of the spy scares of 1914, to be poised to sabotage the utilities of the country by poisoning water or by blowing up gas works, fouling electricity generating stations and sub stations or cutting telephone lines. Not to mention puncturing tyres of the military and officials, impersonating officers from all armed forces, stealing cars and other motorised vehicles, giving poisoned sweets to children, signalling to the enemy by flashing lights and firing flares, planting listening devices or 'bugs' all over the place and flashing lights to enemy vessels out to sea or flying overhead. Some incidents even went to court, in once case from November 1940 the wife of the rector of Horsford was fined £20 and £5 costs after being found guilty of 'recording information which might be useful to the enemy.' Apparently she had written a message on an inside page of a copy of *The Times* which she posted to her cousin who lived in Ardee, Eire.

One persistent rumour is that was that some collaborators were farmers in Norfolk (and I am sure this was said to have occurred in other parts of the country). They were rumoured to be setting up grass landing strips for enemy aircraft and denoting these by painting their barns red. Furthermore, other farmers were said to be directing enemy aircraft to these landing fields or targets for them to bomb by arranging their portable chicken coops into the shape of a swastika or an arrow. On 5 June 1940 Field Marshal Ironside told an important meeting of LDV Commanders 'We have got examples of where there have been people quite definitely preparing aerodromes in this country... We want to know from you what is going on. Is there anything peculiar happening? Are there any peculiar people?' Ironside's statement about people preparing aerodromes failed to survive scrutiny upon closer examination of the information it was presumably based.

Fears about the Fifth Column and traitors were very real and tied up much valuable time for the military and the police but most of the 'emergencies' and suspicions were simply concerns from well-minded, patriotic people and they came to nothing. In *Invasion 1940* Peter Fleming commented: 'Perhaps the fact of the matter is that men's fear of traitors, like their fear of snakes, is seldom based on a realistic estimate of either's power to inflict harm.'

Inland Defences

The second part of Ironside's defence plans was the establishment of inland defensive lines. In the wider defence scheme Britain's most important defensive or 'Stop' line was the GHQ Line that ran around the southern and south west reaches of the county had been constructed to protect London and the industrial Midlands. In Norfolk there were three main Stop Lines; these were to be the buffers for holding up the advance of enemy forces if they managed to penetrate through the coastal crust. The Stop Lines were a system of strategically placed anti-tank ditches, rails and blocks, offensive anti-tank positions (spigot mortars), an array of pillboxes, roadblocks and defended town and villages that traversed the county roughly from west to east and used extant rivers and waterways as part of their defences. The forward stop line 'FI' followed the course of the North Walsham and Dilham Canal and the River Ant and along the Thurne to Horsey. 'FII' Began near Holt and followed the line of the River Bure from just North of Saxthorpe then on through Aylsham, Wroxham and Acle to Great Yarmouth. Behind the forward lines were Corps Line 'A' that ran from Burnham Market to Fakenham and then followed the River Wensum to Norwich where it divided in two, the main line going through Loddon to Beccles and line FIII following the course of the Yare, through Reedham and across the border to Lowestoft. Corps Line B ran from King's Lynn along the Nar to Castle Acre and then turned south and followed the road to Swaffham and then through Attleborough to Harleston.

The bridge crossings over the rivers along the FI, FII and FIII

forward stop lines formed a 'demolition belt' of bridges and key structures that would be blown up to frustrate the advance of enemy invaders. The 287th Field Company, Royal Engineers were charged with the responsibility of the demolitions along the line of the North Walsham-Dilham Canal and the River Bure. Their standing orders dated 13 July 1940 reflect the very real fear of invasion and that the plans for the defence of our county were ready to be carried out in earnest:

Information: The possibility of air and sea invasion continues.
No.1 Section is responsible for the demolition of the following bridges on the River Bure Line:-
No.1 Sub-Section (L/Sgt. Doughty, J.)
Aylsham Rail Bridge
Aylsham Road Bridge
No.2 Sub-Section (Cpl. Southwell, H.)
Burgh Road Bridge
Oxnead Road Bridge
No.3 Sub-Section (L/Cpl. Bacon, D.A.)
Ingworth Road Bridge (1)
Ingworth Road Bridge (2)
Section H.Q. during operations will be in Aylsham, at a spot to be guided by circumstances and notified to Sections.
The truck carrying H.M.G. will be under command of Section Officer and immediately on an alarm will immediately proceed to convoy demolition parties as far as Aylsham. It will then proceed to Section H.Q.
The necessity of demolition being complete need hardly be mentioned. Demolitions are a vital part of military plans and their failure will have most adverse effects on the operation. It is therefore stated that on no account will a complete bridge be allowed to fall into the enemy's hands. Once the charge is laid and the bridge prepared the responsibility of completing the demolition at all cost must rest entirely with the demolition party.

John Westcott
2/Lieut. R.E
Officer i/c No.1 Section
287th Field Company R.E.

In July 1940 Ironside was retired and General Sir Alan Brooke took over as C-in-C Home Forces. He favoured a far less static approach with a greater emphasis on offensive action to repel any enemy attempting invasion and an intricate system of AT islands and defended localities known as 'nodal points' (an expression introduced in Eastern Command and No.12 South Eastern Region in September 1940) was rapidly developed across the country. In Norfolk the most important of these nodal points denoted 'Category A' were a series of towns and villages, not more than 15 miles from the coast, provided anti-tank defence localities and also commanded the nexus of roads.

The units charged with this task were primarily the 8th and 9th (Home Defence) Battalions, The Royal Norfolk Regiment but during 1940 there were insufficient troop numbers to hold a second or reserve line in strength however Home Guard units could be found in every nodal point town, with them could be mustered any available troops, such as fighting personnel from Field Ambulances, Royal Engineer Field Companies, Royal Army Service Corps etc with the Home Guard under operational control, these soldiers would be organised into garrisons for their towns where the local OC troops would have their defence scheme planned. In villages and other localities the defences would be also manned by the available local military forces and Home Guard. The divisional military commanders were in no doubt of the dedication of the Home Guard, particularly in the forward areas on and near the coast; more than one official report stated confidently 'they would, if required, fight to the last round and the last man.'

As defences became more organised it was decided that each nodal point town or village should have its' 'keep' made tank proof by means of road blocks and concrete blocks between houses and that an outpost ring of defences would be constructed on the outskirts. The expression 'fortress' came to be used to designate the main inland towns that were selected for fortification along these lines. Although most of the town defences have now been removed many Norfolk town centres had their own large pillboxes or built into more urban settings and disguised as part of the extant buildings. At Fakenham their town centre pillbox was disguised as a plinth and a statue of Justice was stood on top of it. It should not, however, be assumed that everyone was entirely comfortable about the situation and concerns were voiced through UDCs about the circumstances for introduction and the extent of Martial Law if it was enforced in their town.

Nodal Points (Defended Places) in the County of Norfolk

Category A:
Locations not more than 15 miles from the coast, provided good anti-tank defence localities and commanded the nexus of roads.
Acle, Aylsham, Burnham Market, Coltishall, Cromer, Docking , East Dereham, Fakenham, Holt, King's Lynn, Loddon, Ludham, North Walsham, Norwich, Saxthorpe, Sheringham, Swaffham, Watton, Wymondham, Thetford, Yarmouth

Category B:
Defended towns and villages on routes of re-enforcing formations.
Attleborough, Coltishall, Diss, Harleston, Loddon, Ludham, Wroxham

Category C:
Defended villages of military and /or tactical significance such as road junctions and bridging points
Blakeney, Castle Acre, Cley-next-the Sea, Happisburgh , Ingham, Foulsham, Little Walsingham, Melton Constable, Overstrand, Langham, Mundesley, Reepham, Runton, East, Stiffkey, Thorpe Market, Wells, West Runton, Weybourne

The idea of the stop lines was to hold the enemy at bay rather than deliver a decisive blow against him and buy enough time to establish the direction of the attack and bring up the reserves stationed in Newmarket and Northampton to counter attack as the navy deployed at sea to engage the enemy landing vessels and support craft. GHQ reserves that would have been despatched in response to an enemy landing in East Anglia included 2 Armoured Division in Nottingham and 43 Infantry Division in Hertfordshire. They would be mobilized in such circumstances by a code word that would send them to the required area for example 'Nancy' would send the reinforcements to Attleborough to deploy for a threat from North Norfolk, 'Percy' would despatch them to the Fens to counter invasion forces landed from the Wash or 'George' would send to them to Thetford and Brandon area while 43 Division were told to assemble at Diss to engage any invading force between Great Yarmouth and Aldeburgh.

The infamous 'Cromwell' codeword was assumed by many in the military to announce Britain was being invaded but what it actually requested was an increased state of alert. On Saturday 7 September 1940 'Cromwell' was issued to Eastern and Southern Commands, IV and VII Corps (in GHQ Reserve) and HQ London District. It was assumed by most military officials who received the message that invasion had been announced and they went into full deployment on a war footing. In Eastern Command roads were instantly locked down, defences manned and primed, telephone operators refused

to accept non-official calls and in some areas the church bells were rung but before the immediate action orders could be rescinded or clarified a number of bridges were demolished by Royal Engineers and over the border in Lincolnshire three officers from a Guards Brigade were blown up and killed by mines laid on the road they were driving along.

There were also scares that enemy troops could be landed upon the Norfolk Broads by sea planes. To combat this, a number of broads were closed off and mined, the mines delineated by white posts that stood out of the water. The Norfolk Broads Flotilla was initially crewed by army reservist soldiers under the operational control of the Royal Navy but was taken over by the Army in 1941. The Broads Flotilla consisted of requisitioned motor boats converted into fast patrol craft armed with Lewis guns and crewed by a mixture of soldiers from 8th (Home Defence) Battalion, The Royal Norfolk Regiment and Home Guard. Its continuing task being to patrol inland waterways and guard against German seaplanes using the Broads to drop off undercover agents and teams of saboteurs.

Defence of the Coastal Waters

The defence of our coastal waters and the protection of shipping was provided by the Royal Navy Nore Command. The East Coast convoy route was a mile wide and stretched from the Firth of Forth to the Thames. The merchant vessels that sailed these dangerous waters faced both sea mines and E-Boats. Due to the dangers of enemy action the fishing industry in Great Yarmouth and Gorleston was suspended from the outbreak of war but the valiant fishermen and their vessels did not lie dormant as many of the fishing boats were converted to minesweepers and the fishermen volunteered for the Royal Naval Reserve to become their crews sailing out from Yarmouth undertaking mine sweeping missions as far away as the Dutch coast. The Great Yarmouth base became HMS *Watchful* and provided convoys with protection from MTBs, salvage tugs and Air Sea Rescue boats. In 1940 *HMS Miranda* was established as a dedicated base for the minesweeping trawlers at the Fishwharf.

From 1 January 1941 to 21 July 1945 HMS *Midge* became Yarmouth's coastal forces base under Commander E. R. Lewis DSO, DSC with responsibility for Motor Torpedo Boats, Motor Gun Boats and Mine Layers.

For the period January-May 1941 HMS *Midge* comprised:

HM King George VI inspects a parade of Officers and men from the minesweepers of HMS Miranda at Gorleston, 23 August 1940. (IWM)

Minesweeping trawler – *Cape Melville* (Ty Sk G S Peek RNR)

Minesweeping Group 10 - minesweeping trawlers *Arkwright* (Ty Lt A J W Stead RNVR), *Milford Princess* (Ty Sk J W Cook RNR), *Milford Queen* (Ty Sk R H Soanes DSC RNR)

Minesweeping Group 11 - minesweeping trawlers *Contender* (Ty Sk A E Kettless RNR), *Irvana* (Sk J L Borrett RNR), *Nogi* (Lt Cdr J N Caris), *Solon* (Ty S/Lt J S Watt RNR)

Minesweeping Group 13 - minesweeping trawlers *Blighty* (Ty Lt H Shaw RNVR), *Charles Doran* (Ty Sk R R Snape RNR), *Clothilde* (Ty Lt J D Robinson RNVR), *Cotsmuir* (Ty Sk W C M Ayres RNR)

Minesweeping Group 14 - minesweeping trawlers *Cardiff Castle* (Ty Sk G F H Frosdick RNR), Epine (Lt G A de La Rue RCNVR), *Star of Orkney* (Sk J Flint RNR), *Their Merit* (Ty Sk R W Vann RNR)

Minesweeping Group 15 - minesweeping trawlers Madden (Ty Sk S Amos RNR), *Princess Mary* (Ty Sk C E Parker RNR), *Tamora* (Ty Lt S P Rothon RNVR)

Minesweeping Group 31 - minesweeping trawlers *Bracon Moor* (Ty Lt H N Somerville RNVR), *Carisbrook* (Ty Sk J Moore RNR), *Curtana* (Ty Lt A E Bell RNVR), *George Robb* (Ty Sk J Ormerod RNR)

Minesweeping Group 114 - minesweeping trawlers *Elsie Cam* (Sk D E Coleman RNR), *Lybian* (no CO listed), both at Sheerness, *Valesca* (Ty Lt C W S Barnes RNVR)

Minesweeping Group 115 - minesweeping trawlers *Desiree* (Pbty Sk E L Fiske RNR) at Sheerness, *Marano* (Ty Lt J W G Price RNR), *Orizaba* (no CO listed)

Minesweeping Group 146 - minesweeping trawlers *Hortensia* (Ty S/Lt J K Turnbull RNVR), *Orpheus* (Lt C L Carroll RNR), *Peken* (Ty Lt H McClelland RNVR) damaged.

Minesweeping drifters - *Feasible* (Sk C C Findlay RNR), *Justifier* (Ty Sk R R Russell RNR) repairing, *Silver Crest* (Ty Sk A W J Burwood RNR), *Swift Wing* (Ty Sk R N J Haylett RNR)

Motor minesweeper - MMS.1 at Lowestoft

1st Motor Launch Flotilla - ML.105 at Portland, ML.106 at Yarmouth, ML.107 at Dartmouth repairing, ML.108, ML.110, both at Yarmouth

Echo sounding yacht - *Alicia* (Ty S/Lt A R Friggens RNVR) at Humber

Battle Drill! After disembarking from landing craft, troops of 1st Battalion, Duke of Wellington's Regiment make their assault up the cliffs near Cromer, 21 April 1942. Live machine-gun and mortar fire was used during this exercise. (IWM)

Members of the Royal Army Service Corps on the cliffs at Cromer, 1941. (IWM)

'Y' Service

Military establishments that were to prove extremely valuable to the war effort were also set up in the county. In May 1941 the first Wireless Intercept or 'Y' Service post in the county was set up at Trimingham with more at locations such as at the summit of 'Beeston Bump' at Beeston Regis, Hemsby and Gorleston following soon after. The posts were sometimes situated in requisitioned private dwellings but were always near the cliffs of the location and were run by specialist units of the Royal Navy, Army and RAF staffed by between 12 to 20 personnel. Many of the operators were from the women's services such as the Women's Royal Naval Service ('WReNS'); all of them would have been highly skilled and well-educated young women providing continuous cover working day and night shifts on radios capable of listening to enemy shipping or low flying aircraft radio signals which, if they were in plain German, would be translated and sent to the filtering centre at Harwich or by despatch rider to the Government Code and Cipher School at Bletchley Park in Buckinghamshire to be deciphered if they were in code.

Beyond 1940

In late 1941 with the danger of imminent invasion receded the coastal defences were reappraised. The demands of a widening war put increasing pressure on manpower and the trained troops were withdrawn from the coastal garrisons and were replaced by three county divisions with one mobile field division in reserve. It was also at this time the King's Lynn battery, believed to be situated too distant from deep water to effectively engage a target with a 6" shell was the first coastal battery to be closed.

On 17 August 1941 the Royal Navy Officer at Hunstanton informed Eastern Command's Headquarters Naval Liaison Officer 'that about twelve ships have passed over the Wash minefield without any damage' and as one of the 'principle defences of the Wash' it was requested that the Admiralty relay the minefield as soon as possible.

The reply came back: 'The Admiralty state that it is not their intention to relay the Wash minefield on account of its very doubtful value. Due to the rise of the tide, moderate draught ships could pass over the top of the minefield at high water and due to the dip of the moored mines in the strong tidal streams it is probable that moderate draught ships could pass over the mines at most other states of the tide... it is probable that the majority of the mines no longer exist. It is pointed out that the Wash minefield, could never have been considered one of the principle defences of the Wash; even when first laid it was merely a deterrent to ships entering at or near low water.'

The coastal batteries were manned through 1942 but as the danger of invasion became increasingly remote between 1943 and 1944 the regular troops manning the batteries were removed and replaced by the Home Guard but the Norfolk coast still had a role to play in the preparations for the D-Day landings – Operation Fortitude South. Operation Fortitude was in fact a one of the most successful deception operations of the war, the idea was to convince German intelligence the allies were going to invade two locations other than Normandy. Fortitude North created the lie of a planned invasion of Norway, and Fortitude South, to create a phantom invasion force for the invasion of France at the Pas de Calais rather than Normandy. The deception was created by many cunning devices from deliberate 'careless talk,' to extensive radio traffic to give the impression of massive preparations and troops movements in readiness for the invasions. There were also visiting and movement restrictions imposed from the Wash, around the East Coast and down to Lands End which came into effect on 1 April 1944. Areas affected could be as far as 10 miles inland; in Norfolk the 'protected areas' were: The County Boroughs of Great Yarmouth and King's Lynn and the urban districts of Freebridge Lynn, New Hunstanton, Wells, Cromer, Sheringham, North Walsham and the rural districts of Docking, Walsingham, Erpingham, Smallburgh, Marshland (incl. Loddon), Blofield and Flegg. On 2 April 1944, following a secret reconnaissance around the sectors involved by GHQ, a 'Top Secret' plan was sent to the field commanders and naval officers detailing the construction of buildings and launch sites for fake tank landing craft codenamed 'Bigbobs.' Made of canvas and erected over a metal frame at 25 yards the completed LCTs were indistinguishable from the real thing. A total of six sites were created at Folkestone, Dover, Woolverstone, Waldringfield, Lowestoft and at Great Yarmouth where the dummy LCTs were stored, erected and found their launching hard at Pitchers Quay and the Railway Yard and were berthed upon Breydon Water.

Further reductions among the coastal batteries took place in 1944. The Sheringham battery was closed and the guns at Brancaster, High Cape, Happisburgh and Cley were unmanned and simply kept in maintenance. By late 1944 all the batteries were closed, plans were made to dismantle them and the companies of Royal Engineers and Pioneer Corps set about removing the mines and anti-invasion structures from our beaches. The guns were removed from the batteries in 1945 and scrapped, the only artillery left on the Norfolk coast being the guns of the A.A. Camp at Weybourne, the last rounds being fired by 459 (Essex) HAA Regiment (TA) on 2 October 1958. The minefields of our coastline took considerably longer to clear.

3 Beating the Invader

After seven months of the 'Phoney War' the Battle of France began in earnest on 10 May 1940. Hitler had unleashed his blitzkrieg and by 14 May German Army Group A had broken through the Ardennes, swept west towards Sedan and had set its sights towards the English Channel. Army Group B had invaded the Netherlands and advanced west through Belgium. The blitzkrieg sped through the continent with such apparent ease fears of the fall of Belgium, France and Holland left many in no doubt Britain would face the onslaught next. Particular concerns were shown for the use of German paratroops being dropped in advance of any invasion. Some disparate groups of men in towns and villages were already gathering together to discuss how they would defend their homes, formed irregular units and had begun patrolling country areas after dark armed with shotguns.

Even the most sedate of households saw gentlemen searching in the back of their desk draws for the revolvers they had brought back after their service in the Great War and went out to buy ammunition. Grave conversations were held where husbands and wives agreed to keep the last rounds for themselves. Ex-Army officers were also becoming very vocal in the press, on radio and even on cinema newsreels demanding that they, and many other like-minded men, be given the chance to volunteer to do something practical for the defence of their country, even if only to provide suicide squads against invading forces.

It was to be the fear of the use of paratroops by the enemy that brought matters to a head. An urgent message was circulated from the Air Ministry to all Commands and repeated to the Admiralty, War Office and Ministry of Home Security stating 'Information from Norway shews that German parachute troops, when descending, hold their arms above their heads as if surrendering. The parachutist, however, hold a grenade in each hand. These are thrown at anyone attempting to obstruct the landing. To counter this strategy, parachutists, if the exceeded six in number, are to be treated as hostile and if possible shot in the air.' Although subsequently this information of the offensive tactics used by the enemy has proved to be erroneous the deployment of paratroops was very real. Following a number of high level meetings where the concerns over this matter and what could be done. Among the senior officers at these meetings were General Sir Robert Gordon-Finlayson and General Sir Walter Kirke. Well aware of the rising 'martial enthusiasm' in the country Kirke suggested, if organized properly on a town and village basis, men who were not in military service could make up a volunteer Defence Force to provide a valuable counter measure against the parachute menace. Anthony Eden, the newly appointed Secretary of State for War took a keen interest in this idea and secured official Cabinet approval for the formation of the Local Defence Volunteers, an organization to be placed under Commander-in-Chief Home Forces. The original idea was for the C-in-C to announce the scheme through a radio broadcast but Eden wanted to do this personally. Late on the evening on 13 May Eden drafted the broadcast from notes collated by General Kirke from notes provided by General Gordon-Finlayson. His Majesty's Stationery Office printed thousands of enrolment forms and telegrams were sent from the Under Secretary of State at the Home Office to Chief Constables across the country arranging the use of police stations as centres where volunteers could present themselves and enrol. Delivery of the necessary forms to police stations was given top priority.

The morning papers of 14 May newspapers headlined a 'two thousand tank clash north west of Liege,' fears over the fifth column and spies saw the BBC announced in its German news that any German parachutist found landing in this country in any kit other than a recognized German uniform would be shot. Holland was swarming with troops and Queen Wilhelmina had arrived in London as a refugee, that same evening the Dutch Army surrendered. After a brief announcement Anthony Eden broadcast his radio appeal between the 9 o'clock news and a documentary entitled 'The Voice of the Nazi.' Eden began 'I want to speak to you tonight about the form of warfare which the Germans have been employing so extensively against Holland and Belgium – namely the dropping of parachute troops behind the main defensive lines…In order to leave nothing to chance, and to supplement from sources

'If the Invader Comes' leaflet delivered to every household, June 1940

as yet untapped the means of defence already arranged, we are going to ask you to help us in a manner which I know will be welcome to thousands of you. Since the war began the government have received countless inquiries from all over the kingdom from men of all ages who are for one reason or another not at present engaged in military service, and who wish to do something for the defence of their country. Well, now is your opportunity.

We want large numbers of such men in Great Britain, who are British subjects, between the ages of seventeen and sixty-five to come forward now and offer their services in order to make assurance doubly sure. The name of the new force which is now to be raised will be the Local Defence Volunteers.'

Eden went on to state that the volunteers would be unpaid but they would receive a uniform and would be armed. Those wishing to volunteer were asked to register their names at local police stations. Like a shot from a starting pistol the volunteers poured in, not in hundreds as anticipated but in their thousands through the night and following day; nationally, some 250,000 gave their names in the first 24 hours. Within two weeks 30,000 Norfolk men had volunteered for the LDV.

After the place for enrolment into the Local Defence Volunteers was announced as the local police station many men set off to join immediately, many of them pausing only to grab their discharge books or put on their medals awarded for service in the First World War; some volunteers arrived at police stations even before the broadcast had ended. Many set out with all due speed with the intention of being the very first to volunteer only to find a queue had already formed in front of them. So rapid was the response enrolment forms had not reached every police station but police officers amicably took down names and addresses. In other areas Chief Constables sent instructions that each volunteer was to be asked: Their name and address, Are you familiar with firearms? Your occupation? What military experience have you? Are you prepared to serve away from home? The police were also given clear instructions that they were not concerned with the administration or control of the LDVs, only the registering of the names and addresses of volunteers but they were advised to exercise discretion by 'politely sending way' and not recording the names of those clearly too young or too infirm. In addition to those outlined by Mr Eden the criteria and terms for volunteers were laid down in a War Office circular which stated the period of service volunteers would serve would be 'for the duration of the war' and that 'training and duties could be taken in a volunteer's spare time.' There was no medical examination but men would have to be 'of reasonable physical fitness' and 'capable of free movement,' previous military service and/or a knowledge of firearms (in those days far more country people kept a shot gun to bag a rabbit or pigeon for the pot) were considered advantageous. These points soon evolved into the standard 'Form of Enrolment in the Local Defence Volunteers'. Much to the chagrin of many suitable volunteers already serving in the ARP or in the Special Constabulary they had to be turned down lest the forces they had already been trained in became too depleted. In reality the recruitment terms were flexible, in some small villages men served as both Home Guards and ARP or the HG platoon had an ARP duties section. A Commanding Officer often used his discretion to enrol enthusiastic youngsters as young as fourteen and fifteen as messengers or volunteers if they looked old enough and even went so far as to issue the lad with a dispatch riders army trade badge that many lads wore with great pride as they went speeding off on their bicycles charged with the delivery of another important message. Discretion was also shown towards old soldiers, especially ex-NCOs over the age limit who had valuable experience to impart.

Concurrent with the Eden broadcast each county's Lord Lieutenant a telegram was sent by Eden to the Lord Lieutenant of every county station 'I am sure that we may count on your co-operation and help in connection with the Local Defence Volunteer Force.' Each Lord Lieutenant was expected to begin the county structure of the LDV by appointing an Area Commander with overall command and organization responsibility for the county. On 17 May Norfolk's Lord Lieutenant, Mr Russell Colman, held a conference with his Deputy Lieutenants and began the implementation of the LDV scheme in Norfolk and appointed Colonel R. G. Cubitt TD (later O.C. 5th (T.A.) Battalion, The Royal Norfolk Regiment) for that very task. In each Zone a headquarters had to be established to administer the number of Groups within it. An unpaid Volunteer Organiser was to be put in charge of each Zone and each Group. The numbers involved were not quite like the army, whereas a regular army platoon consists of 30 men the LDV equivalent could range between 10 and 50 men. Most of those appointed to command positions in the LDV had previous military experience but it was not essential as those with respected managerial, organizational and leadership skills from civvy street equally found themselves in positions of command. Eleven battalions, conforming to the areas covered by the extant police divisions, were authorised and their commanders appointed as shown:-

No. 1 Battalion, East Dereham......................Lt.-Col. J F Barclay, TD
No. 2 Battalion, Downham Market.................... Lt-Col E R Pratt, MC
No. 3 Battalion, Harleston.......................... Capt. Sir Robert Bignold
No. 4 Battalion, Holt..............................Lt.-Col. The Lord Hastings
No. 5 Battalion, Nth Walsham.........Col Lord William Percy, CBE DSO
No. 6 Battalion, Norwich................................ Major S W Trafford
No. 7 Battalion, King's Lynn & Sandringham............. Col. O Birkbeck
No. 8 Battalion, Swaffham..................................Capt. F G Buxton
No. 9 Battalion, Wymondham.................Col. The Viscount Bury, MC
No.10 Battalion, Norwich..............................Capt B F Hornor, DSO
No.11 Battalion, Gt. Yarmouth........................Major F R B Hayward

Although the War Office stated it was proposed to issue uniforms of the Denim overall type and field service caps the vast numbers of LDVs meant that the uniforms immediately ready for issue did not go far and uniform for most LDV units in those early weeks and months was almost non-existent. Platoons knew they were coming but enthusiastically set about drilling and training in their civilian clothes with the civilian issue gas mask slung and improvised rifle (often a broomstick) carried at the slope on the march. A units near public or grammar schools in the county sought to alleviate their temporary lack of weaponry by seizing school OTC rifle armouries 'In the Name of the King.' Some such incidents became very heated and required intervention from police and magistrates and even formal legal proceedings were instigated in the most extreme cases. Following a public appeal for old weaponry all manner of firearms and offensive weapons were brought into to police stations for use by the LDV. Local museums were also picked over for serviceable weapons and firearms, this brought out some very serviceable machine guns, pistols and rifles captured during the First World War but with them were also impressed ancient and ethnic weaponry of bewildering vintages. The 10th (City of Norwich) Battalion followed suit with a visit to the Castle Museum where they were able to borrow some Crimean War vintage rifles and were given the option of a sentry box of similar vintage.

The first 'uniform' item to be received by many units in these early days was the 'brassard' – a simple khaki armband stencilled with the black letters LDV. On 22 May Sir Edward Grigg the joint parliamentary Under-Secretary of State for War announced a quarter of a million arm bands were on their way. These supplies were soon consumed so many variations of the LDV armbands were improvised at a local level screen printed or embroidered by patriotic local companies or hand made by local WI or WVS branches.

It is clear from the surviving archives of the LDV in Norfolk and across the country and ably demonstrated by the speed of production that some consideration of what measures should be undertaken to defend town and villages if a unit such as the LDV was formed and many such recorded plans show the unmistakable hand of well experienced officers such as that produced by Major Percival Pickford D.S.O., the Headmaster of the Paston Grammar School and founder of its Cadet Corps who had been appointed LDV Commander for North Walsham Parish. On 23 May 1940 the following was issued as a type written instruction sheet to all Local Defence Volunteers under his command:

DUTIES:
At All times to provide early information of any enemy action and of all suspicious persons. When in uniform [author's note: remember at this time the 'uniform' consisted of an arm band] an LDV is entitled to demand to see the registration card and otherwise to remand in custody anyone whose identity cannot be established.

Information is the primary duty and the first object must be to get into touch at the earliest possible moment with our own infantry, who are prepared to act on information received and with them the closest contact should be maintained. It is also important to get into touch with the LDV HQ at the Grammar School where a reserve force will assemble in an emergency by day or night.

Subsidiary duties are to deny the enemy use of all vehicles and petrol, to provide armed guards at telephone exchanges, to act as guides where required and man road blocks as required.

It must be emphasises that the LDV are only expected to deal with small numbers of the enemy, whose movement must be restricted, while the work of the regular infantry will be to defend local areas from attack.

POSTS: It has been decided for the present to carry out the duties with five posts manned at least from black-out to black-out (dusk to dawn) with reserves at LDV HQ as well as at posts to assemble on the red ARP alarm or other signal by day or by night.

These posts will be manned at night by at least three men armed and uniformed, one of whom at least must be on observation duty at all times of the night and each post must have at least one cycle at the post. The man in charge each night should have had service experience.

For the first week it is expected that the Section Commander will himself post the sentry and explain duties. Posts should not patrol but should always find a sentry outside any hut or shelter.

These posts will be as follows:

    No. 1 : HQ at Col. Besant's, Worstead Lodge, Cromer Rd. (Tel. 181)
    No. 2 : HQ at Mr. Bell's, Lyngate House, Bacton Rd. (Tel. 155)
    No. 3 : HQ at Mr. Farrell's, Long Acre, Hasbro' Rd. (Tel.167)
    No. 4 : HQ at Mr. Randell's, Southcroft, Yarmouth Rd. (Tel. 157)
    No. 5 : HQ at Mr. Brook's, North Walsham Wood, Skeyton Road (Tel. 11)

RESERVE FORCE:
The ten men living nearest to the post will be detailed to proceed at once to the post in the event of alarm by day or night: all the remainder will go at once to the Grammar School Playground and be prepared to act as a reserve (with as many cycles as possible) under the command of the Parish Commander.

POSTS WILL BE MANNED from the night of 23rd May until further orders.

SECTION COMMANDERS are asked to report in writing, on the next morning, any unusual but not urgent matter, and to be at LDV HQ on Tuesday and Friday evenings for a conference.

TRAINING in the use of the ROSS RIFLE [from the Cadet Corps armoury] will be given on Grammar School Field every evening of the week beginning May 26th and all members who have been accepted are required to be there at 7.30 on Thursday May 30th (or as soon afterwards as possible).

It is suggested that until men have had practice in the use of a rifle only the ex-service man in charge of the post will carry the ammunition and that unless an alarm is given rifles should be loaded by nobody. Single loading is recommended.

P. Pickford
LDV Commander
North Walsham Parish

On 24 May 1940 Sir Will Spens, the Civil Defence Commissioner for the Eastern Region placed the

Spot at sight – the German Paratrooper.

Norfolk LDV under the command of the Commander East Anglian Area who, in turn, passed command to the Commander of the 18th Division, whose headquarters were in Norwich.

The first duty of the LDV was observation and posts for this purpose were rapidly established around every town and village in the county. On 9 June, orders were received that 85 road blocks were to be constructed on specially detailed sites and manned in twelve hours. A tall order perhaps but the task was completed as instructed.

Eventually the first issue of denim fatigue uniforms arrived with a separate issue of brown leather gaiters. No cap badges were issued. No boots were supplied at this time and complaints were made about the wear and tear inflicted on the boots of LDVs, many of whom sought some compensation for repairs.

The Battalion level ranks of the LDV consisted of Battalion Commander, Company Commander and Platoon Commander, each rank designated with blue stripes on the epaulette (one for platoon, two for Company and three for Battalion Commanders.) Even at this early stage ex-army officers were raiding their old uniforms for their old rank insignia. There soon followed by the NCO corps equivalents of Section Commander (three chevrons) and Squad Commander (two Chevrons). The official title of the ordinary man in the LDV was Volunteer.

In these early months of the LDV the training schedule of each Battalion varied greatly across the country but suffice to say marching drill bond the men into a disciplined unit was an important factor as was their training on broomsticks and what weaponry they had at their disposal at that time. Crucially, the LDV wanted to set to work on the task it had been set. Most Zones and Groups were rapidly established and their primary function of patrolling set up with duty rotas and their call out alarm system established in the event of an emergency – for most this was to be the ringing of the local church bells, in case this method was prevented by the enemy a 'knock-list' of manual call outs was usually agreed and often typed out and distributed to the platoon.

Later, three Zones conforming to military boundaries were formed in the county viz:-

East Norfolk: Commander, Colonel R. G. Cubitt TD (under operational control of 76 Div.), containing parts of 3rd and 4th Battalions with the complete 5th, 6th, 10th and 11th Battalions.

Mid Norfolk: Commander, Major General E. M. Steward CB, CSI, OBE, consisting of entire 1st Battalion and parts of 3rd, 8th and 9th Battalions.

West Norfolk: Commander: Lt-Col. E. R. Pratt MC, consisting of entire 2nd and 7th Battalions with parts of 4th and 8th Battalions.

Between 26 May and 4 June 1940 the beleaguered British Expeditionary Force was evacuated in Operation 'Dynamo' from the beaches of Dunkirk, an evacuation made more poignant and so typically undaunted as eulogised by J.B. Priestly in his *Postscript to the News* 'Little Ships' broadcast of 5 June 1940. Dunkirk was not just an evacuation but we must not lose sight of the fact that it also heralded a defeat for the BEF. On 18 June Churchill grimly announced in parliament 'What General Weygand called the Battle of France is over. I expect that the Battle of Britain is about to begin. Upon this battle depends the survival of Christian civilization. Upon it depends our own British life, and the long continuity of our institutions and our Empire. The whole fury and might of the enemy must very soon be turned on us.' France capitulated on 25 June and many British households had already received the 'If the Invader Comes' leaflet. The leaflet advised the civilian population to 'stay put,' look out for and report suspicious activity, help our troops and LDV if ordered to do so, suggested the precautions to take which would enable you not to help the enemy such as hiding maps and immobilizing vehicles and suggested if you have a factory to organize its defence 'at once.'

On 23 July 1940 Winston Churchill, who had never liked the cumbersome and somewhat ridiculed title of Local Defence Volunteers, saw it formally announced that the organization be re-named Home Guard (HG). This was not only a change in name but ushered in a new raft of improvements, structured training, uniform and weaponry supplies and official recognition were set in motion for the million HGs across the country. Re-titled and expanding the following additional HG battalions were formed in Norfolk:

No.12 Battalion, Brancaster.......................Lt.-Col. J. Leslie, DSO MC
No.13 Battalion, Sheringham.....................Lt.-Col. W J Spurrell, DSO
No.14 Battalion, Hapton...Lt.-Col. R J Read
No.15 Battalion, Downham Market.........Lt.-Col. Lt.-Col. H. Buchanan
No.16 Battalion, Norwich......................Lt.-Col. H. N. Morgan, M.C.
No.17 Battalion, Reepham.........................Lt.-Col. Q. E. Gurney, T.D.

One great move in the wake of the new changes was on 3 August 1940 when the Home Guard were affiliated to their county regiments and our Norfolk battalions were granted permission to wear the regimental cap badge and the woollen worsted battle dress of their regular and territorial army counterparts in The Royal Norfolk Regiment. There battledress was adorned with a khaki cloth shoulder title with the words Home Guard printed upon it in yellow. Beneath the shoulder title would be letter designations for the county, in our case NK for Norfolk accompanied by the battalion number beside or below it.

The training manuals used by the Home Guard gave a number of helpful tips for improvised anti-tank warfare. After explaining how the enemy tank drivers view is limited to slot sights when the lid is closed the manual explains 'a sheet is disguised to resemble the ground in a narrow lane. On either side of the lane is a man and when the vehicle is about to pass them they each drag on a piece of rope or wire running through the edge of the sheet and passing over tree branches of gate posts. The sheet rises from the ground and before the tank can stop it is completely enveloped and blinded.' He will have to stop of risk an accident, thus cloaked the other waiting 'tank busters' of the HG detachment could then rapidly move in ramming a crow bar between the track and wheel and prise it off or blow it off with his improvised tank charge (4-6lbs of plastic explosive with a Bickford fuse and detonator sheathed in a cocoa tin) thus disabling the tank. It is then a sitting duck for their 'Molotovs' (petrol bombs). Three of these strategically placed on the tank could lead to the fire being taken into the tank's air intake causing it to brew up.

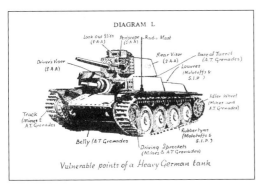

Vulnerable points of a Heavy German tank

Attacking the Track and Delivering a "Sticky."
(These operations are not performed simultaneously.)

Another guide suggests a plentiful supply of metal plates with their undersides painted black could be laid across narrow entrance roadway into a village to given the impression of anti-tank mines. A little straw scattered over them gives the impression of some attempt to hide them, the enemy tank commander stops and opens his hatch to investigate and lo! The waiting HG in the two storey house above him drop a few 'Molotovs' – down the hatch of his tank! Armed with such inspiring methods of improvised anti-tank warfare most Home Guard Companies trained as per these instructions and most of them established their own anti-tank platoons.

The Home Guard Battalions across Norfolk provided a major force for the defence of the nodal points across the county and their dedication was highly regarded by Eastern Command. In August 1940 the following was published in the Eastern Command briefing notes:

> 'The Home Guard are an integral part of the land forces engaged in the battle of Britain. The importance of its part in that battle cannot be exaggerated. The resistance that will be put up in towns and villages will disorganise enemy forces landed by sea or air, isolate their detachments and prevent co-ordination of effort. Of no less importance will be small parties, or even individuals, who knowing every square yard of their country, harry the enemy with skill and determination by day and by night.
>
> The Germans will be well equipped but they don't like opposition, counter attack or night work. They like to rest at night and all successful efforts to disturb their rest will have the greatest effect.
>
> Remember that during their move through France in many parts they met little or no opposition. The Home Guard will see to it that this sort of thing cannot happen in England. Also remember that every successful defence of a village every offensive act carried out by day or night will reduce the area temporarily occupied by the enemy and the numbers of old people and women and children who will have to suffer the indignities or worse of such occupation.
>
> When the battle of Britain is won and its history is written, the part taken by the Home Guard will stand out with the achievements of all other services as evidence to all that Britain refused to be beaten whatever the forces arrayed against her.'

Stanhoe Home Guard Platoon c1941. (PA)

By winter 1940 most HGs at least had access to a great coat and tin helmet for their patrol duties. By early 1941 most units were fully uniformed and even had issue boots. A check list leaflet was soon issued stipulating 'What you must do when the Home Guard is Mustered'

Put on uniform and take the whole of your Arms and Equipment to the place where you have been instructed to report.

Bring the undermentioned articles with you, but no *superfluous* ones:-

Enough food to last 24 hours, drinking mug and plate or mess tin, with knife, fork and spoon.

Razor, lather brush, hairbrush and comb, towel soap and toilet paper.

Change of underclothing, spare pair of socks, handkerchiefs. Have a rucksack or sandbag ready to hold the above.

One blanket rolled bandolier fashion.

Spade or pick if you have them

Identity card bearing battalion stamp

All your own Ration Books

Envelopes, notepaper and pen or pencil,

Tobacco and /or cigarettes

Matches and/or torch

Spare pair bootlaces.

On 1 February 1941 the War Office sanctioned full commissions to Home Guard officers and the old blue stripes of the LDV ranks were replaced with the full military system such as cloth crown and pips with plain khaki backing for officers and chevrons for NCOs. The rank system equated thus: Zone Commander (Brigadier), Group Commander (Colonel), Battalion Commander (Lieutenant Colonel), Company Commander (Major), Platoon Commander (Captain or Lieutenant), Section Commander (Sergeant), Squad Commander (Corporal or Lance Corporal). Volunteers remained so by name until November 1941 when conscription was introduced to ensure the Home Guard was kept up to strength. Each man was expected to attend up to 48 hours training or guard duties a month or face a penalty of a £10 fine or a month in prison. Thus the volunteer character of the Home Guard finally disappeared and Volunteers became Privates.

After the initial issue of rifles in 1940/41 a piecemeal trickle turned into a considerable flow of weaponry dispatched to the Home Guard: bayonets arrived for the rifles, Thompson sub-machine guns, Browning automatic rifles and Bren guns appeared in most platoons and companies often had the likes of Lewis or Vickers machine guns. Thompsons were later recalled from HG units and issued to commandos; the gap in the HG armoury was later filled by an issue of Sten guns. The first weapon received by anti-tank sections was The Blacker Bombard (later retitled Spigot Mortar). Although intended for use by the regular units of the British Army it was quickly replaced by the PIAT and was issued to the Home Guard instead. This was a cumbersome weapon; the three man crew could deploy

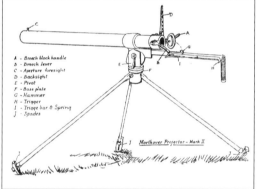

A - Breech block handle
B - Breech lever
C - Aperture foresight
D - Backsight
E - Pivot
F - Base plate
G - Hammer
H - Trigger
I - Trigger bar & Spring
J - Spades

Northover Projector - Mark II

The Northover Projector.

The Atkins Mobile Mounting for the Blacker Bombard ready for transport (left) *and deployed for action* (right) *invented and produced by Corporal (later Lieutenant) Atkins of 7th Battalion, Norfolk Home Guard.*

the weapon to be fired from the ground on its potable mountings or mounted on one of the many concreted spigot mortar mount emplacements (many of these concrete mounts still can be found across Norfolk) fixed at defensive points across the country. The anti-tank round for this weapon was a 20 lb (9 kg) finned bomb full of high explosive, propelled by a black powder charge sufficient to give it a range of over 100 yards albeit with a curved trajectory. Against German tank designs of the early part of the war such a warhead would have been quite effective. There was also an anti-personnel round which weighed 14 lb (about 6 kg) and could be fired out to 500 yards but it remained an unpopular weapon. In 1942, Corporal (later Lieutenant) Atkins of 7th Battalion, Norfolk Home Guard invented and produced the Atkins Mobile Mounting for the Blacker Bombard. Unfortunately, the official policy prevented it from being taken up, though certain 'unofficial' reproductions of this most efficient mounting were by no means and uncommon sight after the original one had completely confounded the official mobile mounting at a demonstration shoot.

Anti-Tank sections were much happier with the arrival of the Northover Projector designed by Major Robert Harry Northover specifically for use by the Home Guard. Northover travelled around the country personally demonstrating his weapon at training events. In effect the Northover was a drainpipe with a breech standing on a tripod, it was the last black powder weapon used by the British Army. It required a crew of three, a gunner and a loader would have sufficed but it was very heavy; the Projector itself weighed about 60lbs, the base plate and legs about 74 lbs consequently rapid movement with the weapon was only possible with three men. A Northover could fire a Self Igniting Phosphorous (SIP) bomb (otherwise known as the Albright and Wilson or AW Bomb) several hundred yards onto a tank and upon its glass case shattering the benzene and phosphor ignite and cloak the enemy armoured vehicle in clouds of thick smoke. The Northover was then capable of firing an AT Grenade or a bombing party could move in on the tank with Molotovs or charges. A lighter Mk II version was devised and introduced later in the war but it was advised that for distance transport it was advisable to mount it on a wheeled carriage.

The Home Guard even had its own 'field gun.' Developed in 1940 as an emergency gun for the

Home Guard it was the product of a private venture by the chief engineer of the Trianco Engineering Company, Sheffield (renowned for its heating appliances). It consisted of a 3-inch smoothbore barrel designed to fire a 3-inch mortar shell, it was mounted on a light gun carriage. There was also a limber for extra ammunition all of which was light enough to be towed by an ordinary motor car. When deployed the carriage was simply up ended onto one of its wheels and was ready for action. Most HGs thought the Smith Gun looked more like an overgrown product from the Tri-ang Toy Company. The Smith Gun was unreliable and could be liable to 'bursting,' such an incident ended in tragic results and claimed the life of a member of the 8th Battalion, Norfolk Home Guard.

Early in 1942 the duties of Zone Commanders became almost entirely advisory and in the same year General Steward was compelled to resign his appointment with Mid Norfolk through ill health and Colonel B.M.M. Edwards M.C. relieved Colonel Cubitt as Commander East Norfolk Home Guard. After years of dedicated drilling, patrolling, exercises and parades the Home Guard was given the order to 'Stand Down' in November 1944. At that time the strength of the Home Guard in Norfolk was 1,141 officers and warrant officers and 30,541 other ranks. The Home Guard was disbanded on 31 December 1945.

What follows are the histories of the individual Norfolk Home Guard battalions based on those submitted by the battalions themselves and first published in *The Britannia: The Journal of The Royal Norfolk Regiment*, Issue 27 (1946).

First Battalion (East Dereham)

Colonel J. F. Barclay T.D. was selected to form and raise this unit. He retained command throughout. Major H. Flower was Second in Command, Major N E D Cartledge was Battalion M.O. while the following Officers acted as Company Commanders during some or all of the unit's active life: Majors H. G. Aldiss, E. C. Chapman, E. Dodds, W. D. Everington, J. H. Garlick, E. C. Keith, A. A. Walker and J. Whitworth. Battalion HQ was in the T.A. Drill Hall at East Dereham.

The battalion's main tasks were the defence of the important road and rail junction at East Dereham and assistance in the defence of airfields. Later particular emphasis was laid on mobile battle platoons and several were formed to deal with any measures the enemy might take to hamper our operations in Normandy.

In 1940 the unit had the honour to send a special party to Thetford for inspection by HM The King.

Officers of the Battalion 1941:
Lieut.-Colonel
 J. F. Barclay T.D.

Majors
 H. G. Aldiss, E. C. Chapman, C. H. Flower M.C., E. C. Keith, J. Whitworth

Captains
 E. Dodds, W.D. Everington, T. B. Probyn, J. A. Sayer, A. A. Walker

Lieutenants
 F. C. S. Allen, W. N. Clarke, T. W. Disdale, S. Farrant, H. Foster, H. J. H. Garlick, T. G. Geddes, C. L. Gorry, L. Greenwood, H. M. Hunter, W. Jones, B. W. A. Keppel, W. J. Monk, F. T. Partridge, A. G. Percival, E. M. Riches, G. R. Smith, R. F. St. B. Wayne

Second Lieutenants
 B. C. Bird, A. F. Burton, F. R. Crane, G. A. Farrow, J. S. Gibbs, H. Greenwood M.M., T. Mack, F. J. Mayes, J. B. Mitchell, J. McClelland, J. R. McGuffie, D. I. Smith, G. H. Vasey, R. Whaites

Colonel Barclay received the OBE for his services and several Army Commander's Certificates were awarded to the battalion, special appreciation was also recorded for Mrs. Wood 'who functioned with great efficiency at Battalion HQ.'

At Stand Down the strength of the unit was 90 Officers and 1,617 Other Ranks.

Second Battalion (Downham Market)

The battalion covered a large area consisting of most of Norfolk west of the Great Ouse and the south west of the county (excluding Swaffham and Thetford). Originally commanded by Lt-Col. Pratt M.C. after his appointment as Zone Commander he was succeeded by Lt-Col. C. A. F. Wingfield. Major A. J. Hawes was Battalion M.O.

Officers of the Battalion 1941:
Lieut.-Colonel
 C. A. F. Wingfield

Majors
 H. Buchanan, Sir John Picton Bagge C.M.G, C. Clarke, F. Clayton, R. Dennis, J. E. T. Hartley, H. H. Teverson M.C., M.M.

Captains
 J. H. Easter, J. W. Hudson, C. S. Monson, C. H. Ray, W. A. Wright

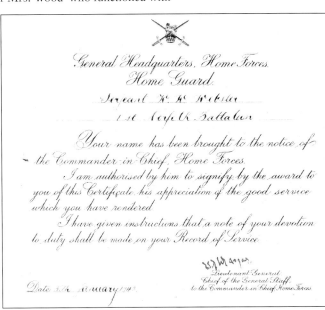

Commander-in-Chief's certificate awarded to Sgt. W. W. Webster, 1st Battalion, Norfolk Home Guard, 5 January 1943

Lieutenants
    H. Bane M.M., H. Clarke, B. N. Doubleday, L. Doubleday, T. Easy M.M., C. A. Ellis, E. Frusher, E. W. Godfrey, J. Greef, A. J. Hawes M.C., S. R. Heyhoe, A. H. Judd, P. A. Leggeri, H. Lindsay-Smith, J. T. Orange, P. G. Roberts, S. Seamer, H. H. Sharp, B. H. West, G. W. Dalton, I. M. D. English, F. Green, V. C. Gutteridge, C. Parkinson, J. W. Spencer

Second Lieutenants
    A. G. Bishop, J. G. A. Carr, C. W. Chilvers, A. A. Dennington, D. Grant M.M., C. A. Holland, C. H. Joyner, R. Peck M.M., J. J. Robinson, A. Turner, H. West.

The following Officers acted as Company Commanders during some or all of the unit's active life: Majors Sir John Picton Bagge, Bart., J. Hartley, J. W. Hudson, J. T. Orange, J. W. Spencer, H. G. Teverson M.C. and W. A, Wright. Battalion HQ was at Downham Market.

The original size of the battalion proved unwieldy for one Headquarters to supervise so the unit was divided in two, the new battalion, the 15th, taking over the battalion sector to the west of the Great Ouse.

The four RAF airfield in the Battalion area called for the provision of aid by the Home Guard in ground defence of these potential enemy objectives and frequent schemes were held to practice and test defences. The terrain to the south east of the battalion area was largely made up of government forest and necessitated special precautions and mobile battle platoons were exercised in operating over this type of ground.

At Stand Down the strength of the unit was 72 Officers and 1,791 Other Ranks.

Third Battalion (Harleston)

This battalion was formally raised at a public meeting held two days after the Antony Eden broadcast and instigated by Colonel C. R. Cadge, O.B.E. and Lt-Col. Stewart Cox, Secretary of the Norfolk Territorial Army Association. Brooke, Poringland and Bixley formed one company with Major Moore as O.C., Captain J. Mann raised another at Diss and Harleston; Major N. G. Sadd, shortly to be succeeded by Major B. Boswell T.D., a third company at Loddon and Major R. J. Read a fourth at Hethersett and Long Stratton.

Officers of the Battalion 1941:
Majors
    A. Beck, E. J. Mann, S. Moore, A. L. Taylor

Captains
    H. S. Foulsham, W.P Pulman, R. J. Read

Lieutenants
    J. L. Brighton, M. R. Formby, H. S. Hall, I. S. Hubbard, M. J. Hunter, H. J. Marshall, W. G. Rutter, S. A. Stimpson, S. J. Cole, W. H. Pursehouse, J. H. McI. Skinner.

Second Lieutenants
    S. T. Ashton, G. W. Boston, A. Bussey, M. M. Downton, W. Foster, H. J. Ives, C. Mutimer, C. Nicholls, G. S. Noy, M.M. Pullen, A. Self M.M., J. L. Perfitt, F. R. Wainwright

In 1941 the battalion area was found to be too large the western portion of the area formed the new 14th Battalion. As the war situation developed the purely defensive role of the battalion was modified and Mobile Battle Platoons were formed for offensive action in the event of enemy airborne landings.

Sir Robert Bignold was appointed to command the unit who was succeeded in this capacity by Lt-Col. V. N. Lockett in 1942. At Stand down Lt.-Col. Lockett was in command with Major Boswell as Second in Command and Major J. Burfield as Battalion M.O. with Company Commanders: Majors H. L. Gray, S. Moore and J. H. Mc. I. Skinner.

At Stand Down the strength of the unit was 53 Officers and 1,329 Other Ranks.

Fourth Battalion (Holt)

The battalion was formed under the command of Lord Hastings with Lord Cozens-Hardy as Second in Command who later retired under the age limit. He was replaced by Lord Leicester until he was appointed Lord Lieutenant and Major P. Hammond D.S.O succeeded him.

At its greatest strength, the battalion numbered 2,300 all ranks and during its service 25 Army Commander's Certificates were awarded to men of the battalion. It also achieved a high state of proficiency, for in the District Battle Platoon Competition and the District Stretcher Bearer Competition the teams from the battalion got second place.

It was commented 'An interesting fact to record is that when the men joined the Home Guard there was no medical inspection and for practical purposes no age limit for recruitment. Yet in four and a half years no serious accident occurred during training and only four deaths were recorded of whom two were transfers from other counties.'

Officers of the Battalion 1941:
Lieut.-Colonel
    The Lord Hastings,

Majors:
    The Lord Cozens-Hardy, P. Hammond, DSO, MC, L. E. Jones, MC TD

Captains
    C.A. Barran, C.V.Scholey,

Lieutenants
    Carter, J.S., W.B.Case, R.F.Deterding, S. H. Mallet, J. S. W. Massey, J.G. Oakden, W. T. Thornton, C. Wainwright, H.J. Pye

The following officers commanded companies of the battalion during the war: Majors P. Hamond D.S.O, L. E. Jones M.C., C. A. Barran, C. V. Scholey, R. Deterding and W. B. Case.

At Stand Down the strength of the unit was 70 Officers and 1, 784 Other Ranks.

Fifth Battalion (North Walsham)

Brig. Gen. W. A. Blake C.B., C.M.G., D.S.O. was Commanding Officer with Lt.-Col. R. G. Cubitt, after ceasing to be Zone Commander, taking over the duties of Second in Command. Major C. G. Taylor was the Battalion M.O.

Officers of the Battalion 1941:
Lieut-Colonel
    Brig. Gen. W. A. Blake C.B., C.M.G., D.S.O.

Majors
    C. R. Gurney, W. Jennings DSO, R.G. Shorter

Captains
    F.M. Bailey, C.I.E., T. R. C. Blofeld, C. Granville O.B.E

Worstead Platoon, 5th Battalion, Norfolk Home Guard

Lieutenants

E. C. Ackerman, R. W. Alston, B. Boyce, P. C. Briscoe, G. M. Duncan O.B.E., A. G. D. Greenshields, F. Gunton, R. F. Kerrison, C. E. Littlewood, Sir Robert W. Lyall-Grant T.D., P. Pickford, D.S.O., M.C., T.D., E. H. Wood, A. L. Taunton, H. V. Taylor, C. B. Wilson M.C.

Second Lieutenants

L. W. Almey, J. Brummage, W. C. Duffield, P. A. Missen, N. F. Pollock, T. W. Purdy T.D., F.R. Bell, A. R. Gurney

The following officers commanded companies of the battalion: Majors C. Gurney, G. E, Milligen, F. M. Place, P. Pickford D.S.O., M.C. and N. Stanley. Captain P. Svenson, originally a LDV, was given an emergency commission and was appointed Adjutant and Capt. S. E. Gurney was Quartermaster.

Battalion HQ	The Grange, North Walsham
No.1 Company HQ	West Lawns, Cliff Avenue, Cromer
No.2 Company HQ	Angel Hotel, North Walsham
No.3 Company HQ	Woods Shop, High Street, Stalham
No.4 Company HQ	Drill Hall, North Walsham
No.5 Company	The Rectory, Ashmanhough
HQ Training (Major A.H.J. Bull MM)	'Cortaigne' Cromer Road, North Walsham

During the latter part of its active life the battalion manned the coastal heavy batteries at Mundesley and Cromer. While all ranks showed great keenness, special mention was made of the Signallers who took second place at the District Signalling Competitions. Several Army Commander's Certificates were awarded to men of the battalion but Second Lieutenant George Mutimer was noted for particular gallantry when he ran to the aid of the crew of an RAF Halifax that had crashed and burst into flames in Westwick Park at 23.00 on 20 January 1944. Mutimer entered the burning plane and initially unaided he was mainly responsible for extricating the whole crew except one who managed to crawl out by himself.

At Stand Down the strength of the unit was 77 Officers and 1, 724 Other Ranks.

Sixth Battalion (Norwich)

North Walsham Platoon, 5th Battalion, Norfolk Home Guard

The Battalion area was to the north-east of Norwich and originally encompassed more country on the far side of the city including Swardeston, Hethersett, Attlebridge and Swannington.

Colonel Bernard Henry Leathes Prior D.S.O. was appointed O.C. from formation until reaching the age limit in 1942. He was succeeded by Lt.-Col. A. R. Taylor. First Adjutant was Major Walter Parsley O.B.E., M.C., who had served for many years with 2nd Battalion, The Norfolk Regiment. He had retired shortly after the end of the First World War and was living at Pieter Maritzburg, Natal. Though well over age, he paid his passage to England to offer his services. He was eventually invalided out after doing much valuable work and gaining the respect and affection of all ranks.

Officers of the Battalion 1941:
Lieut-Colonel

B. H. L. Prior D.S.O., T.D.

Majors

P. J. Mead, B. V. Noel, C. C. H. Twiss D.S.O.
Captains

R. J. Aitken, R. W. Hawke, F. J. Morse, J. de C. Smith

Lieutenants
    H. R. Binnion, S. T. Blink, C. F. Chittleburgh, J. A. Coleman, F. W. Drake M.M., P. S. Ellis, M. Falcon, J. T. Gowing, J. C. Habgood, J. H. Harris, P. W. Jewson, G. H. Kitchener, A. R. Miles, R. Nicholls, A. R. Taylor, C. H. Ward, C. H. Ward, S. C. Ward, T. Wright, H. E. Wray

Second Lieutenants
    F. H. Burbury, J. H. Ellis, W. R. J. Golder, J. C. Harrison, J. C. Harvey, S. F. Hewlett, E. W. Ling, B. L. Misselbrook, H. H. Wilson, T. G. Fowler, C. D. Jones, C. de M. Leathes O.B.E, S. A. Morrish, W. R. Walker, W. W. Tann, B. J. Darby

    The following officers commanded companies of the battalion: Majors R. J. Aitkin, E. D. J. Points, W. C. Duffield, J. T. Gowing, J. H. Harris and J. De Carle Smith. Major A. G. Holman was M.O.

    Colonel Prior related the following story to illustrate the spirit of the rank and file. After lecturing one of the platoons, he was asked, 'Do you think this here Hitler be a coming?' On being told that this was quite possible, the Homeguardsman ruminated, "Well, du if he don't, I shall be wholly put out after all the trouble I've taken."
    At Stand Down the strength of the unit was 90 Officers and 1,905 Other Ranks.

Seventh Battalion (King's Lynn & Sandringham)

Colonel Oliver Birkbeck raised and commanded the battalion throughout. Vice Admiral C. A. Fountaine C. B. was Second in Command. Major C. N. Devlin as Battalion Medical Officer with Captains Fogarty, J. V. Morgan and J. Sexton acting as Company M.Os.

Officers of the Battalion 1941
Lieut.-Colonel
    O. Birkbeck

Majors
    F. Bullen, T. Carlyon D.S.O., C. A. Fountaine C.B., T. P. Melvill D.S.O, R. North

Captains
    C. C. Brown, R. P. Heywood

Lieutenants
    A. Brereton, R. W. Buckley, J. A. Crean, A. F. Culham, A. Dring, T. L. Ground D.S.O, D. W. T. Gurney M.C., H. J. Haggas, J. E. Hancock, A. R. Johnson, S. Kay, E. M. King, F. J. Knight, J. A. Laing, A. L. Marsters, E. H. Ringer, W. Rowe M.C., W. J. Standfield, A. G. Sykes, G. N. Wardle

Second Lieutenants
    A. R. Giles, C. E. Le Grice, A. C. Kiddell, G. J. R. Simpson, P. E. Thain, J. H. W. Terry, A. E. Barrett
    The following were company commanders: Majors D. W. Brown, F. Bullen, A. C. M. Coxon T.D., R. P. Heywood, R. North, W. Rowe M.C. and P. E. Thain. Capt. F. C. Ash D.C.M. served as Quartermaster throughout. Other officers who served as Company Commanders until attaining the age limit were Lieut.-Colonels T. P. Melville, D.S.O. and T. Carlyon D.S.O.

    Two awards for gallantry were obtained, Sergeant E. R. Tipple and Corporal H. C. Smith both received the British Empire Medal; the former for rescuing the crew of an RAF plane which had crashed into a house at Harpley during the night of 23 November 1943. The latter for rescuing the crew of another RAF plane that had crashed and caught fire near North Wootton on 8 August 1941.
    Army Commander's Certificates were presented to Major F. Bullen, Capt. S. Kay, Lieut. O. T. Atkins,

The entire 7th Battalion, Norfolk Home Guard on parade in the Tuesday Market Place, King's Lynn, 16 May 1943

RSM Fuller, Sgts. B.H. Cockrill, R. H. Collins, C. N. Browne, E. Hammond, D. Skipper, J. A. R. Taylor, Cpls. J. S. Hilton, T. R. Offley and J. Warnes.

The battalion won the following competitions: Norfolk and Cambridge Area Identification of Aircraft 1942, Sub-District Battle Platoon 1943 and the Sub-District Smith Gun and District Rifle in 1942.

In 1942, Corporal (later Lieutenant) Atkins invented and produced the Atkins Mobile Mounting for the Blacker Bombard. Unfortunately, the official policy prevented it from being taken up, though certain 'unofficial' reproductions of this most efficient mounting were by no means and uncommon sight after the original one had completely confounded the official mobile mounting at a demonstration shoot.

Another invention to the credit of the battalion was a simple and valuable A.A. mounting for L.M.Gs. It was invented and originally produced by Capt. S. Kay and was set up at vulnerable targets in King's Lynn. In addition to its Home Guard training the battalion was assigned special ARP duties and always turned out parties during air raids, being particularly commended for its promptitude in saving the furniture when King Edward VII School buildings were set on fire by incendiary bombs.

At Stand Down the strength of the unit was 90 Officers and 2, 204 Other Ranks.

Eighth Battalion (Swaffham)

The battalion was formed under the command of Capt. R. G. Buxton (later promoted to Lt.-Col.). Major Lloyd O.B.E., M.C. joined the Permanent Staff as Adjutant and proved a tower of strength to the whole unit. The Battalion's catchment area was similar to that of Swaffham Police. Capt. Makins commanded the Necton-Bradenhams District; Captain Batholomew the Watton District; Major Hawkins the Swaffham District; Major Swann D.S.O, the Feltwell District and Major Lloyd, the Mundford District. Battalion headquarters were situated at Swaffham.

Officers of the Battalion 1941:
Lieut.-Colonel
   R. G. Buxton

Majors
   J. Bartholomew, H. A. Bradley M.C., J. F. Buller M.C., D. Le G. Pitcher C.M.G., C.B.E., D.S.O., W. J. Short

Captains
   G. W. Barnham, E. Makins

Lieutenants
   J. K. W. Broadhead, W. A. R. Mallon, L. Oldroyd, G. Page, D. H. Sanderson, A. A. Saunders, R. G. Warner, G. L. Ashley-Dodd

Second Lieutenants
   A. R. Brunning M.M., C. B.Frost, C. C. Hellicar, G. C. F. Hillier, G. Moreton, P. J. Platten, H. T. Thornton, F. R. Banner, J. S. Hepburn, H. W. Wharf, B. Wiseman, H. J. Watcham

When the Battalion area was altered and 8th Battalion lost all the area west of the Swaffham-Brandon Road but it took over responsibility for Thetford and the villages of Kilverstone, Brettenham and Croxton from 9th Battalion. A large acreage was lost to the battalion when the Stanford Battle Area was formed, all inhabitants being evacuated. This was a constant source of worry as this area was an excellent dropping place for paratroops.

At the time of the Stand Down the Company Commanders were:

     A Company (Bradenham) Major H. A. Bradley M.C.
     B Company (Watton) Major J. Batholomew
     C Company (Thetford) Major Witton
     D Company (Swaffham) Major J. F. Buller MC

The following Officers served with distinction with the Battalion during the war but were not serving at the Stand Down: Air Commodore Pitcher C.M.G, C.B.E., D.S.O, Majors Hawkins, Swann D.S.O. and Hartley.

Major J. Bartholomew and Capt. C. C. Hellicar were both awarded the M.B.E and a large number of Certificates of Good Service were presented. The Carbrooke Battle Platoon won the sub-district Platoon Competition in 1943 and were placed equal second in the District Competition.

It was regretted that the battalion suffered two fatal casualties, one from the bursting of a Smith Gun and one from a Rifle Grenade.

At Stand Down the strength of the unit was 64 Officers and 1,154 Other Ranks.

A bed, with a suitably engraved bronze plaque erected above, was endowed at Swaffham Cottage Hospital to commemorate the raising and service of the 8th Battalion.

Ninth Battalion (Wymondham)

This battalion was originally formed by Colonel The Earl of Albermarle. It was then commanded for a few months by Maj.-Gen. Steward who handed over to Lt.-Col. H.W. Back on 1 February 1941 who remained with the battalion until Stand Down. Major R.G. Hart was Second in Command and Major A.J. Johnson, Battalion M.O.
Officers of the Battalion 1941
Lieut.-Colonel
   H. W. Back

Majors
E. W. Denny D.S.O., D. P. Fagen, J. H. Prior D.S.O., W. E. Salter T.D.

Captains
R. G. Hart, T. A. F. McMillan-Scott, C. R. Russell, T. F. M. Thackeray

Lieutenants
A. E. Bantock, A. Bell, D. P. Claridge, G. R. F. Clarke, L. Fletcher, P. W. J. Fryer, F. N. Garland, G. N. Holmes, R. T. Lawrence, E. C. Partridge, F. H. Swindells, L. Twiddy, M. C. P. Vereker M.C., E. G. Witton

Second Lieutenants
J. D. Alston, P. A. Bainbridge, W. L. Bell, G. Bird, A. M. Blake, F. W. Browne, W. Corbould-Warren, T. Davey, J. Drane, R. J. Dunning, P. R. Friswell M.C., C. N. Garnier O.B.E., E. B. Gowing, G. Green, H. F. Harrison, S. H. Harrold, J. Hedley M.C., P. E. Hinchley, A. D. Howlett, G. C. Howlett, F. E. Hunt, D. Jones, J. S. G. Kay, A. W. J. Keel, J. W. Kemp, E. Larwood D.C.M., F. B. Law M.C., T. H. Lord, G. H. Marwood, J. H. Mayne,, A. L. Melton, J. Norton, R. E. Parker, C. A. Pattinson, E. Pratt, H. L. Smith, A. J. Steed, J. R. Ware, F. C. Woods, A. C. Youngman, J.J. Youngman

The battalion area, with headquarters at Wymondham, included Easton, Hethersett, New Buckenham, South Lopham, East Harling, Attleborough and Hingham. The unit was a very strong one, the greatest strength being 3,033 all ranks in March 1943 and 2,859 at Stand Down.

Majors C. R. Russell and P.W. J. Fryer were awarded the MBE for valuable services and the following received Good Service Certificates: Capt. M.C. Ayton, MC, H.G. Smith, Cpl. H.J.H. Bidewell, Sgts J.S.G. Kay, R.H. Bailey, L.F. Balls, J. Jacobs, CQMS H. Mann, Sjts E.E, Riches, F.W. Roy, Cpl. L.A. Hunt, CSM F Sparrow, L/Cpl R.J. Smith, CQMS E.S. Smith, Cpl. W.F. Wick.

The battalion had the honour of providing 100 men, together with a similar party from 1ˢᵗ Battalion to represent the Norfolk Hone Guard at an inspection by HM The King at Thetford in 1940.

The following officers were Company Commanders at Stand Down: Majors A. Bell, P. Fagan, P.W.J. Fryer M.B.E., C.R. Russell M.B.E. and T. McMillan-Scott. Lt.-Col. J. H. Prior and Major E. W. Denny also commanded companies until they attained the age limit.

Tenth (City of Norwich) Battalion

Lt.-Col. B. F. Hornor D.S.O., was commissioned on 17 May 1940 to raise a City of Norwich unit of the Local Defence Volunteers. Within three days 500 men fell in at the Chapel Field Drill Hall and twenty four hours later nightly guards and patrols were on duty throughout the garrison area.

The shortage of weapons became so acute as number of volunteers increased that old muskets dating back to the Crimean War were borrow from Norwich Castle museum for training purposes.

A signal company under Capt. E.H. Coe M.C. was rapidly formed and established inter-communication between all Headquarters within the garrison. This officer later became Sub-District Signal Officer. Lieut. P. Smyth formed a Tank Hunting Platoon which was later transferred to Auxiliary Units.

In December 1940 the first battalion parade took place where the unit attended a cathedral service afterwards marched past the Corps Commander.

Officers of the Battalion 1941:
Lieut-Colonel
B. F. Hornor M.C.

Majors
Bates, W. E., G. R. J. Bussey, E. H. Coe M.C., B.H. Durrant M.C., H. N. Morgan M.C., F. A. Sexton M.C.

Members of 10ᵗʰ (City of Norwich) Battalion, Norfolk Home Guard on their first full Battalion parade, march past the Corps Commander, Tombland, Norwich, December 1940.

Captains
N. C. Croghan, F. J. Cubitt, C. King. J. H. S. Priestley, A. W. Turnbull, C. C. Tyce M.C.

Lieutenants
E. A. Adcock, G. H. Anderson, E. G. Ball, T. H. Clegg M.B.E., M.C., A. J. Cooper, W. Dunlop, S. T. E. P. Ennion, L. P. Hayman, J. H. W. Jevons, C. B. Johnson, A. P. Lincoln D.C.M., W. S. Lusher, R. R. Matthews, E. W. Mills, F. W. Morris, R. H. Mottram, D. Peden-Wilson, E. W. Pond, H. E. Richens, L. J. Rowbury, A. Ruane, O. P. Smythe, P. J. Spooner, F. R. Standley D.C.M, R. W. Steel, A. Towers M.M., C. E. Turner

Second Lieutenants
H. W. C. Allen, J. F. Barker D.C.M., T. J. Barfield, R. F. Bishop, A. J. Bayliss, J. W. Bellamy, D. H. Brown, W. A. Carter, C. Crofton-Sleigh, H. Cropp, W. G. Cutbush, L. M. Daniels M.M., C. L. Edmunds, W. H. Hurrall, F. G. Ingamells, J. H. Kidd, W. D. Lowden, W. H. McCombie, J. Payne, F. W. Roshier, E. W. Sale, H. W. Sharpe, S. W. Smith, W. L. Sussams, , F. W. Stapley, , H. M. Thompson, P. E. Turner, A. C. W. Wells M.M.

By 1943 the strength of the unit exceeded 4,000 and it was decided to form a second Battalion for Norwich. The 16th Battalion thus came into being, located in the western sector of the city it took half the personnel and Major H.N. Morgan M.C. the Second in Command who was appointed their new O.C.

Company Commanders at Stand Down were: Majors J.H. Priestley, J.F. Morse, W.S. Lusher, G.R.J. Bussey, S.H. Anderson, L. Tungate and C. King M.B.E. commanding companies 1 to 6 and HQ Company respectively. Majors L. Rowberry and W.E. Bates MBE also commanded companies for long periods during the war. Capt. D. B. Hill, late Royal Norfolk Regiment, was Adjutant and Major F. Moor M.C., M.D. was Medical Officer.

The Post Office Home Guard Company commanded by Major S. B. Batch functioned operationally with the battalion though it was actually part of 6th Battalion Cambridgeshire (Post Office) Battalion. Major C. King M.B.E. was W.T.O. Capt. Roshier d succeeded Captain Coe as Signals Officer when the District Commander's Shield for signalling was won by the battalion. Major R.G.C. Carlson the Battalion M.O. trained the Stretcher Bearers who came second (by one point) in the District Stretcher Bearer Competitions.

During evening air raids several A.A. posts in the city were manned by member of the City of Norwich Battalion and several hits were obtained on raiders. In this respect Lieut. E. W. Pond's platoon was specially mentioned:

'In 1941 a company, training on Eaton golf links was bombed by a lone Heinkel without effect. It was heavily engaged with Lewis guns and came down some miles north of the city.'

In 1941 the battalion found a Guard of Honour for the visit of the Chancellor of the Exchequer to Norwich. Detachments paraded for inspection by HRH the late Duke of Kent in 1942 and in 1944 they paraded for HM the King. Captain Miller commanded the Norfolk Home Guard contingent which took part in the final parade in London on Stand Down.

During the Battalion's active life, two men lost their lives when on duty and a number were wounded. Close co-operation was maintained with the ARP Controller and special duties were allotted to the unit. Lieut. Reid formed and commanded a bomb disposal squad. Lieut C. Bell trained a special unarmed combat squad that became so efficient that it regularly gave demonstrations at the Battle School at Moreton Hill, Attlebridge.

The battalion had the help of many ladies who enrolled as drivers, signallers and nurses. Most of the latter were trained by Capt. A. Davidson M.D. and obtained Red Cross Nursing Certificates.

Lt.-Col. Bassett Hornor D.S.O., was awarded the O.B.E. and Major W. E. Bates (Second in Command) and Major C.King the M.B.E. in recognition of their valuable service. Several Army Commander's Certificates were gained by the battalion.

On the evening of 15 June 1944 the battalion suffered a tragic casualty during an unarmed combat display staged on Chapel Field Gardens as part of the 'Salute the Soldier' week. The demonstration was performed in front of a large crowd and the two Home Guards to demonstrate the deflection of a fixed bayonet charge were highly trained and had performed the manoeuvre many times before. At the crucial moment when he should have turned sharply Home Guardsman Terry Wasley (33) slipped causing his body to turn but not his legs and the bayonet entered his thigh severing his femoral artery, despite receiving immediate attention from L/Cpl. Guymer and his removal to the Norfolk and Norwich Hospital within minutes he died later the same evening. The inquest confirmed the death was accidental. Many of the ex-Home Guardmen I have interviewed from the 10th Battalion recalled this particular event with clarity and sadness decades afterwards.

At Stand Down the strength of the unit was 113 Officers and 2,495 Other Ranks.

Eleventh Battalion (Great Yarmouth)

Lt-Col. F.R.B. Haward was originally appointed Officer Commanding Great Yarmouth and District

Norwich Gas Works Platoon, No. 5 Company, 10th (City of Norwich) Battalion, Norfolk Home Guard, 1941

Signals Platoon, 10th (City of Norwich) Battalion, Norfolk Home Guard pictured on Chapel Field Gardens, Norwich 1944.

L.D.V. and he held command throughout the unit's active life.

Poorly armed and equipped the 11th Battalion were charged with the defence of a hight important and vulnerable position – the port, haven and town of Great Yarmouth. Working with the local army units they fostered a great team and efficiency was soon achieved by the battalion. The battalion was granted oneof the first batches of American P.14 and P.17 rifles that had been in store since the First World War. Caked with paraffin wax if took all the efforts of the men, their wives, families and volunteers from the WVS to get the rifles properly cleaned and serviceable. By November 1940 the battalion had also been issued with uniforms.

Training was carried out on Sundays and on most evening during the week and its thoroughness was proved by the battalion's success in competitions held for rifle shooting, stretcher bearing, first aid and signalling. In this last skill the battalion gained first place in Norfolk and second in the Corps.

Officers of the Battalion 1941:
Lieut.-Colonel
    F. R. B. Hayward

Majors
    C. P. Clowes, H. J. Maddieson, W. A. Newman, H. A. C. Salmon D.C.M., S. T. Tunbridge T.D.

Captains
    J. Davey, T. J. Mason, J. E. Parslow

Lieutenants
    E. W. Applegate, W. A. Barfield, P. A. Bond, F. A. Brown, F. R. Chinery, H. Connors, H. Crozier, A. E. V. Durrant, G. A. Flaxman, W. G. Fox, S. G. Gower, H. B. Jones, R. C. Lane, R. F. Lewis, J. G. Palmer, A. R. Pike, W. F. Temple, E. A. H. Thompson, C. Wharton, H. Wharton M.M.

The unit's operational role changed as the war situation developed. Primarily the duties were to hold localities as an anti-invasion task. Then a more mobile role was allotted to it and a Battalion Motor Transport Company was formed under Lieut. C.E. Angel. With the approach of the D-Day the battalion helped in guarding L. of C. to relieve troops to relieve troops and stood by with mobile platoons to meet any enemy counter measures. A battery of .375mm guns was allotted to the unit for use in a fixed role on the coast. Capt. J.G. Palmer trained the required personnel. Later teams were provided for the heavy coastal defence batteries at Winterton and on the North Denes. These teams commanded by Capts. Palmer and E. A. England took their turn in manning the guns. The battalion's activities included coastal patrols from the Suffolk border to Sea Palling, a distance of 15 miles. The Ormesby platoon captured a number of German airman and saved several of our own men.

Senior officers in the battalion were Major S.T. Tunbridge T.D., who was the original Second in Command until relieved by Major F.P. Molineux T.D. Company Commanders were Majors H.A.C. Salmon D.C.M., T. J. Mason, C.P. Clowes, H. J. Maddison, B. V. Noel, and F.S. Taylor. Major A. S. K. Anderson D.S.O., M.C. was Battalion M.O. The rest of the appointments as follows:
    Captain Bodley - Adjutant
    Capt. T.C. Ives - Ammunition Officer
    Capt. T.F. Freeman - W.T.O

No.3 Company, 11th Battalion, Norfolk Home Guard, outside the Hospital School, Great Yarmouth, 1944.

No. 2 Platoon, No. 1 Company (Gorleston), 11th Battalion, Norfolk Home Guard

Officers of 11th Battalion, Norfolk Home Guard at Stand Down 1944

Lieut. J. D. Clarke – Intelligence Officer
Lieut. R. C Hannant – Gas Officer
Lieut. W. Massie – Signals Officer
2/Lieut. A. L. Phillips M.M. – Transport Officer
Captain R. A. Macdonald R.A. succeeded Lieut. S. G. Gower as Quatermaster.

RSM P.E. Amis was appointed Staff Instructor as a result of his valuable work in training recruits. Lt.-Col. Haward was awarded the O.B.E. for his service and several army commanders certificates were give to members of the unit.

At Stand Down Battalion strength was 90 officers and 1,840 other ranks.

After stand down the comradeship carried on with and ex-Officers Association, Great Yarmouth and Gorleston formed Company Associations and a rifle club was created.

Twelfth Battalion (Brancaster)

Formed in June 1940 in the North-West sector of the county with HQ at Brancaster. Lt.-Col. Leslie D.S.O, M.C. commanded for the whole period. Major-General W. Green C.B., D.S.O was Second in Command.

Officers of the Battalion 1941
Lieut.-Colonel
    J. Leslie D.S.O, M.C.

Majors
    S. G. Clarkson, M. Goodall M.B.E., W. Green C. B., D. S. O., The Hon. J. K. E. Howard, H. W. Lamce M.B.E., C. P. Whittaker M.C.
Captains
    J. F. B. Watson, M. Wheatley

Lieutenants
    G. V. Card, Rev. N. D. Fourdrinier, W. W. Frammingham, R. L. Freeman-Taylor, R. D. Hancock, P. H. H. Johnson, J. E. A. Lambert, W. J. Nelson, A. R. Osborne, C. W. Parke, A. Poppleton, J. R. Prior, R. F. Pull, F. Stimpson, E. E. Williamson M.M., G. Woodward, R. L. Leckie

Second Lieutenants
    W. P. W. Holm, W. Humphrey, R. H. Browne

The following were Company Commanders during all or part of the unit's active life: Major S.G. Clarkson, Lieut-Col. M. Goodall O.B.E. and Majors R.D. Hancock, , the Hon. James Howard, R.F.Pull, General Sir Peter Strickland K.C.B., K.B.E., C.M.G., D.S.O.; Majors Bidwell, Watson and C.P. Whitaker M.B.E., MC and Major J. Davidson was M.O.

As a result of particularly valuable services the M.B.E. was awarded to Major Whitaker and Capt. G. V. Card.

The battalion's main responsibility was coast defence and this task was much facilitated by the creation of a platoon of armoured cars. These came into existence soon after Dunkirk when an American friend sent Major Lance a sum of money to be used as he thought fit in the defence of Britain. The officer at once placed the money at the disposal of the commanding officer who, as an armoured car officer of some considerable experience in the First World War, had recognised the urgent need for mobile firepower in his coast defence duties and quickly utilised the money in purchasing high powered second hand cars and fitting them with armour.

At stand down the unit strength was 73 officers and 1,467 other ranks.

Thirteenth Battalion (Sheringham)

The Armoured Cars of 12th Battalion, Norfolk Home Guard, 1940

Lt.-Col. Spurrell D.S.O., M.C. was appointed Officer Commanding and he served in this capacity until Stand Down.

The battalion was formed on 19 February 1941 from sub-units of the 1st, 4th and 5th Battalions. The Battalion HQ was at 'Fornley' St. Peter's Road, Sheringham; No.1 Company HQ was at 'Willow Dean' Church Street, Sheringham and Platoon HQ was at 'Lachaumiere,' West Runton.

Officers of the Battalion 1941:
Lieut.-Colonel

W. J. Spurrell D.S.O, M.C.

Majors
Q. E. Gurney, R. W. Ketton-Cremer, C. H. G. Walker

Captains
J. C. Sale D.S.O., M.C., W. H. F. Wortley

Lieutenants
S. B. Bass, J. W. C. Beeton, E. W. Bray, W. A. Campbell, G. E. Dewing, J. A. Hagen, B. Hammond, R. A. Harden, Rev. R. Meiklejohn, C. F. Mills, R. M. Parker, S. H. Perry-Warnes, B. Stimpson, C. R. Turner, J. W. Underwood, S. B. Winch O.B.E.

Senior Officers and NCOs of 13th Battalion, Norfolk Home Guard 1940

Second Lieutenants
A. W. Garrod, J. T. M. Mee, R. P. Sayer

Subsequently, the 13th Battalion was divided in two again, this time the three southern companies formed the 17th Battalion.

The M.B.E. was awarded to Major F. De W. Harman D.S.O. for valuable services as Adjutant. The following Army Commander's Certificates were awarded for gallantry: Lieut. H. B. Dyball. For Good Service: Major R.W. Ketton Cremer, Lieut D. M. Lilly, C.S.Ms A. Atkins, A.J. Lowe, R. Sanderson, CQMSs J E Blogg, G F Ward, Sjts E. Bartle, A. Bumfrey, G.N. Goff, D.W.F. Long, S. Love, C.B. May, R. R. Pratt, A. E. Tash, S. Wells and Cpl C.J. Basham.

The Sheringham platoon of 3 officers and 80 other ranks were trained as coastal artillery and took over a battery of two 6" naval guns.

No. 1 Company was originally commanded by Major C. H. Walker (late R.A.). He was promoted to the vacant appointment of Battalion Second in Command and succeeded by the late Lord Suffield. On the death of Lord Suffield, Major C.F. Mills commanded the company with Major F. De W. Harman (who had previously been Adjutant) and his Second in Command. The two latterly mentioned officers held these positions until Stand Down.

Major R. W. Ketton-Cremer was in command of No. 2 Company throughout its active life with Captain H. W. Browne as his Second in Command.

At Battalion HQ: Capt. J. Humphries (Welsh Regt.) succeeded Major Harman as Adjutant and held the appointment until after Stand Down. The following served throughout the war:

Quartermaster Captain A. G. Levick
Lieut G. S. Rogers – Signals Officer
Lieut. J. H. Ewing - Intelligence Officer
Lieut F. N. Pollock - Ammunition Officer
Lieut. F. G. Pratt – Liason Officer (Civil Defence)
Major J. A. Eddy – Medical Officer
Capt W. H. F. Wortley – Chief Guide
Lieut R. A. Parker – HQ Commander

Left: Sheringham Company, 13th Battalion, Norfolk Home Guard 1944

Right: 3 Company, 13th Battalion, Norfolk Home Guard, on parade in Reepham Market Place, May 1941.

Topcroft, Harwick and Fritton Company, 14th Battalion, Norfolk Home Guard

Fourteenth Battalion (Hapton)

This unit was formed in February 1941 when the strength of the 3rd Battalion made it necessary to divide the unit in two. The 14th Battalion took over the western sector of the old 3rd Battalion including Newton Flotman, Diss and Harleston. Lt.-Col. R. J. Read was appointed Officer Commanding and remain in position until Stand Down. Major A. Beck was Second in Command. Major J. H. Owens was M.O. and Capt. Horsham Adjutant with the following officers commanding companies: Majors J.L. Brighton, I.S. Hubbard, Sir John Mann, Bart, and A. Lombe Taylor. Battalion HQ was established at Hapton Hall and its environs were used as a weekend camp where intensive field training was carried out.

The battalion was largely concerned with the ground defence of U.S. airfields and close and cordial relations were maintained

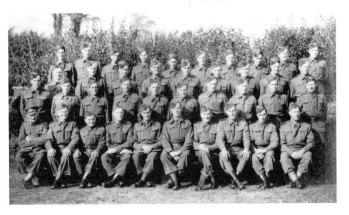

Starston Company, 14th Battalion, Norfolk Home Guard October 1944

with U.S. personnel throughout. One particular incident exemplifies the degree of observation and alertness maintained within the battalion area. One night, one of the observation posts noted a bomber in difficulties. This was reported to the C.O. who turned out just as the aircraft crashed. The plane, a Stirling, was on fire but it was ascertained that the crew had bailed out. A motor ambulance was obtained, stretchers taken from it and some 500 acres of ground combed in the dark by the local Home Guard company. All members of the crew were picked up in one and a half hours and conveyed to hospital.

Mobile battle platoon training was met with great keenness and Lieut. F. R. Wainwright's Platoon from Harleston won the Sub-District Competition on the Battle Area in 1943.

At stand down the unit strength was 62 officers and 1,744 other ranks.

Fifteenth Battalion (Downham Market)

Created in January 1941, this unit was formed from the 2nd Battalion after it was found the size of the area and the strength of the unit was too unwieldy for one Battalion. The 15th Battalion was allotted Norfolk, west of the River Ouse, with certain detachments on the east bank holding bridgeheads.

Lt.-Col. H. Buchanan was the first Commanding Officer and HQ was set up in Downham Market. In 1943 command of the unit passed to Lt.Col. C.S. Monson and battalion HQ moved to Setch.

Valuable work was carried out by a night patrol of the Terrington St. Clement's platoon on 10 March 1941. Cpl. Buffham, Ptes. Hearn and Cooper succeeded in reaching a force landed Junkers 88C-2 at Hay Green so promptly that the crew were prevented from setting fire to the machine. The Junkers was subsequently removed to Farnborough and the members of the patrol received the special tanks of the air ministry as the machine was a new type and intact as (in fact it was the first time a complete Ju 88 night-fighter with a 'solid' nose containing cannon and MG had fallen into British hands in one piece) and also contained certain important documents.

Another incident, while the area was still under 2nd Battalion control occurred near Welney. A patrol discovered one of our airmen who had baled out of a damaged plane. He explained where the other two members of his crew had dropped. The Home Guard at once realised they must have landed in The Wash at Welney, at that time inundated to several feet. In spite of being pitch dark they succeeded, in the nick of time, in rescuing one airman whose parachute cords had caught in a tree and prevented him from trying to save himself. Operationally, the defence of the River Ouse crossing dominated other tasks, with aid in the defence of Sutton Bridge airfield as a secondary role.

The Company Commanders of the battalion were Majors F. Clayton who acted as Second in Command, R.C.C. Dennis and C. Clark.

At stand down the unit strength was 67 officers and 2,175 other ranks.

Sixteenth Battalion (Norwich)

It was decided in May 1943 that 10th (City of Norwich) Battalion had increased in size to such an extent it was necessary for it to be divided into two battalions, the western sector formed the 16th Battalion.

Major H. N. Morgan M.C. the Second in Command of the 10th Battalion was promoted to Lt.-Col. And appointed Commanding Officer of the 16th with Major B. H. Durrant M.C. appointed Second in Command. The following were Company Commanders: Major F. A. Sexton M.B.E., C. G. Tyce M.C., A.P. Lincoln, W.D. Lowden and E.A. Adcock. Major J. S. Whiteside was Battalion M.O. and Capt. E.J. Smith the W.T.O.

The battalion played an energetic role during the bombing of Norwich and special co-operation was arranged with the Civil Defence authorities. Street parties were organised and commanded by Home Guards, while the Civil Defence Rescue Parties were accompanied as it was found the presence of disciplined and uniformed men was a considerable help to the Civil Defence in disembarrassing them of the control of civilians. In addition, aid was given to the hospitals by the provision of stretcher

Men of 16th Battalion, Norfolk Home Guard at Lyng Mill House.

bearers. Major F. A. Sexton was awarded the M.B. E for his services.

At stand down the unit strength was 85 officers and 1,653 other ranks.

Seventeenth Battalion (Reepham)

The 17th Battalion was the last of all the Norfolk Home Guard battalions to be formed in June 1943 with headquarters at Reepham. Carved out of 1st and 13th Battalions but owing to previous changes some of the platoons had already been in at least two other battalions.

Shortly after the new battalion was formed a parade was held at Bawdeswell Hall at which 1,000 men attended and the salute was taken by Field Marshal Lord Ironside who also gave a short address.

Lt.-Col. Q. E. Gurney TD Commanded the Battalion ably assisted by Major B. Stimson his Second in Command. Capt. Raymond Cox (Royal Norfolk Regiment) was Adjutant and Lieut. C. P Dix Signals Officer. The Company Commanders were Majors R.P. Sayer, T.H. Sayer and S.F. Simmons.

At stand down the unit strength was 37 officers and 1,100 other ranks.

After the war the Officers and men of the Norwich Home Guard battalions wanted to perpetuate the spirit and service they had shared. Funds were raised and two proposals were adopted. First, the formation of a Home Guard Club in Norwich and second a gift to The Royal Norfolk Regiment to celebrate their association with it. On 8 December 1945 at the Home Guard Club at Colman House on Pottergate the President, Lt.-Col. Bassett F. Hornor presented the title deeds of a plot of land adjacent to the extant Regimental War Memorial Cottages and a further cheque for £200 to cover any incidental expenses for the site were formally presented to Gen. Sir Ernest Peter Strickland, Colonel of the Regiment by Major F.J. Morse the Chairman of the Memorial Site Committee. Further Regimental Cottages were built on this site to remember the VCs and service of the men of the Regiment during the Second World War with a stone tablet marking 'The site of these memorial cottages was presented by Norwich Home Guard.'

The Secret Home Guard

Although only ever part of the Home Guard for administrative purposes one organization drew on its membership to hand pick men for its very special duties and even adopted HG uniforms to cloak its' members occasional appearances while on manoeuvres or during some of its training with other regular Home Guard units – they were the members of Auxiliary Units, 'Churchill's Secret Army', a top secret organization whose members, in the event of invasion, were to go to ground, allow the enemy to pass over and then would rise up in as a resistance army to harry the army of occupation.

Nationally, the leading light of the resistance army was Major Colin McVean Gubbins a decorated and experienced officer with a particular interest in irregular warfare. He had served with distinction during the First World War and subsequently in both Russia and Ireland. Gubbins compiled three publications for MI(R): *Partisan's Leader's Handbook*, *The Art of Guerilla Warfare* and *How to use High Explosives*. His methods were sneered at by some in the War Office and on the General Staff as 'dirty warfare.' Gubbins preferred that they were quaintly known as 'scallywagging.' In the summer of 1939 he began to approach a few carefully selected British civilians; explorers, mountaineers and linguists all of whom might be 'useful' in a time of war.

In 1940 Gubbins was given the task of creating the underground army soon to be known by the deliberately vague title of 'Auxiliary Units' under the aegis of GHQ Home Forces while Field Marshal Ironside was still C-in-C. Churchill took a personal interest in the development of these units. A letter to him from the offices of the War Cabinet outlined: 'These Auxiliary Units are being formed with two objectives: A) They are intended to provide, within the framework of the Home Guard organization, small bodies of men especially selected and trained, whose role it will be to act offensively on the flanks and in the rear of any enemy troops who may obtain a foothold in this country. Their action will particularly directed against tanks and lorries…ammunition dumps, small enemy posts and stragglers. Their activities will also include sniping. B) The other function of the Auxiliary Units is to provide a system of intelligence whereby Regular Forces in the field can be kept informed of what is happening behind enemy lines.' The letter went on to point out that each unit would comprise no more than a dozen men, they were to be provided with weaponry and equipped with wireless and field telephones apparatus. Each unit was to be accommodated in specially designed camouflaged and concealed (usually underground) operational bases (OBs) where food, water, weapons and ammunition would be stored. Once training got underway the Auxiliaries were also taught how to disrupt enemy railways by blowing up tracks, destruction of petrol and ammunition dumps and how to immobilize enemy aircraft on occupied airfields.

In practice the objective 'A' Aux. Units were to become known as Operational Patrols and usually comprised of between 4-8 men in each unit. Patrols would only operate in an area within 15 miles of their base and they would have no knowledge of the other units in nearby villages. In the event of a successful invasion and enemy occupation they were not to communicate in any way with army command, they had to be isolated and autonomous until a successful counter attack was made or they were wiped out. All Auxiliaries were warned their operational life expectancy was if there was an invasion - about 15 days. If they were lucky.

Objective 'B' units became known as Special Duties Section and Signals. These units contained both men and women who were trained to identify vehicles, high-ranking officers and military units, and were to gather intelligence and leave reports in dead letter drops. The reports would be collected by runners and taken to one of over 200 secret radio transmitters operated by trained civilian signals staff.

Gubbins began his recruitment drive with a team of 12 hand-picked intelligence officers. The officer to be charged with the duty of constructing the first auxiliary units in the East Anglian counties of Norfolk, Suffolk and Essex was Captain Andrew Croft; a very able and intelligent officer with and Oxford degree, proficiency in 10 languages, the ability to ski and fly recent experience of modern military operations in Finland. When the units had taken shape their expansion, recruitment, administration and training was placed in the hands of officers dedicated to each county. Gubbins looked to his cousin, Major Nigel Vernon Oxenden MC who was appointed Auxiliary Units Intelligence Officer (I.O.) for Norfolk in July 1940. Soon to become known simply as 'Oxo' he was well liked by his men. Major Oxenden was later

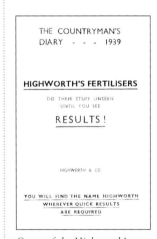

THE COUNTRYMAN'S DIARY - - - 1939

HIGHWORTH'S FERTILISERS

DO THEIR STUFF UNSEEN
UNTIL YOU SEE

RESULTS !

HIGHWORTH & CO

YOU WILL FIND THE NAME HIGHWORTH
WHEREVER QUICK RESULTS
ARE REQUIRED

Cover of the Highworth's Fertilizer's 'Diary.'

THE GALE & POLDEN
TRAINING SERIES

FIGHTING PATROL TACTICS

by COL. G.A.WADE.M.C

Author of "The Defence of Bloodford Village" etc.

Price 1/6 net by post 1/8

transferred to Coleshill House and his duties in Norfolk were carried on by Captain Woodward.

Every man who was to serve in the Auxiliary Units had to be very carefully selected. The Officers and NCO instructors were mostly drawn from the Regular Army while the members of the Aux. Units were drawn from the Home Guard and a huge variety of backgrounds from civvy street as diverse as farm labourers, gamekeepers, factory workers and fishermen to clerics, doctors, dentists and local council officials aged from their teens into their seventies. The one common bond was they had the ability to, above all, keep a secret. Other key factors were that these men were resourceful, could and would, if necessary, blend into the countryside around them and have the willingness to undergo specialist training in guerilla warfare, quickly become proficient in this and follow such orders that they fight as they would be taught to fight – to the last round and to the death if need be. By the end of 1941 201 men of the county had been recruited into the auxiliaries.

The initial approach to these men was very cloak and dagger. Our potential Auxiliary would often be called upon by name at their place of work by a well dressed gentleman claiming to be on 'Government business.' Taken to an unmarked car the true purpose of the visit would be revealed. After a brief explanation of how it was feared that Britain may well be invaded and that an organization was being set up to 'deal with Germans when they get here' the potential recruit would be told he had been highly recommended and would be asked if he would be prepared to join.

If he agreed he would be told to report to the Post Office, Highworth, Wiltshire where he would present proof of identity to its innocuous looking postmistress Mabel Stranks. She would then disappear through a door and upon her return announce 'Somebody's coming to fetch you.' She would then carry on about her business and refuse to answer any questions. It was a simple cover but an effective one. Unmarked transport would arrive and take our man to nearby Coleshill House – GHQ Auxiliary Units. During the war years about 4,000 Auxiliaries were trained in advanced guerrilla warfare including unarmed combat, assassination, sabotage and demolition at Coleshill. The administrative centre for the Norfolk auxiliary units was based at Beeston Hall, near Neatishead with Rackheath Hall operating as their radio communications and control station. Further training was carried out with predominantly regular army instructors on military training areas local to the auxiliary unit. The main training base for the Norfolk auxiliaries Leicester Square Farm, Syderstone. Kept a strict secret it was here that their weekend and annual camps were staged, live firing exercises were carried out and patrols taught how to set and deal with trip wires and work with explosives and all manner of skills and fieldcraft for auxiliaries was taught. There was also a weapons training base at Cawston Common rifle range. Thetford Forest and Lodge Hill, Sheringham also hosted a number of training sessions, there was even a training course in unarmed combat in the field behind the Norwich School led by local strong man Jack Ridgeway. More localised training was also provided by army instructors appointed to the auxiliary units. These men would be met at agreed, secluded locations by members of the local unit, if he needed to go to their OB he would probably be blindfolded and led there to maintain secrecy.

The members of the Norfolk auxiliary units were kept sharp with regular night exercises around their local OB where they would go out and stalk the likes of gamekeepers who worked at night. Some got so close they got their hands trodden on but had to remain still and silent to remain undetected. Some larger exercises were staged such as the test of their 'stand-by' and 'action stations' procedures in 1942. Two units were charged with the recapture Coltishall airfield after a supposed landing by paratroops while others were sent to disrupt the enemy bridgeheads at Wells, Binham and Weybourne.

For most of their existence many Aux. Units had no uniforms and performed their duties in their work clothes or perhaps a set of army denims. In 1943(after a wrangle with the War Office), if Auxiliaries did wear uniforms they were allowed to wear the khaki 'Home Guard' title printed with the standard yellow letters, below that the county letter designations in which they were based and below that the number 201, 202 or 203. 201 signified Scotland and Northumberland 202 units ran from Yorkshire and southwards to the line of the Thames and Wales. 203 covered South and South East Commands thus in Norfolk the designations read 'NK 202.'

The equipment issued to the aux. units was impressive. Initially Patrols improvised with cudgels, hunting or sharpened domestic carving knives, knuckle dusters and cheese cutting wires to act as garrottes. Soon they were provided with rubber truncheons quality pistols such as a Smith and Wesson revolver and a selection of the latest weapons including a variety of grenades, incendiary devices, a silenced pistol, a magnificent .22 calibre sniper rifle, Thompson sub-machines guns and later Sten guns. They were also issued and Fairbairn-Sykes fighting knives, quantities of detonators and plastic explosive. Even today stashes of all the afore mentioned weaponry, including plastic explosives, are still being discovered when the cellars and garages of ex-auxiliaries are cleared out.

In total about 7,000 auxiliaries were recruited and trained and established in groups across Britain. It is thought over 500 Aux Unit operational bases were built in secret in secluded local woodland by Royal Engineers or the men of the patrol themselves, many patrols also had additional concealed observation posts. Some 45 operational bases were constructed. Many of the known OBs and OPs have collapsed or flooded over the years, many still remain undiscovered. When most of the HG units were stood down in 1944 the Aux. Units carried on until 1945. After the war those who had served with Aux. Units were sent small lapel badges as a mark of thanks. These badges are in the shape of a shield divided with a red upper and blue lower (reflecting the colours of GHQ Home Forces). The he centre is surmounted by a crown the number 202 is in the middle with the figure 1 above the zero and the number 3 below. Even years after their exploits many of the auxiliaries never spoke a word of what they did during the war and tragically, despite answering our country's call and training harder than any other civilian unit due to the secret nature of the Auxiliary Units they were unable to claim the Defence Medal. This only changed in 1996 when the Ministry of Defence authorised the award for those men who served at least three years.

The lapel badge issued at the end of the Second World War. to members of the Auxiliary Units in recognition of their services.

4 Air Defence and Bombing

The air defence system in Norfolk had been developed since the mid-1930s; Weybourne Camp had become and Anti-Aircraft Gunnery training camp, extant RAF airfields had been modernised and developed, new airfields had been constructed, Observer Corps posts had been established across the county and the tall radio masts that had drawn the attention of the *Graf Zeppelin* in 1939 were part of the Chain Home Radio Direction Finding (RDF) system of coastal radar stations. Two of the original 15 sites planned for this system in 1937 were in Norfolk, at West Beckham and Stoke Holy Cross. The system otherwise known as AMES Type 1 (Air Ministry Experimental Station) provided long-range detection of aircraft. Each site consisted of four 240ft high wooden receiver, direction finding and elevation-measuring aerials set out in a square around a brick receiver (Rx) block. Nearby were four 350ft high steel construction Transmitter towers strung with transmitter aerial wires between them. On the ground below would be the Transmitter (Tx) Block and generator houses.

The original system was unable to detect aircraft flying at lower altitudes but used in conjunction with the Chain Home Low system, (AMES Type 2) aircraft flying at minimum altitude level of 500 ft. out to 18 miles and aircraft flying at 2,000 ft out to 35 miles could also be detected. One of the first of these new stations to join the chain was built at Happisburgh, complete with its' radar scanner mounted on top of a 185ft high tower. All Chain Home radar stations faced out to sea; once aircraft had crossed the British coast they could no longer be tracked by radar so the interception direction centres had to rely upon visual and aural sightings received from the Observer Corps posts across the county. The Observer Corps in Norfolk (16 Group) had been raised in the 1930s and stood ready for action at the time of the outbreak of war with posts across the county and an established headquarters in Norwich with its plotting table and telephones to communicate the path of enemy aircraft to the appropriate authorities to sound the air raid warning. A warning line was also installed from their Group head-quarters to HM the King's residence at Sandringham House where Gerald and George Lascelles, the two sons of the 6th Earl of Harewood were responsible for the warning operations. Known as the 'S' line it was always regarded as a priority but with special attention when the Royal family were in residence.

The Wardens of Air Raid Warden's Post G6 on The Avenues by Christchurch Road, Earlham Norwich, 1940

Long range German aircraft began mine laying missions and machine gun attacks on merchant shipping over the North Sea in the winter of 1939 and as a consequence of such actions the people of Norfolk were to see one of the most curious sights of the early war years. On Saturday 21 October a Heinkel He115B from 1/Küstenfliegruppe 406 crashed into the sea 5 miles east of Spurn Head, Yorkshire after combat with RAF Hurricanes of No. 46 Squadron. All of the Luftwaffe crew were killed and their bodies were carried on the tide until they were washed ashore at Mundesley and Happisburgh. Thus it was here the first full honours burial of German aircrew in Norfolk was conducted on 2 November 1939. With coffins draped in swastika flags and smart RAF bearer parties the bodies of Oblt. Zur See H. Schlicht, Lt. F. Meyer and Uffz. B. Wessels were given a service inside Happisburgh church and were formally born to their graves in the churchyard. The event drew local and national press interest and was even featured with a photograph in a number of nationals including *The Times*. In retrospect this gesture many seem curious but the reciprocal code of giving honours funerals to aircrew lost over enemy territory by both sides was well established during the First World War and this old tradition was honoured again in 1939.

The first enemy aircraft plot over Norfolk by the Observer Corps was made on Wednesday 6 December 1939 by Observer S. Vincent, a man whose usual job was that of an auctioneer in Norwich. He plotted a Heinkel (He115 float plane (2081) from 3/Küstenfliegruppe (Maritime Group) 506) on a mine laying mission flying across the Wash to Sheringham. The Heinkel collided with the Chain Home radiolocation mast at West Beckham, narrowly missed the Sheringham gas holder and finally crashed onto the West Beach, a short distance from the lifeboat house at 3.15am.

Despite the hour a number of locals went to investigate, a number of them advising their women folk to stay inside and lock the door 'in case there are Germans about.' A number of locals were determined to take a few souvenirs, including the plane's compass and the pilots seat which did sterling

The committal of Oberleutnant zur See W. Wodtke at Sheringham Cemetery, December 1939

service as a comfortable addition to a fishing boat for many years afterwards. A military guard was placed on the site to prevent further losses and the wreckage was soon removed. Upon closer examination the plane's fuel tanks were found to be protected by a rubberised material that was found by the Aircraft Research Establishment at Farnborough to be both fire and puncture resistant and proved to be of interest and value to our own researchers.

The first body from the crew of the crashed Heinkel to be washed up was that of the Observer, Oberfw. Emil Rödel (29) who was buried in Great Bircham churchyard with full military honours including a RAF bearer party on 9 December. The coffin was draped with two swastika flags and there was a large wreath inscribed, 'A tribute to a gallant airman from the officers, NCO's and airmen of the RAF'. Three Volleys were fired, and the last post sounded.

The bodies of Oblt. Zue See W. Wodtke and Oberfw. K. Ullman were washed ashore later in the month and were also given full military funerals at Sheringham. After the War the remains of these airmen and those buried at Happisburgh were exhumed and reinterred at the Soldatenfriedhof German War Cemetery at Cannock Chase, Staffordshire.

On 30 April 1940 a Heinkel He 111H-4 of 1/KG 126, a Luftwaffe coastal unit specialising in mine laying operations, was off the Norfolk coast intent on sowing two parachute mines when it became engulfed with a thick black fog. The Pilot, Oberleutnant and Flugzeugfuhrer Hermann Vagts flew blindly until about 11.15pm when he broke cover near the radar station at Bawdsey. AA Batteries had been put on alert and opened fire damaging the plane which came down at Clacton on Sea, Essex where it crashed causing the first civilian air raid casualties of the Second World War.

Within days of the fall of France the first German bombers flew over Norfolk on their first bombing sorties over the British mainland; the object of their missions being the destruction of our airfields prior to full invasion. The first bombs fell on the county on 25 May 1940. The target was probably RAF West Raynham; 13 High Explosive (HE) bombs were dropped to the north east of the aerodrome shortly after midnight, two further bombs fell on Raveningham with three more falling on Aylsham, Burgh St Peter and on Langley marshes killing a pony and a cow. There would prove to be a number of instances during the war where enemy aircraft would simply 'tip' their bombs out across the countryside, rather than dropping them over the assigned target. There are many reasons for this ranging from the pilot spotting what appeared to be an opportune target, plain and simple error to lightening their load as they fled back across the sea hence. The next two bombs to fall on the county were HEs dropped on a searchlight unit at Strumpshaw on 2 June 1940, this incident caused the first human casualty during the Second World War in Norfolk as the blast caused a soldier to lose his foot. This incident was followed just a few days later on 6 June by an attack aimed at RAF Bircham Newton. Some 200 incendiary bombs were dropped over the area but poor old North Tuddenham suffered worst with 8 HEs landing across the parish.

On 9 July 1940, the city of Norwich suffered its first air raid. The day had begun fine and warm and in the newspapers over the breakfast table folks read of the Luftwaffe tactic of 'glide bombing.' The aeronautical correspondent of *The Times* wrote:

The East Anglia Section highlighted one the German Reconnaissance Guides to Great Britain

'*The enemy appear to be adhering, for the moment at any rate, to their policy of sending over a limited number of aircraft, splitting up some time before they reach the coast and attacking a number of points with small formations. One new feature of yesterday's raids was the employment of 'glide-bombing' in one area. To do this the bomber flies at a great height and shuts off its engines while still some miles from the objective. It then glides noiselessly over its target. The object of this method of attack is to make it difficult for the defences to locate the raider. The machine must, however, come over at a high altitude, because, with its engines off it loses height rapidly, especially when carrying a heavy bomb load. Once the bombs have been discharged the pilot switches on the engines again and regains a safer height with all possible speed.'*

By late afternoon cloud had extended across the sky above Norwich providing excellent cover for any enemy raiders. A few minutes before 5pm a number of employees of Barnards Ltd on Salhouse Road, Mousehold had seen and heard explosions in the distance, about 2 miles away to the North. A 'Yellow' warning signal had been received but not the danger 'Red' so no siren had been sounded, indeed, shortly after 5pm the 'White' safety signal had been received. Percy Moreton, Barnard's Advertising Manager and Warden for No. 20 Office Building recorded what happened next in a remarkable and vivid account he compiled shortly after the incident:

Seven or eight minutes later, employees in the open and in the offices saw two large planes approaching from the north-east, flying low at about 600ft; they were travelling slowly and their engine could be plainly heard. Those who watched the planes were startled to see black markings, in the shape of crosses on the wings.

The approach was unexpected, sudden; it is assumed that the planes glided down from a great height, the pilots opening the engines as bombing level was reached. Within two or three seconds of the recognition of the enemy, the first bombs exploded.

Outside and inside the buildings, employees flung themselves to the ground, by the side of their machines, under desks and tables, next to walls and on the earth over which they were walking. A few, caught in the open, rushed for cover.

The explosions were curiously light in nature, sharp cracks muffled, as it were, at the edges; everyone had expected heavy and prolonged reverberations. The most frightening feature was the vibration of the walls, the sound of glass cracking, the noise of splinters, pebbles and earth hitting the walls and falling on the roofs (Incidental sounds, because of their proximity, give the impression that the building over one's head is about to come toppling down).

Bearing in mind that the first indication of the raid to many was the sound of the exploding bombs, one might have expected signs of extreme fear or panic, but none was evident. There was no hysteria among the girls (most of them in their teens) in fact their behaviour under this violent stress was admirable in every sense. We salute them!

The target was a straight line over the centre hangars running northeast to south west. The precision was remarkable, the bombs falling in a string almost exactly along the predetermined line.

The first bombs to fall, four it is believed, exploded on or near the two central hangars in the Maintenance Depot. As a result the door coverings at the north end of No. 13 Hangar were torn and bomb splinters pierced the walls of the west side. Small round holes in the roof suggested the passage of machine gun bullets.

The first bomb to fall on the Mousehold Works struck a buttress on the east side of No. 12 Hangar, taking away some bricks and digging into the soft earth where it failed to explode. The bomb was later removed by the authorities.

The next bomb fell directly in front of No. 12 Hangar, four paces from the doors. It blew in the doors, badly tearing them and shattered the windows. The roof sheets were blown upwards and this was a singular feature of the explosion. The loading dock by the entrance was destroyed and a wood garage at the side was damaged, collapsing later. A Morris two - ton lorry was wrecked by blast and fire and a Scammell trailer caught fire but subsequently was made serviceable. The bomb landed on the asphalt and must have burst immediately – there was no crater, just a denting and scraping of the surface.

Hereabouts, on the road between No. 12 and No. 9 Hangars, there were three casualties. Harry Leonard Dye [35], packer and Arthur Shreeve [30], driver, were working by the loading dock and received severe injuries from which they died. It is uncertain if they were caught quite unprepared or were in the act of running for cover.

And so they claimed their first victims. One's destiny cannot be foreseen and about this fatal spot at least three persons narrowly escaped death. Ronald Green, Despatch Foreman, was the third casualty. He flung himself on the ground by his office, a wood hut standing to the side of No. 9 Hangar, some twenty paces from where the bomb fell. A bomb fragment tore through his right shoe, cutting the big toe, which later had to be amputated. A boy named Horace Middleton lay near but was untouched.

Arthur Adams of the Despatch Office had a most remarkable escape. He was standing on the steps of the office in full range of the explosion. A bomb splinter went through one of his trouser legs and other splinters pierced the walls on either side of him, one piece entering a drawer of his desk. He felt the rush of air but was miraculously unhurt.

The line of bombing was now over No. 9 Hangar, General Stores, which ran lengthwise directly opposite No. 12. The building was hit twice and almost immediately caught fire. It was soon blazing and the flames rose in a great bellying mass to a height of one hundred feet. They could be seen from many points in the surrounding district. It is fairly certain that incendiary bombs were also dropped and these – or the heat of the high explosives – ignited oil and paint which were stored respectively at the ends of the building.

The only evidence left of the actual structure were isolated bits of broken wall, standing precariously at two or three points. The wrecked and flame licked material, which was mostly of iron and wire resembled a huge scrap-iron dump. Among the tangle of wreckage it was interesting to note the alignment of certain material; blackened by fire but untouched by explosive, steel rods, iron channels and their like stood in neat piles.

The effect of one bomb was devastating. It probably burst within the roof area – a steel girder was struck and the holes in it slanted downwards. Thick coils of wire were cut right through and other heavy material was twisted and thrown about. The doors at the south west end were blown out.

The roadways round the burnt out hangar were strewn with broken glass. Later, as the glass was trampled into tiny pieces, each roadway resembled a carpet of brilliants, glittering and winking in the sun.

Three persons were in the building – Harold Stockwell, chief assistant, was sitting at his desk, which rested against a tier of steel bins containing nuts and bolts. This heavy barrier was an effective safeguard and apart from feeling the shock of the explosion, Stockwell was unharmed. After leaving the building he returned to get his bicycle but owing to the encroaching flames could not get his coat, in which was a wallet containing money and valuable papers.

Reginald Jarvis and a junior, Freddie Phillipo, were in the office at the east side of the hangar. The door which opened into the hangar jammed and Jarvis, who had received a head injury, had difficulty in forcing it open. When this was done the pair had to pass through part of the building to reach and exit but fortunately the way to safety was, at that moment, clear of flames.

The bomb that fell near the south west doors increased the death roll. Opposite that end of the hangar stood the canteen and six workmen were leaving the building as the raid began. Two of them, Gardiner and Cullum, darted back inside, while another named Weevers ran forward and flung himself under a small bush. These men escaped injury but the remaining three caught the force of the blast. Frederick Elvin [32], trimmer and Albert Sayer [53], moulder, rushed for shelter towards the hangar doors; right into the path of the exploding bomb. Frederick Elvin was, it is believed, killed instantly and Albert Sayer died from his injuries within the hour. Sydney Cushion, a boy moulder, was badly lacerated and such was the nature of his wounds, a leg had to be amputated...

The two hangars flanking No. 9 escaped serious damage. Windows in both were shattered and burning material landing on the roof of No. 10 Hangar, the Woodworking Factory partially burnt out a valley gutter and Office partitions were blown down. The two buildings were full of workmen, who sought cover where they stood.

In No. 8 Engineering Works, a number of them got into air raid shelters which they were constructing!

The wall of the canteen facing the south-west doors of No. 9 was ripped and torn by splinters, some of which reached the opposite wall inside. Similar damage was caused on that side by blast from a bomb which burst a few yards outside, near the kitchen. Glass crashed in on all sides, covering the floor. The canteen staff and workmen at tea took cover under tables and amazingly no one was even scratched. The bomb fell on soft earth leaving a crater twelve feet wide and five feet deep.

Above: *Boulton & Paul's Riverside factory, Norwich a clearly identified target in the German Military Objekt-bilder Ost-Anglia.*

Below: *Clouds of smoke billow up after the bombing of Boulton & Paul's Riverside Works after the first air raid on Norwich 9 July 1940*

Here again the nature of certain marks suggested the employment of machine guns; a tea urn, for example, was neatly drilled through. No one heard gun fire and since no spent bullets were found, no final assertion on this point can be made.

The next bomb fell on open ground between the canteen and office building, leaving a fairly deep crater. Leonard Cooper, a boy employed in the Progress Office, was caught between this bomb and that which fell outside the Canteen kitchen. Cycling at his usual quick pace along a nearby path he saw the two planes, and because of his knowledge of aircraft, at once recognised enemy machines. He threw himself off and out of the corner of one eye saw earth and debris from the two craters criss-crossing in the air. Far from being shaken he seemed to revel in the experience. Aeroplanes are his life and he is the type to make a brilliant pilot.

Two girls, Joan Thrower and Vera Daynes, were caught in the open near the Offices and ran for cover. Luckily they were some distance from the path of the bombs although Vera fell, cutting her knee. Both girls came through the ordeal with courage.

The remaining buildings to the south do not run parallel to the main hangar group and set at various angles, they presented an evasive target. Two, semi-detached cottages, flanking the north-west end of the office building were, however, on the line of attack and it is astonishing that they and the occupants, the families of Uden King, Canteen Manager and Samuel Nash, Caretaker, avoided destruction.

Two bombs fell near the building, one in each garden. The largest crater, some twenty-four feet across and ten feet deep, was caused, it was officially stated, by a 500lb bomb. Mrs King, on hearing explosions, rushed from her cottage to find earth raining down on her. Walter Nash (son of the caretaker) who was ill in bed, was shaken by the concussion. Downstairs windows and tiles on the roof were broken and bomb fragments were found here and there about the structure but no serious damage was done and the occupants were unharmed. A few panes of glass were broken in the office building and the roof was splattered with pebbles and earth.

The last of the bombs, four of them, dropped a little further on, in the end of the wood abutting No. 1 Hangar... All told, twelve bombs dropped on the estate (most of them of 250lb calibre) and five or six seconds covered the period of the explosions.'

Moreton noted in his final comments about the attack that: 'One of the planes was seen to bank away to the south...' he was convinced that it was this aircraft, a Junkers 88, that went on to inflict further death and destruction on the city.

Staff were leaving off and pouring out of the gates at Reckitt & Colman's Carrow Works when the raider dived and another bomb whistled down. Some of the men shouted 'Down' as the device crashed through the trees near the old Wilderness Tower at the top of Carrow Hill but tragically many of the girls wheeling their bicycles up the hill did not react quickly

enough and were standing when the bomb exploded killing Bessie Upton (36) and Maud Balaam (40) instantly. Several others were injured by the shrapnel, shattered glass, stones and detritus that ripped through the air with the blast. A number of them were removed to the Norfolk and Norwich Hospital where the severely injured Gladys Sampson (18) and Bertha Playford (19) died shortly after admission. Maud Burrell (37) fought for her life for three days but finally succumbed to her injuries on 12 July.

A further four bombs hammered down upon Boulton & Paul Riverside Works. Direct hits on the large, aged wood-working and paint shop instantly caused a fire to erupt, causing massive columns of smoke to billow skywards; the steel framed building buckled under the heat and truss roof and its corrugated iron covering collapsed. The sheet metal and box making shops were also destroyed here along with the canteen, offices and board-room. Seven died on site namely: Charles Bacon (36), Charles Brooks (39), Herbert Kiddell (44), Walter Smith (23), Arthur Strike (23), George Strowger (27) and Frederick Wright (16). Three were seriously injured and removed to the Norfolk & Norwich Hospital where John McMillan (60) died the same day, Robert Daniels (30) died the following day and Carlos Sewter (46) lost his fight for life on 12 July. Twenty more were injured. Four more bombs were dropped on the neighbouring LNER Locomotive sheds and goods yard at Thorpe Station; only one of these exploded, but it too caused more fatalities, namely: Charles Freeman (44), Stanley Leffling (23), George Payne (37) and Ernest Silom (58). Bertie Hoult (55), William Lord (50) and Richard Parker (37) were removed to the Norfolk and Norwich Hospital but sadly they also succumbed to their injuries. Many more were wounded to lesser extents. When the dust settled the and the adjacent railway lines were found to have become a twisted and mangled mess of iron, many of the shattered rails being left pointing skyward in some a gaunt and silent memorial of the blast.

The greatest and hard learned lesson from this first raid was the need to provide a supplementary watch or in addition to the extant public warning system. Messrs. Boulton & Paul, Laurence Scott & Electromotors and Reckitt & Colman came together to pool resources and set up their own team of spotters and a spotting post was rigged up on top of Carrow House. The firm's internal air raid signal system was then coupled up and controlled by a switch on the staging.

The spotters proved their worth over two subsequent raids but it was felt that the efficiency of the spotters could be greatly improved if they had an unobstructed view of the entire horizon. The Joint committee worked on the problem of a more favourable location and a property on some of the highest ground in the area at No. 15 Bracondale that had been leased to Boulton & Paul was found to be ideal for the placement of a stand-alone observation post. The 'Post' took the form of a steel pylon tower surmounted by a cabin with a gallery around it from which the observers could operate – some 82ft above ground level. The spotters on the tower also proved themselves in helping to keep the factories running. In 1940 if these Norwich factories had stopped work and taken cover based on the public warning alerts there would have been 580 warnings and 640 hours and 19 minutes taken out of the working year through taking shelter whereas the spotters would only activate an alert if their factories faced imminent danger and thus just 238 'crash' warnings were given from the spotters post with a total duration of 26 hours and 7 minutes. Other businesses in the city such as F. W. Harmer clothing manufacturers on St Andrew's soon followed suit with their own spotter teams and 'crash' alert systems.

The Thorpe Electricity Generating Station, another target illustrated in Objektbilder Ost-Anglia.

The operators of the private air raid spotting post funded by Boulton & Paul, Colman's and LNER at Bracondale, Norwich.

'We will fight them in the Air' – Norfolk airfields during the Battle of Britain

Barton Bendish
Dispersal airfield constructed in 1939 serving 3 Group Bomber bases (parent station RAF Marham) in the event of enemy attack on the main airfields.

Bircham Newton
Served continuously as an operational airfield since 1916, it was enlarged and improved in the 1930s

| 206 Squadron | June 1936 – July 1941 | Avro Anson G.R.I and Lockheed Hudson Mk 1 |
Flew coastal patrols over the North Sea. On 8 November 1939 F/O H. E. M. Featherstone was flying his Avro Anson aircraft on convoy protection duties when it was attacked by a German He115 floatplane. His gunner (ACI Brtton) shot down the German aircraft, one of the first German aircraft to be shot down during the War and was awarded the DFM.

| 235 Squadron | April 1940 – June 1941 | Bristol Blenheim Mk IV F |
Coastal Command Squadron flying anti-enemy shipping and convoy protection patrols over the North Sea and making sweeps off Holland.

| 826 Squadron | April- December 1940 | Fairey Albacore Mk 1 |
RN Squadron attached to RAF Coastal Command carrying flying night shipping patrols for the protection of shipping convoys and operations in Holland, Belgium and France.

| 815 Squadron | April – June 1940 | Fairey Swordfish Mk 1 |
RN Squadron attached to RAF Coastal Command flew operations in support of the Dunkirk evacuation May 1940.

| 812 Squadron | May– June 1940 | Fairey Swordfish Mk 1 |
RN Squadron attached to RAF Coastal Command for night-time mine laying missions off the North Fresian Islands.

Bodney
Opened in March 1940 as a grass satellite airfield for RAF Watton.

Coltishall
Building commenced in February 1939, known initially as Scottow Aerodrome it was intended to be a bomber airfield but in practice it served as a fighter base. If the RAF had followed their established tradition, the station would have been named after the nearest railway station, which would have made it "RAF Buxton", but to avoid possible confusion with Buxton, Derbyshire, it was named after the next local village with a station, hence RAF Coltishall. Opened as fully operational at 0001 hours on 23 June 1940

| 66 Squadron | May – September 1940 | Supermarine Spitfire Mk 1 |
The first fighter squadron to use Coltishall as a forward base from 29 May, its duties consisted mainly of North Sea Patrols. Flew covering patrols during the Dunkirk evacuation.

| 242 Squadron | June – December 1940 | Hawker Hurricane Mk 1 |
Squadron comprised mostly Canadian pilots; returned demoralised and battered from France. Upon their return the squadron became part of 12 Group, received new Hurricanes and a new Commanding Officer – Squadron Leader Douglas Bader. By his singular leadership and determination Bader rebuilt 242 and achieved operational readiness for his squadron to play its part with distinction in the Battle of Britain. Once fully operational 242 began to operate from Duxford as part of the famous 'Big Wing.'

| 604 Squadron ('B' Flight) | July 1940 – August 1942 | Bristol Blenheim Mk I F |
Night Fighter Detachment based at Coltishall for the defence of Norwich against enemy night intruders.

| 616 Squadron | September 1940 | Supermarine Spitfire Mk I |
Commanded by the legendary Squadron Leader A. G. 'Sailor' Malan; their duty was to intercept daylight enemy intruders.

| 74 Squadron | September – October 1940 | Supermarine Spitfire Mk IIA |
Replaced 616 as the daytime interceptor unit

Docking
Known locally as 'Sunderland Airfield,' came into use as a satellite and overflow for the Coastal Command station at Bircham Newton in spring 1940.

East Wretham
Constructed late 1939 as a grass runway satellite airfield for RAF Honington in Suffolk.

Feltwell
First World War airfield retained until 1936 when the site was reconstructed as a RAF bomber base with a grass runway

| 75 (NZ) Squadron | April 1940 – August 1942 | Vickers Wellington Mks 1 and 1a |
No 3 Group bomber squadron and saw action over Norway, France, Belgium, Italy, Sweden and Germany.

Great Massingham
Opened July 1940 with grass runways as a satellite for RAF West Raynham.

| 18 Squadron | September 1940 – April 1941 | Bristol Blenheim Mk. IV |
Light bomber squadron flying low level raids against shipping and land targets.

Horsham St Faith
First constructed as a bomber station with grass runways in 1939 and officially opened on 1 June 1940.

| 19 Squadron | April – May 194 | Supermarine Spitfire Mk 1 |
Squadron was part of 12 Group Fighter Command based at Duxford but used Horsham as a forward base from which to fly patrols over the North Sea to intercept enemy raiders in daylight.

| 264 Squadron | May - July 1940 | Boulton Paul Defiant Mk. 1 |
Squadron was part of 12 Group Fighter Command based at Duxford but used Horsham as a forward base for operations during the German invasion of the Low Countries.

| 66 Squadron | May 1940 | Supermarine Spitfire Mk 1 |
Fighter squadron flying North Sea patrols. Flew mission in support of the Dunkirk evacuation.

114 Squadron   June – August 1940   Bristol Blenheim Mk IV
Returned from the Battle of France where it has suffered badly. Re-equipped and flew low level operations against shipping, ports and other coastal targets in German occupied Holland as part of 2 Group's Light Bomber Force.

139 Squadron   June 1940 – July 1941   Bristol Blenheim Mk IV
Lost most of its aircraft during the Battle of France, returned and re-equipped with Blenheims the squadron flew low level operations against shipping, ports and other coastal targets in German occupied Holland as part of 2 Group's Light Bomber Force.

Langham
Opened in May 1940 with three grass runways as an emergency landing field and satellite for RAF Bircham Newton.

Marham
An aerodrome from 1916-19, in 1935 work started on a new airfield with 'C' Type hangars, technical staff buildings and domestic quarters re-opening as a two squadron heavy bomber station on 1 April 1937.

38 Squadron   May 1937 – November 1940   Vickers Wellington Mk 1
Flew propaganda leaflet raids on Germany and bombing raids with the Channel ports and the Ruhr as regular targets.

115 Squadron   June 1937 – September 1942   Vickers Wellington Mk 1
Flew propaganda leaflet, mine laying and bombing raids on Germany and German airfields in occupied Norway. In April 1940, while on temporary loan to RAF Coastal Command, 115 Squadron gained the distinction of making the RAF's first bombing raid of the war on a mainland target-the enemy-held Norwegian airfield of Stavanger Airport, Sola.

Matlaske
Constructed with grass runways and opened as a satellite for RAF Coltishall in 1940. Used as an advanced landing ground for fighter squadrons flying from Duxford.

Methwold
Opened as a dispersal airfield for RAF Feltwell in the winter of 1938. 214 Squadron flying Vickers Wellington Mk 1 and 1A moved here from Feltwell on 3 September 1939 until February 1940. Between this time and the summer of 1942 no squadrons were based at Methwold but the Wellingtons from Feltwell were regularly dispersed here. The grass airfield was transferred to No. 2 Group in the exchange of bases with No. 3 Group, in the summer of 1942

Oulton
Construction commenced in 1939 and opened on 31 July 1940 as a bomber airfield with T2 type hangars and grass runways. Operated as a satellite airfield for RAF Horsham St. Faith between July 1940 and September 1942

114 Squadron   August 1940 – March 1941   Bristol Blenheim Mk IV
Flew cloud cover day missions on airfields, Channel Ports and other targets in Germany and occupied Europe.

Swanton Morley
Construction commenced early 1939 and the station was opened in September 1940 as a grass runway light bomber airfield in 2 (Bomber) Group.

105 Squadron   October 1940 - December 1941   Bristol Blenheim Mk IV
Played an active role in the 2 Group day and night bombing campaign flying mostly low level missions against coastal targets and ports in Belgium, Holland and Northern France.

Watton
Construction began in 1937 as a bomber base with C Type hangars and grass runways. Airfield became active in 1939. The Blenheims of 2 Group at Watton served with great distinction and brought numerous honours to the station.

21 Squadron   March 1939 – December 1941   Bristol Blenheim Mk IV
A 2 Group light bomber squadron predominantly flying shipping patrols over the North Sea. 82 Squadron was almost wiped out during an attack on enemy formations in Gembloux in May 1940. Later missions were flown against troop movements and armoured train in German occupied Holland and Belgium. Transferred to Coastal Command (operating from RAF Lossiemouth, Scotland) June - October 1940.

82 Squadron   August 1939 – March 1942   Bristol Blenheim Mk IV
A 2 Group light bomber squadron predominantly flying shipping patrols over the North Sea.

18 Squadron   May 1940   Bristol Blenheim Mk IV
Squadron had suffered badly during the Battle of France. Re-equipped and recuperated here.

105 Squadron   July – October 1940   Bristol Blenheim Mk IV
Took the place of 21 Squadron while they were transferred to Coastal Command (June – October 1940). Flew missions against ports, airfields and troop movements in Holland and Northern France.

West Raynham
Opened in 1939 with four C Type hangars and grass runways.

101 Squadron   May 1939 – July 1941   Bristol Blenheim Mk IV
A 2 Group Bomber Squadron reserve unit involved in training.

2 Group T. T. Flight   February 1940 – January 1942   Bristol Blenheim Mk IV
Target Towing unit that provided gunnery training for local squadrons.

76 Squadron   April 1940 – May 1940   Avro Anson Mk 1 and Handley Page Hampden Mk 1
Part of 16 O. T. U. Training as a Hampden bomber unit. Plans changed and unit was disbanded before it was fully trained or equipped.

139 Squadron   May 1940 – June 1940   Bristol Blenheim Mk IV
Suffered severe losses and came direct to West Raynham to recuperate and re-equip upon their return from the Battle for France.

18 Squadron   June 1940 – September 1940   Bristol Blenheim Mk IV
Suffered severe losses and came direct to West Raynham to recuperate and re-equip upon their return from the Battle for France.

Members of 8 Section, No. 4 Bomb Disposal Company, Royal Engineers carefully remove the 250kg bomb from outside No. 4 Theatre Street, September 1940.

As the Battle of Britain reached its climax in September 1940 Norwich suffered more air raids, the raid of 18/19 September saw just four bombs dropped on Norwich two of them were 1kg Incendiaries that were swiftly dealt with, the other two were time sensitive SD 250kg bombs. One of these fell on heath land at Long Valley, Mousehold and detonated 12 hours later. The other 250kg bomb smashed through the path and embedded itself 30 ft into the soft subsoil outside No. 4 Theatre Street. Residents were evacuated from the immediate vicinity and notices posted around the area restricting entrance. The men from 8 Section, No. 4 Bomb Disposal Company, Royal Engineers arrived on 24 September . They knew the device could detonate anything up to 96 hours after it was dropped and even the slightest movement could start the clockwork fuse ticking again. In 1940 there was little kit for the brave men of bomb disposal, let alone a manual to help them, so they set about digging out the bomb with their picks and shovels. It took the best part of a day's digging before the tail fin of the bomb was sighted. It took a total of four days to uncover and defuse the bomb, no easy task and one that could result in death and destruction. After defusal, even when the bomb was roped around and began to be hauled up the crew took no chances in case a secondary fuse remained hidden inside Lieutenant Patton RAMC carefully placed a piece of cloth on the casing and gently pressed his stethoscope on top to listen for the activation of any hidden mechanisms as the bomb was manually hauled out by block and tackle. Having been made safe the bomb was then loaded onto an army lorry and was removed to Harford tip.

By a remarkable coincidence the George Medal was introduced on 24 September 1940, the very same day the men of 8 Section went to work on the unexploded bomb. In December 1940, in an unparalleled award ceremony for one single act during the Norwich blitz, three members of the section were awarded the George Medal for their roles in the disposal of the Theatre Street bomb.

Beyond the Battle of Britain

The chain Home RDF system and Observer Corps provided sterling service during the Battle of Britain and was awarded the title 'Royal' in April 1941 but as German tactics changed to night bombing blitz the extant system proved inadequate. In 1941 GCI (Ground Controlled Interception) radar stations brought new technology to guide interceptor night fighters to locate specific enemy aircraft from the ground and by directing searchlights onto intruders. The GCI station at Neatishead opened in 1941. In that same year Coastal Defence and Chain Home Low radar became joint and 120 new sites were identified for the new stations, including Bard Hill, Hopton, Hunstanton, Trimingham and Winterton; their construction was carried out between 1942 and 1943. Another development from the RDF system was IFF (Identification, Friend or Foe) which enabled incoming aircraft to be identified; the IFF equipment housed in brick 'huts' were erected near the aerial bases at most CH stations and GL radar was issued to a number of ROC posts such as Brundall, Docking and Melton Constable other posts received High Frequency radios termed 'Darky' for communication with aircraft lost or in distress. The German military attempted were made to jam the CH system, their efforts were monitored by 'J Watch' mobile equipment set up near CH stations, The Avenue at Stoke Holy Cross was one such location. The offensive scheme to jam Knickebein (the navigational beams of German bombers) involved a number of stations across the county and a Meacon (masking beacon) long range jamming operation was established at Scole.

Air Raid!

After the initial raids of 1940 the aerial attacks on the county carried on until 1945, (a complete list of all air raids appear in *Appendix I*); the following accounts relate some of the most significant incidents.

The year 1941 saw Great Yarmouth suffer its worst year of bombing. A total 767 alerts were sounded and 1, 328 'crash' warnings given. A total of 167 raids were conducted on the town during the course of which 803 High Explosive bombs and 6 mines exploded in the borough destroying many of the old 'Rows'; an estimated 7,020 incendiary bombs rained down and 55 UXBs had to be dealt with by bomb disposal squads. A hundred and nine people lost their lives, 329 were injured and the historic townscape of Great Yarmouth was changed forever.

In *Great Yarmouth – Front Line Town*, Charles Box the Borough Chief Constable and ARP Controller wrote:

> *During the night, [7 – 8 April 1941] Great Yarmouth experienced its worst raid. It would appear that at 12.30am enemy aircraft commenced a series of attacks by dropping incendiary bombs on open ground west of the Borough. These were followed at 12.32am by two parachute mines at the north end of the borough, in the Collingwood Road district. Considerable damage was caused to houses but owing to the fact that many of the occupants had evacuated, the casualties were only two killed and seven injured. This incident was well in hand when at 1.00am a huge shower of incendiary bombs was dropped, extending from the Market Place in a southerly direction across the Row area along South Quay to Gorleston.*
>
> *At this time the Fire Brigade and A.F.S. were still under my control and within a very short space of time all the units were involved and at 2.08am assistance was requested from Lowestoft and Beccles. At 2.57am a further request for assistance was made to the Regional Office and this was sent from Norwich and Cromer districts. In the meantime, many of the bombs and resultant fires were tackled by Supplementary Fire Parties, Wardens, Special Constables and Police and members of the public but in spite of all this effort the fires were so numerous and*

Site of Reynold's Garage on the corner of Apsley Road and Rodney Road, Great Yarmouth destroyed by a direct hit from a High Explosive bomb during the afternoon of 27 February 1941.

widespread, that some of them began to assume large proportions and to add to the difficulties, whilst fire fighting was in progress, hostile planes were continually flying overhead, dropping further incendiary bombs over the area, thereby causing further fires.

During the same period, two large calibre H.E. bombs were dropped on Southtown Road, thereby causing craters which cut off vehicular communication between Yarmouth and Gorleston. However, such an emergency having been foreseen, sufficient personnel were available in Gorleston to deal with the fire occurring there. These bombs added further difficulties to the fire fighting as the water mains were broken, resulting in a considerable reduction in the pressure of water available in Yarmouth.

The assisting pumps and crews duly arrived and reasonably good progress was being made when, at 5.02am, two parachute mines were dropped at the south end of the Borough, one at the junction of Blackfriars Road and Queen's Road and the other in the Row area at the south end of Middlegate Street. Both exploded, causing great havoc. In the first case, a Special Constabulary Sub-Station received the full effects of the blast and five special constables unfortunately lost their lives. The effect of the second mine in the Row area was appalling and as soon as I realised the magnitude of the task of rescue, I requested three Rescue Parties from Norwich.

Among the premises which were seriously damaged or gutted were Marks & Spencer's, Rose's Fashions, Boot's Chemists, Hill's Restaurant, Johnson's Clothing, the Museum and Library, Education Offices, the Science School and the Seaman's Mission and Institute. In all it is estimated that there were 65 major fires and nearly 200 other fires. Military assistance was given to clear the debris.

All services worked magnificently and valuable assistance was rendered by the public and all branches of His Majesty's Forces. All were united under one common object and any thought of seeking protection from missiles which were continually falling seemed to be farthest from their minds.

Human memory is short but I shall never forget the appalling sight that Yarmouth presented that night and with the additional fires that continually broke out, it seemed that nothing could prevent the destruction of the centre of the Town and South Quay but when day broke, owing to the untiring efforts of all concerned, all fires were under control and the situation, although bade, saved from becoming any worse. It is estimated 4,000 Incendiary Bombs were dropped during this night.

An interesting feature of these raids was that so far as I am aware, no casualties were caused by the Incendiary Bombs, or resulting fires, but the casualties for the night were 17 killed and 68 injured.

All the following day strenuous efforts were made to tidy up the streets and prepare the Services for the next night. As anticipated, the enemy returned at 9.30pm, dropping 4 HE bombs

The junction of Blackfriars Road and Queen's Road, Great Yarmouth after the raid of 8 April 1941. A Special Constabulary Sub-Station received the full blast of the parachute mine that landed here and five Special Constables lost their lives.

at the south end of the Borough followed by at 11.07pm by many incendiary bombs on premises both sides of the river Yare. These were immediately tackled and with the exception of a fire at the Salt Union premises, which were gutted, the resulting fires were soon extinguished and a repetition of the previous night's ordeal prevented.

(Author's Note: The raid had been carried out by Junkers 88 and Heinkel III from Luftwaffe Squadrons II/KG I Ju 88 based at Rosieres en Santerre III/KG 26 Lion Geschwader and KG 76 and 77.)

The worst of the raids on Yarmouth was far from the last and raids were conducted on the consecutive nights of 9, 10 and 11 April causing further damage and loss of life, Charles Box continues:

April 9th 1941
Another attack with HE bombs was made at 2.32am but most of these fell on the beach at the south end of the town. More HE Bombs were dropped in the River Yare at 2.44 am, and the final attack of the night was at 3.07 am when 4 HE bombs were dropped at Nelson and Upper Cliff Roads at Gorleston. This last attack destroyed 10 houses and caused considerable damage to others. Casualties were 6 killed and 5 injured.

April 10th 1941
At 12.12am Nelson Road, Springfield Road and Lowestoft Road. 2 HE bombs. Casualties: 2 killed, 3 injured.
At 1.29am On sea front south of Borough. 2 HE bombs and 14 HE bombs in a line from south end of Nelson Road Central to North Drive, one of which fell on the Royal Aquarium but caused little damage.

April 11th 1941
At 12.17 am 4 Heavy HE bombs were dropped across the George Street Row area. Considerable damage was done to dwelling houses and a number of people were trapped. A communal Anderson Shelter received almost a direct hit and seven bodies were removed from it. The Rescue Parties did some excellent work here. The total casualties were 13 killed and 12 injured.'

The bombing of Norfolk during April 1941 was a month marked by tragic civilian casualties, among them the worst loss of life in a single incident in the country areas of the county occurred when Horning Ferry Inn was bombed. The incident was recalled in *A Norfolk Village in Wartime* edited by Charles F. Carrodus (Clarke 1946):

'*The Ferry raid took place on April 26th 1941, on a busy Saturday night at a quarter to ten o'clock. Most licensed houses would be at their busiest at that hour and the Ferry Inn was no exception to that rule. The belief that the bomber was attracted to the spot by a display of light seems generally accepted. It was a dark, moonless night, several cars were parked outside and a fresh one had just arrived in some haste. It was near closing time. If no light was shown what could have induced the raider to shovel out his bombs on a lonely house on the edge of the marshes?*

Four bombs were dropped on the property but only one of them hit the house. Altogether, however, fifteen were released. The bulk of them falling aimlessly on the surrounding marshland. Later investigation by the experts proved they were 112-pounders and so of comparatively light calibre. Of the four which fell on the Ferry Inn property, one dropped on the pontoon ferry-boat, ten on the Woodbastwick side of the river and one in the river itself, as shown by the number of dead fish afterwards found afloat. But the one which found its target – it was the second of the series – could not have been more accurately aimed if the object of the crew had been to produce the greatest possible destruction. Twenty-one lives were lost and several more or less serious cases of personal injury also occurred. The house was wrecked and the pontoon ferry was still out of action nearly four years later. Twenty four people were in the bar at the time and of these only three escaped serious injury. Two had retired to for the night, were blown out of bed and dropped on the thatched roof, which had been lifted by the blast on to the lawn.'

The manageress, Miss Olive Leighton had been in the kitchen at the time the bomb hit but managed to clamber out of the wreckage and choking dust in pitch black, helping others find their way out as

she did so. Showing selfless presence of mind she found a motorist outside and sent him to summon the ARP from their station at Grove Farm, Upper Horning. Despite being dishevelled, bruised and cut she then set off on foot but soon found a lift in a car to raise the alarm at the Swan Hotel.

Among the first to respond to the call for help were the local Special Constables under Sergeant P. Page and Acting Sergeant A. Edmunds who was assisted in the rescue work by his son Arthur along with the especially valued help of Miss Betty Tallowin and Mr Fred Purdy. Superintendent P. E. Levick of North Walsham police soon arrived and played a prominent role in the search of the wreckage. He was soon joined a number of the locally garrisoned troops and ARP rescue squads from Aylsham and Sprowston who worked through the wreckage until daylight. Four people, namely Mrs Dorothy Sutton, Mr A R Stringer, the proprietor of the Ferry Boat, Miss Daisy Almond and Mrs Kathleen Adlington all suffered such injuries they were removed to the Norfolk and Norwich Hospital.

Local troops and emergency services searching through the wreckage in the morning light after the bombing of The Ferry Inn, Horning.

Major Leathes of the Home Guard organised an improvised mortuary where each of the bodies were laid out and covered with a rug. Among them three members of the Sutton family, another was to die from her wounds in hospital.

Casualty Roll from the bombing of Horning Ferry 26 April 1941

Flying Officer John Anthony Atwill (26) 222 Squadron RAF
Miss Patricia Almond (20) Resident of Horning
Mr Thomas Henry Bell (24) Drayton resident
Miss Nellie Blomfield 26) Private Secretary, Horning
Wren Freda Coralie Coates (35) Women's Royal Naval Service (HMS *Minos*)
Mr Fred Crisp (60) Barman at the Ferry Inn
Aircraftsman First Class Ian Fiddes (26) 222 Squadron RAF
Second Hand Harvey Gilbert Hall (29) Royal Naval Patrol Service (HMS *Europa*)
Mr Russell Charles Larkman (35) Norwich resident
Mr Kingswell Leggett Meek (20) Farm Pupil, Sycamore Farm, Hoveton
Flying Officer Brian van Mentz DFC (24) 222 Squadron RAF
Mr Joseph Gillian Clement Lejune (49) Horning resident
Aircraftsman Second Class William Joseph Pearsall (27) RAFVR
Mr Abraham Lincoln Rhodes (66) Resident of Horning and Doncaster
Flying Officer Harold Paul Roberts (44) 222 Squadron RAFVR
Aircraftsman Second Class William Joseph Smith 222 Squadron RAFVR
Mr Douglas Leonard Sutton (27) Resident of Great Yarmouth
Mr Henry Sutton (65) Resident of Horning and Great Yarmouth
Mr Henry Sutton jnr (35) Resident of Horning and Great Yarmouth
Mr Douglas Watson (56) Special Constable, Horning

Died in Hosptal
Mrs Dorothy Rosalie Sutton (31) wife of Henry Sutton jnr. Resident of Horning.

In the aftermath of the Ferry Boat Inn bombing the published news of the event was heavily censored and cloaked in the press as an incident at an undisclosed location in East Anglia, it was over a month before a photograph of the devastated pub was released and appeared in the local press. But it only took 'Lord Haw Haw' until the following Sunday to gloat and proclaim in his broadcast that 'an establishment on the Broads for building war-ships had been successfully raided from the air.'

Katherine Adlington, wife of respected Yarmouth GP, Dr Basil Adlington, was eventually released from hospital but she suffered from her injuries for many years afterwards and her memories of that fateful night were printed in *Norfolk Fair* some forty years later. Significantly she recalled just moments before the bomb dropped in the Ferry Boat Inn two men had entered the bar and the barman had cause to ask them 'Have you put your car lights off?'

Horning Ferry Inn was rebuilt and re-opened by Wing Commander Bob Stanford Tuck DSO, DFC, AFC representing the many airmen from Coltishall who had frequented the inn during the war.

The Baedeker Blitz

After the failure of the bombing campaigns to destroy airfields and London Hitler planned to break British morale by attempting to destroy the picturesque and historic cities of England. The cities were reputedly selected from the German *Baedeker* Tourist Guide to Britain. The first attack was launched against Exeter on 23 April 1942, a direct reprisal raid for the bombing of Lübeck. German propagandist Baron Gustav Braun von Sturm is reported to have said after the first attack of the campaign 'We shall go out and bomb every building in Britain marked with three stars in the Baedeker Guide' and thus the so called 'Three Star Blitz' or 'Baedeker blitz' became

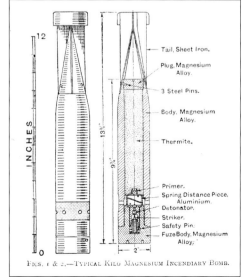

FIGS. 1 & 2.—TYPICAL KILO MAGNESIUM INCENDIARY BOMB.

the name given by the British to these infamous raids on Exeter, Bath, Norwich, York and Canterbury April-June 1942. On the nights of 27/28 and 29/30 April 1942 Norwich received its' heaviest raids of the war.

The briefing notes issued to the Luftwaffe squadrons involved in the raids stated:

> *'NORWICH is the capital of the County of NORFOLK with 126,200 inhabitants. The city lies on the East coast of England on the hill of the Yare surrounded by many orchards. In the City besides the old Cathedral, a further 30 churches, Norman Castle, City Hall and the St. Andrew's Hall. Furthermore Norwich has important rail junctions and is the central hub for several roads. There is an Aircraft parts manufacturer 'Boulton & Paul' (L 74 44). A bus and car factory, together with numerous other important factories.'*

The first priority targets in Norwich were the factory installations, the secondary target was the inner city centre, no doubt an attempt to destroy the new City Hall.

The first indication of the incoming raiders was a radio interception as they flew over the North Sea at 20.15 hours. Fighter Command scrambled night fighters to engage the raiders but no aircraft were shot down. At 23.21 on the bright moonlit night of 27 April their first alert was sounded as two He111's 'X' and 'Y' Pathfinders from the 2nd Staffel of Bomber Gruppe 100 (2/KGr. 100) flew steadily over Norwich and dropped their parachute flares that combined with the moonlight to illuminate the city streets 'as bright as day.' The Heinkels then went into a shallow dive dropping the first incendiary bombs and opening up with their machine guns.

Within minutes they were followed by the next wave of bombers and over the next two hours Dorniers, Heinkels and Ju88s bombers from Luftflotte 3, comprising KG2, Gruppes 1-4 from Gilze Rijen; Gruppe II, Gruppe III, a trainee crew from Gruppe IV and II/KG40 in Do217s; Kgr.506 and IV/KG30 in Ju88s and He111's from IV/KG55 and IV/KG4 dropped high explosive bombs and incendiaries over the city and surrounding suburbs.

The incendiaries that hailed down on the city started a number of large fires that were recorded as visible from a distance of 150km by the last of the Luftwaffe bomber crews. With their target so clearly marked the Luftwaffe bombers could treat this as a 'tip and run' raid, a total of 185 High Explosive bombs fell on the city that night killing 162 and injuring 600. The damage on that night included the city's main water pumping station which was put out of action and the M&GN Station that was turned into an fiery inferno and completely destroyed. Among the casualties was popular National Fire Service Company Officer Sam Bussey (39) was trying to save horses from blazing stables on nearby Oak Street when a bomb fell close by wounding fireman Len Strivens and Malcolm Pease but Sam lost his life; he was the only full-time fireman to be killed during the Norwich Blitz.

Four 500kg HE bombs fell on Chapel Field Gardens, two of them direct hits upon the underground air raid shelter. Fortunately one of these failed to explode and was defused at 7.00 the following morning – meanwhile the rescue of many of those who were trapped in the wreckage of the bombed shelter carried on regardless.

After just one night of respite the bombers of the Luftwaffe resumed the attack on Norwich shortly after the siren was sounded at 21.11 on 29 April 1942. This attack was led by 7 He111 Pathfinders from Chartres. The main bomber force that followed comprised 17 Do217 of II/KG2 from Soesterberg and 11 from III/KG2 at Schiphol. A further eight Do217 of I and IV flew from Gilze Rijen. Nine crews came from IV/KG55 and 9 from II/KG40 from Soesterberg; five of IV/KG4 and fifteen Ju88 drawn from IV Gruppen of KG3, KG30 and KG77 all operating from Chievres. The raid lasted about an hour and a quarter during which 112 HE bombs were dropped along with thousands of incendiaries. In this raid about half of the 90 tonnes of bombs that were dropped met their mark in the city, far more incendiaries were used, severe damage was sustained and made more severe because the Heigham Street water works had been disabled in the previous raid causing major problems for the fire service in this raid. A total of 69 people lost their lives and 89 were injured. The target was the city centre with Thorpe Station and Goods Yard, Bishop Bridge Gas Works, the Water Tower and Boulton & Paul's works as the secondary targets. The city centre and City Hall remained remarkably undamaged, the nearest bomb landing on the Clover Leaf Cafe on Guildhall Hill.

The flames from the Wincarnis Works, Westwick Street, Norwich were so intense they scorched George Swain's camera when he took this photograph on the night of 29/30 April 1942.

The Hippodrome was also hit blowing two house managers down the stage door steps without hurting them, ripped the back out of photographer George Swain's adjoining studio (narrowly missing George who was on the premises at the time) and killed the stage manager, his wife and two Danish performers. One of the sea lions from their act was released from its cage by the falling wreckage, George Swain recalled the sound made by Buddy 'The World's Greatest Comedy Seal' was worse than the whistle of a bomb as he flapped in his ungainly way through the theatre crying for his master. Buddy died shortly afterwards, many said it was from a broken heart.

Across the Market Place, Brigg Street, St Stephens and Rampant Horse Street area were the scene of dreadful devastation including the gutting of Curl's and Bunting's department stores, Peacock's Stores and the ancient thatched Boar's Head pub on the corner of Surrey Street. Further up Chapel Field Road Caley's chocolate factory was also burnt out. Many local children risked life and limb over the ensuing days to get amongst the rubble and into the lower stories of the building where the vats of chocolate had ended up releasing their precious contents. Despite being riddled with dust and masonry children grabbed the chunk of chocolate which had been rationed and gorged themselves; many of them eating so much they were sick.

The burnt out shell of Bunting's Store, Rampant Horse Street, Norwich after the raid of 29/30 April 1942

The area of the city from St Benedict's Street and up along Dereham Road was badly hit in both raids. The area around and including the historic St Benedict's Gates was reduced to rubble, as were the nearby Wincarnis and Odol works off Westwick Street and large sections of Grape's Hill and Barn Road. St Benedict's church was reduced to little more than the remnants of a wall and its tower. To give an idea of the level of destruction here, among the rubble there appeared to be a pillbox that no-one could recall being there before, then it clicked, it was the strong room of the Midland Bank!

Edward LeGrice, The author of *Norwich, The Ordeal of 1942* recalled:

> The outstanding remembrance is of the choking dust and smell of soot and gas, for the blast certainly acted as a chimney sweeper par excellence. On the night of April 29th, our family sheltered under the stairs – I had been told by an expert that a cupboard under a strong staircase offered the best possible protection – and so it proved in our case, and in many others... Bomb after bomb fell shaking the house to its foundations, for we counted 29 HE bombs within a few hundred yards of us. Windows were shattered, ceilings crashed down, the crockery on the cupboard shelves was shaken off, a sugar basin emptied itself on my daughter's head, to be followed by the milk jug and finally when one bomb fell just opposite, the voice of a warden was heard to say 'Don't you think you had better come out of there?'

The ruins and scarred tower of St Benedict's Church, St Benedict's Street after the raid of 29/30 April 1942.

Many people who recall those dreadful nights freely confess they not only thought that when the daylight came there would be no city left, indeed some though the end of the world had come. The symbolic historic buildings of Norwich such as the Cathedral, Castle, Guildhall and City Hall all stood proud after the raid (the cathedral did have a narrow escape incendiary bombs fell on both North and South transepts but the fire watchers of the cathedral close and when firemen were rapidly on hand and managed to extinguish the fire in June 1942) but whole streets, businesses, churches, pubs were destroyed, burnt out or damaged beyond repair. As a result of these two raids a total of 14,000 buildings suffered bomb damage ranging from broken widows to roof tiles to the loss of an entire wall, of which 1,200 had to be demolished.

The year 1943 was marked in Norfolk by a tragic loss of female military personnel in two separate air raids on Great Yarmouth. The first occurred at 6.28am when and enemy aircraft dropped 6 High Explosive bombs across the southern part of the town; one of these received a direct hit on the HMS *Midge* WRNS billet at the corner of Queen's Road and Nelson Road South. Rescue Parties were rapidly on the scene and despite their work being hampered by a fire breaking out in the debris they managed to recover thirteen Wrens

Left: The scene on Rupert Street after the night of 29/30 April 1942 sums up the devastation inflicted on Norwich by the Baedeker Blitz.

Right: The WRNS hostel on the corner of Queens Road and Nelson Road South, Great Yarmouth after suffering a direct hit on 18 March 1943 killing 8 Wrens.

Wren Joan M. Hughes (20) killed in the Wren holstel bombing, Great Yarmouth on 18 March 1943. (GC)

alive from the wreckage. The bodies of eight Wrens were also recovered, namely Sec. Off. Mrs A.E. Jago Brown and WRNS ratings: Anne A Drummond, Joan M. Hughes, Violet B. Powell, Aileen M. Kilburn, Muriel A. Rainton, Ellen E. Regan and Rita M.R. Turner who died of wounds.

In early May 1943 Luftwaffe attacks changed from strategic bombing to rapid in and out terror raids on specific targets conducted by squadrons of Fokker Wolfe 190s flying low to avoid detection by radar. The first of these new attacks on Great Yarmouth occurred on 7 May 1943 resulting in 13 killed and 51 injured.

Four days later on 11 May 1943 twenty FW 190s sped across the sea again appearing over Great Yarmouth at 8.45am. Despite having the advantage of early morning sea mist cover and the sun low in the sky behind them one was shot down by F/O Townsend in one of four Mustang fighters from 613 Squadron (Coltishall) who had been on their way to recce shipping off the Dutch coast. Another was brought down by AA fire but the rest flew over the north end of the town machine gunning and dropping high explosive bombs as they did so. On North Drive a Company of thirty ATS girls were marching briskly back to their billet at Sefton House (site now occupied by the swimming pool of the Burlington Palm Hotel) after taking part in physical recreation on the nearby Wellesley Road recreation ground when the raiders screamed towards them, one of them opening up with his machine guns. The girls ran towards the hostel for cover, one of them tripped and hit the deck, this accident undoubtedly saved her life, as moments later a bomb was dropped on the building.

James Dean was an eye witness and told a *Yarmouth Mercury* reporter: 'I heard the roar of the planes and right in front of me a crashing sound. Then there was another and I saw a building burst apart about five hundred yards in front of me just as five planes came screaming over my head. The blast lifted me off the motor roller I was driving. The planes were so low I could see the black crosses on them. They seemed to lift themselves up to clear the roof tops. I was on the ground when the bombs fell and when I looked towards the billet I saw the awful wreckage.' In fact upon later examination bomb fragments were found to have hit the motor roller Mr Dean was driving. He rushed over and assisted with the rescue effort. Soldiers from 1st Battalion, The Sherwood Foresters manning the AA mounted Bren gun position on the shore end of the Britannia Pier were also among the first on the scene and were soon working with rescue squads tearing through the wreckage. The young soldiers and the rescuers worked for hours digging through the rubble had not seen carnage involving so many young women before and the sights they saw haunted them for the rest of their lives. The name of only one that was dug out alive was reported at the time, that of Pte. Doreen Chappel (22) of Cinderford, Yorkshire who was removed to the General Hospital. A total of 26 girls lost their lives as a result of the bomb on Sefton House. Twenty three other people, mostly mothers and children, were killed and 41 injured by the other bombs that fell on the town in the same raid.

Three members of the ATS were commended by General Sir Frederick Pile, G.O.C-in-C AA Command for their bravery and conduct in the rescue. Subaltern Anne Green (23) of New Barnet Hertfordshire, a London secretary in peace-time, helped to remove two ATS girls from the wreckage,

Memorial to the 26 ATS girls killed in the bombing of Sefton House on 11 May 1943, erected on a wall overlooking the site and unveiled by Lady Soames DBE on 11 May 1994.

IN SEFTON HOUSE WHICH STOOD ON THIS SITE
TWENTY-SIX MEMBERS OF THE AUXILIARY TERRITORIAL SERVICE
LOST THEIR LIVES BY ENEMY AIR ACTION ON

11 MAY 1943

Pte BERNADETTE BELL	MANCHESTER	Pte ELIZABETH MACKAY	RARICHIE NIGG
L/Cpl MOLLIE CARTER	SHEFFIELD	L/Cpl ANNA MACLEOD	STORNOWAY
Pte JEAN COPLEY	ASTON SHEFFIELD	Pte VERA MANN	LEEDS
Pte LOUISA FARNES	STOCKTON ON TEES	Pte LOUISA MAXWELL	GOSFORTH
Pte DOROTHY FAWKES	HEXHAM	Pte JANE MCAULAY	GLASGOW
Cpl MARGARET GALBRAITH	NEW MILLS DERBY	Pte IVY MOORE	GRIMSBY
Pte KATHLEEN GAUNT	BINGLEY YORKS	Pte ROMA PEARSON	GRIMSBY
Pte LILIAN GRIMMER	GREAT YARMOUTH	Pte JEAN SCOUGALL	EDINBURGH
L/Cpl EILEEN HUNT	BESTHORPE NOTTS	Pte JESSIE SHARPE	HESSLE YORKS
Pte NORAH JAMES	ROLLESTON STAFFS	Pte MARJORIE SUTTON	FULSTOW LINCS
Pte MAY JOHNSON	LOUTH LINCS	Pte DORIS TRAVERS	NORTHAMPTON
Pte JESSICA LEWIS	BOURNEMOUTH	Sgt VIOLA WELLS	GRIMSBY
Cpl ENID LINE	CROUCH END	Pte DORIS WIMBUSH	DONCASTER

IN THEIR MEMORY THIS PLAQUE WAS UNVEILED BY
THE LADY SOAMES DBE 11 MAY 1994

completed a roll of missing girls for the use of the rescue parties and as her citation stated 'worked incessantly and calmly, organising and encouraging the few survivors and rendering invaluable aid with the task of clearing the debris. She set a magnificent example to all ranks.' Pte E. Corless (22) of Royston Avenue, Bentley near Doncaster and Pte E. M. Norcup (23) of Dean Street, Breewood, Staffordshire were also commended for setting 'a very fine example of coolness and courage and carried out their duties without a sign of nervousness.'

This incident has been described as the largest single military loss of servicewomen. The youngest victim was a local girl, Lillian Grimmer (19), of Cobholm, she and a number of her comrades were buried with full military honours in Commonwealth War Graves in Great Yarmouth (Caister) Cemetery and a memorial listing the names of all those killed in the incident was unveiled on a wall overlooking the site of Sefton House by Lady Soames DBE on 11 May 1994.

The raid of 11 May 1943 was to prove to be the last FW 190 raid on Great Yarmouth. Chief Constable and Town ARP Controller Charles Box made urgent representations to Will Spens The Regional Commissioner for Civil Defence during his visit to the Borough later in the day on 11 May and within hours of his visit a balloon barrage was installed and flying over the town. Another raid was attempted on 6 July but the raiders were driven off before they reached the town by four Typhoons from 56 Squadron (RAF Matlaske).

The Turning of the Tide

After the Battle of Britain new RAF bases opened and some of the grass strip satellite landing grounds became operational bases in their own right and some extant airfield developed more specialist flight training or developed roles within and co-operation with coastal command and air sea rescue. The following shows the RAF airfields in Norfolk for the period 1942-43:

Fighter Command	**Bomber Command (No 3 Group)**
Coltishall	Downham Market
Ludham	East Wretham
Matlaske	Feltwell
	Little Snoring
Bomber Command (No 2 Group)	
Attlebridge	**No. 100 (Bomber Support) Group**
Bodney	North Creake
Docking	
Foulsham	**Coastal Command**
Great Massingham	Bircham Newton
Horsham St Faith	
Marham	
Methwold	
Oulton	
Sculthorpe	
Swanton Morley	
West Raynham	

Fighter Squadrons

The squadrons flying from the county's RAF airfields served with distinction and honour and included aircrew and squadrons from a variety of nations, including Free French, Polish, Czech, Australia, New Zealand, Canada and American volunteers in the RAF 'Eagle' Squadron. The fighter squadrons sought out and engaged the enemy raiders over our county, flew coastal and 'kipper' patrols over the North Sea fishing fleet and later flew both day and night escort flights for bombers, 'Ranger' patrols over the continent and sweeps over the channel, during one of which in February 1942 pilots from 137 Squadron (Matlaske) discovered the German battle cruisers *Scharnhorst* and *Gneisenau* as they dared to dash through the English Channel. In 1944 they flew operations over France during Operation Overlord and over Holland during the fight for the liberation of North Western Europe and in the pursuit of launch sites of the formidable V2 rockets. There were also those whose legendary gallantry and leadership saw them heralded as heroes during the war at Coltishall, for example, after Douglas Badger and 'Sailor' Malan came Bob Stanford-Tuck with 257 'Burma' Squadron flying Hurricanes (he later returned to become Coltishall's Station Commander 1947-48) and those who later rose to fame such as TV presenter Raymond Baxter who flew Spitfires on 'Ranger' sorties with 602 Squadron from Ludham.

Pilot Officer Cecil Thomas Kingsborough Cody of 167 Squadron, RAF Ludham is carried shoulder high after scoring his first kill of a Ju88 of KG6 on 28 January 1943. Quite an achievement but celebrated all the more because it coincided with a visit from no lesser VIPs than HM King George VI and Queen Elizabeth. (IWM)

Bomber Command

The achievements of Norfolk bomber command squadrons can sometimes be somewhat lost in the shadow of the 'Mighty Eighth' US Army Air Force but this should not be the case. Bomber squadrons flying out from Norfolk attacked enemy shipping and e-boats and flew operations deep into enemy territory from the early years of the war when the likes of 75 (NZ) Squadron (Feltwell) that were flying night raids to Berlin and Northern Italy.

The bomber squadrons were involved in many significant actions and special operations. The

The de Havilland Mosquito B.IVs of 105 Squadron taxi out for take-off at RAF Marham, December 1942.

Hudsons from 320 and 407 Squadrons (Bircham Newton), the Stirlings of 218 and the Wellington IIIs of 115 Squadrons (both from Marham) took part in the 1,000 bomber raid against Bremen on 31 March 1942.

The Bristol Blenheims and Douglas Bostons of 107 Squadron (Great Massingham) gained a distinguished reputation for daring low-level raids against shipping and land targets over Holland and Belgium between May 1941 and August 1943. Among the pilots of 107 was Bill Edrich, a Norfolk man (born at Lingwood in 1916) and already an accomplished cricketer, he gained the DFC while flying with the squadron.

In 1942, 105 Squadron (Horsham St Faith) was the first bomber squadron in the RAF to be fully equipped with the Mosquito. The first one was delivered to the squadron by Geoffrey de Havilland personally. The squadrons of Mosquitos flying out from Norfolk acquired a remarkable reputation for their work as pathfinders on night raids into Germany between the latter half of 1944 and into 1945. 105 and 139 Squadrons flying Mosquitos out of Marham were both daring and notable in their actions, flying daylight and dusk raids guided by 'OBOE' equipment to pin point and precision bomb their target and enjoyed such success that during 1943 they were regularly featured in the press and were described as 'two of the most famous squadrons in the RAF'

The 100 (Bomber Support) Group was formed in 1943 but much of their work was classified 'Top Secret' until long after the war. Initially based at West Raynham but soon moved headquarters to Bylaugh Hall in January 1944. The squadrons that formed the group were based on airfields across the county, namely: Foulsham, Great Massingham, North Creake, Little Snoring, Oulton, Sculthorpe, West Raynham, Swanton Morley and Swannington. As the other squadrons were built up and trained and the specialised equipment was developed, 192 Squadron (Foulsham) began seeking out and identifying German radio and radar signals and 141 Squadron undertook the Group's first bomber support operation on 16 December. Once the equipped the bombers of 100 Group were carrying the latest R.C.M (Radio Counter Measures) equipment designed to jam enemy radio signals (some of them were fitted with 'MANDREL' devices to swamp the German early warning system) they flew night intruder patrols and they played a major role in support of Operation Overlord flying ground attack sorties over the Normandy beachheads until the allies established a firm foothold in Northern France. From late 1944, 100 Group Bomber squadrons were equipped with a veritable armoury of deception and jamming devices and inventions, notably, the squadrons took part in 'SPOOF' raids and drops of 'WINDOW'. WINDOW was particularly effective – bundles of aluminised-paper strips (treated-paper was used to minimise the weight and maximise the time that the strips would remain in the air, prolonging the effect), one every minute through a flare chute, using a stopwatch to time them. The results were spectacular. The radar guided master searchlights wandered aimlessly across the sky. The AA guns fired randomly or not at all and the night fighters, their radar displays swamped with false echoes, utterly failed to find the bomber stream rendering ground-controlled fighters of unable to track their targets in the night sky and left radar-guided guns and spotlights useless.

Four of the eighteen Victoria Crosses awarded to Bomber Command were awarded to aircrew flying from Norfolk airfields:

Flight Sergeant Arthur Louis Aaron VC DFM RAFVR
No. 218 Squadron (RAF Downham Market)

On the night of 12 Aug 1943 Flight Sergeant Aaron (21) was captain and pilot of a Stirling bomber on a mission to bomb Turin. His plane was hit by an enemy fighter, three engine were hit, the windscreen shattered and the front and rear turrets put out of action and the aircraft became unstable and difficult to control. Aaron had been hit in the face breaking his jaw, his lung and arm were also hit and consequently he was unable to speak or use his right arm. With his navigator dead and other crewmen wounded, he signed to the bomb aimer to take the controls and set a course for the nearest air bases North Africa. Assisted to the rear of the aircraft morphia was administered to him but he insisted on returning to the cockpit where he attempted to resume control but he was too weak so he helped to navigate by writing instructions with his left hand. Five hours later with the fuel getting low, the flare path at Bone airfield in Algeria was sighted and Aaron summoned enough strength to direct the bomb aimer in the hazardous task of landing the damaged aircraft in darkness and with the undercarriage retracted. Four attempts to land failed, on the fifth he was nearing collapse but the landing was completed by the bomb aimer.

Nine hours after landing Flight Sergeant Aaron died from exhaustion. Had he been content to rest and conserve his strength he would have stood a good chance of recovering but his determination and sense of responsibility for his aircraft and crew enabled him to confront the crisis and give generously of himself until he could give no more. He is buried in Bone War Cemetery, Algeria, North Africa.

Flight Sergeant Arthur Louis Aaron VC DFM RAFVR

Acting Squadron Leader Ian Willoughby Bazalgette VC DFC RAFVR
635 Squadron (RAF Downham Market)

The citation for Squadron Leader Bazalgette's valiant action was published in the *London Gazette* on 17 August 1945:

> *On 4th August 1944, Squadron-Leader Bazalgette was master bomber of a Pathfinder squadron detailed to mark an important target at Trossy St. Maximin for the main bomber force.*
>
> *When nearing the target his Lancaster came under heavy anti-aircraft fire. Both starboard engines were put out of action and serious fires broke out in the fuselage and the starboard mainplane. The bomb aimer was badly wounded.*
>
> *As the deputy master bomber had already been shot down, the success of the attack depended on Squadron-Leader Bazalgette and this he knew. Despite the appalling conditions in his burning aircraft, he pressed on gallantly to the target, marking and bombing it accurately. That the attack was successful was due to his magnificent effort.*
>
> *After the bombs had been dropped the Lancaster dived, practically out of control. By expert airmanship and great exertion Squadron-Leader Bazalgette regained control. But the port inner engine then failed and the whole of the starboard main-plane became a mass of flames.*
>
> *Squadron-Leader Bazalgette fought bravely to bring his aircraft and crew to safety. The mid-upper gunner was overcome by fumes. Squadron-Leader Bazalgette then ordered those of his crew who were able to leave by parachute to do so. He remained at the controls and attempted the almost hopeless task of landing the crippled and blazing aircraft in a last effort to save the wounded bomb aimer and helpless air gunner. With superb skill, and taking great care to avoid a small French village nearby, he brought the aircraft down safely. Unfortunately it then exploded and this gallant officer and his two comrades perished.*
>
> *His heroic sacrifice marked the climax of a long career of operations against the enemy. He always chose the more dangerous and exacting roles. His courage and devotion to duty were beyond praise."*

Acting Squadron Leader Ian Willoughby Bazalgette VC DFC RAFVR

His heroic sacrifice marked the climax of a long career during which he chose the more dangerous and exacting roles showing remarkable courage and devotion to duty. He is buried in a Commonwealth War Grave in Senantes Churchyard, Oise, France.

Acting Wing Commander Hughie Idwal Edwards VC DSO DFC
105 Squadron (RAF Swanton Morley)

On 4 July 1941, Edwards, an Australian born in Fremantle in 1914, led a daylight attack (Operation Wreckage) against the port of Bremen, one of the most heavily-defended towns in Germany; the citation for his Victoria Cross was published in the *London Gazette* on 22 July, 1941.

> *Wing Commander Edwards, although handicapped by a physical disability resulting from a flying accident, has repeatedly displayed gallantry of the highest order in pressing home bombing attacks from very low heights against strongly defended objectives.*
>
> *On 4th July, 1941, he led an important attack on the Port of Bremen, one of the most heavily defended towns in Germany. This attack had to be made in daylight and there were no clouds to*

afford concealment. During the approach to the German coast several enemy ships were sighted and Wing Commander Edwards knew that his aircraft would be reported and that the defences would be in a state of readiness. Undaunted by this misfortune he brought his formation 50 miles overland to the target, flying at a height of little more than 50 feet, passing under high-tension cables, carrying away telegraph wires and finally passing through a formidable balloon barrage. On reaching Bremen he was met with a hail of fire, all his aircraft being hit and four of them being destroyed. Nevertheless he made a most successful attack, and then with the greatest skill and coolness withdrew the surviving aircraft without further loss.

Throughout the execution of this operation which he had planned personally with full knowledge of the risks entailed, Wing Commander Edwards displayed the highest possible standard of gallantry and determination.

Squadron Leader Edwards was decorated with the Victoria Cross at a ceremony in Buckingham Palace, he survived the war and retired from the RAF in 1963 with the rank of Air Commodore and was appointed the twenty third Governor of Western Australia. He died in 1975.

Sergeant James Allen Ward VC, 75 (NZ) Squadron, (RAF Feltwell)

In July 1941 Sergeant Ward (22) was gaining experience as a co-pilot on the squadron's Vickers Wellington bombers, the London Gazette of 5 August 1941 published his Victoria Cross Citation:

Sergeant James Allen Ward VC, 75 (NZ) Squadron

On the night of 7th July 1941, Sergeant Ward was second pilot of a Wellington returning from an attack on Munster. When flying over the Zuider Zee at 13,000 feet, the aircraft was attacked from beneath by a Messerschmitt which secured hits with cannon shell and incendiary bullets. The rear gunner was wounded in the foot but delivered a burst of fire which sent the enemy fighter down, apparently out of control. Fire then broke out near the starboard engine and, fed by petrol from a split pipe, quickly gained an alarming hold and threatened to spread to the entire wing. The crew forced a hole in the fuselage and made strenuous efforts to reduce the fire with extinguishers and even the coffee in their vacuum flasks, but without success. They were then warned to be ready to abandon the aircraft.

As a last resort, Sergeant Ward volunteered to make an attempt to smother the fire with an engine cover which happened to be in use as a cushion. At first he proposed to discard his parachute to reduce wind resistance, but was finally persuaded to take it. A rope from the dinghy was tied to him, though this was of little help and might have become a danger had he been blown off the aircraft. With the help of the navigator, he then climbed through the narrow astro-hatch and put on his parachute.

The bomber was flying at a reduced speed but the wind pressure must have been sufficient to render the operation one of extreme difficulty. Breaking the fabric to make hand and foot holds where necessary, and also taking advantage of existing holes in the fabric, Sergeant Ward succeeded in descending three feet to the wing and proceeding another three feet to a position behind the engine, despite the slipstream from the airscrew, which nearly blew him off the wing. Lying in this precarious position, he smothered the fire in the wing fabric and tried to push the cover into the hole in the wing and on to the leaking pipe from which the fire came. As soon as he removed his hand, however, the terrific wind blew the cover out and when he tried again it was lost. Tired as he was, he was able with the navigator's assistance, to make successfully the perilous journey back into the aircraft. There was now no danger of the fire spreading from the petrol pipe as there was no fabric left nearby, and in due course burnt itself out.

When the aircraft was nearly home some petrol which had collected in the wing blazed up furiously but died down quite suddenly. A safe landing was then made despite the damage sustained by the aircraft. The flight home had been made possible by the gallant action of Sergeant Ward in extinguishing the fire on the wing, in circumstances of the greatest difficulty and at the risk of his life.

Just ten weeks after his VC citation Sergeant Ward was killed after his Wellington bomber was hit by flak over Hamburg and came down in flames on 15 September 1941. He is buried in the Commonwealth War Grave Cemetery at Ohlsdorf, Hamburg, Germany.

Coastal Command

The squadrons of Coastal Command frequently maintained elements of their squadrons flying out from Norfolk airfields to maintain their high level of quick response both in attack and for air sea rescue work.

Between April and October 1944, 455 (RAAF) Squadron and 499 (RNZAF) Squadrons acquired the most formidable reputation in Coastal Command flew out from Langham as a 'Strike Wing' which staged combined attacks and sunk an impressive tonnage of shipping including an impressive range of 'U', 'E' and 'R' boats

The largest Coastal Command base in Norfolk was at Bircham Newton. Operational sorties against enemy shipping were flown predominantly by Bristol Beaufighters and Lockheed Hudsons (1942-43). Not forgetting 811 Squadron who flew Fairey Swordfish on mine laying duties. 280 (Air Sea Rescue) Squadron had their Avro Anson ASR I aircraft based at Bircham Newton, Langham and Docking. Their job being to search for pilots who had bailed out over or ditched in the sea, would drop a dinghy and supplies and then direct the rescue launches to his location. Air-Sea Rescue squadrons were also based at Matlaske, flying Supermarine Walrus that could alight on the sea in calm conditions. A detachment from 278 (Air Sea Rescue) Squadron (Matlaske) kept a detachment at Coltishall to cover the sea area between Cromer to Lowestoft from April 1942. There was also 521 Squadron, the meteorological unit. Their work did not grab headlines but it was a difficult and dangerous task in the days before satellite when sorties would have to be flown over the enemy territory to ascertain the weather conditions or information gathering for forecasting before a raid was attempted.

The B-17s of the 100 Bomb Group (Thorpe Abbotts) dodging the flak over enemy territory.

Welcome America

After an initial reconnaissance in February 1942, the first American B17 bombers and P38 fighters and crews arrived in Britain in July and by mid 1944 the Eighth Air Force had grown to become the biggest military air fleet ever seen with 122 bases, 200,000 personnel, 2,000 four engine bombers and 1,000 fighter aircraft and entered into history as the 'Mighty Eighth.'

Two American Air Divisions had bases in Norfolk with a total of eighteen USAAF airfields across the county. The 2nd Air Division had the largest presence in the county predominantly flying Consolidated B-24 Liberators. The Division's first headquarters was at Camp Thomas, Old Catton (September 1942 - October 1943) and later Ketteringham Hall (December 1943 - June 1945)

Eighth USAAF Bomb Groups & Fighter Bases
Norfolk, June 1944
Second Air Division

Group	Base	BG Aircraft Letter Identifiers
466th Bomb Group	Attlebridge	Circle - L
93rd Bomb Group	Hardwick	Circle - B
389th Bomb Group	Hethel	Circle - C
458th Bomb Group	Horsham St Faith	Circle - K
491st Bomb Group	Metfield	Circle - Z
492nd Bomb Group	North Pickenham	Circle - U
453rd Bomb Group	Old Buckenham	Circle - J
467th Bomb Group	Rackheath	Circle - P
448th Bomb Group	Seething	Circle - I
44th Bomb Group	Shipdam	Circle - A
445th Bomb Group	Tibenham	Circle-F
392nd Bomb Group	Wendling	Circle - D

The 3rd Air Division had bases in both Norfolk and Suffolk with Elveden Hall, just over the border in Suffolk as its Headquarters. The Division predominantly flew Boeing B-17 Fortress bombers out of the county with some of them flying Consolidated B-24 Liberators for short periods.

Third Air Division

Group	Base	BG Aircraft Letter Identifiers
452nd Bomb Group	Deopham Green	Square - L
96th Bomb Group	Snetterton Heath	Square - C
100th Bomb Group	Thorpe Abbotts	Square – D

Eighth Army Air Force Fighter Group Stations
352 FG   Bodney
359 FG   East Wretham

Reconnaissance Group
802 RG   Watton

The arrival of the Eighth Air Force bombers saw a number of airfields under construction for RAF bombers such as Tibenham, Snetterton Heath and Wendling rescheduled for USAAF use and an unprecedented programme of new build airfields roll out across the county. Extant RAF bases such as Horsham St Faith, East Wretham or Watton were also occupied by the USAAF. The work had been begun by civilian contractors such as John Laing & Sons, George Wimpey & Co Ltd or Taylor-Woodrow Ltd, joined by US Army Engineer Battalions from July 1942. It was a massive undertaking; heavy bombers required concrete runways and hard standing, the individual costs of which often surpassed £1million. Once completed, each airfield was occupied by a single Bombardment Group consisting of four flying Bombardment Squadrons; a Squadron had an average compliment of 12 to 16 bombers with 200 combat airmen. The total personnel on a bomber station varied between two and three thousand. With such a massive and sudden influx of foreign service personnel in the county it is hardly surprising the arrival of the Americans was known as 'The Friendly Invasion' and their bases as the 'Fields of Little America.'

The first heavy bomber base to open in the county was at Shipdam in October 1942, indeed it was to prove to be the host to B-24 Liberators for longer than any other combat airfield of the 'Mighty Eighth' in Britain. The first bombing mission flown by the Second Air Division commenced on 7 November 1942. The strategic bombing campaigns of the 'Mighty Eighth' aimed to destroy the industries, communications, transport and fuel supplies that directly or indirectly supported the German war effort. RAF Bomber Command concentrated on night attacks while, significantly, its American counterpart, the 8th Air Force, operated mainly in daylight. When setting set off on their mission twenty to forty heavy bombers would take off from a single airfield and would assemble into formation as they climbed to their operation altitude of 20,000 to 25,000ft. Joined with other formations they would form a division column of about 500 – 600 bombers; an impressive and unforgettable sight for anyone who saw them above the county.

Full operational fighter support began in September 1943 from 352nd Fighter Group with 328th, 486th and 487th Fighter Squadrons flying out of Bodney (they were known as 'The Blue Nosed Bastards of Bodney.') Major George Preddy, the top scoring P-51 ace with 8th USAAF who could claim twenty seven victories, was based at Bodney until his death by 'friendly' AA fire on Christmas day 1944. The 352nd were followed in October by 359th Fighter Group consisting of 368th, 369th and 370th Fighter Squadrons flying from the old RAF East Wretham airfield. Both units came under the command of 67th Fighter Wing of VIII AAF Fighter Command.

Airmen and ground crew of 'Blonds Away' of 389 Bomb Group (Hethel) 1943.

Many of the American men got to know and be known in the surrounding towns and villages around their bases . Initially there were problems, the British people had been at war since 1939, on the home front they had suffered air raids and rationing had bitten hard by late 1942/43. The American servicemen had not experienced any of this and were seen by some as 'swanking,' they seemed to have a lot of money, their uniforms were 'flash' and if they were invited to tea although their manners were good they had no concept of moderation necessitated by rations. Women who were parted from their husbands, particularly those who were prisoners of war did not appreciate the 'advances' of some of the servicemen if they went to a dance; for some folks in Norfolk the culture shock was too much. Fights and missives such as 'Go home Yanks' were chalked graffiti on some walls in towns and villages near the bases. A sea change was needed, a guide had been produced for American servicemen coming to Britain and now information films were produced for American servicemen to learn more about British culture and how the war had affected us. Once a little time had passed the natural curiosity of many Norfolk people and the warmth and good manners of the American servicemen saw friendships emerge that were to last for decades beyond the end of the war.

Some Important Do's and Don'ts for American Servicemen in Great Britain
(Issued by US Military Authority)

BE FRIENDLY – but don't intrude anywhere it seems you are not wanted.

You are paid higher than the British 'Tommy.' Don't rub it in. Play fair with him. He can be a pal in need.

Don't show off or brag or bluster – 'swank' as the British say. If someone looks in your direction and says 'He's chucking his weight about,' you can be pretty sure you're off base. That's the time to pull in your ears.

If you are invited to eat with a family don't eat too much. Otherwise you may eat up their weekly rations.

Don't make fun of British speech or accents. You sound just as funny to them but they will be too polite to show it.

Avoid comments on the British government or politics.

Don't try to tell the British that America won the last war or make wisecracks about the war debts or about British defeats in this war.

NEVER criticise the King or Queen.

Don't criticise the food, beer or cigarettes to the British. Remember they have been at war since 1939.

Use commonsense on all occasions. By your conduct you have great power to bring about a better understanding between the two countries after the war is over.

You will soon find yourself among a kindly, quiet, hard-working people who have been living under a strain such as few people in the world have ever known. In your dealings with them, let this be your slogan:

> *It is always impolite to criticise your hosts;*
> *It is militarily stupid to criticise your allies.*

American servicemen often took some of their leave in Norwich, dancing at Samson and Hercules and taking in a movie at cinemas like the Regent and Electric on Prince of Wales Road, Odeon on Botolph Street or Haymarket or a show at the Hippodrome Theatre or Theatre Royal or at the YMCA on St Giles where free concerts were given on Sunday evenings. Many just enjoyed a day strolling around the historic sites of the city and in the parks at Eaton and Earlham. The American Red Cross Service Club was set up in the Bishop's Palace and US Servicemen were provided with dormitories for their visits in the city at 13, The Close and at an annex on Bethel Street. Often 120,000 men and women passed through the club in a single month with up to a thousand staying in the city overnight. There was usually a good presence of American Military Policemen known as 'Snowdrops' (after their white helmets) to help maintain order. Many children loved meeting the Americans who always made a fuss of them and often carried a few sticks of gum, sweets or 'candy' as they called them to give away. There were also special children's dances and teas held on the bases where children could try hot dogs, burgers and ice cream. Christmas was especially good with red coated and bearded Santa there were treats for the local children and a few tinned turkeys found their way onto the festive tables of folks around the bases. Some of the big sisters of these children also found friendship and love with the American servicemen. These men fathered about seventy thousand of the three hundred thousand illegitimate babies born during the war years (three times the pre-war rate). There were an estimated 50,000 British girls who had married American servicemen, many of them came from East Anglia. In Norfolk a GI Brides club was formed in 1945. Admittedly there were a number of divorces when the practicalities of moving 'State Side' set in or marriages did not endure but many of them did eventually get over to America to join their husbands.

In December 1943 the 445th Bombardment Group flew its B-24 Liberators bombers to Tibenham, among them was 703rd Squadron Commander, Captain James Stewart. An accomplished pre-war pilot, Stewart had been concerned that his celebrity status would mean he would be relegated to non-operational service but after an appeal to his commander he was assigned overseas to an active service unit flying missions over Germany; including the infamous mission to bomb the ball bearing factories at Schweinfurt on 14 October 1943. The mission became known as 'Black Thursday' after the high number of casualties sustained; out of 291 aircraft that left for the mission 60 aircraft were lost. Stewart was promoted to Major and in March 1944 and was transferred 453rd Bombardment Group at Old Buckenham as their Group Executive Officer. This was a new B-24 unit that had been experiencing difficulties, so to inspire confidence in these men Stewart flew as command pilot in the lead B-24 on numerous missions deep into Nazi-occupied Europe. In 1944, Stewart was twice decorated with the Distinguished Flying Cross for actions in combat; he was also awarded the Croix de Guerre and the Air Medal with three oak leaf clusters. In July 1944, after flying 20 combat missions, Stewart was made Chief of Staff of the 2nd Combat Bombardment Wing of the Eighth Air Force.

The American Air bases were also visited by a number of Hollywood stars including Jack Benny, Larry Adler, Martha Raye, Kay Francis and Marlene Dietrich came over on 'meet the troops' visits or to entertain with on base concerts and shows. In June 1944 Major Glenn Miller and the 8th AAF Band began a half months tour across the airfields and venues of East Anglia. Seventy-one concerts were performed, a number of them in Norfolk, including the bases at Attlebridge, Hardwick, Thorpe Abbotts and Wendling.

Above all, the American servicemen in East Anglia had a job to do. The targets for the heavy bombers of 2nd and 3rd Air Divisions flying out from Norfolk ranged from Norway in the north, over Poland and Romania to the east and deep into Germany often flying low and facing intense opposition from both enemy flak guns and fighters to attack such infamous targets as Bremen, Munster, Marienburg and Schweinfurt. Operations as far away as the Mediterranean were also conducted using temporary bases in North Africa. The missions they undertook included support for the invasion of Sicily and the D-Day landings and beyond as well as submarine facilities and V weapon launch sites, indeed, aircraft from Norfolk airfield were among the first to conduct a daylight raid over Berlin, the very heart of Nazi Germany on 4 March 1944.

Some specific missions, the action and sacrifice of the men of the 8th USAAF are etched bold into history such as the oil installations at Ploesti in Romania in August 1943. During this raid the lead B-24 was flown by group commander Lt. Col. Addison E. Baker of the 93rd Bomb Group (Hardwick) with Major John L. Jerstad as his co-pilot. The bomber was damaged but they refused to make a forced landing electing instead to lead the group to the oil facilities before their plane crashed in the target area. Both men were posthumously awarded the highest award for bravery awarded by the United States, the Medal of Honor. The group leader of the raid, the legendary Colonel Leon W. Johnson, was also awarded a Medal of Honour, presented to him in front of a special parade of surviving aircrews of 44th Bomb Group in front of the control tower at Shipdam on 23 November 1943.

At one period the chance of an individual airman completing the 25 (later 30-35) missions in a tour of operations, was as little as one in three. Although they did not have the highest overall loss rate of any group in the 'Mighty Eighth' (that fate befell the 492nd at 'North Pick' who lost 57 aircraft during its three months of operational flying between May and August 1944) the 100 Bomb Group at Thorpe Abbotts suffered the loss 84 aircraft over eight missions into Germany, including such targets as Bremen, Berlin and Hamburg between August 1943 and December 1944 and thus earned the nickname of 'The Bloody Hundredth.'

Norfolk also had some of the 'luckiest' aircraft. The 733rd Squadron, 453rd BG at Old Buckenham set an unbeaten record of 82 missions without a loss. The 467th BG at Rackheath flew 212 combat missions in the closing months of the war and led the 'Mighty Eighth' in bombing accuracy and also had the distinction of the B-24H 'Witchcraft' that held the record for the highest number of combat missions (130) for this type of bomber in the entire Eighth Air Force.

On 25 April 25 1945 the 2nd Air Division flew its last offensive raid. A total of 95, 948 sorties had

The entrance to Samson and Hercules House Dance Hall, Norwich a popular venue for many American servicemen.

Major James Stewart

Major Glenn Miller. Glen and his dance band also played at the Samson and Hercules Ballroom, Norwich on 18 August. (JG)

Airmen and ground crew of 'Rosies Riveters' of 100 Bomb Group (Thorpe Abbotts) 'The Bloody Hundredth'

been flown in 493 operational missions by the division's B-24s, dropping 199,883 tons of bombs. Six 2nd Air Division groups received special presidential citations for outstanding actions and five airmen (four of them posthumously) received the Medal of Honor. In combat the 2nd Air Division gunners claimed 1,079 enemy fighters destroyed against losses of 1,458 B-24s missing in action and many others were lost in accidents. A total of 6,700 men serving with the 2nd Air Division lost their lives during the conflict.

Deadly Postscript

As the war turned in favour of the allies after the D-Day landings Hitler needed a new strategy to boost German morale and show he could still fight back. Despite being unimpressed by the tests he had observed, the jet powered flying bombs, known in Germany *Vergeltungswaffe 1* (Vengeance Weapon 1) were his best option and so from mid-June 1944 these weapons were fired at allied population centres such as Antwerp and London. Only about 25% of these pilotless aircraft hit their intended targets. A combination of defensive measures, mechanical unreliability or guidance errors saw may V1s crash harmlessly into the sea but for the same reasons many of them also landed across the country. In the opening stages of this offensive three V1s fell on Norfolk: the first at Ovington on 10 July 1944, second at Whinbugh on 31 July and the third at Mulbarton on 24 September. This new weapon became a familiar sound to many as it passed overhead, the simple pulse jet engine with its characteristic buzzing sound gave rise to the colloquial name of buzz bomb or doodlebug.

The British counter measures against the V-weapon menace was code-named as Operation Crossbow. In a combined land and air operation barrage balloon defences were deployed to defence cities. The Royal Observer Corps fired 'Snowflake' illuminating rocket flares from the ground to identify V1 flying bombs and RAF Fighter Command deployed numerous squadrons with high speed fighters to intercept doodlebugs, the brave pilots having to 'flip' the flying bomb off course or shoot it down; the Mosquitos of 85 and 157 Squadrons flying out from RAF Swannington did particularly well, claiming they had shot down a combined tally of seventy V1s between July and August 1944. The Spitfire IXs of 229 Squadron, Coltishall took up the offensive and mounted armed reconnaissance flights to attack V2 launch sites pursuing them to around the Hague in 1945.

TOP SECRET – Operation Aphrodite

RAF Fersfield (originally known as RAF Winfarthing) was constructed in 1943-1944 as a satellite of RAF Knettishall (Suffolk) but became the operational base for the top secret Operation Aphrodite. The idea was to develop war tired B-17 Fortresses into stripped down drones packed with explosives (redesignated BQ-7s) to be used against enemy V-1 sites, deep fortifications that had resisted conventional bombing and submarine pens.

Approximately twenty five Fortresses were assigned to the 562nd Bomb Squadron, 388th Bomb Group, along with two B-24s from the United States Navy (PB4Y-1), to be used in Aphrodite missions. The idea was that pilots would get the planes in the air and then parachute out leaving the bomber under the control of another flying aircraft that would then guide it to its' target on the European mainland. The first mission took place on 4 August 1944; their target was a V-1 site in Pas-de-Calais. Although eminently possible, in theory, the technology at the disposal of the allies at the time was simply not advanced enough and the drones were not accurate. Later missions proved little or no better and only reiterated the same problems. Lt. Joseph P. Kennedy, Jr., the brother of future American President John F. Kennedy was killed in a subsequent mission when his Navy PB4Y-1 exploded over Blythburgh, Suffolk. Operation Aphrodite was declared 'unfeasible' early in 1945.

Anti-aircraft guns were redeployed in several movements to counter the new threats from the air: first, in mid-June 1944 from positions on the North Downs to the south coast of England then a cordon closing the Thames Estuary to attacks from the east. In September 1944 a new linear defence line was formed on the coast of East Anglia.

The Anti-Aircraft and Mobile Artillery Defences of Norfolk 1944

Unit	Base
56 Medium Regiment RA	Colne House, Cromer
96 Medium Battery RA	Cliftonville Hotel, Cromer
174 Medium Battery	Shelley House, Cadogan Road, Cromer
221 Medium Battery	Marlborough Hotel, Prince of Wales Road, Cromer
7 Heavy Battery	Cliffdale Hotel, Cabell Road, Cromer
173 Field Regiment RA H.Q.	Kings Mill School, Cromwell Road, Cromer
138 Field Battery	Royal Links Hotel, Cromer
156 Field Battery	The Warren, Overstrand Avenue, Cromer
157 Field Battery	Newhaven Court, Norwich Road, Cromer
158 Field Battery	Linkside, Cromer
192 Light AA Battery HQ	The Croft, Cromer Road, Sheringham
B Troop, 192 Light AA Battery	Cadogan House, Cadogan Road, Cromer

Searchlight Regiments and Batteries

82 SL Regiment HQ	The Orchards, Raveningham
510 SL Battery HQ	Red Clyffe, Brundall
Detachment 510 SL Battery	Tunstead
Detachment 510 SL Battery	Lessingham
72 SL Regiment HQ	Whitwell Hall, Reepham
466 SL Battery HQ	Aylsham
Detachment 466 SL Battery	Bradfield
Detachment 466 SL Battery	Colby
Detachment 466 SL Battery	Mundesley
Detachment 466 SL Battery	Cromer
Detachment 466 SL Battery	Honing
Detachment 466 SL Battery	Felmingham Hall
Detachment 466 SL Battery	Westwick
Detachment 466 SL Battery	Walcott
Detachment 466 SL Battery	Edingthorpe
Detachment 466 SL Battery	Sidestrand
Detachment 466 SL Battery	Thorpe Market

By September 1944, when a total of 4,261 V-1s had been destroyed by fighters, anti-aircraft fire and barrage balloons, the V1 threat to England was temporarily halted when the launch sites on the French coast were overrun by the advancing Allied armies. But it was this month that was to be marked by the arrival of the first V2 to land on the county. The V2 (officially designated as the A4) was a long range rocket known in Germany as the *Vergeltungswaffe 2*, retaliation weapon. London was the main target, 'short falls' of V-2s could occur over much of South East England but there were other targets including the City of Norwich. Operated by Versuchs Artillerie Batterie 444 under the command of Oberst Gerhard Stegmeier the launch site for the attacks on the Norwich was in a wood near Rijs in South West Friesland, Holland.

ATS women operate a predictor at the anti-aircraft training camp at Weybourne, October 1941. A 3.7-inch gun and concrete emplacement can be seen in the background.

The first V2 that fell on Norfolk crashed into a field near Ranworth at 4.25pm on 26 September 1944 causing a great explosion and crater and sent a column of smoke 2000ft in the air. The only casualty was a man who required treatment for shock after the blast. Many more rockets followed (See Appendix 3 for a complete listing of all air raids on the county, including V1 and V2 rockets fired from Rijs) in some cases damage was caused, people were injured and there were many narrow escapes; notably the Rockland St Mary V2 blast on 4 October 1944 when 21 children and 1 teacher suffered cuts caused by flying glass as the widows of the school were blown in, seven children required hospital treatment and a man leading horses in a nearby field was badly injured when he was struck on the neck by a piece of the rocket. By some miracle no-one was killed in any of the V2 landings on the county and the City of Norwich never received a hit by a V2, the nearest the rockets came was the V2 that crashed on the golf course at Hellesdon on 3 October 1944 leaving a crater 33'x37' and 12 ft deep, causing minor damage to some 400 homes in the area between Dereham Road and Boundary Road. Only one casualty was an elderly lady that was treated for shock. This was undoubtedly a sobering near miss; if any of the V2 had hit its target the story would have been very different.

The last V2 aimed at Norwich fell on a field at Manor Farm, Ingworth on 12 October causing minor damage to 24 houses and the church. The very last V2 to fall on Norfolk was a 'short fall' aimed at London that crashed at Welborne, near Mattishall on 26 October 1944. Landing on open ground at 10.12am, the explosion caused minor damage to nearby farm buildings, the local school, about 20 houses and brought down the telephone wires. Two men were slightly hurt when horses took fright.

This was, however, not to be the last offensive, enemy action over the county, air raids continued until 1945 when piloted enemy air attacks resumed. On the evening of Monday March twenty Mosquitos returning to the county from raids on Berlin were joined by enemy intruder bombers that machine gunned Sustead and Thornage and attacked airfields at Langham, Wendling and finally

Swanton Morley, where the very last bombs fell on the county at 9.30pm causing only minor damage. The Mosquitos of 125 Squadron at RAF Coltishall were scrambled to intercept the enemy intruders. Among them was Flight Lieutenant Kennedy and Flying Officer Morgan in their Mosquito N.F. Mk XXX; they brought down a Ju 88 which crashed into the sea 10 miles north-east of Cromer, thus claiming the distinction of shooting down the last enemy aircraft shot down by a defensive fighter operating over Britain during the Second World War.

Crew 4, Norwich Centre, Royal Observer Corps, 25 July 1944

Royal Observer Corps (Norfolk) 1934-1945
No. 16 Group HQ
GPO (basement), Dove Street, Norwich 1934-1940
GPO (new premises), St Andrews, Norwich 1940-1942
"Fairfield," Lime Tree Road, Norwich 1942-1947

From 1942 onwards the St Andrews premises was retained as emergency accommodation and used operationally in late 1942 after main cable to 'Fairfield' had been damaged by enemy action. They were again used in 1943 while structural alterations to accommodate a long range plotting board were carried out at 'Fairfield'.

Aldeby	Post D. 1	Opened October 1938
Aylsham	Post R. 3	Opened 1934
Brancaster	Post N. 1	Opened 1934
Brundall	Post V. 2	Opened 1934
Caister	Post T. 4	Opened November 1934
Cley	Post P. 2	Opened November 1934
Coltishall	Post V. 1	Opened November 1934
Cromer	Post Q. 1	Opened November 1934
Dersingham	Post O. 3	Opened November 1934
Diss	Post G. 1	Opened June 1939
Docking	Post N. 2	Opened June 1939
Downham Market	Post K. 1	Opened March 1936
East Dereham	Post Y. 2	Opened November 1934
Elmham	Post W. 3	Opened November 1934
Fakenham	Post P. 3	Opened November 1934
Freethorpe	Post T. 1	Opened November 1934
Garboldisham	Post D. 3	Opened September 1939
Gressenhall	Post Y. 1	Opened November 1934
Harleston	Post C. 3	Opened October 1939
Hellesdon	Post W. 2	Opened November 1934
Hingham	Post X. 3	Opened November 1934
Honingham	Post X. 1	Opened November 1934
Hockham	Post B. 1	Opened November 1938
Hunstanton	Post N. 3	Opened November 1934
King's Lynn	Post H. 2	Opened November 1934
Loddon	Post T. 3	Opened October 1934
Long Stratton	Post C. 1	Opened October 1938
Martham	Post S. 1	Opened 1934
Massingham	Post O. 2	Opened November 1934
Melton Constable	Post Q. 3	Opened November 1934
Mundesley	Post H. 1	Opened January 1934
Mundford	Post A. 1	Opened June 1939
Narborough	Post Z. 1	Opened November 1934
New Buckenham	Post B. 2	Opened October 1938
Reepham	Post W. 1	Opened November 1934
Runham	Post S. 3	Opened November 1934
South Creake	Post O. 1	Opened November 1934
Southery	Post K. 2	Opened September 1936
Stalham	Post S. 1	Opened November 1934
Stoke Ferry	Post Z. 3	Opened May 1940
Swaffham	Post Z. 2	Opened November 1934
Thetford	Post A. 2	Opened December 1938
Walcott	Post R. 2	Opened November 1934
Watton	Post Y. 3	Opened November 1939
Wells	Post P. 1	Opened November 1934
Wymondham	Post K. 2	Opened July 1934

5 On the Home Front

When war was declared on 3 September 1939 those who had not completed their refuge room or garden shelter set out to complete their tasks. For factories, hospitals and homes to remain operational in the black out meant the windows would have to be screened or properly fitted with shutters of black-out curtains, no mean feat in any home but think about places such as the Norfolk and Norwich Hospital where there were 1,600 windows to black-out.

The ARP organisation had developed apace and now had a structure with a number of its own specialist 'arms' as shown in the *National Service* booklet (1939):

Air Raid Wardens

Rescue(Later further delineated to Rescue (General), and specialist Light Rescue and Heavy Rescue) and Demolition Parties

First Aid Parties

First Aid Posts

Ambulance Drivers and Attendants

Decontamination Squads (Trained to removed all traces of dangerous or persistent gas dropped or sprayed from enemy aircraft from streets, vehicles and buildings)

Report Centres, Communications and Messenger Service

To become an Air Raid Warden firstly one would have to apply to Norfolk County Council, the *National Service* booklet outlined the qualifications for acceptance as 'Air Raid Wardens should preferably be people who live in the district where their duties will lie. Men who are over the age of 30 are needed, and men between 25 and 30 may also apply if not available for more active service. Some women over the age of 25 are also needed.' Over the course of the war the age stipulation for female volunteers was reduced. The rule of thumb used by many recruiters for the ARP was 'if they are fit enough and keen enough to do the job – we'll train 'em to do it'

In *ARP: A Practical* Guide (1939) the type of person suitable for Warden's work was described: 'The Air Raid Warden occupies a most important place in the general scheme of Air Raid Precautions. He should be a responsible and reliable member of the public, free from physical or tempera-

Franklyn Horsley, Fire Guard Staff Officer at ARP Post A1, Rackham Road, Division 3 (Angel and Woodcock Estates) Norwich, 1940

Norfolk County Council Casualty Service Mobile Unit with Ambulance and First Aid Party crews, North Walsham, 1940.

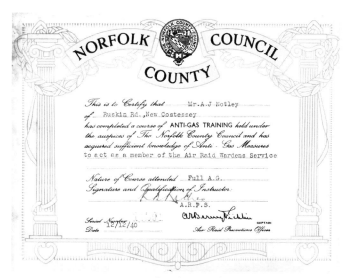

*Norfolk County Council
certificate awarded to Mr A.J.
Notley of New Costessey on
completion of an Anti-Gas
Training Course to act as a
member of the Air Raid
Warden's Service, 12
December 1940.*

mental disability, whose duty is to advise and instruct his neighbours how to protect themselves against injury from air attack, and to this end to fit them with the necessary respirators, and make known the precautions available to safeguard life and property.

In war time the warden is expected to act with courage and presence of mind a: as leader and helper of the people in his immediate neighbourhood and b: as a link between such people and the local ARP services'

All Air Raid Wardens were trained (usually in part time courses outside of working hours) in anti-gas, basic first aid, elementary fire fighting and instructed in how to receive, record and send messages. If passed proficient after one month service with their unit the new warden would be presented with their silver ARP badge. Wardens would also be given a Card of Appointment, signed by the ARP Officer and/or the Clerk to the Local Authority to prove his authority to householders or others he may visit in the course of his duties and with that (before uniforms were issued in 1941) and, in the absence of a uniform, a screen printed on a white cloth arm band produced by Norfolk County Council marked NCC Warden for county areas to be worn on the left arm when on duty in civilian clothes. Along with this came their 'appointments' of Civilian Duty Respirator, Tin Helmet (Painted, black with a white 'W' for most wardens; white helmets with diamonds or stripes denoted the more senior ranks among the wardens and ARP Officers) and ARP issue whistle suspended from a chain or lanyard – all of which must be carried by a Warden when on duty. Whistles and sirens were used to sound and enforce the Air Raid Warning, at the post there would also be a rattle for each warden on duty to sound the warning for poison gas attack, and a hand bell to sound and enforce the siren's single rising note for 'All Clear' raiders passed.

The intention of the Wardens Service was to provide a warden's post of five or six wardens for every 400 to 500 inhabitants. Wardens would have to acquire an thorough knowledge of their sector and inhabitants (for example, a young mother with baby twins and toddlers with husband away at the war would need assistance putting on and operating the babies gas masks in the event of a gas attack.) The warden would also need to know the location of gas mains, electric cables, telephones, shelters and trenches. Wardens needed to keep in touch with residents in their sector and given then necessary advice. Wardens would probably be first on the scene if air raid damage had occurred and would be responsible for summoning the proper form of help e.g. Fire Service, Heavy or Light Rescue squads, Ambulance, emergency utility repair crews etc. Such procedures were rehearsed by staging regular drills and exercises, these operations also taught the wardens to work together and fostered strong team skills.

The problem was, from the point of view of many of the population, in the years up to the outbreak of war and indeed through the 'Phoney War' period of 1939-40 before the bombers of the Luftwaffe began their bombing campaign on Britain wardens were sometimes viewed by their neighbours with suspicion. Dressed in just tin helmet and arm band with their civvy clothes the wardens did not look 'official' or 'properly appointed.' The attempts of the wardens to get to know their area were often seen as prying and their behaviour after dark as 'lurking'. Some undoubtedly did become overzealous in their duties while striving to be thorough; the public often saw this as 'interfering' and viewed the wardens' authority to act as 'busy-bodies charter,' especially after some upheld minor blackout infringements to magistrates court and resulted in the offending house or vehicle owner being fined really didn't make them any more popular. Due to shortages in official supplies uniforms for ARP Wardens only began to arrive from October 1939. The first issue was that of a 'bluette' light denim overall for men and Macintosh type overcoats for women with white metal buttons marked ARP. In a number of areas where shortages persisted the local authorities privately purchased blue overalls for their wardens.

Another emergency service created in the late 1930s was the Auxiliary Fire Service, founded during the Munich Crisis in 1938, it men were recruited to supplement the work of established fire brigades at a local level. Each recruit would fill in an application form

That would be was scrutinised by the Chief Constable. If the man appeared suitable he would be issued with a boiler suit, peaked cap and a Pair of Wellington Boots. Recruitment was such the Norwich AFS could not cope with the training schedule so Chief Officer Underwood of Colman's Carrow Works Brigade took over some of the workload and by 1941 had trained half the total number of recruits. Other businesses such as Laurence & Scott and Steward and Patteson brewery raised their own AFS units. Every AFS unit had the authority to requisition or hire either lorries or cars to adapt to tow trailer pumps. By 1940 there were approximately one hundred Coventry Victor trailer pumps stationed

*Below left: ARP Wardens of
Post H8, Group I, Division I
(Dereham and Heigham
Roads) based at the children's
home in Turner's Road,
Norwich 1940.*

*Below right: Auxiliary
firemen demonstrate the use
of a stirrup pump in front of
the Agricultural Hall during
Norwich Civic Week,
October 1938.*

in the Norwich area with approximately 100 full-time auxiliary firemen and 200 part time auxiliary firemen to man them. Across the county every town and many villages now had their own AFS units with a trailer pump and number of AFS units sent pumps and crews to attend the London blitz in 1940.

The local fire authorities were taken over by the National Fire Service (NFS) in 1941. The Fire Service became an entity in its own right, broke away from police control and established a new HQ at Whitegates, Hethersett. Norfolk was now officially titled Fire Force 13. The Fire Force was controlled by a Commander with the assistance of a Deputy. Each Fire Force was sub-divided into divisions under the command of a Divisional Officer with his Division divided into two columns, commanded by Column Officers. Hours of duty were standardised to 12 hours on then 12 hours off (later amended to 48 on and 24 off) then finally amended to 24 on and 24 off for firemen, while ranks above Section Officer were more or less on a continuous duty rota.

Even though there were trained ARP wardens in most towns and most ARP appointment cards were endorsed by the local senior police officer in the early months of the war the Special Constables patrolled and ensured the blackout was maintained in many towns in the county. With so many police officers being ex-forces their numbers rapidly fell with the call up of the Reserve in 1939 and further recruitment through the war, thus the membership of the Special Constabulary had to be expanded and a Police War Reserve was established. In October 1939 a *Norfolk Chronicle* reporter joined two of the Holt town 'Specials' which he named as S.C. Y and S.C. Z on their beat during the black out:

> 'Sharp at 8.30pm we set out – after they had 'signed on' at the police station – first down Station Road towards High Street. Suddenly a bright light shone behind us. Case No. 1 happened within a few yards of the police station. The offender was a cyclist with too bright a light; the first case went to S.C. Z who stopped the cyclist and explained to him the offence. 'This is the first time I have been out on a bicycle since the war started.' The offender explained but promised to 'see to it.'
>
> On through the High Street where no dangerous lights were visible; up Norwich Road, but no lights; doubled back through the High Street up part of New Street (all clear); through Cross Street (several chinks of light could be seen but they were not serious); down Albert Street to Tower Street and Shirehall Plain. Here again everything was blacked out. We continued down Tower Street when two cyclists were seen approaching with bright lights. Here S.C. Y shouted out to the offenders, who however, pedalled off quicker.
>
> Through White Lion Street (all clear) down Peacock Lane and Jubilee Road. Here one rather bright light was quickly extinguished. Except for this one light this part of the town was clear. We then continued up Cromer Road, S.C. Z gave a small yard the 'once over' as he termed it. Cromer Road was showing no lights. Suddenly S.C. Z saw one. It seemed small enough as we approached but as we got nearer we saw a window measuring roughly 3ft by 5ft completely uncovered and light streaming from it. This so far had been the worst offender of them all. S.C. Y went to the door and explained what was wrong. Suddenly the light went out and it was explained that there was a covering over the window – which we could just see – but the 'boys'

Left: *The Steward & Patteson Brewery Auxiliary Fire Service Patrol (Norwich City No.21) with their Coventry Victor trailer pump 1940.*

Right: *Norwich City firemen 'going in' with their hose 1940*

Chief Officer G. W. Underdown of Carrow Works Fire Brigade

Holt Special Constables 1940

had knocked it down. Here I expected to see S.C.s Y and Z take down the offender's name and address but Z said to me (and this is worthy of public notice) 'We are not out to catch people but to help them. We find that many of the lights that are seen are left on through carelessness, it is for their own good as well as for other people's.'

During the blackouts of the 'Phoney War' many expressed scepticism for their necessity on the streets and in the columns of the newspapers; this excerpt of a letter from Carthage Caldcleugh of Fakenham published in the *Norfolk Chronicle* in October 1939 was particularly scathing:

> *'The general feeling in this town is that various Sanhedrims of religion are making a serious blunder in fixing the last devotions of Sunday in the afternoon instead of night, on account of the stupid acts of Westminster, that of 'blacking-out' completely at an hour when most people are just beginning to wake. To begin with, why black out in broad daylight? Our observers can give us seven minutes warning of the approach of enemy aircraft; and we can all black out now in two. Make no mistake about it but by this time 'Jerry' has every town, city and hamlet near any military objective taped' to a nicety and if our 'Archies' and our aircraft can't prevent his approaching he will find you all, even though you drape yourselves and your houses in the very deepest crape. Personally, I don't think he will come near us; that he couldn't if he attempted. The why close God's House to His people at the very hour they feel they need Him most?*

The black-out not only cause many inconveniences it led to unprecedented numbers of road traffic accidents; nationally 4,000 people were killed on Britain's roads between September and December 1939 add to that injuries to pedestrians and even fatalities occurring to those left stumbling around the blackened streets. On 4 November 1939 the Yarmouth docks were the scene of some of the first tragedies. Royal Norfolk Regiment soldier Pte. John Randall Ablett (20) of Thurlton and Phyllis Watson (19) of Great Yarmouth were walking along the quayside when they both fell into the harbour. Phyllis was saved with a boat hook but John was drowned. On the other side of the river, Charles Frith (38), a Grimsby skipper also tumbled into the water, a friend dived in after him but the current proved too strong and Frith was carried away and drowned.

The members of the Women's Voluntary Service and Women's Institute had played a key role during the evacuation of children in September 1939 not only ensuring the day ran smoothly but sorting out feeding and helping find billets and after care for the children. The following month they played a major role in the appeal and distribution of clothing for those in need. In the editorial of the Norfolk Women's Institute Supplement to *Home & Country* (October 1939) the following article entitled '*Our Visitors*' reflects much of the mood of the county in the immediate wake of the first great evacuation:

Evacuees from Edmonton and Bethnal Green shortly after their arrival in North Walsham Market Place, 1 September 1939.

Many problems face our Local Authorities following the arrival of thousands of evacuees in Norfolk, and hundreds of our members who volunteered for, and were looking forward to, the reception and care of school children, received a nasty shock when called upon to provide lodging for mothers and young children in their stead.

Dirt, disease and ingratitude have been depressing elements in a scheme which from a transport point of view was a marvel or organisation. Out of evil good may come, for citizens are already asking 'are the vast millions spent on social services in this county being put to their right use?' Out sympathy goes out in full measure to those householders who have received shock upon shock and we hope they will take comfort and gather courage with the realisation that these troubles, great as they are, fade into insignificance compared with stupendous problems the world is facing today.

Nor must it be supposed for one moment that all our visitors come within this category, far from it. We have records of delightful visitors it is a joy to welcome to the county, who's co-operation with their hostesses to overcome domestic difficulties makes life worthwhile.

We must remember the evacuees also have their problems to face. They are parted from members of their family, they have had to leave their homes, the countryside in many cases is irksome to them, so much so in some cases they have disappeared suddenly and returned to their homes! Mothers who do this are running a great risk for their children and taking a great responsibility and it is our duty to try to persuade them to leave their children with us even if they will not stay.

Misfits in billeting are being rapidly adjusted but apart from interchanges arranged by the senior regional officers, changes in billets can only be made with the approval of the Local Authority, and school accommodation can only be exchanged by the sanction of the Secretary of Education.

Many members complain of damage to their homes. These complaints should be referred to the Local Authority, the Local Welfare Committee or the Billeting Offices.

Several Institutes have suggested forming working parties to mend and make clothes for their visitors. This is very commendable and necessitous cases and for emergencies but we all must remember that the responsibility for clothing remains with the parents and they should be appealed to in the first place. Where there are many mothers in a district it is much hoped the W.I. will arrange a Mother's Club.

If we can exercise patience and bring tact and understanding to our aid, we shall surmount our difficulties.'

During the 'Phoney War' of 1939 and early 1940 many children did return home from evacuation, especially when there was a chance to spend Christmas with their families. Across the country every city, town and village organised a wide variety of activities for the war effort, a report from the Burnham Market Women's Institute recounted their village efforts between September 1939 and March 1940:

'On September 1st we received our Evacuees, 160 children and 16 married teachers. The children were easy to billet but the teachers, married ones – were something no-one had expected. However, billets for them and after some re-shuffling they have settled down. The foster parents are not all W. I. Members, but a very great number are.

We had a sick bay in the village where difficult cases from all the surrounding district were dealt with. Members made 25 nightgowns, several small overcoats and dresses boys' knitted suits and socks for the children.

At Christmas we felt we should like to send a parcel to each of the men from the village who were in the Services. However, when we came to enquire of the names, we found there were more than we could afford to send to. But some of the older men in the village volunteered to make a collection and we members undertook to knit sufficient woollies for each parcel and do the packing.

In the end our efforts exceeded all expectations. We actually packed 73 parcels. In each were the following: one or two woollies, most had 2, 2 razor blades, a cake of soap, a small lighter case (hand made) and a Christmas card (these were from the Institute), 50 cigarettes, 2 handerkerchiefs and ½ lb. of chocolate and the postage was covered by the men's very generous Fund. We have had many letters of appreciation from those receiving them.

Now we have started a 1d. a week Fund for wool and are busy knitting sea boot stockings. But these are expensive to make – 6s. each pair.

Some of our members have fitted up one of the military units with woollies and we are busy knitting for the second unit. In the meantime we send them something home-made each week, cakes or scones.

There are three Working Parties, who have been busy since September and one of them has already sent away 120 hospital garments and 26 pairs of operations stockings or bed socks. Another member has made herself responsible for operation stocking and bed-socks and had collected over a hundred already from her friends. We have four First Aid Posts, all run by W.I. members. Most of us have passed the Red Cross examination in First Aid.

Our first parcels resulting from our 1d. Fund were despatched today, one to the R.N.M.D.S. F. Stores containing – 3 pairs sea boot stockings, 1 pair socks, 3 balaclava helmets, 1 scarf, 1 pair mittens, 3 pairs cuffs and another with khaki things in went to Reading.

The whole village is united in its effort to help in whatever way possible.'

Parents of evacuees arrive in Wymondham Market Place to visit their children billeted in the town and surrounding area shortly before Christmas 1939.

As more and more men were called up to serve 'in the forces' the war effort was extended on the Home Front in unprecedented ways. Many servicemen, especially those who had to leave their wife with a young family at home voiced the opinion that their wives and sweethearts had endured the harder share of the war. Many of them were to recall receiving photographs of those they loved from home and how, although obviously well and not starving, their concerns were that their sweethearts and wives looked 'war weary.' This is hardly surprising with homes to run, children to care for and with an ever increasing number of food and clothing items being rationed that was quite enough to contend with but add to that the regular sounding of sirens hailing air raids, false alarms or not and the fact that many men leaving factories and businesses more and more women were required to take their place and increase the workforce to fulfil the increased demand for military supplies; especially in the factories such as Harmers on St Stephen's where they made uniforms for the military and civil defence, in the city's boot and shoe factories making footwear for the forces and at Boulton & Paul making prefabricated buildings for the military or munitions at Laurence & Scott. As in the First World War, women also worked on public transport working on buses or on the railways. Then it makes it all the more remarkable that so many of them were also voluntarily 'doing their bit' on the Home Front.

One of the organisations often omitted from wartime histories are the Hospital Supply Depots. By March 1940 there were 70 of these established in the county along with and 152 Working Parties. Run under the auspices of the Joint War Committee of the British Red Cross Society & Order of St. John under the inspired direction of Mrs. Lance and working in co-operation with the Women's Voluntary Services the organisation drew on volunteers from Women's Institutes, local groups women's groups and individuals. All Depots were affiliated to the national Central Hospital Supply Service. The Norfolk depots were certainly kept busy in those early months of 1940 with Emergency Hospitals being opened by the military authorities to cope with the influenza epidemic. All emergency hospitals were supplied with a large number of bed jackets, pyjamas, pillow cases etc amounting to well over 1000 garments. A consignment of 6000 bandages were also sent to Finland together with other medical supplies. Between 1939 and 1940 the Depots executed government orders including the likes of shirts for Polish refugees and over 1000 nightshirts and cardigans. Knitting was also done at the Depots for the ship-

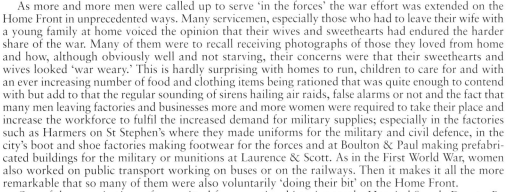

Stibbard Girl Guides and their grand paper salvage collection, August 1940

An Eastern Counties Bus Company 'clippie' 1942.

Left: *A Central Hospital Supply Service Depot Staff, Norfolk*

Right: *WVS Officer and her van, a gift of The British War Relief Association of Northern California, Great Yarmouth, 1940.*

wrecked persons landed on the coast and several hundred knitted garments were sent to the Sailors' Home at Great Yarmouth and elsewhere. When no special work in hand, bandages and surgical dressings were made for stock.

Another oft forgotten organisation was the National Pigeon Service that provided message carrying birds to the services from British racing pigeon breeders. A number of the birds recorded on the Meritorious Performance List include those bred by Norfolk breeders such as, Messrs Thurlby and Haynes of King's Lynn; H. Leamon of Lawson Road, Norwich; S. Rowbotham and T. Franklin on Gresham Road, Drayton Estate and J. Cowles of Beecheno Road, Norwich who provided the Dark Cheq. Pied Cock 'Neilson' (NURP.41.EAN) who was trained at RAF Gillingham and reliably flew missions of distances between 300 and 500 miles in good time over five years. In 1945 'Neilson' was selected for a very hazardous task and was dropped in the Ruhr Pocket more than 300 miles distant and after several days detention homed successfully. Most notable of all was Blue Cock 'Royal Blue' (NURP.40.GVIS.453) bred by and trained at HM King George VI's Pigeon Loft, Sandringham and operating out of Bircham Newton, 'Royal Blue' was the first pigeon to bring a message from a force-landed aircrew on the continent during the Second World War. Released by the crew in Holland on 10 October 1940 at 07.20 hours, the young bird arrived with its message at Sandringham at 11.30 hours the same day. This efficient pigeon was recognised for this action by the award of the Dickin Medal 'the animal's VC' in March 1945.

Throughout nation's darkest hours the women of Norfolk's Women's Institute was the backbone of the war effort on the home front. Between January and March 1941 a record of the special war activities of some of the Institutes from across the county was published in their *Home & Country* supplement - a remarkable account that reveals so much about the wartime activities in towns and villages across Norfolk, note in particular the number of evacuees received, often in very small villages. The WVS was responsible for the welfare of evacuees but the WI took a keen interest in 'the visitors' and in very many areas the WVS representatives and the WI member was one and the same person;

★─────────────────────────────────────★

10 Points about the Scrap Iron Campaign

1. In the whole output of steel in this country, 65 per cent of the raw material used is scrap iron and steel.

2. Every ton of scrap salvaged at home saves the importation of a ton from overseas.

3. There are thousands of tons of scrap iron and steel rusting away in the fields, farms, and cottages of England and Wales.

4. The Iron and Steel Control, Ministry of Supply, Caxton House East, Tothill Street, London, S.W.1, is now organizing the collection of this iron and steel scrap from villages.

5. Voluntary canvassers and organizers are needed. THIS IS WHERE WOMEN'S INSTITUTES CAN BE PARTICULARLY HELPFUL.

6. A noticeable site for a dump should be selected on a road that can be used by heavy lorries.

7. Notices (which the Iron and Steel Control will supply) should be put near the dump and in all places commonly used for public notices. Householders and farmers in and around the village should be personally canvassed.

8. Obsolete iron and steel articles of all kinds are required—old stoves, flat irons, bedsteads, obsolete tools, farm and garden implements, and machinery, old railings : things that at present wastefully clutter up yards, corners of fields, attics, and outhouses can be turned into valuable munitions of war.

9. When the dump contains a worthwhile load— three or four tons—the local organizer should inform the Iron and Steel Control, **which will arrange for the dump to be cleared.**

10. Standard prices have been laid down by the Government, and profits made out of the Iron and Steel Control's village collection scheme will be handed to the Red Cross Agricultural Fund.

If a scrap iron and steel collection scheme has not yet been started in your village, write at once to the Iron and Steel Control at the address given above and get one going.

★─────────────────────────────────────★

Alburgh (38 members)
Knitted 140 comforts supplied to men serving in the Forces from the village, Minesweepers, Territorial Welfare, BEF in France, RAF and WVS. Raised £10 for wool. Received 50 evacuees, collected clothes, gave concerts and socials for their benefit. Savings Group started by WI, open to village, 23 members saved £2 1s 9d in first two weeks. Helped with salvage and the Preservation Centre made 957 lbs of jam. The Leader, Deputy Leader, Secretary and majority of the personnel of the local First Aid Post are WI members, two are Air Raid Wardens and a large number work for WVS.

Bradenham (31 members)
Knitted 100 comforts supplied to men serving from the village. Raised money for wool. Received 160 evacuees, staged entertainments collected clothes, mended and washed them for their benefit. Provided a weekly whist drive, a social and private hospitality for local Forces. Savings Group for village and WI holiday Savings Club, 190 members saved £450. Helped with salvage and the Preservation Centre made 1066 lbs of jam. Sent Christmas parcels to men serving from the village, ARP and Red Cross services. Provided volunteers for blood transfusion service. Members helped with fruit picking, potato raising and general land work.

Burgh St Peter (18 members)
Knitted 64 comforts supplied to men serving from the village, territorial welfare and RAF. Raised £5 9s 8d for wool. Savings Group started by WI in August, members had saved £18. Helped with salvage and the Preservation Centre made 150lbs of jam.

Feltwell (50 members)
Knitted comforts and sent Christmas gifts to men serving from village and Territorial Welfare. Raised money for the wool. Accumulated crockery and clothes for evacuees. Savings Group started by WI, open to village, 150 members, saved £134. Members worked in the village First Aid Post, helped with salvage and started an 'Emergency Fund' for the village.

Fincham (36 members)
Knitted 86 comforts and helped WVS with theirs and supplied these to servicemen from the village and prisoners of war. Raised £10 for wool. Received 40 unaccompanied evacuees and 40 mothers and children. Collected clothes, carried out washing and mending and helped with communal feeding. Savings Groups in the village, 43 members, saved £183 18s 0d.

Fulmodeston (30 members)

Knitted 34 comforts and masses of knitting as WVS workers. Received a large number of evacuees but only had 4 mothers and 10 children (3 of them unaccompanied) by December 1940. Accumulated and supplied clothes to evacuees. Members were part of the village and next village Savings Group – 54 members, £408 15s 0d were saved in 4 months. Members helped with salvage. Preservation centre preserved 2cwt. 89lbs plums and 6lbs. blackberries. Sent 7 Christmas parcels to men of the village in the forces in 1939 and co-operated with the village effort for 12 men at Christmas 1940. Institute staged Ministry of Information Film shows for all village and visitors.

Guist (20 members)

Knitted comforts for the men serving from the village. Raised £8 for wool. Received evacuees and held 'socials' for their local forces. The village Savings Group had 76 members. Supplied material and made up 130 articles for hospital.

Hellesdon (68 members)

Knitted 250 comforts, supplied to WI centre and adopted a Minesweeper. Savings Groups started by WI, 24 members saved £134 4s 6d. Helped with salvage, worked for Hospital Supplies and collected knee rugs and walking sticks for hospital. The Preservation Centre made 1,300 lbs of jam.

Hockham (35 members)

The WI and WVS have a joint knitting club that made 181 comforts supplied to the men of the village, the WVS and their WI's adopted Minesweeper. Raised £26 18s 4d for wool. Received 17 evacuees. Provided entertainments, baths, vegetables, fruit and even mended sock for locally based forces. Village Savings Group in the charge if WI saved £900. Worked for Norfolk & Norwich Hospital, made and supplied 17 articles. Helped with salvage. Subscribed to War Charities, Cigarette Fund and Ambulance Fund.

Houghton (60 members)

Knitted 150 comforts supplied to men from the village, Territorial Welfare and Navy. Raised £20 for wool. Received 30 evacuees and entertained members of the local forces to whist drives and dances. Members in the village Savings Group. Helped with salvage and the canteen for the Forces.

Hoveton & District (132 members)

Made 144 comforts supplied to local servicemen, the RAF and Mission to Seaman. Raised £11 5s 2d for wool. Received 248 evacuees and accumulated 200 articles for their benefit. Helped the local committee in the entertainment of soldiers. Savings group started by WI, 200 members, saved £1253

Left: *The village iron dump collected during the salvage drive, in front of the George and Dragon pub North Elmham, July 1940. (GFWM)*

Right: *Pots, pants and kettles for salvage, St Giles Street, Norwich 1940*

The Martham scrap metal salvage collectors 1940

17s 6d. Members belong to the local hospital supply depot working party. Salvaged 12 tons of waste paper. Preserving Centre made 500lbs of jam and 664 cans of fruit. Collected for War Charities and members helped the local Red Cross and Canteen.

Lopham (41 members)
Knitted 140 comforts supplied to men from the village in the Forces and WVS. Raised £6 10s 0d for wool. Received 50 evacuees – mothers and children and collected clothes, did washing and mending for their benefit. Savings Group started by WI, open to village, 21 members, saved £27 10s 6d. Supplied material and made 39 articles working for local hospital groups, and made up 40 articles. Helped with salvage and the Preservation Centre made 930 lbs of jam. Whist drives were held for local Home Guard and refreshments were supplied every night they were on duty.

Melton Constable (40 members)
Made 73 comforts supplied to Territorial Welfare and servicemen from the village. Raised £15 for wool. Received 36 evacuees and accumulated clothes for their benefit and provided a mending and washing service for both evacuees and local military forces. Entertained servicemen to light meals, worked for Hospital Groups and salvage.

Melton Constable Park and Swanton Novers (20 members)
Knitted 403 comforts supplied to Royal Norfolk Regiment, Cold stream Guards, Territorial Welfare, Minesweepers, Searchlight Party, Home Guards and men serving from the village. Raised £7 7s 0d for wool. Received about 60 evacuees. Entertained local forces at whist drives, tea parties and tennis. Savings Group started by WI, open to village, 46 members saved £32 9s 6d in its first six months. Made 270 articles working for Red Cross Hospital Supplies. Helped with salvage collection. Preservation centre made 480 lbs of jam. Members of Melton Park WI worked in WVS canteen for Newfoundland Gunners billeted in the park.

Morningthorpe, Fritton and District (48 members)
Knitted approximately 1000 comforts and 16 knitted blankets supplied to men serving in the forces from the village, Red Cross and St John, Royal Navy and Minesweepers. Raised £22 for wool. Received 30 evacuees and collected clothing for their benefit. Sent supplies of vegetables weekly to the forces. Savings Groups started by WI, 40 members, saved £150 15s 0d. Made up articles for hospitals, helped with salvage and the Preserving Centre made 1,650 lbs of jam and jelly.

Mundford (33 members)
Knitted 190 comforts (with help from the village) and supplied to Regiments, Hospital and Territorial Welfare and raised the money for wool. Received 60 evacuees. Assisted in various activities to entertain locally stationed forces. Savings Group started by WI, 18 members, open to village, saved £16 7s 6d. Worked for hospital, supplied material and made 21 garments. Helped with salvage and local canteen for five months. Sent 75 parcels to men from villages serving with the Forces. Collected books and periodicals for army camps.

*Little Cressingham Sunday
School outing, Spring 1942.*

North Walsham & District (148 members)
Knitted 167 comforts supplied to Army, RAF and Mission to Seamen. Raised £25 1s 6d for wool. Received 700 evacuees in September 1939 (many have since returned home) but for six months many WI members housed, clothed and fed them. Mended socks for the Forces. Savings Group started by WI, 12 members, saved about £700 (there were also other Savings Groups). Worked with Hospital Group and at two canteens. A large parcel of toys and another of great coats etc was sent to the collection for those in bombed areas.

Old Hunstanton (184 members)
Knitted 1400 comforts supplied to men serving from the village, Minesweepers, Army, Navy, RAF and hospitals. Raised £35 for wool. Evacuees received and a collection was made for clothes and toys. There was a Savings Group in the village and members ran a WI Canteen.

Poringland (44 members)

Members helped with the village working party which had made 1,000 comforts sent to men of the village and Minesweepers. Raised £5 for wool. Received 60 evacuees. WI started Savings Group open to people from the village and had 25 members and saved £45 between July and December 1940. Collected waste paper for salvage.

Roughton and District (33 members)

Made 29 comforts supplied to men serving from the village. Raised £1 11s for wool. Received 96 evacuees. Savings Group started by WI, 36 members saved £16. Helped with salvage and the Preserving Centre made 600 lbs of jam. Sent 53 Christmas parcels to men of the village serving in the Forces. Raised 27s towards a stretcher for the First Aid Post and 32s 6d for the Red Cross.

Runtons & District (52 members)

Approximate number of comforts made 450, supplied men serving from the village and the County Centre. Adopted a Minesweeper and sent 292 comforts. Raised £27 18s. 6d for the purchase of wool. Received 160 evacuees in the village and set up working parties to make clothes for them. Carried out the mending of clothes for forces for three months and treated the local forces to a weekly sing-song. Practically all members belonged to the National Savings Groups and had saved approximately £400 to December 1940. Made 52 pairs of soft slippers for hospitals. Made 6 pairs of pyjamas for WVS and helped the WVS with salvage.

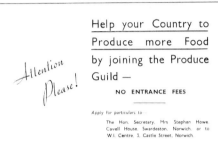

Help your Country to Produce more Food by joining the Produce Guild —

Attention Please!

NO ENTRANCE FEES

Apply for particulars to
The Hon. Secretary, Mrs Stephen Howe,
Cavell House, Swardeston, Norwich, or to
W.I. Centre, 3, Castle Street, Norwich.

Sandringham (75 members)

Knitted 482 comforts and supplied men from village, Navy, RAF, Minesweepers and the County Centre. Raised £26 for wool. Received 45 evacuees (31 remaining). Raised £8 8s 6d for War Charities. Members were also part of the village War Savings Groups. Made 13 helpless case sheets to Red Cross and 9 pairs of pyjamas. Members also collected salvage.

Southrepps (60 members)

Knitted 300 comforts supplied to RAF, Territorial Welfare and Minesweepers. Raised £11 for wool. Received 200 evacuees and carried out mending for them. Savings Group started by WI, open to village, 132 members saved £162

Stanhoe and Barwick (38 members)

Made 80 comforts supplied to servicemen from the village and various depots. Raised £4 10s for wool. Received 40 evacuees. Accumulated clothes, helping with feeding, entertaining, washing and mending. Held fortnightly dances for forces. Members help the Red Cross Working Party and sort salvage paper for WVS.

Thuxton with Garveston (20 members)

Knitted 200 comforts (with help from the village and local WVS) supplied to local men serving in the forces. Raised £8 6s 0d for wool. Received 52 evacuees. Helped with salvage. Provided entertainment for evacuees, collected books for the forces and provided hot drinks for the Home Guard.

Tilney St Lawrence (80 members)

Knitted 8 comforts supplied to Territorial Welfare Committee. Received 100 evacuees. Savings Group started by WI and open to the village, 19 members saved £24 8s 0d.

Wendling (24 members)

Knitted 93 comforts supplied to men from the village in the Forces, Territorial Welfare and Minesweepers. Received 50 evacuees and collected clothes for their benefit. Savings Group started by WI, open to village, 30 members, saved £16 10s 0d. Also helped with salvage.

Whitlingham (23 members)

Knitted 294 comforts for men serving from the village, Red Cross, Seaman and WVS. Received 2 evacuees. Collected a large amount of clothes for emergency hospital and evacuees. The local Savings Group was formed by the WI and was open to the village and had 125 members who saved £150 by December 1940. Members collected of salvage.

Doing 'their bit' in Holt - knitting garments for servicemen

Whissonsett and Horningtoft (49 members)

Knitted 137 comforts supplied to men from the village. Raised £16 6s 0d for wool. Received 75 evacuees and gave them a Christmas party from funds provided out of Preservation Scheme. Started the local Savings Scheme and had saved £3 17s 6d (School Savings £200). Helped with salvage and the Preservation Centre made 2,092 lbs. of jam.

Worstead (86 members)

Knitted 160 comforts and supplied the Norfolk Regiment and the County Centre. Received 20 adults and 40 children evacuees and helped supply them with clothes. Provided baths for a local Searchlight unit. Savings Group was started by WI and had saved £55 15s 6d. Worked for the Red Cross hospital. Made 55 articles from own material and made up 62 articles. Helped with salvage and was a Branch of Norfolk and Norwich War Charities Appeal Council.

Many members of the WI were also members of the Women's Voluntary Service, which had done so much to help in the evacuation schemes set up and ran rest centres for blitz casualties (the also provided relief cover for Incident Inquiry Points during the blitz freeing members of the ARP to do more hands on duties) as well as running a fleet of mobile canteens, their spirit, like that of so many women's services on the home front was indomitable.

In 1941 national WVS membership stood at over a million women and a notable venture was opened by the Norwich branch. A problem had emerged that despite being in uniformed organisations such as the Women's Land Army were not permitted to use forces canteens so The Elm Hill Club for 'Women in the Services, The Land Army and Nursing Services.' Excellent meals could be obtained here, there was also an information bureau, supplies of chocolate and cigarettes to buy and a lounge with a radio, newspapers and magazines, even a bath could be taken for 1/-. The club Superintendent was Molly Kent, a former Land Girl who was always especially pleased to welcome members of her 'old mob.' One Sunday is particularly recalled when the club was opened when members of the WLA from across the county attended a Church Parade at Norwich Cathedral during War Charities Week and they managed to feed over 100 Land Girls – a very welcome meal after some of them had travelled over 40 miles after doing the morning milking to attend the service! In the latter war years WVS established local centres with mobile Salvage Officer to supervise the various collections for the likes of rags, metal or paper. There would also be a Food Leader to co-ordinate local efforts and help people get to grips with rationing. The WVS also helped organise campaigns such as 'Warship Week', 'Wings for Victory' and 'Salute the Soldier'.

While on the subject of canteens and restaurants, it is now almost forgotten that restaurants were exempt from rationing, which led to a certain amount of resentment as the more affluent could supplement their food allowance by eating out. To restrict this, certain rules were put into force. No meal could cost more than five shillings; no meal could consist of more than three courses; meat and fish could not be served at the same sitting. For those who had not managed their coupons so-called 'Community Feeding Centres' later re-named British Restaurants were set up by the Ministry of Food across the country. Run by local committees on a non-profit making basis meals in British Restaurants came with their own restrictions. No customer could be served with a meal of more than one serving of meat, fish, game, poultry, eggs, or cheese purchased for maximum price of 9d or less. The standard of food was very dependent on the skill of the cooks and what food stuff were available; when all other meat sources were drying up there was always rabbit and wonders were often achieved with its creative use. Some restaurants certainly had their humour; one menu seen in Norwich, chalked on a restaurant black board promised 'Sea Pie – buy it and *See* what is in it!'

From late 1940 the Civil Defence organisation developed a more professional appearance. Berets were also issued (upon which could be worn the ARP badge) to be worn when not wearing the tin helmet and from early 1941 the distinctive dark navy 'battle dress' style blouse and trousers were issued to the men and fabric belted four pocket tunics with white metal buttons and trousers or skirts were issued to women. The ARP organization also phased out its old name in favour of 'Civil Defence' and upon these new uniforms a cloth roundel bearing the letters CD surmounted by a crown was sewn upon the pocket of the left breast, normally with a county designation 'Norfolk' displayed in a semi-circular box patch underneath.

In December 1941 Parliament passed the National Service Act, which called up unmarried women between 20 and 30 years old to join one of the auxiliary services. These were the ATS, the Women's Royal Naval Service (WRNS), the Women's Auxiliary Air Force (WAAF) and the Women's Transport Service. Married women were also later called up, although pregnant women and those with young children were exempt. Other options under the Act included joining the Women's Voluntary Service (WVS), which supplemented the emergency services at home, the British Red Cross Society, St John Ambulance Brigade or the Women's Land Army, helping on farms.

Below left: The temporary Cloverleaf Cafe at 29, St. Giles Street opened shortly after the original cafe was destroyed by a direct hit on the night of 30 April 1942

Below right: Civil Defence drivers, workers and rescue crews Coltishall c1944

There was also provision made in the Act for objection to service on moral grounds, as about a third of those on the conscientious objectors list were women. A number of women were prosecuted as a result of the Act, some even being imprisoned. Despite this, by 1943 about 9 out of 10 women were taking an active part in the war effort.

The St John Ambulance Brigade and British Red Cross Society came together again in the Joint War Organisation for the duration of the Second World War. Both organisations carried on their work running the county's ambulances. The *Report of The British Red Cross Society, Norfolk Branch* (1941) was keen to point out their members had maintained their peacetime duties in addition to those taken on for wartime:

'helping with tonsils and adenoids at the Jenny Lind Hospital and the Medical Officers of Health with Diphtheria Immunisation and the treatment of scabies, assisting with Hospital Libraries, working at Child Welfare clinics, sewing for the Norfolk and Norwich Hospital, manning and cleaning ambulances and helping the Village Nurse are also working full and part time in Convalescent Homes and Maternity Homes, relieving the permanent staff in Shelters and First Aid Posts.'

St John Ambulance men and a Red Cross Nurse at a casualty handling exercise at West Garth, North Walsham 1940

Thanks was also given in the Red Cross report to Miss Griffith and her band of helpers who had sorted, listed and packed the extra Hospital Supplies for the Invasion Committees of 678 villages in 'an amazingly short time' and had arranged their delivery through the First Aid Commandants.

Mobile Voluntary Aid Detachment volunteers were drawn from nearly every Red Cross Detachment and 178 of them had been posted to Naval, Military and Air Force Hospitals by 1941, a number of male members from St John Ambulance were also mobilized as members of the Auxiliary Sick Berth Reserve. Many members also worked in Civil Hospitals as Civil Nursing Reserves.

Although the call to the forces depleted their numbers, both Red Cross and St John Ambulance played a key role in the Civil Defence organisation in Norfolk. With so many men leaving for war women were trained as ambulance drivers. These girls were remarkable, they had to learn to drive very quickly, often under blackout conditions, and 'on the job' so as not to waste petrol. Along with male drivers they too drove and crewed ambulances sent by their Divisions and Detachments to help the rescue efforts during the blitz on London in 1940 and brought their ambulances to places in need across our own county, when it too was bombed. The ambulances were often the first emergency vehicles on the scene at many air crashes.

Red Cross and St John Ambulance units from across the county had instructors giving lectures to members, civil defence organisations and the general public in First Aid and Anti-Gas, they staffed Mobile Units, First Aid Posts, Air Raid Relief Vans and organised a Messenger Service staffed by cadets. The Thorpe Station Canteen was staffed by Red Cross and St John members between the hours of 9pm and 6am. When the canteen was destroyed by enemy action they carried on in a mobile van until new accommodation was found. Those who worked in the canteen gave up remarkable amounts of their time when they could be sleeping or at leisure; walking two or three miles in the blackout in all weathers to take their turn on the rota. Members also helped at the St Andrew's Hall Sick Bay and various centres of the Blood Transfusion Service, where many were themselves donors. There were Regimental Sick Quarters staffed by local Detachments at Sheringham, Holt and Blakeney and Auxiliary Hospitals staffed by volunteers from The British Red Cross Society and St John Ambulance J.W.O with army nurses and RAMC personnel at: Blofield Hall; Broome Place; Cranmer Hall, Sculthorpe; Denton House; Felthorpe Hall; Hardingham Hall; Hilborough Hall; Stow Bardolph Hall; Wroxham Hall; Pickenham Hall, South Pickenham and Woodbastwick Hall. Locally, the Red Cross and St John Joint War Organisation also did much to collect food items and comforts to be sent in 'Red Cross Parcels' to our Prisoners of War. A number of Red Cross Officers also undertook the duties of Liaison Officers who would assist and comfort families and Searchers who would undertake the necessary paperwork find the whereabouts of missing service relatives. Their efforts were greatly assisted by the fund raising events and mutual moral support of The Norfolk Prisoners of War Committee.

Below left: The nurses at Blofield Hall War Hospital

Below right: Some of the convalescent soldiers and three of the nurses at Pickenham Hall War Hospital, September 1942.

King's Lynn ambulance drivers, crew and depot team c1940

Norfolk St John & Red Cross Ambulances 1942

Reg. Number	Station	Garage	Officer –in –Charge
BAH 632	Attleborough	Dingle's Garage, High Street	Mrs Goodwille
BFN 972	Aylsham	Watt's Garage	Mrs. Carter
BFN 973	Cromer	East Coast Garage	Mr R. L. Randall
NG 5799	Cromer	East Coast Garage	Mr R. L. Randall
AAH 200	Downham Market	Church Road	Mr A. D. Marchant
BAH 171	East Dereham	J.J. Wright, High Street	Mr W C Pryke
DVF 551	Fakenham	Dr. Arthur's Yard	Mr C. B. Andrews
NG 9623	Fakenham	Dr. Arthur's Yard	Mr C. B. Andrews
DNG 919	Flegg	Francis' Garage, Martham	Mr F. S. Taylor
CPW 150	Holt	Holt Garage, Cromer Road	A/Supt. A.H. Colman
BNG 483	Hunstanton	Ducker's Garage	Mrs. A. S. Goddard
BNG 197	King's Lynn	Messrs. Johnson, James Street	Mr A. G. Williamson
NG 5168	North Walsham	Brentnall Plain	Supt. G. B. Fuller
ACL 100	Norwich	N&N Hospital	Mrs Sargent
ACL 929	Norwich	N&N Hospital	Mrs Sargent
NG 7554	Swaffham	White Hart Lane	Mr. W. B. Rix
BPW 516	Thetford	Earls Street	Mr N. C. Ley

Another remarkable, but in this case very local organisation, was established in Norwich between July 1940 and August 1941. The Mutual Aid Good Neighbours Association (M.A.G.N.A) was raised with the intention of co-operating with the ARP and other allied organisations to provide aid and assistance for the victims of air raids, particularly those who were suffering from shock and to alleviate the distress of those rendered homeless after an air raid. Staffed along the lines of the ARP an appeal was launched for over 2,000 volunteers to find a 'Street Mother' for every street. Her duty being to compile a list of aged and infirm residents and organise the householders to become good neighbours, finding out who could and would be prepared to help by temporarily offering their home to those in need after an air raid. The Organiser for the City was the indefatigable Mrs Ruth Hardy who saw MAGNA grow to over 30,000 Norwich women who offered their home as shelter and temporary accommodation to their neighbours; many of them also attended a course in basic first aid. Every one of them displayed a small yellow poster in their window stating 'A good neighbour lives here.'

Local wartime organisations and emergency services on parade in Reepham Market Place for their War Weapons Week, May 1941

Norfolk had suffered air raids and casualties since 1940 but the greatest challenge to all the volunteer organisations across the county on the home front came between 1941 and 1942 when Norfolk suffered its' most severe and sustained attacks from the air, especially in Great Yarmouth and in Norwich during the 'Baedeker Blitz' of 1942. The number of people who had been rendered homeless as a result of the first two 'Baedeker' raids on Norwich during the nights of 27/28 April and 29/30 April 1942 ran into the thousands but the relief efforts provided by the voluntary wartime organisations was truly magnificent. Among them the six YMCA vans who worked in relays to keep a constant flow of refreshment – their crews continued to report for duty even when the bombs were falling. The twenty Church Army vans in the city served 10,000 cups of tea during the raids as did the Salvation Army canteens and hundreds of meals were served by the eleven Rest Centres established by the Education Authority and welfare organisations.

A mobile unit consisting of three travelling vans and marquees was sent up from the City of London. Staffed by helpers who had honed their skills and experience during the London blitz, they established a relief depot at the Model Senior Girl's School on Dereham Road to provide shelter, replacement clothing and personal requisites to those who had been 'bombed out.' The Women's Voluntary Service also did sterling work serving tea to casualties at the hospital, provided the majority of the staff for the Rest Centres, supervised the removal of good furniture from bombed houses and distributed vast quantities of emergency clothing. MAGNA was also to the fore, many had sheltered people in their own homes, 400 temporary homes were found for the homeless and valuable assistance, advice and first aid was rendered by members across the city.

There were numerous acts of gallantry by both uniformed services and civilians during those nights of the blitz, many will go unrecognised but meant so much, sometimes even life and death, to many. One who was recognised was John Grix, one of our nation's youngest recipients of the British Empire Medal, one of the city's brave Civil Defence Messengers. He had lied about his age at the time of his deed, Messenger Service boys had to be 16 but John was just 15 years old when the sirens wailed on the nights of the blitz. Joan Banger relates his story in *Norwich at War*:

'He cycled two miles to duty through the heaviest bombed area, repeatedly jumping from his machine to lay flat as bombs whistled down, and, when passing one building that was blazing furiously, his hands were sprayed with acid shooting from its windows into the street. On arrival at his centre he reported for duty and throughout the night he obeyed instructions which included travelling through devastated parts of the City to lead firemen from the County to the various reported incidents.

The Messengers, unlike the other Civil Defence Services did their work singly. Not until hours later did this boy mention that first aid was necessary for his acid-burnt hands, and afterwards, when daylight came, he volunteered to join parties of rescue workers. That night he slept at the Report Centre and the following day helped wherever he could in the city. When the siren again sounded he once more made many nightmare journeys during which he was blown from his machine five times.'

The King shares a smile with Civil Defence Messenger hero John Grix BEM (16) during his surprise visit to Norwich 13 October 1942

On Tuesday 13 October 1942 HM King George VI paid a surprise visit to the city of Norwich to inspect the damage and meet some of those who had done so much to help others during the bombing of the city. All manner of personnel from St John Ambulance and Civil Defence Workers to Home Guard, Nurses, Salvation Army workers, National Fire Service, Police and members of the WVS paraded in front of Norwich City Hall. Such was the secrecy many of them did not realise they were to be inspected by the King. The King paused and shared a few words with young John Grix and Police Inspector Buttle who had also been awarded the BEM for his work in bomb reconnaissance. His Majesty then spoke to Mrs Ruth Hardy, the MAGNA organiser. The King was unfamiliar with the MAGNA badge she wore on her Civil Defence uniform, when she explained it stood for Mutual Aid Good Neighbours' Association the King smiled and said 'Mrs Hardy, there is too little friendship in the world today, do keep up this wonderful work.'

The work of all the home front organisations carried on throughout the war years, their efforts often taking different directions as various demands arose or schemes and initiatives were introduced by the various government ministries. By the latter years of the war many of the children who had been evacuated had returned home again only to have to be evacuated from the London area again during V-Weapon attacks of 1944 and the Billeting Officers, WVS, WI, Red Cross and St John rose to the challenge again. During July 1944 over 3,000 evacuees arrived by train at Norwich, Diss, King's Lynn and Thetford and were found homes with families in the city, town and surrounding villages. Thousand more followed over the ensuing weeks and problems with re-homing them soon developed and evacuees had to sleep in rest centres and ex-military billets as pressure was applied on unwilling households. By

*The King's Lynn Civil
Defence wardens, report and
control and rescue workers
1944*

the first week in September 1944 an estimated 20,000 evacuees had come to the county and with the situation becoming intolerable government announcements were made to the effect that they anticipated the flying bomb attacks would end within a fortnight and within a week evacuees had begun to return home to London again.

In April 1945, the Government sent out travel arrangement information for the return of evacuees to their homes after the cessation of hostilities in Europe. The scheme commenced in early May and by July 1945 most evacuees had returned to London. In August 1945 there were still a number of evacuated children and adults who remained in reception areas; most of them had no home to return to because it had been destroyed in the blitz or in the case of evacuee children their parents had been killed or they simply did not wish to return. The evacuation scheme was officially terminated in March 1946.

*The Queen Elizabeth appreciation scroll sent after the war
to all those who shared their home with evacuees in 1939.*

6 On the Land

The farming lessons of the First World War were well observed in 1939. The long cold winters, flooding and subsequent bad harvests saw our food supply become a matter of concern in the latter years of the Great War so every effort was going to be made to ensure this Second World War did not become a war of attrition. Just one month after the outbreak of war the Ministry of Agriculture launched the 'Dig for Victory' scheme that saw private gardens, park land and estates turned into allotments not only provide essential crops for families and neighbourhoods alike, but help the war effort by freeing up valuable space for war materials on the merchant shipping convoys.

Leading the way in the county was the estate of HM King George VI at Sandringham where 50 acres were put under the plough in October with another 50 planned soon after. Norfolk farmers, in the main, entered into the spirit of the scheme and at a meeting of the Norfolk War Agricultural Executive Committee in April 1940 it was announced that more than the county's quota of 25,000 acres of new land had been ploughed and that farmer had promised to plough another 12,000. Matter became far more pressing in May 1940 as the situation in France deteriorated and few were left in any doubt that Britain would soon be standing alone and the ploughing of land would no longer be a patriotic gesture but a necessity and the War Agricultural Executive Committees (WAEC) across the country were given greater powers to ensure this was done. This process began with a quick but detailed survey of the county's farms to assess their produce potential and to decide if the farm was properly equipped and efficiently managed to fulfil that potential.

If there was a problem the WAEC could arrange the loan of machinery or supply seed, fertilizers or lime on deferred terms if necessary, indeed some farmers productivity increased by 200 – 300 per cent. There were even some instances of the WAEC making an agreement with the farmer to farm his land themselves. Farmers who failed to comply with cultivation orders could face a court appearance and a fine; in one instance in May 1940 a Fincham farmer was brought before Downham Market Petty Sessions for failing to cultivate 100 acres of land ordered by the Norfolk War Agricultural Committee under the Defence of the Realm Act. The farmer pleaded 'Guilty of a technical offence' but the chairman

Tractor and binder harvesting a field 'somewhere in North Norfolk' August 1940. (GFWM)

Queen Elizabeth talks with one of the Land Army girls on the Sandringham Estate, August 1942

of the Bench left him in no doubt: 'We are of the opinion that more than a technical offence has been committed and that it was a deliberate attempt to evade the law.' The farmer was fined £100 and ordered to pay costs. If all else failed the WAEC had the power to requisition the farmer's land, it would then be farmed under the auspices of the War Ag or let to an approved tenant. There was no means of appeal against the decision of the War Agricultural Committee.

The successful farms flourished including Sandringham. During their visit in August 1943 The King, Queen Elizabeth and Princesses Elizabeth and Margaret inspected the results of the Sandringham Estate's war-time food production. The harvest of wheat produced 60 to 70 bushels an acre and potatoes showed yields up to 12 tons to the acre – the result of a comprehensive plan carried out with the help and advice of the Norfolk War Agricultural Committee and was followed keenly and personally by the King who had received detailed monthly progress reports. Altogether some 1,433 acres were being farmed on the estate of which 977 were arable – 537 of which had been ploughed since the beginning of the war. A new dairy herd had also been started and was showing an increase in milk production. All suitable grass in Sandringham Park had been put to the plough. Six acres of lawn in front of the house were producing rye while beetroot and parsnips filled the beds of the ornamental flower garden. Beside the church was growing a fine crop of oats and the golf course in the park was growing oats and rye.

The King and Queen with the young Princesses watch as Land Girl demonstrates a mechanised bailer on the Sandringham Estate, August 1942

The flax crop produced over 3½ tons of high quality flax to the acre but the most impressive achievement was the ditching, draining and ploughing of 476 acres of Sandringham Marshes. This land was rich permanent pasture but by 1943 it was all food production including peas, beans, mustard, wheat and oats. The farms were highly mechanised with corn crops gathered in by combine harvester and a mechanised bailer that the Royal party observed being operated by a Land Girl, just one of 14 members of the Women's Land Army working on the estate.

The Fen country between Thetford and Downham Market had also proved to be a worthwhile venture and 1,500 acres near Feltwell were cultivated by the War Ag and handed over to a private enterprise farming company. Including extant farm land, well over 750,000 acres of Norfolk farmland was brought under the plough during the Second World War. Although some farm jobs such as experienced cow or pig men were protected as 'reserved occupations' many members of the agricultural workforce were mobilised and called away to war so if farming was to carry on and expand in wartime the shortfall in the workforce had to be addressed.

The valuable role played by the members of the Women's Land Army during the First World War was not forgotten and plans for the establishment of a Women's Land Army (WLA) to fill the gap left by farm workers called up to military service were laid early in 1938, when the organisation began a register of volunteers. It was always made clear that the WLA would be headed, managed, administered and staffed entirely by women under the aegis of the Ministry of Agriculture and Fisheries. By June 1938, WLA county committees for local administration, recruitment, enlistment and placement were established. In February 1939 Lady Gertrude Denman, a First World War stalwart and leading light of the National Federation of Women's Institutes since 1917, accepted the post of Honorary Director of the WLA, and offered her home at Balcombe Place, near Haywards Heath in West Sussex, for its headquarters. In Norfolk the County Committee consisting of a Chairman and eight members was established during the Spring of 1939. All of them had a connection with the land, a number of them were wives of farmers, some had Women's Institute connections; the original members were: Chairman: The Dowager Lady Suffield (Cromer), Miss M. Betts (Bramerton), Miss B. Burgess (Brooke), Mrs W D Everington (Little Dunham), Mrs Hafen (Hempstead by Holt), Mrs Harrison (Tilney St Lawrence), Mrs Jameson (Thetford), Mrs A M Keith (West Barsham) and Miss K Waters (Herringby). Miss Iris Tillett was appointed Country Secretary, (one of the youngest women to receive such an appointment in the country) a position she maintained with enthusiasm and great vigour through the war and into peacetime and it was to her that were issued the first batches of forms for interviews, enrolment, uniform measurements and medicals. The Norfolk WLA County Office was courtesy of the Norfolk Federation of Women's Institutes who gave the use of a large room on the second floor of their offices and two of their staff at 3 Castle Street, Norwich (removed in 1941 to larger premises on Price of Wales Road). The Women's Land Army was officially formed on 1 June 1939, and a grand recruitment campaign was launched, which included a prominent section appealing for volunteers in the *National Service* booklet of 1939, sent to every household in Great Britain. This was quite a coup.

The title Women's Land Army was always something of a misnomer because this was always a civilian organisation, operating under the auspices of the Ministry of Agriculture, and not subject to military discipline. However, some Land Girls did work in secure areas and came under military law. Some were bound by the provisions of the Official Secrets Act if they worked on sites such as Thetford Forest where camouflage experiments and tank manoeuvres were carried out. When war broke out, some 17,000 volunteers had registered with the 52 county offices and over 1,000 girls were dispatched immediately to placements on farms. More girls joined during the massive recruitment campaign during the last week of April 1940. A grand exhibition of the work of the WLA was staged in St Andrew's Hall, Norwich; even the County Office moved to the Hall for the week and recruiting meetings were held at King's Lynn and Great Yarmouth.

WLA recruits came from a wide variety of backgrounds. There were both city and country girls among them, and most were young, often in their late teens, and officially joining 'for patriotic reasons'. Most will admit today that they chose the WLA in preference to military call-up or work in a munitions factory. Above all, Land Girls wanted to 'get away from it all' - a good enough reason to escape from humdrum jobs and stifling homes. Many female conscientious objectors joined the WLA. After sending off a written application, girls would be invited to an interview to assess their suitability. They were questioned by a board of at least two members of their local Agricultural Committee. The minimum age for enlistment in the WLA was seventeen and a half, but it appears that girls of 17 were often accepted, and even 16-year-olds if they looked as if they were strong enough to do the work. A medical examination was required, but in many cases this was a quick question and answer session with the doctor when he would ask about 'wheeziness,' flat feet and varicose veins. The successful applicant would then be required to commit herself to the Land Army for the duration of the war by signing a form upon which she would 'promise to abide by the conditions of training and employment of the Women's Land Army' which then entrusted 'its good name' into her hands. Girls could leave if they married, or transferred to other war work. The upper age limit seems to have been 50, but many older women with relevant experience or social position occupied management positions in the organisation.

In the early years of the war Norfolk farmers preferred to have an extra pair of willing hands to 'lend a hand on the land' and the girls could be found a place on a farm without any previous training and would be taught by practical experience as they went along. A uniform was issued, consisting of two short-sleeved Aertex shirts, one green ribbed V-neck pullover, one pair of brown corduroy breeches, two

One of the Norfolk Land Girls

pairs of fawn coloured knee-length socks, one pair of shoes, one bib and brace overall, one hat (described as a brown 'pork pie' type), one pair of rubber boots, a short mackintosh (never desperately well waterproofed), a belted 'duster coat' and an armband, normally worn only on parade (although they were often slipped on work clothing for publicity photographs.) Awards were made of half 'diamond' cloth service badges representing six months of service – a full diamond denoting a full year. Proficiency tests in separate specialist skills as general farm work, milking, poultry keeping, tractor driving and market gardening – if the candidate proved herself proficient she would receive a certificate and a proficiency badge. Later in the war, a smart three-quarter length brown Melton overcoat, designed by the couturier Worth, was issued. A green necktie, with the letters WLA striped across it, was also issued, but had to be bought in some counties.

Uniforms were normally sent to the girl's home in a parcel, but some got a rapid placement and only received their uniform after they had arrived at a farm. Although far from flattering, the girls did what they could to make the best of their uniform for 'walking out' and parades. Some strung a bootlace through the hat to stop it blowing off in the wind, enabling them to wear it 'cowgirl' style, perched on the back to the head like a heroine in a Tom Mix film. Many girls found their bib and brace overalls too hot in the summer and cut the legs down to shorts. The 'city girls' (all those with no knowledge of working the countryside) certainly made a song and dance of getting into and walking around in gumboots. The sheer ineptitude of some city girls led to many funny tales and cartoons in local and national newspapers, but the farmers found their antics both frustrating and costly. They damaged tractors and machinery, while some even confused male and female livestock, with unfortunate results. Most of these girls were also shocked at the lack of toilet facilities in the fields. Iris Tillett, the Norfolk County Secretary recalled "...country life was in some ways rather primitive by town standards; water had to be drawn from a well, there was an earth closet down the garden path instead of an indoor lavatory, no bathroom but occasionally a tub in front of the kitchen fire and neither gas nor electricity. We always tried to warn volunteers of this during their interview but to one who had never lived outside a crowded city, this was beyond imagination and the story is told of the recruit who returned to her County Office in tears after three weeks saying 'It's just like you said it was and I can't stand it.'

Training the girls before placing them on farms was the only answer, and soon four- to six-week training programmes on four farms in the county and at agricultural colleges in the Midlands or Suffolk. Standard training consisted of milking by hand and machine, animal husbandry, tractor driving and hand work such as 'chopping out' with a hoe, followed by oral, practical and written examinations. Later, training establishments developed regimes that were tailored to regional requirements as well as running specialist courses in hedge laying, pest control and even thatching. However, if there was a great demand for help on the land, often at harvest time, girls would still be sent off without training.

At first, each county had its own rate of wages were paid by the farmers who employed Land Girls, the minimum weekly wage (for 48 hours work) for girls over the age of 18 of 28s 0d.. After 1942 the County War Agricultural Executive Committees took over the employment and payment of WLA girls and a National minimum wage of 32s 0d was set, of which 12s 6d was to be left over for each girl's personal needs after paying for her lodgings. The girls were supposed to be employed on the same terms and conditions as other farm employees. A maximum working week of 48 hours in the winter and 50 in the summer was agreed, although most girls and farm labourers working for far longer. Some girls were even expected to do their field work *and* help the farmer's wife around the house, carrying coal and cleaning grates. This was strictly against WLA rules, for Land Girls were 'outdoor workers'. It was also agreed that the girls should have guaranteed holidays and sick pay, most girls working a five and a half day week, with Saturday afternoons and Sundays off. The farmer might even show his appreciation with an extra couple of bob, or a few fresh eggs. There were, however, concerns over the land girls being lonely and isolated. With a sterling contribution from the Norfolk Federation of WIs a system of WLA Local Representatives was established across the county from the summer of 1940. The name of the local representative was given to all land girls in the village as a person she could go to for friendship and help. Representatives would also be asked to make contact with potential employers and check her lodgings were acceptable and would visit the land girl at least once a month and report back to county headquarters. All WLA girls stationed more than 20 miles from home were also granted a railway warrant for a visit home every six months.

The girls worked the same day, from sun up to sundown, as the men on the farm, but many were not housed on the farms where they worked, but in hostels which were often country houses converted for the purpose. So the girls had to get up very early to be bussed in, often on the back of a lorry or in an open trailer behind a tractor. Their work varied, like all farm work through the year, from ploughing and sowing and planting to harvesting. The most popular tasks were haymaking, looking after chickens, milking or working with livestock but, as ever, mucking out and the hard, dusty job of harvesting cereals was never popular. Many farms were not able to replace their worn-out machinery, and some even had to resort to horse power and long redundant reaper-binders and hand ploughs when petrol was short. Crops such as sugar beet and potatoes were lifted by hand.

It would also be remiss of me not to mention the forestry workers working for the forestry commission in Thetford Forest. Originally members of the WLA this work grew so much a Women's Timber Corps was formed as separate arm of the WLA in April 1942 and were seconded to the Home Timber Production Department of the Ministry of Supply who took over responsibility for their placement, billeting and welfare for the duration of the war. The Timber Corps girls or 'Lumber Jills' as they were affectionately known, would have attended a four week training course to learn use of the saw, bill hook and axe. Once given their placement much of their work was extremely hard, cutting wood for railway sleepers and pit props. The Timber Corps had 6,000 members nationally, had their own cap badge and distinctive green beret.

In Norfolk and a number of other counties, women who could only give a limited amount of time to working on the land formed their own organisation; in our county it was known as the Norfolk Women's Auxiliary Land Corps (NWALC) often affectionately referred to as the 'Home Guard of the Land'. Formed under the guidance of the Norfolk War Agricultural Committee with Miss I. M. Hoare as Women's Organiser and offices at 26, The Close, Norwich and representatives in many villages across the county membership was open to any women who could give some time away from their normal work such as soldier's wives living temporarily in the villages, women evacuated from bombed areas, school teachers, older girls in their holidays. There were also a large body of members of the NWALC who were women considered too old for the WLA, many of these ladies had also served in the Land Army or similar organisations during the First World War.

Unlike the WLA the Auxiliaries could not be deployed away from their home locale but their work was very similar as they found themselves employed in the likes of weeding, hoeing. Sugar beet singling, pea, fruit and potato picking, carrot pulling and harvesting and they carried a membership card and wore an orange arm band (stencilled with 'Norfolk Women's Auxiliary Land Corps' the arms of the county backed by hoe, sickle, pitch fork and surmounted by a what sheaf) when they were working. Applications could also be sent to Miss Hoare for a place at one of four fruit-picking camps for holiday makers established in the county at Westwick Fruit Farm, Emneth, Terrington St John and Upwell in June and running to September 1943. It was a bumper fruit harvest year and an appeal was launched for 3,000 pickers at a rate of 300 a week. Holidaymakers were asked to give no fewer than four days at a time, longer if possible. Living costs were fixed at 4s a day for men and 3s 6d for women, uptake was remarkable with all places were filled by civilians and by both British and Commonwealth troops on leave.

After a number of bad experiences in living conditions and to help alleviate the old problem of loneliness for Land Girls hostels for between 12 -50 girls were set up across the county with their own wardens, cooks and domestics. The original hostels were: Longland House at Holkham Park (first to open on 29 June 1942 with accommodation for 32 girls), Crow Hall in Downham Market, Bale Rectory, West Rudham Vicarage and Lingwood Rectory. These were soon followed by the Shooting Box

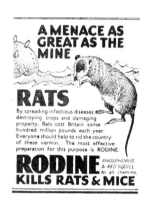

Women's Land Army Rally at Mannington Hall c1942

at North Creake, Barton Bendish Hall, Thurning Hall, Dilham House and Woodton Old Hall. There were also four county organisers in the North, South and East of the county working from bases in their own areas. Their duties were to oversee the employers (particularly addressing the perennial problem of the employers not paying the wages correctly), employees and the hostels for their local land girls; they made a daily telephone report to county headquarters and would come in once a week to see the County Secretary.

At its peak in 1943, the WLA counted 80,000 active members in its ranks. In that same year Norfolk WLA got its first commodious premises all of its own in a requisitioned house at 9 Christchurch Road with, at its height, some 21 staff. By May 1944 there were over 1,650 land girls working in Norfolk.

Although Land Girls did join in the stand-down and Victory parades, the WLA did not stop working in peacetime. Many girls did return home, and others left to marry in the years after 1945 - the Women's Timber Corps was disbanded in 1946 - but 8,000 members of the WLA carried on through the darkest days of post-war austerity and rationing. The Women's Land Army was finally disbanded in 1950.

Members of the Women's Land Army from across Norfolk after a Thanksgiving Service at Norwich Cathedral 1945.

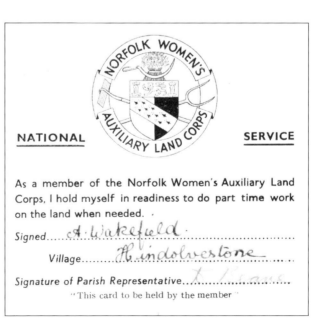

Membership Card for the Norfolk Women's Auxiliary Land Corps

7 The Royal Norfolk Regiment and The Norfolk Yeomanry 1939–1945

The following accounts are based on the short accounts supplied by the officers of the battalions of The Royal Norfolk Regiment published in The Britannia (1946)

Regular Army
1st Battalion

When war was declared 1 Royal Norfolk were in Delhi, India and did not return to the UK until May 1940 after nearly 17 years in foreign stations. On 6 November after completion of foreign service leave, the battalion mobilized and formed part of 20 Guards Independent Brigade and entered into a comprehensive training programme. In August 1941 battalion moved to 24 Guards (Independent) Brigade Group and moved to Wimbledon to man the 'Brown Line' Defences of London and remained there until September 1942. During this time many Londoners filled the ranks of the battalion. Despite the war widening and great strides being made in the Western Desert 1 Royal Norfolk were still not deployed for active service but yet more changes of location and training at home with 79 Armoured Division in Northern Command in the Knaresborough area. In March 1943 the battalion and the other units serving in 185 Brigade were to be transferred to 3 Infantry Division and the spirits of the men surged high as it was known that 'Iron Division' was earmarked as a high priority for overseas service and was being specially trained for mountain warfare. Proceeding to Belford in Northumberland the training was even more arduous than before – forty eight hour treks and full war scale were carried out with our boys carrying 60lb loads over mountainous country, and not one of them fell out. On 30 May 1943 the battalion arrived at Inverary to begin assault training. The course continued for 17 days and by the end of it the battalion was well versed in the undertaking required by combined operations and the tasks required for consolidating a beachhead in the face of enemy opposition. After more exercises at Forres in Morayshire in January and 'Exercise Crown' in February where the battalion moved to Invergordon in 1944. April saw the end of the assault exercises in Scotland and the battalion left for the south of England on 12 April and arrived the following day at Camp J.9 at Haywards Heath in Sussex. One last exercise, Operation Fabius, was staged in the Chichester area in May and then the battalion was returned to camp for the final preparations before they departed on the greatest task - Operation Overlord.

Sergeants Mess, 1st Battalion, The Royal Norfolk Regiment, Halleaths, Dumfrieshire, Christmas 1943.

At 22.15 hours on 3 June the battalion proceeded to Newhaven and embarked in three LCI's with the transport in LCT's, the first crossing was postponed and the men disembarked. Their morale was not diminished, keyed up and ready to go at 23.00 hours on 4 June a signal was received that the convoy would weigh and proceed the following morning and at 1000 hours on 5 June the craft put to sea. It was a rough crossing and many of the men were seasick before they were half way across the Channel – then and only then the seals on the maps were broken and for the first time they saw exactly where they were going (previously the terrain and maps had been studied in detail but all objectives had been given code names.

1 Royal Norfolk landed on Queen Red Sector of Sword Beach at 09.50, as the ramps of the landing craft were dropped the men poured out and were expecting a wade ashore but for most it was almost a dry landing and the men scrambled ashore amid shell and mortar fire. For most of the battalion it was their first experience of enemy fire. The battalion reached its concentration area near Periers-sur-le-Dan in good order and at 1200 hours proceeded towards their first objective, high ground over-looking Caen to the left and Lebisey Wood to the right but were A and B Company were held up by machine gun fire from an enemy strongpoint on a feature known on the operations map as 'Hillman'. In the meantime the remainder of the battalion had moved farther round the left flank and by-passing the opposition captured a feature which later became known as 'Norfolk House' on the Caen canal. It took until 8 July for Lebisey Wood to be cleared of enemy; casualties had been heavy and occurred mainly during the severe shelling and mortar fire the men of the battalion had come under as they consolidated the gains. On 11 July the battalion was pulled back to Blainville for four all too brief days of rest (the first since they landed). On 15 July they were in action again to consolidate the capture of Caen with the final objective of Falaise; they faced heavy opposition as they fought through Ranville, Heronville and Manneville Wood.

On 3 August the advance to the east saw the battalion attack and consolidate La Chapelle. On the following day they attacked La Bistiere, a victory that was to prove to be hard won. Major Ian MacGillivray commanding 'A' Company came under heavy shell fire as they approached the start line and incurred a number of casualties. Major MacGillivray, despite being under fire, immediately went round his men restoring confidence by his personal disregard of the danger and brought them to the line on time. During the attack his personal leadership and encouragement came to the fore again as he led and cheered the men on to their objective.

Major Hubert Holden was in command of 'D' Company and he personally led his men throughout the advance. He located one enemy tank which was holding up the company and his example of cool courage inspired his men, although they had suffered very heavily pressing home their attack. The Spirit of his company never faltered, due to his personal bravery in the face of heavy odds his company reached their objective and drove the enemy back. In the same action Sgt Hanson was in command of a forward platoon of D Company, his leadership and courage had brought his depleted platoon almost to their objective when they were held up by a road swept by enemy fire. Hanson led eight of his men across, losing four while doing so, but forced the German tank that had been holding up the company to withdraw. For their outstanding bravery in this action Major MacGillivray, Major Holden were each awarded the Military Cross and Sgt. Hanson, the Military Medal for Bravery in the Field.

The 11 Armoured Division had been pushing towards the Vire - Vassy Road, ahead of the Division were 3 Monmouth at Sourdevalle and 1 Royal Norfolk were ordered to relieve them on 6 August. Two companies had taken over but before the remainder could do so the enemy opened up with a heavy artillery bombardment followed by a counter attack led by Tiger tanks supported by infantry from the Panzergrenadiers of 10 SS Panzer Division. Facing them near the hamlet of Pavee hidden deep in the bocage about 5 miles east of Vire were the men of 'B' and 'C' Companies.

Cockney Londoner Acting Corporal Sidney Bates (23) was commanding the right forward section of 'B' Company which had already suffered casualties as the counter attack came in. There were some 50-60 enemy in this attack, supported by mortars and machine guns. Seeing the situation had become desperate Bates got up and charged at them firing his Bren gun from the hip and despite being almost immediately wounded and knocked down by machine gun fire he recovered himself quickly and continue his advance towards the enemy spraying a deadly hail from his Bren as he went. His action had silenced much of the enemy machine gun and rifle fire but mortar bombs continued to fall all around him. He was then hit for the second time and much more seriously and painfully wounded. Undaunted, he staggered to his feet again and continued towards the enemy. His constant firing continued until the enemy started to withdraw before him. At this moment, he was hit for the third time by mortar bomb splinters - a wound that was to prove mortal. He again fell to the ground but continued to fire his weapon until his strength left him. This was not, however, until the enemy had withdrawn and the situation in this locality had been restored. Two stretcher-bearers risked their lives to bring the mortally wounded Sidney Bates in from the battlefield, one of them was a well-loved regimental and local character, L/Cpl. Ernie Seaman (he was later awarded the Military Medal). But nothing could be done for Corporal Bates who died shortly afterwards of the wounds he had received but by his supreme gallantry and self-sacrifice he had personally restored what had been a critical situation and he was posthumously awarded the Victoria Cross.

Later in August the battalion received reinforcements including the equivalent of an entire company from 7 Royal Norfolk after their battalion was disbanded after receiving severe casualties during the Battle of Epron. With rest, reinforcements and re-equipment the battalion was back to strength and ready for action. The German retreat had seen them fall back through France, Belgium and half of Holland. The battalion crossed from Belgium to Holland over the Escaut Canal in September and only a few days after their cross were ordered forward to occupy the town of Helmond. The men of 1 Royal Norfolk approached with caution, every weapon at the ready but were met with rapturous joy from an immense crowd of cheering civilians who gave our boys a flag waving welcome

In October the battalion were ordered forward to concentrate in a wooded area on the edge of the Reichwald Forest. On 4 October 10 Platoon 'B' Company was pinned down by snipers and L/Sjt. Ted Shepherd (22) was sent forward with his section to locate and destroy them, this he did, then rejoined the platoon for the final attack. Ted was a tall and powerfully built man, what happened next is recorded in his citation:

A/Cpl. Sidney Bates VC

In the assault on the main strongpoint, this NCO led his men forward with the utmost courage and coolness. Heavy small-arms fire was encountered and a 5cn mortar was active. As he assaulted the enemy trenches his Sten gun jammed. Confronted by 2 of the enemy, he threw it at them and then leaped after it empty handed into the trench. Sgt. Shepherd seized both by the neck and banged their heads together with such force that they temporarily lost control. He dragged them out, assisted by another member of his section, and using his fists rendered them completely docile. The Platoon, having completed its task, returned with the prisoners.

Sgt Shepherd was later evacuated as it was discovered he had fractured his knuckles while dealing bare-fisted with the enemy. His courage, cool-headedness and leadership were of outstanding quality and an inspiration to his section, which was 75% untried in battle. His control was remarkable throughout, and the success of the whole operation was mainly due to the two actions fought within the framework of the play by this NCOs Section.'

CSM Ted Shepherd MM

Ted was awarded the Military Medal for Bravery in the Field and was later promoted to CSM, the youngest in 1 Royal Norfolk.

Beyond the Reichswald forest and towards the heart of Nazi Germany the Allied advance slowed down as the German resistance became stronger. After numerous moves 1 Royal Norfolk settled at Overloon where it was ordered to take up a position astride the Overloon - Venraij road. The advance was a difficult one and hard fighting occurred at the Molan Book waterway near Venraij. In just 4 days the battalion suffered 211 men killed, wounded and missing. After weeks of local patrolling and small attacks the Battalion captured Ouisterham and Wanssum and by Christmas they had found themselves at Haps occupying a length of the River Maas. In January, after a period in reserve, the Battalion was again on the advance and entered Goch in Germany on 25 February 1945. From here an attack was made on Kervenheim where it had to fight its way over a rectangular sward 1,000yds by 800yds, which lay between it and the objective. After a severe battle 1 Royal Norfolk incurred 165 casualties but the enemy was beaten and retired from his strong position.

The next attack was on the village of Kapellin which was surrounded by a natural water obstacle on almost all sides. By a well-planned night attack the battalion moved through the outer defences of the Siegfried Line and threatened the German's positions to such an extent they eventually retired. After a period of rest the battalion marched on towards the Rhine. On 23 March the Allies crossed the Rhine , the 1 Royal Norfolk crossing on the 29 March and halting at Rees. They then moved back into Holland, via Lichtenvoorde and Enschende, for an attack on Lingen, a small German town on the east bank of the Ems

Men of 1st Battalion, The Royal Norfolk Regiment listening to the radio and examining maps for the forthcoming night's patrols, Venraij, Holland, November 1944.

Canal. The battalion crossed an intact bridge and following fierce house to house combat took the town the following day. From Lingen and after a stiff fight for Brinkum, where the battalion sustained 12 casualties (the enemy suffered 60 dead and 5 Officers and 203 other ranks were taken prisoner), the Battalion headed for Bremen.

On 25 April the battalion were due to cross the flooded plain to the city, but at the last minute were diverted through Arsten and attack Habenhausen. The attack was a success and on the 26 April the battalion marched into Bremen. There was no more serious fighting and by 5 May 1945 all offensive operations had been cancelled. Luckily when the news of VE Day arrived the men if 1 Royal Norfolk were at the gates of Becks Brewery. Of that day the late Captain John Talbot, the battalion's Royal Artillery Liaison Officer simply recorded: 'Becks Brewery emptied.' After VE Day the Battalion moved to Minden where it ended its campaign as part of the Army of Occupation in Germany.

2nd Battalion

The 2nd battalion had been on Garrison duties in Gibraltar since March 1937 when it set sail to return to Britain again on 18 January 1939. On arrival at Southampton it came under Aldershot Command and was stationed at Guardeloupe Barracks, Bordon Camp as part of 4 Infantry Brigade. The spring and summer of 1939 were spent on hard and continuous training and was at a high state of fitness and efficiency when the order to mobilize was received at 1640 hours on 1 September 1939.

Movement orders were received on 13 September and a small advance party left for Southampton. On 16 September the battalion's motor transport left for Avonmouth where they were to embark for St. Nazaire. The remainder of the battalion left for Southampton on 20 September where it embarked aboard the M.V.'s Royal Daffodil and Royal Sovereign and landed at Cherbourg in the early hours of 21 September becoming the first complete infantry unit of the B.E.F. to land in France. On the same day the battalion entrained for the brigade assembly area at Noyen and marched to its billets in the Commune of Pirmil (Sarthe).

In early October the battalion moved up to the forward area on the Franco-Belgian border, near Rumigies where it took over from the French 201st Regt. d'Infanterie. The next two and a half months were spent digging trenches and anti-tank ditches to continue the defensive system beyond the Maginot Line. On 24 December the battalion entrained for the Saar and arrived at Metz on 25 December. It took a further five days marching in the freezing cold by night and laying up by day to reach the front relieving 1 Black Watch on 1 January 1940.

This sector was on the extreme left of the Maginot Line and consisted of three lines; the *Ligne de Contact* was the front line, the *Ligne de Recuil* or fall back position and the *Ligne de Resistance* which comprised the Maginot Forts proper. During the brigade's stay in this sector each battalion occupied each line in rotation for a period of five days at a time.

Field Marshal Montgomery decorating CSM Tom Catlin for his bravery at the Battle of Sourdeval on 6 August 1944.

Men of 1ˢᵗ Battalion, The Royal Norfolk Regiment entering Wanssum, November 1944

General Georges inspecting a Guard of Honour from 2ⁿᵈ Battalion, The Royal Norfolk Regiment at Marchiennes, France, early 1940.

The duties of the battalion consisted mainly of wiring, reinforcement of defences and night patrols. One of these patrols on the bright moonlit night of January 3-4 1940 consisted of three men under Captain Peter Barclay and Lieut. C. R. Murray-Brown, sent to reconnoitre the enemy positions around the railway station at Waldwisse. After crossing about half a mile of no-man's land Captain Barclay led the search of a house that proved to be empty. Leaving the rest of the patrol behind to give covering fire if required, Captain Barclay took L/Cpl. M. H. 'Mick' Davis with him to penetrate further to ascertain the location and strength of the enemy's defensive posts. They ran into barbed wire and were at once subjected to rifle fire which effectively gave away the German positions. After a sharp exchange of grenades and small arms fire Captain Barclay and L/Cpl Davis managed to work their way clear and the patrol withdrew without loss. For their coolness and resource Captain Barclay and L/Cpl. Davis were given immediate awards of The Military Cross and the Military Medal respectively, while the remainder of the patrol were Mentioned in Despatches. These were the very first gallantry awards made to any members of the BEF in the Second World War.

The battalion returned to Rumigies on 20 January and were again engaged improving defences until the enemy offensive of early May 1940. Hitler had unleashed his blitzkrieg (lightening war) and the men of the 2nd Battalion were soon deployed to a variety of positions along the River Dyle to counter the enemy attacks. By 20 May the situation for the entire BEF had become critical and the battalion had fallen back and was lining the banks of the River Escaut, south of Tournai. Fighting was hard and many Officers and men were wounded and had to be evacuated. The following day the attack continued, one incident was recorded in the *London Gazette* of 23 August, 1940:

On 21 May, 1940, when his company was holding a position on the line of the River Escaut, south of Tournai. The enemy succeeded in breaking through beyond the company's right flank, which was consequently threatened. C.S.M. Gristock organised a party of eight and went forward to cover the right flank. An enemy machine gun was inflicting heavy casualties on his company, and he went on to try to put it out of action. Advancing under heavy fire, he was severely wounded in both legs. He nevertheless gained his fire position, and by well aimed rapid fire killed the crew and put the machine gun out of action. He dragged himself back, but refused to be evacuated until the line had been made good. By his gallant action the position of the company was secured and many casualties prevented. C.S.M. Gristock has since died of his wounds.' For his supreme gallantry and sacrifice CSM George Gristock (35) was awarded the Victoria Cross. A good CSM and a tough fighting man, remembered for his mess trick of taking a bite from a beer glass, was buried in Brighton City Cemetery, Sussex. After the war his parents, George and Edith Emily Gristock, of Sandhurst, Berkshire presented his VC and medals to the Regiment.

CSM George Gristock VC

On 22 May the enemy attacked in strength and further casualties were sustained by the battalion. Orders were then received to withdraw to the Gort Line at midnight. The battalion proceeded to route march to Bois de Wannenhein where it was embossed for La Bassée in the Béthune sector. After a few hours rest the battalion took up position on the Béthune-Estaires Canal in the locale of Paradis. Over the ensuing days the fighting and the opposing enemy troop concentrations grew more intense. By 26 May the BEF was in fighting retreat and the 2nd Battalion Royal Norfolk Regiment were part of the rear guard of the BEF evacuating from Dunkirk. Casualties had steadily increased but orders came the position was to be held to the last man and the last man and the men of the battalion fought on with grim determination, they knew what their duty, the battalion's part in stemming the German advance was helping to save countless lives and the men never showed a sign of wavering in the face of such terrific odds.

After a brief lull when the troops were able to eat a hot meal on the night of 26-27 May, the dawn of 27 May was hailed by a by a massive enemy barrage and a full-scale attack by the enemy reinforced enemy made a full scale attack. The fighting became confused, pockets of soldiers were being lost or taken prisoner, by the late afternoon the remaining total battalion strength had been reduced to about 100 all ranks, many of them taking to the cover of battalion headquarters at Duries farmhouse, Le Paradis.

Final scene at Battalion HQ, 2ⁿᵈ Battalion, The Royal Norfolk Regiment, Le Rue de Paradis at approximately 17.00 hours, 27 May 1940. Lt.-Col. Ryder ordered the burning farmhouse to be evacuated and the defence to be continued in the ditches and outbuildings. All walking wounded went into action again and the seriously wounded were brought into the yard. The surrender was made at 17.15 hours. (From a sketch by Major C. W. H. Long, who was Adjutant at the time.)

Massacre at Le Paradis

On 27 May 1940 the remaining men of 2ⁿᵈ Battalion, The Royal Norfolk Regiment bravely held on at Duries Farmhouse in Le Paradis through gunfire, mortars and shelling and only removed themselves to a cow shed after the building finally caught fire and collapsed. They fought on until 5.15pm when they finally ran out of ammunition. The remaining men were then ordered to surrender by their commanding officer Major Lisle Ryder who fell wounded as he did so. They left the cowshed under a white flag and the 99 remaining soldiers surrendered to No. 4 Company, 1st Battalion, 2nd S.S. Totenkopf (Deathshead) Regiment, under the command of SS Hauptsturmführer Fritz Knöchlein.

Disarmed and paraded on the Rue du Paradis they were marched toward Petit Cornet Malo, hastened by kicks and blows from the rifle butts of their captors as they did so. Meanwhile, two machine guns from No.4 Machine Gun Company were set up on a paddock facing a barn, Private Albert Pooley recalled:

'we turned off the dusty French road, through a gateway and into a meadow beside the buildings of a farm. I saw with one of the nastiest feelings I have ever had in my life two heavy machine guns inside the meadow... pointing at the head of our column. The guns began to spit fire... for a few seconds the cries and shrieks of our stricken men drowned the crackling of the guns. Men fell like grass before a scythe... I felt a searing pain and pitched forward... my scream of pain mingled with the cries of my mates, but even before I fell into the heap of dying men, the thought stabbed my brain 'If I ever get out of here, the swine that did this will pay for it.'

Once all the Norfolk lads had fallen Knöchlein ordered his men to go through the mound of bodies with bayonets to ensure all were dead. Laying motionless until it was dark and the enemy gone and although badly wounded, there were two survivors from this hellish experience – Privates Pooley and Bill O'Callaghan. They managed to drag themselves out from under the bodies of their murdered comrades and hid in the nearby farm of Madame Duquenne-Creton, who risked a similar fate by helping both men. Pooley's leg wound was too severe to carry on and both Pooley and O'Callaghan gave themselves up and became prisoners of war. Pooley was repatriated in 1943 but found it difficult to find anyone from the military authorities to believe his story. His did not give up and after the war managed to persuade one officer to come and see for himself. The bodies from the mass grave had been exhumed from the mass grave where they were buried where they fell in 1942 and had been reburied in graves in the far extension of Le Paradis churchyard. Tended by the local people, white crosses had been erected and soldier's helmets left poignantly on some of the graves of those 97 brave soldiers who had been cut down by the hail of bullets on that fateful day. Today their graves are marked by Commonwealth War Graves headstones but because many of them had been forced to remove their dog tags before they were shot they remain unknown soldiers. My first visit to the graves of these men was one of the most moving moments of my life. I rested my hand on every headstone. This small cemetery with so many good Royal Norfolk Regiment men who died with their heads held high, is a corner of a foreign field that will remain forever England.

Albert Pooley pressed on, evidence was gathered and Fritz Knöchlein, the German Officer responsible for ordering the massacre was traced and arrested in Germany in 1947. Tried before the Curiohaus War Crimes Court in Rotherbaum in October 1948. Found guilty, he was hanged on 28 January 1949 in Hamburg. No other German soldiers or officers were prosecuted for their roles in the massacre.

After 27 May the battalion had been decimated. The following morning those who had been taken prisoner by other German units were brought to a barn at Locon, among them was Captain Long who had been wounded and captured in the final action, he counted seventy members of the battalion all facing an uncertain future as Prisoners of War.

Two men had managed to escape namely Private Ernie 'Strips' Farrow, who narrowly missed the massacre by being ordered a few hours earlier to demolish a bridge where he was wounded and taken prisoner. He escaped a few weeks later with Les Chamberlain they spent 14 months 'on the run' but finding resistance units who could help them they made an epic journey returning via Paris, Marseilles, Spain and Gibraltar to England.

Many others did not put up and shut up with captivity either, men like Sgt Verdun Storey made a number of escape bids but sadly did not make it home, they were punished and put into even more secure camps – where they tried to escape again.

Out of a unit that had set off to war with almost a thousand men just five officers and 134 other ranks of 2nd Battalion, The Royal Norfolk Regiment returned to Britain during the Dunkirk evacuation.

The men of the 2nd Battalion who returned to England were sent to Horton Park, Bradford and by 7 June the battalion was being reformed from this nucleus. As it reconstituted the battalion trained and took on a health shape again thanks to stalwarts such as CSM Slaughter and RSM 'Tick-Tock' Wright. The battalion proceeded to India with 2 Infantry Division, landing at Bombay on 10 June 1942. Here the battalion trained in both combined operation and jungle warfare.

Early in 1944 the Japanese invaded India in the Arakan and made good ground in their offensive. At that time the battalion was 1,500 miles away in Western India but was moved rapidly by air, rail and road to the Indo-Burma frontier where they made their first contact with the Japanese on 14 April 1944 where the men of 'D' Company drove off the enemy killing 30 to our three wounded, one of them later died of his wounds in hospital. Trekking through the jungle it was difficult going and there was constant danger from Japanese surprise attack and snipers. Between 4-6 May the Battalion was to fight its most bitter engagement of the far eastern war, the Battle of Kohima. The battalion was to lead a group assault on a high point of known as GPT Ridge. The fighting was hard but excellent progress was made, through jungle where visibility was rarely more than five yards; Japanese positions were rushed and overrun with good shooting accounting for large numbers of the enemy and casualties for the battalion were light, thanks in no small part to the efforts of Colour Sergeant Bert 'Winkie' Fitt who was commanding the right forward platoon of 'B' Company. His able handling of his sections resulted in the capture of three enemy bunkers in quick succession and maintained the impetus of the attack. Further advances were made and the final objective was captured but in the end the battle had taken its toll; 3 officers and 19 other ranks killed and six officers and 50 other ranks wounded. Much gallant work was carried out by the stretcher bearers and Captain Mather RAMC.

The following day, 5 May, was reasonably quiet, ration and ammunition parties had a chance to bring up supplies and a small battalion cemetery was created for the fallen. Still one objective remained, the bunker christened 'Norfolk Bunker' that dominated the track to the main road and an attack was mounted at dawn on 6 May. During the previous night, despite being wounded in the knee Captain Jack

Members of 2nd Battalion, The Royal Norfolk Regiment and some of their pals as Prisoners of War in Stalag VIIIb, Lamsdorf (now called Łambinowice) in Silesia, 1940.

Officer, Senior NCOs and Sergeants, 2nd Battalion, The Royal Norfolk Regiment 1941.

Randle made a daring reconnaissance of the positioned and settled the axis for advance for each platoon. Unfortunately, when the attack was made the left platoon was unable to keep far enough to the left and forced the other into open slopes on the right. Here they ran into deadly machine gun fire from and undetected machine gun post (they dug into the hillsides and camouflages their entrances only revealing themselves when the battalion attacked). Platoon Commander, Lieutenant Charles Roberts was killed almost instantly. Upon seeing Lieutenant Roberts fall, Colour Sergeant Fitt went forward alone and succeeded in destroying it, at the second attempt, with a well placed grenade. In the next instant, Fitt was caught by a burst of fire which shattered his jaw. He later recounted, 'It felt like a severe punch. I spat out what was left of my teeth and sprayed the foxhole with my light machine-gun. When it jammed, I threw it in the face of a Jap who was still alive.' In the hand-to-hand struggle that followed Fitt managed to kill his enemy with his own bayonet. As he led his men across the top of the enemy position, Fitt witnessed the last, courageous charge of his Company Commander, Captain Jack Randle.

Randle's platoon was pinned down by the intensity of the machine gun fire. Appreciating that the destruction of this enemy post was imperative, if the operation was to succeed, twenty six year old Captain Randle charged the Japanese post single-handed. His citation published in the *London Gazette* on 8 December 1944 continued:

'Although now mortally wounded, he silenced the gun with a grenade thrown through the bunker slit. He then flung his body across the slit so that the aperture should be completely sealed. The bravery shown by this officer could not have been surpassed, and by his self-sacrifice he saved the lives of many of his men and enabled not only his own company but the whole battalion to gain its objective and win a decisive victory over the enemy.'

Captain John 'Jack' Randle VC

Captain John Niel 'Jack' Randle was awarded a posthumous Victoria Cross for his outstanding gallantry and sacrifice. He is buried in the Kohima War Cemetery, India.

After bringing the survivors out after the battle C.Sgt Fitt was met by his CO, the redoubtable Lieut.-Col. Robert Scott. Fitt recalled: 'I had an old field dressing wrapped around my face, and he said, 'They've got you then. Let's have a look.' The MO took of the bandage and Colonel Scott laughed and said, 'Well, you never were an oil painting!' Whether or not it was due to shock, despite his painful injury Fitt burst out laughing. C.Sgt Fitt was awarded the Distinguished Conduct Medal for his gallantry and went on to be the very last Depot Regimental Sergeant Major of The Royal Norfolk Regiment and he remained a well respected legend among the men; 2nd Battalion veteran Arthur Storey, who served with him, recalled: 'He was a soldier first and last. Like everybody he liked his beer and a bit of fun but he was a real fighting man. He was the sort of man you'd follow to hell and back. He never asked anyone to do anything he wouldn't do himself.' Evacuated to hospital after being wounded at Kohima, Fitt managed to wangle his way out after only three days and returned to the battalion under his own steam.

From 6 to 28 May the battalion remained in a perimeter camp and was much troubled with snipers. On 28 May they went into action again in the advance on Aradura Spur, a steep climb to a knife edge where the enemy held a very strong position. An attack was delivered but it was unsuccessful, the battalion suffering around 50 casualties. The cumulative losses in battle and through sickness through malaria, dysentery and other tropical diseases left the battalion with just 14 Officers and 366 other ranks but still morale remained high and they would fight again.

Carriers of 2nd Battalion, The Royal Norfolk Regiment, advancing up the Dimapur - Kohima Road, Nagaland, India, 1944

Returning to Dimapur the battalion reorganised and took part in the advance on Imphal. At Viswema it encountered the enemy and had a sharp fight for a road block. The advance continued and in two months 104 miles had been covered.

At the end of 1944 the 14th Army began a general offensive. The battalion marched with the rest of the Division across the Indo-Burma border to Tamu, down the Kabaw Valley and over the Chindwin River. In the first month of this advance the battalion covered 300 miles. A battle developed in the village of Ondaw, which blocked the main road down to the Irrawaddy opposite Mandalay. Before the 14th Army crossed the Irrawaddy in strength the battalion was ten miles from Mandalay. In reaching this position in the bend of the river it had covered 500 miles, excluding patrolling, in 70 days, crossed tow of the world's largest rivers and had existed the whole time from supplies dropped from the air.

In the bend of the Irrawaddy between the battalion and Mandalay were a large number of Japanese and it was the battalion's job to keep them occupied while other units of 2 Division manoeuvred to secure a crossing of the Irrawaddy to the south. The Division had a tough crossing but the battalion got across then took part in bitter fighting in Central Burma which resulted in the destruction of one Japanese army.

On 13 April 1945 the battalion was withdrawn from Burma and flew to India arriving at Calcutta on 18 April to prepare for the new offensive on Rangoon in May. The battalion trained but the offensive was not required. The battalion was committed to no further operations, in June the battalion moved to Kamareddi, about 60 miles from Secunderabad. It was here the news of Japan's final capitulation was received and on 18 October the first eight officers and 464 other ranks all due for release left for Kaylan Transit camp on the first leg of their return journey back to England. The *Regimental History* acknowledged the men of the 2nd battalion '*had fought one of the hardest battles of the war. Burma, probably the most difficult of all the theatres of action had called for extreme endurance from every man and for a high degree of personal courage in the specialized fighting necessary in the jungle.*' Some measure of the service of the 2nd Battalion in the Burma campaign may be grasped by the fact the battalion was awarded more individual awards for courage than any other in 2 Division.

Most poignant of all, however, was the memorial erected by 2nd Battalion to their fallen comrades on one of the lonely hills near the town of Kohima. Here is a large teak cross cut from one of the huge

Men of 2nd Battalion, The Royal Norfolk Regiment, India 1945

jungle trees was erected upon a base of native rock, with a pathway of the same stone leading to it. On the cross piece is carved 'The Royal Norfolk Regiment,' upon the base is a plaque bearing the three battle honours 'GPT Ridge,' 'Aradura Spur' and 'Viswema' and the dates April-June 1944. Not far away, on the slopes of Garrison Hill, is the Divisional Cemetery, now in the care of the Commonwealth War Graves Commission. Here lie the 108 men of the battalion who were killed in those actions. In the cemetery is the memorial to 2 Division, upon it are inscribed the words:

When You Go Home, Tell Them Of Us And Say,
For Your Tomorrow, We Gave Our Today.

Territorial Army

4th Battalion

The battalion was embodied on 3 September 1939 with Battalion HQ and HQ Company at Chapel Field Drill Hall, Norwich; A and D Companies at Great Yarmouth; B Company with detachments at Wymondham, Attleborough, Thetford and Watton; C Company with detachments at Diss, Harleston and Long Stratton. The Commanding Officer was Lt.-Col. J H Jewson MC TD with Major A E 'Flicker' Knights MC MM TD as his Second in Command.

The first weeks of the war were spent guarding aerodromes and other vulnerable points. In late September Battalion HQ and HQ Company moved to Great Yarmouth and in late October to Gorleston. During the Battalion's occupation of Great Yarmouth and Gorleston defences, visits were received from a number of VIPs and the Racecourse Company's post on the east side of Caister Road became known as 'General's Corner.' Among the visitors were Prince Henry, General Sir Edmund Ironside, then Chief of the Imperial General Staff, the Rt. Hon. Neville Chamberlain, Mr Anthony Eden, General Sir Alan Brooke and most notably in August HM King George VI, visited Battalion HQ and inspected a detachment of 19 officers and 323 other ranks at Gorleston Holiday Camp.

The battalion remained in the Yarmouth area on coastal defence duties until September 1940 when it moved under canvas to Langley Park. At the beginning of October companies went into billets in various villages nearby and Battalion HQ moved to Brooke Hall. In November 1940 the whole battalion moved to Cambridge. In December it received the order to mobilize and in order to do that and complete Brigade and Divisional training it moved to Stobs Camp, about five miles from Hawick Scotland in January 1941. The battalion remained there until April when it moved to Blackburn and

Officers of 4th Battalion, The Royal Norfolk Regiment (TA), 1940

HM King George VI, accompanied by Lt.-Col. J H Jewson MC TD, inspecting members of 4th Battalion, The Royal Norfolk Regiment (TA), 23 August 1940.

then on to Ross-on-Wye, Herefordshire in July. Lt.-Col. Jewson was promoted on 9 September and was succeeded in command of the Battalion by Lt.-Col. Knights and Major J N Packard became Second-in-Command.

The battalion sailed from Liverpool on 20 October 1941 and joined a convoy just North of the Clyde. Half way across the Atlantic the British Escort handed over to an American Escort consisting of one battleship, one aircraft carrier, two cruisers and several destroyers. At Halifax, Nova Scotia, the battalion was transhipped to the USS *Wakefield*. It then called at Trinidad and Cape Town. Landing at Bombay on 29 December and they went into camp at Ahmednagar.

7 Platoon, A Company, 4th Battalion, The Royal Norfolk Regiment (TA) Duckworth Mill, Blackburn 1941.

On 19 January 1942 it re-embarked at Bombay and landed at Keppel Harbour, Singapore on 29 January, which was, at this time, being raided day and night by enemy aircraft.

The battalion was given a sector to defend in the North East of the Island until the Japanese made a landing in the North West Coast, when it was taken from 54th Brigade and formed part of 'Tom Force' under Lieut.- Colonel Thomas, Northumberland Fusiliers. This force, consisting of 4 Royal Norfolk, Sherwood Forsters and the Divisional Reconnaissance Battalion, moved to Bukit Timah, some 5 miles West of Singapore Town. On 11 February the battalion it went into action West of the Racecourse and met a strong Japanese attack on Singapore from the North West. Heavy fighting ensued with no air support, whilst the Japanese had plenty of aircraft which harried our troops continually. A move was then made to Adam Road which was in the perimeter defences of Singapore City. Most of the food dumps had to be abandoned together with stores of water and ammunition and by 15 February supplies of all kinds were running short. On that date the order to surrender was received.

Two days later the battalion was moved into the crowded area of Changi. During the next three and a half years practically all the men were made to work on the railway of death and in other labour camps. Conditions in Thailand were terrible and over 124 men of the battalion died from disease and starvation alone. When the Japanese surrendered only 88 men of the battalion were found on Singapore Island, the rest having been dispersed over Thailand and the surrounding country.

5th Battalion

The battalion, under the command of Lieut.-Colonel Scott-Chad, mobilized at East Dereham on 3 September 1939 and embodied at East Dereham, Aylsham, North Walsham and Holt.

During early October the battalion was concentrated at Holt in billets. In November 1939 the colours of the battalion were laid up in Sandringham Church. Shortly afterwards the battalion moved to the military camp at Weybourne where it was responsible for a sector of the East Coast Defences.

At Christmas the Battalion had the honour of proving a guard for HM King George VI during his stay for about six weeks at Sandringham. The guard were about a company strong under Major E. Thistleton-Smith, Capt E P Hansell, Capt T D Savory and Lt J M Woodhouse (The Essex Regt. attached). It was quartered in York Cottage and its duties consisted of manning LMG Anti-Aircraft posts and patrolling the grounds.

In March 1940 Lt-Col. E C Prattley came from the 2nd Battalion in France to take over from Lt Col G N Scott-Chad. In the same month section training was begun. After Dunkirk and the threat of invasion hung over the country the Battalion occupied their beach defence positions at Weybourne almost continually. Additional defence posts were constructed, barbed wire entanglements erected, anti-tank ditches were dug and a field of fire cleared.

In September the battalion went into Brigade Reserve and was billeted in Holt. The bulk of the

battalion were in Gresham's School. The battalion was now brigaded with the 6th Battalion and the 2nd Battalion, The Cambridgeshire Regiment to form 53rd Brigade of the 18th Division. In November the Battalion was moved to King's Lynn to relieve 4 King's Own Scottish Borderers. The men of 4 Royal Norfolk did not have a comfortable time at Lynn. They were billeted in cold, dark and uncomfortable warehouses on the Docks and while they were here a several air raids were carried out on the town. After a peaceful but somewhat uncomfortable Christmas and New Year at Lynn, in January 1941, the 18th Division was ordered to mobilise in South Scotland. After training there the move was made to Northwich, Cheshire and it was here the battalion was brought fully up to strength, continued to train, men developed specialisms and the battalion prepared to proceed overseas for active service with a total of 40 Officers and 922 Other Ranks.

The battalion embarked the HMT *Duchess of Atholl* at Gourock on 29 October and arrived at Halifax, Nova Scotia where they transferred to USS *Mount Vernon* which carried the entire 53 Brigade group. Leaving Halifax the ship called at Trinidad, Cape Town and Mombassa and arrived at Singapore on 13 January 1942.

The battalion moved into Woodlands Camp in the North East of the Island where it was hoped that a few days would be spent to get used to the new surroundings. Within three days the Commanding Officer and a reconnaissance group moved up to Jemalung in South Johore. The Battalion followed later, taking over a defensive position from the 2/19th Battalion, Australian Infantry. On 20 January orders were received to move into Divisional Reserve ay Ayer Hitam.

The next day patrols had their first brush with the enemy and a few casualties occurred. In endeavouring to keep the road open from Ayer Hitam to Batu Pahat, the first real contact was made with the Japanese on 22 to 23 January and severe casualties resulted in the close fighting in the jungle. The Battalion then relieved 2 Cambridgeshire Regiment (Lt. Col. G C Thorne, Royal Norfolk Regiment Commanding) at Batu Pahat and on 25 January a withdrawal to Sangarrang was successfully carried out. The next day the battalion with other troops found themselves cut off by the Japanese and in consequence they had to retire across country and sea leaving all transport behind.

The battalion under Major C P Wood (less D Company who were rescued by the Royal Navy) succeeded in reaching Singapore, with very few casualties. Lt Col E C Prattley, who stayed to see a bridge blown succeeded with a few other men in escaping and reaching Singapore by sea.

On arrival at Singapore a few days were spent in re-organisation and the preparation of defences. on 3 February the battalion was ordered to defend the Naval Base at Seletar but on 12 February it was withdrawn to the outskirts of Singapore City as the Japanese had made a successful landing on the front held by the Australians.

On 13 February the battalion took up a defensive position in the Braddell Road area. The fighting was close and the action intense. It was soon deduced the Japanese grenades being used had a fuse just long enough to pick it up and hurl it back – still an extremely hazardous action for which Pte C. Frost was awarded the Military Medal. Heavy firing and shelling continued all night. It was from the fighting, much of which was hand to hand in this area, that the battalion sustained heavy casualties.

In the early hours of Saturday 14 February, many men from the Battalion were evacuated to Alexandra Military Hospital. The water supply to the hospital had been cut off in the early hours, and shelling from the air, mortar and artillery, became intense. Having penetrated from the Ayer Rajah area the first Japanese attacks were seen towards the Sister's Quarters, the Japanese fighting troops were about to enter the hospital from the rear. Lieut E. Weston went from the Recreation Room to the rear entrance with a white flag to indicate surrender of the hospital. The Japanese took no notice and bayoneted him to death. Then they entered the ground floor of the hospital and ran amok and neither incumbents pointing to the Red Cross Brassards or shouting the word 'Hospital!' had any effect.

Next a Japanese party entered the Theatre Block where operations were being prepared. In the corridors male and female personnel held up their hands but the Japs, for no reason, set among them, flailing bayonets. Even a soldier on the operating table was bayoneted to death. Sgt Oswald Griffin, was prewar NCO and keen 5th Battalion boxer realising the situation, although already wounded in combat on Braddell Road and ordered to hospital, mustered those he could to hold back the attackers and assisted those able to escape to get out and run for the British lines. By their selfless act several lives were saved but Sgt Griffin and his small group of brave men fighting off the enemy with their fists could only

Some of the fallen defenders of the Island of Singapore.

L/Sgt. Oswald Griffin

hold on for so long; they did not make their own escape and were never seen again. Captain Hamond recorded of Sgt Griffin 'He was a stalwart NCO but above all a tough, courageous soldier for whom I had great admiration.'

The situation was becoming more desperate by the hour so it was also on 13 February, with a heavy heart, the officers of the Battalion saw to it to maintain the old tradition that the British army never lets a complete unit be taken prisoners of war and the official escape party consisting of three officers and about eight other ranks were ordered away. They were lucky and all, except one who was recaptured, eventually reached India via Java. The rest of the battalion had to fight on.

It was on 15 February with the battalion had been in close combat with the enemy and our men were becoming fatigued to the degree some could hardly stand that the order came to cease fire from GOC, Malaya. Despite all of their trials during battle for Singapore morale had remained high and this new came as a bitter blow to all the men of the battalion and so the men of 5th Battalion, The Royal Norfolk Regiment went into Japanese captivity.

6th Battalion

April 1939 saw the foundation of the new 6th Battalion; the first parade being attended at the Chapel Field Drill Hall, Norwich by 250 recruits, all in civilian clothes. There were no NCOs and these had to be borrowed from the 4th Battalion and their first serious training commenced at Falmer Camp, near Brighton in July. On 1 September 1939, the unit, then known as The City of Norwich Battalion, was mobilised under the command of Lt-Col. D G Buxton at the Aylsham Road Drill Hall, Norwich. The Battalion was then at a very weak strength, specifically, 24 Officers, 27 Warrant Officers and Sergeants and 283 other ranks.

Immediately after mobilisation A and B companies were despatched to Hemsby, where they were billeted in the holiday camp adjoining the village. C Company took over guard duties at Watton aerodrome, and the remainder of the unit remained in billets in Norwich with HQ at the Aylsham Road Drill Hall.

The battalion being so weak in strength, the transfer of 16 of its best NCOs to the Depot at Britannia Barracks as instructors, created some difficulties in the training of the young soldiers. These troubles were, however, soon overcome by the promotion of keen and promising men, so that when the first draft of 'Army Class' or Militiamen arrived on 19 October , it was possible to 'squad' the whole 100 recruits and commence their training without delay.

Towards the middle of November, the battalion was ordered to Aylsham and were quartered in billets in the town and training was carried out on Blickling Park, which was found a most useful area. After a fortnight in Aylsham a quick move was made to Sheringham, the 287 Field Company Royal Engineers arriving in the town at the same time. The battalion took up defensive positions along the coast from Cromer to Weybourne with specific orders to prevent seaborne landings.

The first Christmas of the war was celebrated here and the whole battalion sat down to a fine dinners of turkey and plum pudding in the basement of the Grand Hotel. The C.O., Lt-Col. Buxton, visited each company in turn, and 'took wine' with each mess room. He was afterwards entertained in the Sergeant's Mess. On the evening of Christmas Day, when 25 per cent of the unit were on leave, a 'stand-to' was ordered, and positions on the coast were manned for several hours.

January 1940 was a cold and bitter month with heavy snowfalls in early February that saw working parties sent out from the battalion to clear the roads of snowdrifts, some of them 10-12ft deep, to assist the County Council and make way for battalion transport (which consisted of impressed civilian vehicles) to get through to Dereham to collect the rations. The bad weather caused an outbreak of sore throats and mild influenza among the troops. A temporary hospital stocked and staffed mainly by the Sheringham Branch of the British Red Cross was opened in two rooms of the Grand Hotel.

As the weather improved, considerable use was made of the golf course for training, and the hills and rough ground to the south of the town towards Cromer for both day and night exercises, and, in spite of the location of two rifle companies at various aerodromes in North Norfolk, On 10th May

Bren carrier passing through a road block manned by members of 6th Battalion, The Royal Norfolk Regiment (TA) on Cromer Road, Sheringham, 1940.

1940 the battalion was directed to send a platoon to guard Cromer Pier with all companies ordered to battle stations the following day on a front from Sheringham to Overstrand and serious works were carried out installing road blocks, digging weapons pits, sandbagging and reinforcing defensive emplacements at vulnerable points across the area and on the main roads. Special watch was to be maintained for enemy parachutists. Battle headquarters was moved from St Bernards in North Street to Ledbury in Abbey Road. A Lewis gun post located at East Runton claimed a German aeroplane which was brought down to the east of Cromer.

Shades of the invasion scares of 1914 were relived on 14 May when a baker's roundsman put the battalion on alert when he reported seeing German parachutists landing at Felbrigg. A platoon from A company made an exhaustive search of the woods in the vicinity but drew a blank. A further search at dusk was equally unproductive. A cross-examination of the roundsman proved he was suffering from nothing more than 'hallucinations.'

During July orders arrived stating there would be no withdrawal from any position and full preparations were to be made to repel the anticipated German invasion. Mines were laid in the gaps in the cliffs and at all exits from beaches that were potentially passable by enemy infantry. An armoured train was brought up from Melton Constable to support local defences and beach lights (in fact adapted car headlamps) were issued to D Company. Installed at Lifeboat House Gap and Dead Man's Gap the strict instructions for their deployment were that 'they were only to be used as fighting lights and to be sited not less than 10 nor more than 50 yards from any emplacement. They were not to be exposed until any leading invasion craft had struck the beach and were to be used in close co-operation with Bren gun positions, with great care to be taken when fixing the lights to ensure they did not blind or impair the vision of other weapons or defensive position crews.'

At the end of August the Battalion was relieved by 2nd Battalion, The Cambridgeshire Regiment, and moved into Brigade Reserve at Holt and were quartered, principally, in the grounds of Gresham's School. Here there were no obstacles to training and with the assistance of a platoon of Irish Guards, who were attached to the Battalion for a while, great strides were made in drill and soldierly bearing which had been neglected during the more pressing activities on the coast. On 21 September the Battalion moved to Weybourne and took over the coastal defences from the 5th Battalion who, in turn, moved into reserve. The ensuing month was spent in defensive positions and much work was carried out in making improvements to the trenches and courses and demonstrations continued until the end of October.

In November the whole brigade moved back into reserve and the battalion was stationed in Swaffham where they spent the second Christmas of the war. The rifle companies were billeted in the town with Battalion HQ and HQ Company at Petyards, a large farm some three miles from the town. The generosity of local people saw to it that the battalion enjoyed another very fine Christmas dinner. In early January 1941 the battalion moved to Scotland on 5 January, preparatory, it was thought, to it proceeding overseas. During the loading of the battalion stores onto the train the following day a German aeroplane suddenly appeared out of low cloud and dropped several bombs on the station yard. Owing to the low visibility the teams of Bren gunners positioned around the station yard did not see the plane until it was over them and it was out of sight before effective fire could be brought to bear. Unfortunately, five men from the fatigue party; Privates Gordon Stevens, Leonard Batch, Frederick Smith, Albert Sewell and Christian Cobbold were killed and Pte James Furness died the following day from the wounds he sustained as a result of this incident.

In the spring the battalion moved again to Hartford, Cheshire and in August a move was made to Knowsley Park, the seat of Lord Derby, near Liverpool. There were many large scale exercises during the time. The Battalion moved out for overseas deployment on 27 October 1941. After a long night journey the Battalion detrained at Gourock, and at once embarked the HMT *Duchess of Atholl*.

As the convoy steamed up the estuary towards Halifax the early morning sun was rising and a good view of the harbour and town was obtained. Immediately on arrival at the docks all personnel were transferred to the USS *Mount Vernon* which was to take them to Singapore, landing at the naval base on 13 January 1942. A tropical rainstorm providentially prevented the convoy from being bombed at anchor by the Japanese planes that we heard passing overhead. However, the rain successfully soaked all personnel and their baggage during transit to Tyersall Park Camp, where the battalion spent its first two days. On 16 January the battalion embossed for the journey to the mainland of Malaya, to a ridge 10 miles south of Muar forward of Yong Peng.

On 19 January the battalion was attacked by Japanese forces and after two successful counter-attacks by 3/16 Punjabis and 2nd Loyals, the battalion covered the withdrawal. The battalion then moved to Sengarrang and Rengit, near the west coast, where it was cut off and after an unsuccessful attempt by 15 Infantry Brigade to clear the enemy it was ordered to take to the jungle and endeavour to get back. By a lucky contact with the Navy the 200 remaining men of the battalion was evacuated to Singapore on 31 January 1942 where the battalion was reorganised and re-equipped in preparation for the defence of the Island. On 3 February 53 Brigade took up a position on the north coast of Singapore Island from the naval base to the River Seletar. From this time until 12 February all ranks worked feverishly in the construction of defences, which were non-existent when the battalion arrived in the area. Most of this work was carried out under the cover of darkness because the enemy had good observation posts on the Johore side of the Straits opposite and made easy pickings for the Japanese shelling from the northern side of the Johore Straits. In spite of the 'mauling' the battalion had suffered its morale was high, as at last the measure of jungle warfare had been taken, and the role of coast defence was far more familiar. With the defences prepared, the impending Japanese attack was anticipated with confidence.

The Japanese attacked on the west coast of the causeway and on 12 February the brigade was ordered to withdraw as quickly as possible, as the enemy had all but gained possession of the bridge at Nee Soon. The 6th Battalion now covered the withdrawal of the brigade over the Seletar and took up position at the seventh milestone on the Naval Base – Singapore road. Next day, the enemy made a particularly aggressive attack in the dense jungle, managed to penetrate defensive positions. At dawn on 14 February the battalion withdrew to a position on Braddell Road in reserve behind the 5th Battalion. On 15 February, orders were received at 1400 hours that hostilities would cease at 1600 hours that day. Later, information was received that the British forces had capitulated and that the battalion was to concentrate in its present position and await orders. Casualties had been severe in the fighting and tragically there were still more to come.

Thus ended the short campaign, and it is fair to say that the battalion fought with considerable merit, especially as it had received no training in jungle warfare, and did not act as a motorised battalion, for which role in 18 Division the battalion had been training so long in England. Capt. W R Jackson RAMC carried out the evacuation of casualties under extremely difficult conditions; the Battalion M.O. Sergeant A. Branson was awarded the Military Medal for his conspicuous gallantry in the evacuation of the wounded.

On 17 February 1942, the battalion marched to Changi Barracks on the east coast of the Island and there started the three and a half years of life as prisoners of war. At the end of the fighting the battalion had suffered 179 Officers and men killed and 75 wounded.

Prisoners of War

On 17 February all three territorial battalions of The Royal Norfolk Regiment marched about 17 miles to Changi Barracks on the east coast of Singapore Island. Some men, however, found transport hidden in rubber plantations and were relayed to Changi without interference from the Japanese and joined the rest of 18 Division in captivity. The barracks had escaped serious bombing and remained in excellent condition but there was no water or light; a situation soon rectified by the Royal Engineers. There was, however, serious overcrowding and huts had to be erected as overspill. Many of the Norfolks were crammed into the NAAFI of Robertson Barracks.

Food was scarce, there was practically no meat and rice appeared to be the main diet – the shape of things to come! And this change of diet did not help the constitution of many soldiers and resulted in many of them not going to the toilet for over 20 days. Attempts were made to organise concerts to relieve the boredom of captivity and vegetable gardens were started whenever possible to supplement the meagre rations. There were also various forms of study and education for all ranks in the form of a 'university.' It was also during the incarceration at Changi that a renegade Sikh battalion mutinied and was put in charge, they put up roadblocks, demanded stringent respect and made the situation even more difficult.

Soon dysentery became prevalent and one of the early deaths was the popular thirty five year old Padre, Captain the Reverend John Oswald Dean. He was sadly missed by all ranks. At the end of April men were marched to Singapore and accommodated in tents in Farrar Park Camp. Here food improved considerably. Also some pay was issued to those who worked, about 25 cents a day, the equivalent of about 4d, so that a little extra food, especially bananas and pineapples could be bought. It was often possible to steal food from the Japanese, and other items that were sold to the Chinese. During this period there were practically no medical supplies, but the health of the battalion remained good. As an example of the Japanese mentality, a Japanese store was raided one night by a party of Malays and some were killed in the ensuing fight. The heads of these were put up in about eight prominent places such as the railway station.

During the summer the Japanese issued paper declarations to every many upon which he was expected to sign his name and agree not to escape. At first the men refused so the prisoners were ordered to Selerang Barracks where the Australians were held. Prisoners held in the southern area of Singapore had to travel the furthest, approximately two miles, over steep hills to Selerang. The two roads to Selerang were soon covered with troops from 18 and 11 Divisions, many of them in teams pushing trailers, handcarts and even wheelbarrows, piled dangerously high with rations, cooking stoves, fuel, utensils and bedding. Lads who were beri-beri cases or recovering amputees struggled along on crutches and for so many reasons men, who could only just walk, remained determined to get there – somehow. Some men took over four hours to cover just one mile. Spirits were kept high, after struggling to the top of a hill, men would simply laugh and joke and cries like 'Off to Brighton for the weekend!' were heard. All these men were crammed into a barracks built for just *one battalion* of British infantry. After a couple of days all supplies, including those for medical needs were cut. Diphtheria and dysentery rapidly became epidemic and nobody was allowed to be removed to hospital. One poor man had to be operated on for appendicitis. In these dire conditions the British Commander ordered all ranks to sign the declaration saying of course, that as it was done under duress, it had no meaning. The men having pacified their captors were then allowed to trek back to their original camps.

The senior British and Australian Commanders were made to witness the shooting of two British and two Australian soldiers who had previously attempted to escape. Subsequently the Japanese General responsible was himself sentenced to be shot, and the sentence was carried out in the same place. Many Eurasians and Chinese gave great help to the battalion such as gifts of food, medical supplies, musical instruments and later wireless parts. The Japanese camp commander in Farrar Park at this time was a Sergeant Asouki, who also did a great deal to help.

A railway was ordered by Japanese High Command to support their troops deep into Burma and Siam. It was to be built in 18 months, however this order was counter-commanded and construction was to be completed in one year – which it was, but at a horrific cost in life. At this point to recount the experiences of all three battalions as bodies of The Royal Norfolk Regiment becomes difficult because men from all battalions in captivity made up the railway work parties that were constantly demanded. Latterly even very sick men were sent from Singapore up country to work during 'Speedo,' notably F and H Forces, which consisted of large numbers of Norfolk men, experienced tremendous hardships and casualties. Towards the end of June the camp at Changi began to split up. The first party to go was from the 6th Battalion, under the command of Capt. Goddard, its' destination was Thailand, where it was to assist in building a railway. At the time of its departure it was rather envied by those they left behind. None as yet knew what the railway was to cost in human life and suffering.

In September 1942, the 5th Battalion was removed a mile distant to Serangoon Road where a camp was being rebuilt. The accommodation consisted of palm leaf huts. The men had to sleep in very crowded conditions on wooden platforms in two tiers, which very soon became full of bedbugs. This camp was 2000 strong and commanded by a Japanese Officer. The guards were now changed from fighting soldiers to Prisoner of War guards who were Koreans with Japanese NCOs – all of these were 'a very bad lot.' Lt-Col. Prattley was British Camp Commander. One evening he was beaten over the back with a rifle by a drunken Japanese lance corporal.

In September the Officers, at last, got a little pay, about $10 a month. The British Commander laid down certain contributions towards men's messing and hospital upkeep. A good concert party and band were now forming. Also a few selected canteen suppliers were allowed into camp once a week. Eventually electric light and shower baths were erected. In October a Red Cross ship was allowed in, and a very welcome issue of clothes, medical stores, food and cigarettes was made. It was also in October that the move to Thailand was accelerated. Further parties were ordered there, including a large one from the 4th Battalion under Lt-Col. Knights while others were sent off to Burma, Indo-China, Formosa, the Philippines and the Japanese mainland. It was impossible to keep a check on all men in the three battalions as they became split up, a factor that caused many regrets among both officers and men.

After Christmas the 5th Battalion moved back to Changi and were accommodated in a barrack room block in Roberts Barracks. There was now much more room after the working groups had been despatched. Some really good concerts and plays were performed in Changi. During this period of captivity the Battalion Medical Officer was Captain Chopping RAMC, who apart from being a very good doctor, was also a wireless expert, and had made a very fine compact wireless set so there was no lack of news from the outside world. As 1943 progressed more and more men were shunted up to Thailand for work on the railway, only the sick, the wounded and those attending to them remained in Singapore.

On 18 March 1943, a party of 550 other ranks (400 5th Battalion and 150 6th Battalion) and five officers, namely Major Crane, Captain Hamond, Captain Self and Lieutenants Curtis and Batterby were ordered to go to Siam to work on the railway which was being made from Bangkok to Rangoon. The party was taken by MT to Singapore and then put into steel goods wagons, twenty-five men plus kit to a wagon. The railway was a metre gauge, so the overcrowding and heat turned the wagon into ovens. The journey took five days and the men ate two meals a day, chiefly rice. By the time the men arrived at Non Pradok they were completely exhausted. The Japanese issued five unripe bananas per man and a close-by prisoner of war camp was able to provide tea. The party was moved into another train of open trucks, 50 men were put in each truck and were wedged in like sardines. The track was very uneven and the train proceeded very slowly at 5-10 miles per hour, a speed that was not enough to provide any cooling draught. It was blazing hot, which was not made any better when the train stopped for about an hour and a half at noon whilst the guards went and had a meal. No prisoners were allowed to leave the trucks. The party arrived at Kanburi and were marched one mile and ordered into the jungle. This had to be cleared and everyone bivouacked in the open. Just before dark rations were delivered which were much better than had ever been issued before; rice, vegetables, pork and eggs. The great difficulty was cooking, as the Japanese would not allow any cooking pots to be taken from Singapore, and only a few were issued. The next day working parties had to be found to work on the railway. Troops were allowed to bathe in the river about a mile away. In the evenings it rained and everyone got soaking wet. It was not until after about eight days that some tents and tarpaulins were issued. In the meantime, further parties from Singapore arrived daily until there were about 5000 troops in the area. About 3 April 1943, the party was ordered to move on again. It was transported by the trolleys that carried the rails for laying and were drawn by diesel rail cars that could also be converted for road use. About 50 men were left behind suffering from malaria and dysentery, and these were moved to the base hospital nearby, run by a British Medical Officer and staff.

This journey was not too bad as the trucks went faster and the day was cooler. In the evening the party was detrained at Wompo, which was then the railhead, further progress being stopped by a viaduct that had to be quarried out of a cliff face. Five tents, each about 14ft x 18ft were issued and a camp was made on the riverbank. The following day the work started from daylight and carried on until dark. One party had to work for 24 hours on end. The guards here were Koreans. Beatings by guards and Japanese railway engineers were frequent. No pay had been issued since leaving Singapore until the last evening in this camp. The pay issued in Singapore was no use in Siam as it too three months to get this changed. On about 14 April the party had to march about 10 miles to Tarso. About fifty men were left behind for evacuation to base hospital. No transport of any sort was provided and everything had to be carried; this was a very hard march. The stay in Tarso was only for a few days; again men were just put into a jungle clearing without cover. On around 17th April the party started to be moved by MT in three lifts' one going each day, to Takanun. In this, the party was very lucky because every subsequent party had to march about 90 miles.

On arrival at Takanun, tents were issued on a scale of one per 25 men. All ranks were made to work on the railway and also on a Japanese camp. No men were allowed to build a cookhouse or dig latrines. The food was very bad, practically rice only. The camp was situated on the riverbank with the trace of the railway on the other side. The surrounding jungle was of very dense, prickly bamboo and practically impenetrable. More parties started to arrive and pass through the camp daily. Meanwhile the hard work, exposure, lack of proper food and medical supplies began to take its toll upon everyone. The tow Medical Officers with the party, Captains Donaldson and Petrovski RAMC, did wonderful work with what little medicine they had. When the monsoon broke at the end of May, conditions became terrible as the tents were made of very poor quality material and not only did they fail to keep the wet out but became completely rotten after about a month. Cholera hit the camp causing a great many deaths. Not for some time did the Japanese allow the camp to build any hospital huts to cope with the growing number of sick men with other ailments such as bronchitis, beri-beri, malaria, amœbic dysentery and diphtheria. All the fit men of the camp were moved out to another camp about 20km above Takanun and 2km above Tameroh Parh. Capt Robert Hamond was in command of the fit men of the Norfolk party that consisted of two other officers; Lt. Bill Battersby and Lt Ned Holiday and 100 men. Captain Hamond and Captain Self both had cholera (Capt Hamond had also suffered Tropical Typhus) but managed successful recoveries but after the move Capt Hamond went down with scrotal beri-beri and could not walk for a time so Bill Battersby took over the running of the camp. In ten weeks 98% of the men suffered from Malaria. It was several days before the Japanese would allow any sick to be evacuated to base hospitals. This was a long journey by barge. Altogether during this period, the entire Norfolk party in captivity in the two camps suffered about 170 deaths.

We must also remember the constant abuse and torture of prisoners took a horrific toll. The work was murderously hard. In places the railway ran through rocky hills, here the track had to be levelled by hand with crowbars and sledgehammers. The tools provided for the work were primitive in the extreme adding to the labours of the construction. So the work went on and the 'Railway of Death' forged its way through the jungle – for every sleeper laid a British, Australian or Dutch life was taken (about 13,000). Add to this toll add inestimable thousands of coolies from Malaya.

Most of the Norfolk's role in completion of the railway was done by October 1943. Conditions became much better and huts were built of bamboo and palm leaves. Parties were organised to work in the cemeteries, a stage was built for entertainments and the food improved considerably. During that winter it used to be very heartening to hear our bombers fly overhead at night on their way to and from objectives such as Bangkok and Saigon. Quite a good amount of food was available for Christmas, and all ranks had a riceless day and a pantomime in the evening.

In February, all fit men were organised to go to Japan, no officers of the 5th Battalion were allowed to or detailed to go by the Japanese, so RSM Spencer was put in command of the men in this party. Early in March 1944, Takanun camp was evacuated and everyone was moved by rail down towards Bangkok to a base camp at Chunki. This was a large camp accommodating about 11,000 prisoners of war. The place was very well organised although everything was improvised because the Japanese supplied nothing. There were tailors, boot makers, laundry, theatre, a band, good cookhouses and canteens. The hospital, although it had very little equipment and practically no medical supplies, did wonderful work. The cemetery at that time was looked after by senior officers and was very well laid out in grass and tropical flowering shrubs.

Men evacuated sick from up country working parties were, when discharged from hospital, taken into a combined Norfolk battalion commanded by Lt-Col. Alan Cubitt. In May working parties were sent up country again for railway maintenance and firewood cutting for the locomotives. During the monsoon, owing to washouts and bombing, the railway did not operate at all efficiently. In the summer, some American Red Cross parcels arrived and were distributed: about six men shared each parcel. Some other camps did not receive any because the Japanese guards took the contents of the Red Cross boxes for themselves. At the same time quite a good amount of medical supplies also came. These were very much needed and made the critical difference between life and death for many sick and injured men.

In November, twenty-one Liberators flew low over the camp. The sight of our own bombers put all ranks in very good heart but when they dropped a few bombs on a bridge a few miles away some fell on Tamakan camp and caused casualties. Tamakan was later evacuated and the nearby big girder bridge on concrete piles was soon completely destroyed by allied bombing. Christmas 1944 was spent at Chunki in much the same style as the festivities of the previous year.

In February 1945, all officers were taken away from the men and put in Kanburi camp, about six miles distant. When the end finally came the battalions were scattered in small parties on different parts of the railway, some also on the Japanese mainland as forced labour down the salt mines. The parties on the railway were taken to either Bangkok or Petburi aerodromes and as they arrived were flown to Rangoon. Petburi had been built by prisoners of war but, ironically, the first planes to use it were allied Dakotas sent by the Americans who were magnificent in evacuation the camp – even in monsoon.

Some of the men of the 4th, 5th and 6th Battalions who had survived Japanese captivity at Aomi Hall, Japan 1945

The end itself is remembered as coming with dramatic suddenness. It had been heard over the secret wireless sets hidden around the camp that Germany had gone down to total defeat in May 1945, and all realised that now the Allies could concentrate the whole of their energies on the war in the Far East; and by that token, the days of the Japanese were numbered. By early August there was a distinct change in the attitude from the Japanese prison guards and their former brutality changed to a cringing servility. On 15 August all camps were buzzing with rumours and it could hardly be believed that Japan had actually surrendered. But within a few days relieving officers and supplies from Burma were parachuted on to the camps brining vivid reality to the fact of freedom. Gradually all prisoners were brought down to centres where they could be re-equipped with clothing and properly housed, preparatory to a return to England. The long months of captivity had at last come to an end. The first one hundred and forty soldiers of the Royal Norfolk Regiment liberated from the hands of their Japanese captors landed at Southampton aboard the *Corfu* on 13 October 1945, the rest soon followed from camps all over the Far East; many had to wait weeks and months for transport and shipping, some were in such a bad state they were sent to Canada to be 'fattened up' before coming home at last.

Going home! Some of the men of 4th, 5th and 6th Battalions who had survived Japanese captivity pictured on Bangkok airfield beside the plane that was to take them on the first leg of their long journey home, September 1945

Colonel 'Flicker' Knights was later to record: 'In spite of all the Japanese could do, the brutality of the guards, frequent beatings, humiliation and torture suffered, the men of the 4th, 5th and 6th Battalions of The Royal Norfolk Regiment never forgot they were soldiers. It was their steady discipline, inflexible courage through adversity and native dignity that could withstand every provocation and comradeship unique to Norfolk men that brought them through their horrific ordeal.' Theirs was a triumph through death and disablement, may they never be forgotten and those of us who are left with their legacy remember the motto of the Far Eastern Prisoners Of War Association and 'keep going the spirit that kept them going.'

7th Battalion

When the TA was ordered to double in size in the spring of 1939 the 5th Battalion recruited up to double strength allowing the new unit (the 7th Battalion) to grow up alongside the trained one. In July the new battalion began to take shape during summer camp at Falmer near Brighton. Recruits had been joining almost up to the time they left so for training purposes the battalion was divided into two halves, one of trained men under Lt-Col. Debenham and the other made up of recruits under Lt-Col. Scott-Chad. Within a short period of time the unit was turned into a pioneer battalion. After receipt of orders at 19.30 hours on 1 September 1939 the 7th Battalion was embodied as a unit in its own right and immediately moved its HQ to King's Lynn. Battalion strength was 23 Officers and 621 ORs.

On 30 December 1939 an advance part of the battalion was sent to Southampton to prepare for embarkation. Motor Transport removed the Battalion to Southampton on the 7th and 13th but the men of the battalion were dogged by sickness after an epidemic of German measles broke out at the time of sailing causing great consternation at Cherbourg and sick men were evacuated at every stopping place. The journey had been bitterly cold but, thankfully, uneventful and the Battalion arrived at the concentration area of St Remy-du-Plain (Sarthe) on 15 January 1940 and thus the most junior of all the Royal Norfolk Regiment Territorial Battalions was the first to be deployed to an active theatre in the Second World War.

Minor movements of companies and platoons took place at frequent intervals and much training had to be carried out and because the battalion had been sent to France as a Pioneer unit additional equipment had to be sourced and issued to make the battalion fit to fight. By 21 May the whole of 51

Officers of 7th Battalion, The Royal Norfolk Regiment (TA) 1939

Division had moved to General Reserve. When the BEF moved up to combat the onrush of Germans through Belgium the battalion entrained at Mars La Tour and eventually arrived at Rouen. From here it moved to Clais where on arrival 'A' Company was attached to 154 Brigade, 'C' to 152 and 'D' to 153 while 'B' Company, Battalion HQ and HQ Company remained in the town. For some time the companies moved and fought with the Brigades and Battalions to which they were attached. Battalion HQ and 'B' Company moved with HQ to 51 Division.

One platoon of 'A' Company were in action at Belloy with 'D' Company, 1/8ᵗʰ Argyll and Sutherland Highlanders and were surrounded after a very hard fight. Another platoon of the same company was also engaged with 'A' Company of the same regiment at Franleu where it fought on after troops in the vicinity had surrendered but eventually they too were forced to surrender. 'C' Company took part in the attack on Abbeville but had to withdraw with the rest of the attacking troops. 'D' Company had the task of defending Toeffles during the attack on Abbeville. It repulsed a strong attack made by the Germans but had to conform to the general withdrawal of our own troops.

A general retirement of all troops now took place and by 10 June, Battalion HQ, 'A' and 'C' Companies were at St Denis; 'B' Company had moved to Ouvilliers with Divisional HQ, whilst 'D' Company was still attached to 153 Brigade.

At St Denis the battalion was ordered to destroy all kit not essential for fighting to enable the men to be carried in the mechanical transport. The battalion, less 'D' and 'B' Companies then received orders to move to St Riquier but it was much delayed on approaching St Valery by traffic blocks. 'B' Company, less one platoon, rejoined the battalion at St Valery and on 11 June St Riquier was reached and dispositions made for defence. However, the battalion was ordered to move quickly to Cailleville where Divisional HQ had been established. An advance party from 'D' Company joined the battalion here as did one platoon from 'B' Company.

The Battalion Commander, Lieut.-Col. C A Debenham was then ordered to reconnoitre a defence line to cover the embarkation of the Division. He left the battalion in the charge of the Adjutant, Captain Jickling, who realising that the enemy were drawing close to the town ordered companies out to the defensive position, where they soon came under fire from machine guns and artillery but no serious attack developed.

During the night the battalion was ordered to assemble for embarkation at 23.45 hours on 11 June. HQ Company, 'A' and 'B' Companies took up a position in a sunken road near the station of St Valery, whilst 'C' Company went to the beach. At 02.00 hours on 12 June the Commanding Officer was informed that as the troops could not embark they were to move out of the town before daybreak and take up a line to protect Divisional HQ. This line was occupied at dawn. At 10.30 hours orders were received to lay down arms.

'D' Company who had been attached to 153 Brigade eventually placed themselves under the command of 1 Gordon Highlanders. During the retirement to St Valery it was surrounded by enemy tanks about one mile North West of the town and were forced to surrender.

Earlier, as dawn was breaking at about 02.30 hours on 12 June Captain Anthony Colley, convinced the Navy were lying off the coast and not having received any orders, showed great initiative and split C Company into parties of about 18, with the idea of trying to reach the naval ships by means of a few fishing boats moored in the river. After a hazardous walk parties led by Capt. Colley and Second Lieutenant Jim Walker managed to secure boats but not finding any oars improvised with spades. Tragically the progress of Captain Colley's boat was hampered because its mast would not pass under a low bridge and were forced to return to the beach where Captain Colley was killed trying to get further parties off at Val-Les-Roses. Second Lieutenant Walker's party, after a number of alarms and close calls after bursts from enemy machine gun fire, reached units of the fleet and were taken aboard HMS *Harvester* and landed at Southampton the following day, where eleven men of 'C' Company had also arrived. This latter party had been taken aboard by the Navy at Val-Les-Roses, about one and a half mile from St Valery with several other parties from the division. Thus, out of the entire 7ᵗʰ Battalion just 29 other ranks and one officer (Lt. H J Walker) returned to England.

The 7ᵗʰ Battalion was reconstituted and after undergoing specialist training it proceeded overseas under the command of Lieut. Colonel Ian Freeland and landed in Normandy as part of 176ᵗʰ Brigade, 59 Division on 28 June 1944 and moved to the concentration area near Bayeux. On 8 July the battalion moved up to the vicinity of Epron for the attack on Caen which it attacked with 1 Royal Norfolk on its left. Unfortunately the success signal was sent up from La Bijude in error before the battalion had

Officers, Senior NCOs and Sergeants of 7ᵗʰ Battalion, The Royal Norfolk Regiment (TA) shortly before their departure to Normandy 1944.

consolidated on its objective, it was counter attacked and driven back; this resulted in the right flank of 7 Royal Norfolk being exposed and it suffered heavy casualties.

The CO went forward himself and decided to attack La Bijude, the battalion's other objective but this attack was held up by enemy positions which had not been located. By this time the strength of the battalion was very much reduced but since the Divisional Commander had said that it was vital to capture the objectives the CO, with 'D' Company attacked again that evening with a Company of 7 South Staffordshire in support. This operation was successful; La Bijude and Epron were captured and cleared. By this time 7 Royal Norfolk had suffered about 200 casualties and had to be withdrawn and reorganised.

The battalion's greatest battle was to come next, the crossing of the River Orne. The reconnaissance for this crossing was made by Capt. David Jamieson, Captain Jim Walker and a sapper. They found a suitable place for infantry and tanks but the only approach was through a thick wood and the banks on both sides were very steep. The two leading battalions crossed without much opposition and 7 Royal Norfolk waded over after them but 'A' Company lost direction and finished up 700 yards from their intended position, they dug in, but in the morning they found themselves surrounded and had to surrender.

In the early evening the enemy counter attacked from the forest directly opposite D and C Companies and Battalion HQ. The ground was thick and the fields of fire were short. Heavy mortar and artillery fire came down and tanks suddenly appeared at close range. Sgt. Arthur Courtman's section of 6 pdrs was sited in the area of D Company's right forward platoon. The guns were 40 yards apart, and as the crews had already suffered heavy casualties crossing the bridge. Sgt Courtman planned to fire the guns himself if possible. He blew up his first tank at 60 yards with his first shot. Next, a Panther approached, Courtman ran to his second gun and with his first shot, over 100 yards knocked it out too! These successes achieved under intense fire so raised the morale of D Company the enemy met with such stiff opposition they did not penetrate. Lt-Col Freeland recorded 'Throughout this action Capt Jamieson's company gave magnificent account of itself under very heavy fire.' Despite the fierce fighting and a number of anxious moments the battalion was still in firm possession of its positions at last light. Everyone was feeling very pleased with how they accounted for themselves during the day but all ranks knew there was still plenty more fighting to come. With the enemy dominating the bridge there could be no evacuation.

At 0800 hours on the morning of 8 August the enemy began its second counter attack. This time special attention was paid by the enemy to Sgt Courtman's guns and one was soon knocked out along with two of the three Churchill tanks with D Company taking the full brunt of the attack. A strong enemy force had worked its way around the north of Grimbosq and attacked D Company from two sides. Rapidly, they overran the forward platoon and Lieut Bushell was killed while Sgt. Courtman, firing his last remaining gun alone under intense fire of all kinds was finally killed by a tank shell. Lt-Col. Freeland recorded of Sgt Courtman: 'So died one of the bravest men of all times, who by his magnificent example had inspired the men of the D Company around him to superhuman efforts.' Sergeant Arthur Courtman, a 31 year old King's Lynn man was directly mourned by his wife and parents and of course his comrades in the battalion, they never forgot him or his bravery. In the light of his valour many were disappointed to learn Sgt Courtman was only recognised with a posthumous Mention in Despatches.

The fighting was conducted at close range and was ferocious. The situation was confused and the enemy attack began to tell. Captain Jamieson was the only Officer from D Company left alive but kept his cool and reorganised his men in a tight formation around the single remaining Churchill tank. But to Jamieson's dismay they manoeuvred directly into the line of fire of a concealed enemy tank. Jamieson tried desperately to signal the tank commander, but to no avail. He then ran and tried to use the phone at the back of the tank but could not get through. Ignoring incoming fire he clambered on to the tank. As he did so an armour piercing shell drilled a hole through the driver's compartment. Jamieson was thrown off peppered with shrapnel and badly shaken. Jamieson received wounds near his right eye and in his left forearm. CSM Jones took command while Capt Jamieson was having his wounds dressed. At the Regimental Aid Post Captain Payne and his staff he under extreme pressure and despite at one stage of the battle having 75 wounded there performed a 'miraculous' evacuation of injured men to the safety of a stable. After directing the battle with skill for some time, CSM Jones was also badly wounded and had to be evacuated. It appeared the position would be overrun but the 18 set radio operators, Pte Pennington assisted by Pte Nicholson, although without a Company Commander, continued to relay accurate and essential information to their CO, Lt-Col Freeland. Despite being in great pain Captain Jamieson his eye dressed and his arm in a sling returned and took command again and with complete disregard for his safety walked about amongst his men encouraging them to greater efforts. He sent back targets for the artillery over the radio. At one stage the position being so serious the fire had to be brought down on the company itself. Luckily they were well dug in and the accuracy of the guns of 116 Field Regiment was outstanding – it was later recorded each gun fired about 1000 shells during the 24 hours of the battle. Lt-Col. Freeland records 'So successful was Capt Jamieson in his direction of the battle and so magnificently did D Company fight that the enemy was held and heavy casualties inflicted upon him.' There was constant fire, the enemy had attacked several times but each time they were repulsed.

Freeland continues 'Capt Jamieson's outstanding leadership and personal bravery was largely responsible for the defeat of these determined attacks. He refused to be evacuated and stayed with his company until the company were relieved in the evening.'

Jamieson's VC citation concludes: 'Throughout this 36 hours of bitter and close fighting, and despite the pain of his wounds, Captain Jamieson showed superb qualities of leadership and great personal bravery. There were times when the position appeared hopeless, but on each occasion it was restored by his coolness and determination. He personally was largely responsible for the holding of this important bridgehead over the river Orne and the repulse of seven German counter-attacks with great loss to the enemy.'

Casualties in the battalion during this action were 13 officer and 213 other ranks killed, wounded or missing. Shortly afterwards the battalion was disbanded and the remaining officers and men were

Captain David Jamieson VC

All that was left of them – the 7th Battalion men who were still serving with 1st Battalion, The Royal Norfolk Regiment, 1945

All that was left of them – the 7th Battalion men who were still serving with 1st Battalion, The Royal Norfolk Regiment, 1945

sent as reinforcements to other units, many of them joined 1 Royal Norfolk. Lt-Col Freeland concluded his account of the battalion:

> 'During its short active service career for the second time in the War the 7th Battalion had made a name for itself which was in keeping with the highest traditions of the Regiment. At the time of its dispersal, in spite of severe casualties, its morale and fighting record was of such high order that it was singled out for special praise by not only the Divisional Commander, but the Commander-in-Chief himself. In the two months fighting the battalion had been awarded one VC, two DSOs, one MC, ten MMs and five Mentions in Despatches. Many more deserved decorations.'

As the *Britannia* commented: 'Thus ended for the second time in the War the 7th Battalion of the Regiment, which, by its fine achievements, would appear to have merited a worthier fate.'

The last VC

Men from The Royal Norfolk Regiment were awarded a total of five Victoria Crosses, a record unsurpassed by any other county regiment during the Second World War. The final VC to the Regiment was awarded to Lieut. George Knowland (22), attached No. 1 Commando for action at Kangaw, Burma on 31 January 1945. Lieutenant Knowland was commanding the forward platoon of a Troop positioned on the extreme North of a hill that had been subjected to heavy and repeated enemy attacks throughout the day. Before the first attack started, Lieutenant Knowland's platoon was heavily mortared and machine gunned, yet he moved about among his men keeping them alert and encouraging them, though under fire himself at the time.

When the enemy, some 300 strong in all, made their first assault they concentrated all their efforts on his platoon of 24 men but in spite of the ferocity of the attack, he moved about from trench to trench distributing ammunition, and firing his rifle and throwing grenades at the enemy, often from completely exposed positions. Later, when the crew of one of his forward Bren guns had all been wounded, he sent back to Troop Headquarters for another crew and ran forward to man the gun himself until they arrived. The enemy was then less than 10 yards from him in dead ground down the hill so in order to get a better field of fire, he stood on top of the trench, firing the light machine gun from his hip and successfully keeping them at a distance until a Medical Orderly had dressed and evacuated the wounded men behind him. The new Bren gun team also became casualties on the way up and Lieutenant Knowland continued to fire the gun until another team took over.

Later, when a fresh attack came in he took over a 2-inch Mortar and in spite of heavy fire and the closeness of the enemy, he stood up in the open to face them, firing the mortar from his hip and killing six of them with his first bomb. When all the bombs were expended he went back through heavy grenade, mortar and machine gun fire to get more, which he fired in the same way from the open in front of his platoon positions. When those bombs were finished he went back to his own trench and still standing up fired his rifle at them. Being hard pressed and with the enemy closing in on him from only 10 yards away, he had no time to re-charge his magazine. Snatching up the Tommy gun of a casualty, he sprayed the enemy and was mortally wounded stemming this assault, though not before he had killed and wounded many of the enemy.

Such was the inspiration of his magnificent heroism, that, though fourteen out of twenty-four of his platoon became casualties at an early stage, and six of his positions were over-run by the enemy, his men held on through twelve hours of continuous and fierce fighting until reinforcements arrived. If this Northern end of the hill had fallen the rest of the hill would have been endangered, the beach-head dominated by the enemy and other units farther inland cut off from their source of supplies. As it was, the final successful counter-attack was later launched from the vital ground which Lieutenant Knowland had taken such a gallant part in holding.

Lieutenant Knowland is buried in the Commonwealth War Graves Commission Cemetery at Taukkyan, Burma.

Lieut. George Knowland VC

8th and 30th Battalions

The 8th and 30th Battalions are direct descendants from the 9th (Norfolk Group) Defence Companies raised by Lieut.-Col. The Lord Walsingham DSO in July 1939. These early defence companies had no establishment of officers of other ranks, no uniform except a red brassard with 'TA' stencilled upon it, no equipment and no transport.

The men of 8th (Home Defence) Battalion, The Royal Norfolk Regiment serving with the Broads Flotilla, November 1940

Originally the companies were raised to defend vital points in their own localities and the men could not be transferred to other companies. This condition was cancelled when the group became the 8th Battalion and men could accept the new conditions or be discharged. Very few took their discharge.

The Key Party started work in August 1939 with headquarters at Tottington and consisted solely of officers. Recruiting started at once and companies were situated at Norwich, Yarmouth, Lynn and Attleborough. The recruits were all old soldiers and with no refresher training were sent off at once to various vulnerable places.

On 2 November 1939 the defence companies all over England were converted into Home Defence Battalions thus originated the 8th (Home Defence) Battalion, The Royal Norfolk Regiment.

In 1940 the May intake from Infantry Training Centres at Norwich and Lincoln were transferred to the 8th Battalion which continued to carry out defence duties over a gradually widening area. It also had transferred to it the personnel of the 'Broads Flotilla' which consisted of armed motor boats manned by Regular Army Reservists (previously under the command of the Royal Navy). The anti-para-troop landing duties of the flotilla soon occupied a whole company of the battalion.

One of the biggest units in the Regiment at one period the battalion strength was 85 Officers, 2,400 other ranks with 5 Home Defence Companies and 5 Young Soldier Companies.

Early in 1940 the 8th (HD) Battalion was renamed 30th Battalion but its duties remained the same. In August 1943 orders to mobilise were received and the battalion collected its units from across the county and concentrated at Caister, leaving on 12 September 1943.

Reaching Algiers, North Africa, without incident, the Battalion moved out 15 miles to 'Z' Area where they undertook duties guarding Italian POWs who worked as dock parties and protection patrols of water supplies. In October the battalion moved to Sicily and soon settled in as a Garrison Battalion with detachments at Pozzallo guarding the Malta Cable and the important anchorage at Augusta.

In March 1944 the battalion moved to Vasto and Termoli on the Italian mainland. Ultimately the Termoli platoon went to Ortona which had not fallen at the time the move took place. 'Y' Company went to Foggia and in May 1944 Battalion HQ and the remainder of the battalion moved to Barletta.

The battalion, less one company at Vasto and Ortona moved to Ancona in August 1944. One company moved to Falconana where Battalion HQ was later established. Later, two companies were moved; one to Terni to guard Fascist internees and the other to Perugia. The battalion remained on Garrison duties until August 1945 when Battalion HQ was at Rimini with companies at Ancona (Y), Falconana ('U'), Padua ('T'), Forli and Bologna ('K').

9th Battalion

On 27 May 1940, 50th (Holding) Battalion was formed in Norwich under the command of Lieut.-Col. H F Watling. It originally consisted on selected NCOs from 4th, 5th and 6th Battalions, survivors from Dunkirk, selected other ranks from the Depot and a company from the 10th (Holding) Battalion. It had hardly begun to function when a large number of officers and other ranks were sent to 2nd Battalion.

Drafts were soon despatched to the battalion and by the middle of July 1940 it was 1,200 strong and training was carried out on the Eaton Golf Course. In the Autumn it moved to North Walsham where it ceased to be a Holding Battalion and was formed into a Field Force Battalion and renumbered 9th Battalion.

Christmas 1940 was spent near Cromer where the battalion was engaged in manning and improving the coastal defences. During this time the battalion was absorbed into 76 Division and placed in 220 Brigade. In April 1941 the battalion was moved to Brandon, Suffolk where hard training was carried out for a month, then returned to Norfolk and based at Happisburgh they erected steel anti-tank scaffolding along the beaches. In October 1941 large drafts were taken for the Territorial Battalions to bring enable them to complete mobilization. By Christmas the battalion was back in North Walsham.

In July 1942 field training and battle drill were carried out across the Holt Hall estate and in Blakeney and by December the battalion had been transferred to 47 (London) Division and had been moved to Winchester Barracks where many of the NCOs and men were able to drill on a barrack square for the first time.

Early in 1943 a move was made to Bournemouth where many of the men assisted in air raid duties.

June 1943 saw the battalion move to the Isle of Wight for further training and took over as 'house-keeper' for a number of invasion camps. In January 1944 the battalion travelled to the North where it took part in large scale exercises on the Yorkshire Moors. Returning to the Isle of Wight by 'D' Day highly trained teams had been established for despatching personnel to the battle front.

In August 1944 9th battalion was disbanded and drafts were sent to Field Force Battalions in Italy, Africa and India.

70th (Young Soldier) Battalion

In May 1940, it was announced that the Army would receive volunteers under the call-up age. A limited response was forthcoming and the young soldier recruits were posted to the Regimental 30th Battalions. With the Battle of Britain came a vast increase in the number of volunteers and on 19 September 1940 Young Soldier Battalions were formed by detaching all the young soldiers from the 30th Battalions together with a proportionate number of First World War NCOs and emergency commissioned officers. These were designated 70th Battalions.

The strength of 70th Battalion, commanded by Lieut.-Col. E. Thistleton-Smith was about 500 and men were scattered on vulnerable points and aerodromes from Hopton in the East to Marham in the West, from Happisburgh in the North to Feltwell in the South. Battalion HQ was in a small house in The Crescent, Chapel Field Gardens, Norwich. Recruits arrived at an average of twenty a day and with few stores and no accommodation they were found billets at Reepham, Cawston and Aylsham, issued a rifle and after six weeks rather perfunctory training, given live ammunition and sent to guard vulnerable points (VPs).

The duties were simple- just guard duties, mostly 24 hours on and 24 hours off, living, in most cases, under the most primitive conditions. Lack of transport added to the difficulties. The Commanding Officer managed to get a car out of the RASC by quoting a non-existing authority. The platoon commander of the Broads Flotilla guard had six VPs with 40 all ranks. He was lucky to obtain a motor cycle as it was nearly an 80 mile round trip to visit all his posts.

In November 1940 battalion HQ moved to Taverham Hall and teething troubles became less acute. Young, enthusiastic games-playing officers and NCOs from other battalions began to arrive and the number of VPs to guard were cut down. A hutted camp was erected in the grounds of the hall in the winter for a training company and essential equipment began to trickle through. Lieut.-Col. Shand MC, from Britannia Barracks, ran courses for cooks, young NCOs and instructors and he loaned RSM Swingler who deserves more credit than any other single person for the grand reputation the battalion obtained.

Members of 70th (Young Serviceman) Battalion, all of them aged between eighteen and twenty take a break from training, Taverham Hall, June 1940

When the battalion was over 1,100 strong the War Office brought out an establishment and by the summer of 1941, it had one company (150 strong) on each of 4 aerodromes, one training company at Taverham and a Recruit Intake Company. The young soldiers came from every walk of life and many of them gave false ages on enlistment but many of those involved with the battalion looked back with great pride in its standards of fitness and training achieved as well as its remarkable *espirit de corps*. One private soldier, aged just 17, shot down a Junkers 88 at Watton with 76 rounds from a Lewis Gun and his hits scored on an enemy plane at Hopton.

In December 1941 the battalion changed places with the Sherwood Foresters in the 3rd Infantry Brigade for one month at Yarmouth. The Forester left their transport, carriers, mortars, signal equipment etc and a cadre of instructors in every subject the result being our boys were turned from a static unit with little training into a field force unit.

In the spring of 1942 two old carriers, one 3" mortar and some miscellaneous signal equipment arrived and 'B' Company were very proud to be turned into Headquarter Company. More transport arrived and the last was seen of civilian cars and lorries which had been clung to for so long. The next move was to Wolterton Park and soon after to Peterborough to provide a counter attack role if any aerodrome was invaded by the enemy.

By summer of 1943 this role was considered unnecessary and the battalion was moved to Leighton Buzzard where, like all other Young Soldier Battalions, it was disbanded. Young Soldiers from this battalion went on to serve with practically every regiment of the British Army in all theatres of war.

The Depot

The Depot at Britannia Barracks was used with the Nelson (Cavalry) Barracks and hutments adjoining as an Infantry Training Centre. From September 1939 until August 1941 recruits were trained on a 16 week infantry syllabus and were destined to be posted to one of the battalions of the Regiment. In August 1941 the Northamptonshire Regiment sent its training staff to the Depot because its own centre was required for other purposes and the name was changed to No. 2 Infantry Training Centre (No. 2 ITC) with the combined staffs working together.

On 2 July 1942 Primary Training for all recruits entering the army was instituted and No. 2 ITC was given an allotment of this class of training and a new addition was made known as No. 52 Primary Training Wing. The recruits that passed through Britannia Barracks were dispersed to all branches of the Service.

Lieut.-Col. Shand MC took over command of the Depot in September 1939 and remained in command until March 1943 when he was relieved by Lieut.-Col. Cochrane of the Northamptonshire Regiment. Early in 1942 the Northamptonshire Regiment returned to its Depot and was replaced by the training staff of the Dorsetshire Regiment from Colchester and Command was assumed by

40th Norfolk Company ATS, Britannia Barracks, Norwich c1940.

Lt-Col. Thywaites, he was replaced by Lieut.-Col. J S Hewick who remained until after the end of hostilities with Major J G Steward as Officer in Charge, Royal Norfolk Regiment Depot Party. The efficiency of the Depot owed much to the clerks, cooks, stores workers and drivers of the 40th (Norfolk) Company Auxiliary Territorial Service. Raised during Autumn 1938 the company served at the Depot throughout the duration of The Second World War.

No. 2 Infantry Holding Battalion

This battalion cane into existence at Ludham in mid-November 1944 under the command of Lieut.-Col. P H Cadeux Hudson MC (Hampshire Regiment) as a composite battalion made up of both Royal Norfolk Regiment and Dorsetshire Regiment soldiers. Holding battalions were formed in the Autumn of 1944 to relieve the congestion at Infantry Training Centres; to take in sick and wounded after hospital treatment; to collect floating personnel from home and abroad; to supply drafts and to supply personnel for general demands when required. Ludham was not a popular station owing to a lack of accommodation and facilities for games but it became bearable because it was a meeting place for Officers and Other Ranks from all battalions.

In mid-March 1945 the battalion moved to Great Yarmouth where it was accommodated in hotels and boarding houses. A very pleasant summer was spent there and a first rate concert party was formed under Captains Longe and Houseman with Bandmaster D. Harvey. At the end of August 1945 the battalion moved to Dorchester and command passed to Lieut.-Col. G. Winter. The battalion was finally disbanded in July 1946.

The Norfolk Yeomanry

Reformed after the First World War in conjunction with the Suffolk Yeomanry as 108th (Suffolk & Norfolk Yeomanry) Army Field Brigade RA the regiment was converted to the 65th Anti-Tank Regiment in 1938 and when the TA was doubled became a regiment in its own right again in April 1939 as the Suffolk Yeomanry split away to became 55th Suffolk Yeomanry Anti-Tank Regiment.

The Norfolk Yeomanry joined the BEF in France in February 1940 serving with 50 (Northumbrian) Division and was involved in considerable fighting around Arras 21-22 May 1940. The regiment evacuated in fair order via Dunkirk and returned to Britain but lost all of its equipment in the process.

The Yeomanry was re-equipped and sailed for the Middle East aboard HMT *Costa Rica* in December 1940 arriving on Suez on 16 February 1941 in time to assist in halting Rommels' advance on the Libyan border in action at Halfaya Pass. So began a period of intensive service that did not end until the fall of Tunis in 1943. During this time the batteries of the Norfolk Yeomanry had only one period of six weeks rest. Their major operations began with Operation Battleaxe, the first attempt to relieve Torbruk in the summer of 1941. The operation did not succeed but at Capurezzo one battery knocked out sixteen enemy tanks.

In November 1941 the Regiment was serving with 4 Indian Division and took part in the relief of Torbruk and the capture of Benghazi where they spent the Christmas of 1941. Rommel's counter attack cut off part of the Division in Benghazi including Yeomanry RHQ and some of the Battery 'B' Echelons. Most of these troops managed to get away but RHQ suffered heavily, however, eight men of the regiment managed to walk back 300 miles across across the desert to Gazala and into British lines.

At the battle of Gazala the Swaffham Battery was tragically overrun and lost. During the retreat to El Alamein the batteries suffered some nasty moments, including one battery losing all its troop commanders when they were taken prisoner. The Norfolk Yeomanry was with 10 Armoured Division at the battle of Alam Halfa, when Rommel's last attack on Alamein was repulsed. At the end of this battle the regiment was transferred to 7 Armoured Division with whom it was destined to remain to the rest of the war. With this division, the 'Desert Rats' fought at Alamein.

One of the great characters of the Norfolk Yeomanry who distinguished himself twice during these key desert battles was Sgt 'Dolly' Gray of 258 Battery. He had been awarded the Military Medal during the advance to Benghazi in December 1941. Then during the opening days of the Second Battle of El Alamein he won the Distinguished Conduct Medal, his citation, countersigned by both Montgomery and Alexander reads:

Anti-Tank Gunners and portee of The Norfolk Yeomanry near Carpurezzo, where the Regiment first destroyed tanks in the desert, 1941

'For gallantry and devotion to duty in the 'January' Bridgehead on 25 October, Sgt. Gray was troops sergeant of 'G' Troop of 258 A/T Battery. At first light the enemy armour was seen to be grouping for an attack. The troop commander himself went off to contact the tanks commander of the tanks with which he was working and ordered Sgt Gray to liaise with what was thought to be an infantry post on the flank of the Troop. The post turned out to be one the enemy had reoccupied during the night, but Sgt Gray, quite undaunted, went up and brought back first 6 fully armed Italian Officers and later about 200 Italian other ranks. Whilst conducting them back from the Troop to the rear the party was shelled and Sgt Gray was wounded and had to be evacuated. The enemy post was found to contain 3 anti-tank guns, 3 heavy MGs, 1 4-inch mortar and a number of light machine guns, grenades and rifles. By his fearless example and aggressive spirit, with which he imbued the whole Troop, he was to a large degree responsible for both saving the whole Troop from a difficult situation and for capturing about 200 prisoners.'

During the long pursuit that followed the battle of El Alamein, 7 Armoured Division never lost contact with the enemy and took part in the battle at El Agheila; the capture of Tripoli, the defensive battle at Medenine, at which the Germans lost 52 tanks to anti-tank guns without one of our tanks being lost; Mareth and finally, the assault on Tunis under the command of the First Army.

In the invasion of Italy the Regiment, with 7 Armoured Division, formed part of the 'follow up' for the Salerno landing which began on 9 September 1943. On 15 September the division started landing and the Regiment was all on shore by 17 September. The bridgehead was still very small and all of it under shell fire and crammed with equipment. Gradually the advance of the Eighth Army from the heel of Italy helped to ease the situation and on 27 September the division was able to break out in the direction of Scafah, which was eventually captured after confused battles in the streets. One brigade of the division was directed on Naples which was entered on 1 October. The Yeomanry, however, skirted Naples going by way of Afragola and Aversa, both of which were fair sized town from which the enemy needed to be flushed out. They pushed steadily on to the Volturno river, which was crossed, and a bridgehead formed only after great difficulty. The banks of the river were very steep and the current very rapid. The Yeomanry here did good work getting the infantry anti-tank guns and ammunition across by rafts.

Churchill tanks of 25th Army Tank Brigade advance over open country near Thetford in Norfolk, November 1942.

The advance was pressed on until the river Garigliano was reached, The division, together with the Yeomanry, were then withdrawn and sent back to England; while on that journey they spent Christmas 1943 at sea. On reaching England the regiment was stationed in Norfolk in Thetford Forest and the surrounding area. Regimental HQ, 257 and 260 Batteries were billeted in Kimberley Hall near Wymondham, 258 Battery in Attleborough and 258 Battery at Wymondham. While in this area the Yeomanry, along with the rest of 7 Armoured Division prepared for the invasion of North Western Europe, their tanks and vehicles rolling over the battle area and getting used to country roads while batches of the men managed to enjoy some well-earned leave.

The invasion plan was that 7 Armoured Division was to follow up 50 (Northumbrian) Division, The Norfolk Yeomanry were ashore on D+3 concentrating around Ryes. Villars Bocage, about 12 miles to the south, was their first objective. The town was reached but a fierce tank battle with 21 Panzer Division developed in and around the town and eventually 7 Armoured Division was forced to withdraw. At this time the Yeomanry were heavily engaged with tanks. They bagged some but lost some guns and had some men taken POW. There followed a long battle for the bridgehead until the build up could be completed.

After the fall of Caen an attempt was made to break out from the bridgehead by the three armoured divisions south-west of Caen; this was initially successful but was halted before anything decisive was accomplished. Finally the breakthrough came and the pursuit started. The Seine was crossed at St Pierre Vauvray, from there on the pace quickened and the division swept on to Ghent in Belgium.

A rest period followed in the Malines area. The next operation was the protection of the Guard's Armoured Division left flank in their attempt to reach Arnhem to relieve the Airborne Division. Following on this the Regiment fought up the outskirts of St Hertogenbosch. It then moved south-west and captured Tillberg and Loon-Opzand. At this time the Regiment was frequently employed destroying buildings and church towers used by the enemy as observation posts.

Senior NCOs of The Norfolk Yeomanry, Germany 1945

When the line was carried to the Maas the Division was moved to the Lomburg province of Holland. On the night of 23 March the Rhine crossings began and on 28 March the Regiment crossed at Xanton, on bridges built by 15 (Scottish) Division. Thus began the final rout of Nazi Germany. The Division was directed first on to Bremen which was then by-passed, then Hamburg, which was not captured but surrendered to 7 Armoured Division after heavy fighting around the bridges over the Elbe at Harburg. On 2 May General Wolz arrived at 7 Division HQ to discuss arrangements for surrender. On 3 May RHQ drove into Hamburg and moved into billets near the zoo. Although the official surrender was a few hours away members of the German forces were surrendering by the thousand. Hostilities were to cease from 8.00am on 5 May and VE Day was officially announced on 8 May 1945. The Norfolk Yeomanry remained in Germany forming part of the Army of Occupation for a further eighteen months and the Regiment formally disbanded in Germany in February 1946.

8 A Time to Remember

VE Day arrived on 8 May 1945 and with the announcement of this day by Winston Churchill he said 'we may allow ourselves a brief period of rejoicing.' In Norwich Gentleman's Walk rapidly filled with revellers in both civvies and uniforms of every hue and celebrations were held across the county as streets dusted off the coronation bunting and local folks clubbed together to pool their ration coupons to get a few treats for the children at their street party. Most children had a great time, so did many adults but look closer at the faces of many ladies – mothers, sisters, wives and girlfriends; their smiles are not as wide as they might be because their special relative is not there to share the day. For many Norfolk families their loved one's fight was still going on in the Far East in India and Burma or still the men waited for freedom from captivity in the hands of the Japanese, a freedom that would only be made possible by the defeat of Japan. Six days after atomic bombs were dropped on Hiroshima and Nagasaki, on 15 August 1945, Japan announced its surrender to the allied powers and the soldiers and captives of the Far East could begin to look forward to making the long journey home again. Delays due to the regulations in 'demob' release schemes and spaces available on shipping prevented many men in the Far East from returning until 1946. For some of those called up late in the war the situation was similar in Germany and they ended up serving in the occupation forces, a number of Norfolk men were also present when some of the major concentration camps were opened. Even after experiencing years of war previously, for many of them it was the sights they saw in the camps that lingered in their nightmares. With the return of our local heroes special dinners and welcome home events were held and the men tried to settle back into civvy life. For some the reunion with children they had not seen for years and vice versa proved difficult but then they were fortunate; there were some children who never saw Daddy again.

Airfields across the county were left in silence after years of aero engines spluttering into life and roaring away, the hangars where the concerts were held now echoed with bird song and the clang of agricultural machinery as the farmers reclaimed their land. Many of them still stand today, some of their buildings ruinous, the runways divided by tall grass through the gaps in the concrete or simply ploughed up while others have been lovingly restored and opened as museums by enthusiasts or used for other purposes. Many of the fixed defences, the anti-tank blocks and spigot mortar mounts across the county were removed or are overgrown and almost forgotten; the pillboxes and defensive emplacements demolished or left again as unblinking silent sentinels, reminders of an invasion that threatened but never came.

Borough of King's Lynn

VICTORY CELEBRATIONS

SATURDAY, 8th JUNE, 1946

✵ PROGRAMME ✵

Committee:
THE WORSHIPFUL THE MAYOR (ALDERMAN R. BUNNETT, J.P.), *Chairman*; ALDERMEN CATLEUGH, ERRINGTON and RABY; COUNCILLORS BURLINGHAM, FISHER, JERMYN and PAINE, with the TOWN CLERK, BOROUGH SURVEYOR, BOROUGH ELECTRICAL ENGINEER and MR. E. H. BRADFORD.

Secretary:
MR. F. G. REEVES, Town Clerk.

Assistant Secretary:
MR. F. J. COMER, Town Clerk's Department.

Hon. Treasurer:
MR. E. H. BRADFORD.

Organisers:
MORNING PROCESSION.—THE CHIEF CONSTABLE (MR. F. Calvert).
SERVICE.—REV. H. B. J. ARMSTRONG and REV. W. E. PAULSON, Adpt. A. PRICE (Salvation Army).
VICTORY GALA.—CORPORATION DEPOT SPORTS CLUB.
CHILDREN'S SPORTS.—MR. A. SAUVAIN and COMMITTEE of Head and Assistant Teachers.
GRAND VICTORY PARADE.—MR. E. PAINE and COMMITTEE.
BONFIRE & FIREWORKS.—THE BOROUGH SURVEYOR (MR. H. G. Ridler).

VE Day street party, Kings Road, Fakenham 8 May 1945

The most dangerous remnant of the war in Norfolk were the minefields of our coastline that remained a hazard for decade after the end of hostilities. The initial bulk of the clearance work was completed between 1944 and 1947 with many of the military disposal teams incorporating German ex-prisoners of war labourers who chose to say in this country rather than return to their war torn homes and were allowed to do so if they volunteered to work in bomb disposal. However, there were some areas where it was considered too dangerous to clear the mines because maps showing their where-abouts had been lost or the areas where they had been laid had changed due to coastal erosion and extensive cliff falls. One such place was the stretch of coast from the Trimingham border with Mundesley to Overstrand that consisted mainly of sandy cliffs rising in parts to 200 ft. In the late 1940s a decision was made by the military authorities to rope the area off and leave the minefield for a consid-erable period to let the terrain settle and hopefully reduce the danger to the Sappers of the Royal Engi-neers whose task it would be to clear the mines.

In the early 1950s only the Mundesley minefield and a similar stretch of coast at Fairlight Green in Sussex remained uncleared and so it was decided to complete the task. The project at Mundesley was allocated to No.1 Bomb Disposal Troop, Royal Engineers then based in Totteridge, North London. The first team consisted on one Officer, Captain Hough, Staff Sergeant 'Taffy' Thomas, Sergeant Robert O'Doherty and Corporal Ken Braddock and about ten ex-POW German labourers. Their mission being

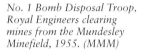
No. 1 Bomb Disposal Troop, Royal Engineers clearing mines from the Mundesley Minefield, 1955. (MMM)

to deal with any bombs or mines still in position resulting from wartime hostilities in the London area and the East of England. After new reconnaissance they began the long process in April 1953. Based in Mundesley their work commenced at the Trimingham end.

Work progressed steadily for about two weeks until 6 May 1953 when a mine exploded killing Sergeant O'Doherty and Corporal Braddock. Captain Hough and Staff Sergeant Thomas crawled onto the minefield without protection to try and rescue their comrades but they found them both dead. For their heroic action Captain Hough was awarded the George Medal and Staff Sergeant Thomas the BEM.

The work recommenced with a second team from London with Sergeant Laverty and L/Cpl. Bruce Hogg. Because of the nature of the terrain the project developed into a major engineering exercise using heavy plant such as bulldozers to cut away the cliff that had fallen onto the beach and exposing the mines and the use of high pressure water jets to wash the surface of the sandy cliffs and dislodge the mines. The methods were successful but it was a long process and personnel remained on site until the early 1970s when the beach and cliffs were finally returned to the local community.

Memorial to the Royal Engineer Bomb Disposal personnel who were killed while clearing land mines on the Norfolk Coast 1944-1953, dedicated by Sir Timothy Colman KG, HM Lord Lieutenant of Norfolk at Mundesley on 2 May 2004.

Appendix 1
The Civilian Casualties of Norfolk during the Second World War
Reproduced by kind permission of the Commonwealth War Graves Commission

BLOFIELD AND FLEGG, RURAL DISTRICT,
Norfolk, Civilian War Dead

BROWN, Civilian, KATHERINE JANE, Civilian War Dead. 7 May 1943. Age 52. of Calgarian, Beach Road, Winterton. Widow of Henry Robert Brown. Died at Albion House, Back Road, Winterton.

COLMAN, Civilian, ALICE JANE, Civilian War Dead. 11 May 1943. Age 67. Wife of Robert Jonathan Colman, of Manships Farm, Ormesby St. Michael. Died at Manships Farm.

FOX, Civilian, BERTIE, Civilian War Dead. 22 July 1941. Age 56. of 74 Lawn Avenue, Great Yarmouth. Husband of Caroline Lucy Fox. Died at Ferry Farm, Reedham.

FOX, Civilian, CAROLINE LUCY, Civilian War Dead. 22 July 1941. Age 56. of 74 Lawn Avenue, Great Yarmouth. Wife of Bertie Fox. Died at Ferry Farm, Reedham.

GAILIS, Civilian, JANIS, Civilian War Dead. 30 January 1940. Age 26. Latvian National; Merchant Navy; of Matioa 101, Riga, Latvia. on beach at Hemsby.

HODDS, Civilian, EDNA MAUD, Civilian War Dead. 7 May 1943. Age 45. Wife of Alfred James Hodds. Died at Back Road, Winterton.

NELSON, Civilian, ERIC VICTOR, Civilian War Dead. 29 March 1941. Age 17. Son of Mr. and Mrs. Horatio Charles Nelson, of 22 Lichfield Road, Great Yarmouth. Died at Postwick.

SMITH, Civilian, SIDNEY SAMUEL, Civilian War Dead. 18 May 1942. Age 51. Son of Samuel and Florence Smith, of 258 Heigham Street, Norwich; husband of Eva Smith, of 133 Nelson Street, Norwich. Injured 29 April 1942, at Norwich; died at St. Andrew's Hospital, Thorpe-next-Norwich.

THIRTLE, Civilian, HERBERT RICHARD, Civilian War Dead. 27 June 1942. Age 58. of The Green, Little Plumstead. Husband of Rose Alice Thirtle. Died at The Green.

THIRTLE, Civilian, ROSE ALICE, Civilian War Dead Link. see NORWICH list.

TOLMAN, Civilian, CUBITT, Civilian War Dead. 1 April 1941. Age 28. Husband of Violet Florence Tolman. in field adjoining Wood Farm, Mautby.

TOLMAN, Civilian, VIOLET FLORENCE, Civilian War Dead. 1 April 1941. Age 30. Wife of Cubitt Tolman. Died at field adjoining Wood Farm, Mautby.

WROE, Civilian, JOYCE MARGARET, Civilian War Dead. 19 November 1940. Age 3. of 4 South Beach Parade, Great Yarmouth. Daughter of Arthur Stanley and Dorothy Emily Wroe. Died at Thrigby Road, Filby.

CROMER, URBAN DISTRICT,
Norfolk, Civilian War Dead

BOWDITCH, Civilian, ALICE MAUDE, Civilian War Dead. 22 July 1942. Age 58. of 13 Garden Street. Wife of Robert Bowditch. Died at 13 Garden Street.

Memorial plaque at the Garden of Remembrance, Earlham Cemetery

BOWDITCH, Civilian, ROBERT, Civilian War Dead. 22 July 1942. Age 63. of 13 Garden Street. Husband of Alice Maude Bowditch. Died at 13 Garden Street.

BUMFREY, Civilian, JAMES ROBERT, Civilian War Dead. 19 October 1942. Age 45. Son of Mr. and Mrs. J. H. Bumfrey, of 6 York Terrace, Suffield Park. Died at St. Margaret's Road.

CLARKE, Civilian, EDITH BERTHA SOPHIA, Civilian War Dead. 22 July 1942. Age 57. of 40 Church Street. Daughter of Mary Ann Clarke, and of the late John Adam Clarke. Died at 40 Church Street.

DAVIES, Civilian, ANN, Civilian War Dead. 22 July 1942. Age 5. of 13 Garden Street. Daughter of William Henry and Ellen Richenda Davies. Died at 13 Garden Street.

DAVIES, Civilian, ELLEN RICHENDA, Civilian War Dead. 22 July 1942. Age 32. of 13 Garden Street. Daughter of Robert and Alice Maude Bowditch; wife of William Henry Davies. Died at 13 Garden Street.

DAVIES, Civilian, JOHN ROBERT, Civilian War Dead. 22 July 1942. Aged 7 months; of 13 Garden Street. Son of William Henry and Ellen Richenda Davies. Died at 13 Garden Street.

DAVIES, Civilian, WILLIAM HENRY, Civilian War Dead. 22 July 1942. Age 30. member of Cromer Lifeboat crew; of 13 Garden Street. Son of John James and Beatrice Davies, of 8 New Street; husband of Ellen Richenda Davies. Died at 13 Garden Street.

DOUGHTY, Civilian, THOMAS WILLIAM, Civilian War Dead. 23 July 1942. Age 49. A.R.P. Casualty Service. Son of Mr. and Mrs. W. Doughty. Died at Thurgarton Dairy, Church Square.

DUGDALE, Civilian, EDITH, Civilian War Dead. 23 July 1942. Age 51. of 15 Garden Street. Wife of Frederick Dugdale. Injured 22 July, 1942, at Garden Street; died at District Hospital.

DUGDALE, Civilian, KENNETH FREDERICK, Civilian War Dead. 23 July 1942. Age 16. A.R.P. Messenger; of 15 Garden Street. Son of Frederick Dugdale, and of Edith Dugdale. Injured 22 July 1942, at 15 Garden Street; died at District Hospital.

JILLINGS, Civilian, JAMES PETER, Civilian War Dead. 18 April 1941. Age 85. of 7 Alfred Road. Injured 11 April 1941, at 7 Alfred Road; died at 12 Bernard Road.

KING, Civilian, DORIS EMMA, Civilian War Dead. 17 November 1940. Age 12. Daughter of Arthur William King, of Bower Cottage, Lower Common, East Runton. Died at 18 Central Road.

PRYER, Civilian, FREDERICK WILLIAM, Civilian War Dead. 19 October 1942. Age 50. Senior Air Raid Warden. Husband of Maude Sarah Clorinda Pryer, of Post Office, Thorpe Market. Injured at Cromer; died same day at District Hospital.

WESTRUP, Civilian, BEATRICE HELEN, Civilian War Dead. 23 July 1942. Age 45. of Thurgarton Dairy, Church Square. Daughter of Charlotte May and of the late Ernest Horace Samuel Westrup. Died at Thurgarton Dairy.

WESTRUP, Civilian, CHARLOTTE MAY, Civilian War Dead. 23 July 1942. Age 74. of Thurgarton Dairy, Church Square. Widow of Ernest Horace Samuel Westrup. Died at Thurgarton Dairy.

DEPWADE, RURAL DISTRICT,
Norfolk, Civilian War Dead

BRAND, Civilian, FRANCES LILIAN, Civilian War Dead. 23 September 1940. Age 44. Daughter of Walter William and Frances Ruth Key Brand, of South View, Mellis, Suffolk. Died at The Hall, Roydon.

COOK, Civilian, HELEN BEATRICE, Civilian War Dead. 22 February 1943. Age 47. of Hill Farm, Great Moulton. Daughter of Alfred and Sarah Stimpson, of Rookery Cottages, Potter Heigham; wife of Charles James Cook. Died at Hill Farm.

COXALL, Civilian, ALBERT EDWARD, Civilian War Dead. 25 November 1944. Husband of Florence Coxall, of 132 Gertrude Road, Norwich. Died at Hardwick Aerodrome.

DOWNHAM, RURAL DISTRICT,
Norfolk, Civilian War Dead

BACON, Civilian, ALFRED EDWARD, Civilian War Dead. 29 October 1940. Age 57. of High Street, Fincham. Died at Fincham Men's Club.

ERPINGHAM, RURAL DISTRICT, Norfolk, Civilian War Dead

ALLEN, Civilian, JAMES, Civilian War Dead. 6 July 1943. Age 39. Fireman, N.F.S. Husband of Blanche Allen, of Avenue Cottages, Watlington, King's Lynn. Died at Kelling Sanatorium, Holt, as the result of an illness contracted while on duty during air raids.

BYGRAVE, Civilian, ALBERT WILLIAM, Civilian War Dead. 29 October 1940. Age 41. Husband of Lily Violet Bygrave, of 100 Bignold Road, Drayton Estate, Norwich. Died at Matlaske Aerodrome.

KING, Civilian, JANE, Civilian War Dead. 19 January 1941. Age 66. Daughter of Mr. and Mrs. Thomas Hatt, of Market Street, Shipdham; wife of S. King, of 159 Malpas Road, Brockley, London. Died at Beckham House, West Beckham.

MARTIN, Civilian, FREDERICK, Civilian War Dead. 29 October 1940. Age 46. Husband of Rosetta Martin, of 1 Pinder Close, Drayton Estate, Norwich. Died at Matlaske Aerodrome.

SPAVEN, Civilian, CORNELIUS, Civilian War Dead. 4 April 1943. Husband of Rebecca Spaven, of 4 Crystal Villas, Victor Street, Hull, Yorkshire. Died at Holt.

FOREHOE AND HENSTEAD, RURAL DISTRICT, Norfolk, Civilian War Dead

EASTER, Civilian, KIT, Civilian War Dead. 14 May 1942. Age 62. of 11 St. Margaret Alley, Norwich. Widow of G. E. Easter. Died at Parish Hall Rest Centre, Poringham.

FREEBRIDGE LYNN, RURAL DISTRICT, Norfolk, Civilian War Dead

PRATT, Civilian, RONALD EDWARD BADEN, Civilian War Dead. 1 May 1945. Age 16. Sea Cadet Corps. Son of Mr. and Mrs. Edward Pratt, of 5 Lansdowne Street, King's Lynn. Died at Seal Sand.

GREAT YARMOUTH, COUNTY BOROUGH, Norfolk, Civilian War Dead

ALGAR, Civilian, ARTHUR, Civilian War Dead. 14 July 1941. Age 42. of 14 St. Luke's Terrace, Cobholm. Husband of Edith Maud Algar. Died at 14 St. Luke s Terrace.

ALGAR, Civilian, EDITH MAUD, Civilian War Dead. 14 July 1941. Age 44. of 14 St. Luke's Terrace, Cobholm. Wife of Arthur Algar. Died at 14 St. Luke's Terrace.

ANNISON, Civilian, GEORGE FREDERICK, Civilian War Dead. 8 April 1941. Age 41. of 1 Havelock Place, Havelock Road. Son of Samuel and Emily Annison, of 2 English Buildings, North Market Road; husband of Mary Ann Caroline Annison. Died at Middlegate Street.

ARBON, Civilian, EDWARD, Civilian War Dead. 14 July 1941. Age 56. of 104 Mill Road, Cobholm. Son of the late Charles and Sarah Elizabeth Arbon, of Row 125; husband of Florence Arbon. Died at 104 Mill Road.

ARBON, Civilian, FLORENCE, Civilian War Dead. 14 July 1941. Age 50. of 104 Mill Road, Cobholm. Daughter of Mr. and Mrs. Thurston, of Row 11; wife of Edward Arbon. Died at 104 Mill Road.

AYERS, Civilian, BERTIE, Civilian War Dead. 9 July 1941. Age 26. of 12 Amis Buildings, St. Nicholas Road. Son of William Arthur and Rose Elizabeth Ayers, of SA Withybed Lane, Alvechurch, Birmingham; husband of Dorothy Ayers. Died at St. Mary's Lane, Southtown.

BALLS, Civilian, MARY, Civilian War Dead. 27 February 1941. Age 52. of 19 York Road. Wife of Charles Arthur Balls. Died at 19 York Road.

BALLS, Civilian, MOLLY MARGARET, Civilian War Dead. 27 February 1941. Age 19. of 19 York Road. Daughter of Charles Arthur Balls, and of Mary Balls. Died at 19 York Road.

BANHAM, Civilian, BENJAMIN GEORGE, Civilian War Dead. 18 March 1943. Age 38. Firewatcher; of 122 Burgh Road, Gorleston. Son of Mr. and Mrs. G. Banham, of Low Common, Reedham; husband of Ivy V. Banham. Died at Southtown Maltings.

BARHAM, Civilian, NELLIE CHARLOTTE, Civilian War Dead. 7 July 1941. Age 35. of 196 Northgate Street. Daughter of the late Mr. and Mrs. Walter Brown, of Norwich; wife of Russell Henry Barham. Died at 196 Northgate Street.

BARHAM, Civilian, RUSSELL HENRY, Civilian War Dead. 7 July 1941. Age 38. of 196 Northgate Street. Son of Henry Barham, of 125 Lincoln Street, Norwich; husband of Nellie Carlotte Barham. Died at 196 Northgate Street.

BATLEY, Civilian, JOHN PERCIVAL, Civilian War Dead. 11 July 1940. Aged 13 months; of 25 Gordon Road, Southtown. Son of A.B. P. C. Batley, R.N., and of Vera Adeline Batley. Died at 25 Gordon Road.

BATLEY, Civilian, VERA ADELINE, Civilian War Dead. 11 July 1940. Age 19. of 25 Gordon Road, Southtown. Wife of A.B. P. C. Batley, R.N. Injured at 25 Gordon Road; died same day at General Hospital.

BERRY, Civilian, WINIFRED DAISY, Civilian War Dead. 16 February 1941. Age 47. Wife of William Robert Berry. Died at 5 Queen's Place, Albion Road.

BETTS, Civilian, FREDERICK, Civilian War Dead. 7 May 1943. Age 45. Husband of D. M. Betts, of 24 Brooke Avenue, Caister-on-Sea. Died at Vauxhall Station.

BISHOP, Civilian, FRANCES, Civilian War Dead. 11 April 1941. Age 30. Wife of James Bishop. Died at 7 Row 39.

BLYTH, Civilian, FREDA DORIS, Civilian War Dead. 13 May 1941. Age 29. of 15 Colomb Road, Gorleston. Wife of R. J. Blyth. Died at 15 Colomb Road.

BONNY, Civilian, HENRY, Civilian War Dead. 16 April 1941. Age 74. of 31 Bells Marsh Road, Gorleston. Husband of Harriet Sarah Bonny. Died at 31 Bells Marsh Road.

BONNY, Civilian, HARRIET SARAH, Civilian War Dead. 27 April 1941. Age 73. of 31 Bells Marsh Road, Gorleston. Wife of Henry Bonny. Injured 16 April 1941, at 31 Bells Marsh Road; died at General Hospital.

BOYCE, Civilian, EDWARD WILLIAM, Civilian War Dead. 12 June 1941. Age 53. of 1 Lowestoft Road, Gorleston. Son of the late Mr. and Mrs. Edward Boyce; husband of Rose Ellen Boyce. Died at 1 Lowestoft Road.

BOYCE, Civilian, ROSE ELLEN, Civilian War Dead. 12 June 1941. Age 53. of 1 Lowestoft Road, Gorleston. Daughter of William George and of the late Rose Alice Hacon; wife of Edward William Boyce. Died at Lowestoft Road.

BRADFORD, Civilian, WILLIAM, Civilian War Dead. 11 April 1941. Age 72. at 19 Row 47.

BREED, Civilian, ERNEST, Civilian War Dead. 10 October 1944. Age 3. Fireman, N.F.S. Husband of Margaret Breed, of 9 Pondcroft Road, Knebworth, Hertfordshire. Injured 1 October 1944, at N.F.S. Beach Approach Camp, Hopton; died at Gorleston Hospital.

BROWN, Civilian, GEORGE WILLIAM, Civilian War Dead. 8 April 1941. Age 41. Special Constable. Husband of Olive Rose Brown, of 12 Harbord Crescent. Died at Seagull Garage, Queen's Road.

BROWNE, Civilian, ELLEN, Civilian War Dead. 24 December 1942. Age 70. of 82 St. Nicholas Road. Daughter of the late Richard Matthews; wife of George A. Brown. Injured 22 December 1942, at 82 St. Nicholas Road; died at General Hospital.

BROWNE, Civilian, FREDERICK JAMES, Civilian War Dead. 25 January 1941. Age 56. Husband of Eliza Maud Browne, of 11 Century Road, Southtown. Died at Jewson's Quay.

BUSH, Civilian, ELLEN CAROLINE, Civilian War Dead. 24 August 1940. Age 75. of 55 Cliff Hill, Gorleston. Widow of James Bush. Died at Beach Road, Gorleston.

CAPON, Civilian, ALBERT EDWARD, Civilian War Dead. 18 April 1941. Age 52. of 22 Elsie Road, Southtown. Husband of Annie Edith Capon. Died at 22 Elsie Road.

CAPON, Civilian, ANNIE EDITH, Civilian War Dead. 18 April 1941. Age 50. of 22 Elsie Road, Southtown. Daughter of Priscilla Todd, of 11 Row 130; wife of Albert Edward Capon. Died at 22 Elsie Road.

CAPON, Civilian, JOYCE PRISCILLA, Civilian War Dead. 18 April 1941. Age 18. of 22 Elsie Road, Southtown. Daughter of Albert Edward and Annie Edith Capon. Died at 22 Elsie Road.

CATLING, Civilian, ADA JANE, Civilian War Dead. 22 December 1942. Age 58. of 1 Higham Place, St. Nicholas Road. Died at 1 Higham Place.

CATLING, Civilian, ELLEN ROSE, Civilian War Dead. 22 December 1942. Age 66. of 1 Higham Place, St. Nicholas Road. Died at 1 Higham Place.

CLARKE, Civilian, HARRY GEORGE, Civilian War Dead. 13 May 1941. Age 56. of 13 Colomb Road, Gorleston. Husband of Isobel Clarke. Died at 13 Colomb Road.

CLARKE, Civilian, ISOBEL, Civilian War Dead. 13 May 1941. Age 57. of 13 Colomb Road, Gorleston. Wife of Harry George Clarke. Died at 13 Colomb Road.

COCKLE, Civilian, HARRY THOMAS, Civilian War Dead. 9 April 1941. Age 47. of 51 Nelson Road, Gorleston. Husband of Rose Elizabeth Cockle. Died at 51 Nelson Road.

COCKLE, Civilian, MURIEL FLORENCE, Civilian War Dead. 9 April 1941. Age 16. W.V.S.; of 51 Nelson Road, Gorleston. Daughter of Harry Thomas and Rose Elizabeth Cockle. Died at 51 Nelson Road.

COCKLE, Civilian, ROSE ELIZABETH, Civilian War Dead. 9 April 1941. Age 47. of 41 Nelson Road, Gorleston. Daughter of George William Darkins, of St. Thomas Cottages, Great Glen, Leicester, and of the late Phoebe Darkins; wife of Harry Thomas Cockle. Died at 51 Nelson Road.

COOPER, Civilian, OWEN PATRICK, Civilian War Dead. 11 May 1943. Age 5. Son of Clifford and Mary Maud Cooper, of 19 Seymour Avenue. Died at 28 Seymour Avenue.

DAVY, Civilian, HERBERT CECIL, Civilian War Dead. 8 April 1941. Age 55. Special Constable; of 84 Nelson Road Central. Son of

W. J. and P. M. Davy, of 30 Nelson Road Central; husband of L. E. Davy. Died at Seagull Garage, Queen's Road.

DRAVINS, Civilian, ARVIDO KARLIS, Civilian War Dead. 10 February 1940. Age 30. Latvian National, Merchant Navy; of Laidzes, Latvia. Died at North Beach.

FINCH, Civilian, NELLIE MARY ANN, Civilian War Dead. 16 April 1941. Age 52. of 107 Alderson Road. Daughter of Mr. and Mrs. T. W. Graves, of Silk Mill, Davey; wife of Albert Finch. Died at 107 Alderson Road.

FORD, Civilian, GEORGE ALFRED, Civilian War Dead. 30 May 1942. Age 56. Husband of Alice Ford, of 30 Maygrove Road. Died at Jewson's Yard.

GALLANT, Civilian, ALICE HARRIET, Civilian War Dead. 11 May 1943. Age 64. Wife of Ethelbert Gallant. Died at 90 Caister Road.

GOTTS, Civilian, ROBERT GEORGE, Civilian War Dead. 30 May 1942. Age 58. Firewatcher. Husband of Alice Maude Gotts, of 24 Granville Road, Southtown. Died at Jewson's Yard.

GRAVES, Civilian, THOMAS WILLIAM, Civilian War Dead. 4 February 1941. Age 60. of 204 Palgrave Road. Died at General Hospital.

GREEN, Civilian, GEORGE SEPTIMUS, Civilian War Dead. 1 February 1941. Age 59. Husband of Edith May Green, of 16 Wolseley Road, Southtown. Died at Grouts Factory, St. Nicholas Road.

GROOM, Civilian, DONALD, Civilian War Dead. 7 May 1943. Age 47. of 12 Anson Road, Southtown. Husband of Lily Groom. Died at General Hospital.

GROOM, Civilian, LILY, Civilian War Dead. 7 May 1943. Age 48. of 12 Anson Road, Southtown. Wife of Donald Groom. Died at General Hospital.

HACON, Civilian, WILLIAM GEORGE, Civilian War Dead. 12 June 1941. Age 84. of 1 Lowestoft Road, Gorleston. Husband of the late Rose Alice Hacon. Died at 1 Lowestoft Road.

HALL, Civilian, ALFRED, Civilian War Dead. 29 July 1942. Age 77. of 42 Hamilton Road. Died at 42 Hamilton Road.

HAMMOND, Civilian, PRUDENCE MAY, Civilian War Dead. 30 May 1942. Age 21. of 2 Albany Road, Southtown. Wife of Arthur Leslie Hammond. Died at 2 Albany Road.

HANNANT, Civilian, FLORENCE MAY, Civilian War Dead. 9 April 1941. Age 27. W.V.S.; of 6 Alexandra Cottages, Nelson Road. Daughter of John Robert William and Elizabeth Scott, of 61 Trafalgar Road, Gorleston; wife of Frederick Joseph Hannant. Died at 6 Alexandra Cottages.

HARMAN, Civilian, HARRIET, Civilian War Dead. 25 January 1941. Age 68. Daughter of the late Mr. and Mrs. John Harman. Died at 13 Queen Street.

HARRISON, Civilian, WILLIAM JOHN, Civilian War Dead. 8 April 1941. Age 70. Special Constable. Husband of Elizabeth C. Harrison of 10 Kimberley Terrace. Died at Seagull Garage, Queen's Road.

HAYMAN, Civilian, ROGER BERNARD, Civilian War Dead. 11 May 1943. Age 5. Son of Cpl. Bernard Edward Hayman, Royal Army Service Corps, and Verna Mary Hayman, of 316 Beccles Road, Gorleston. Died at 71 North Denes Road.

HODDS, Civilian, CAROLINE, Civilian War Dead. 16 February 1941. Age 78. of 4 Queen's Place, Albion Road. Widow of John Edward Hodds. Died at 4 Queen's Place.

HOLMES, Civilian, BRENDA VERA, Civilian War Dead. 18 February 1942. Age 16. Daughter of Mr. and Mrs. E. A. Holmes, of 105 Havelock Road. Died at 39 Northgate Street.

HOWE, Civilian, LENA MAY, Civilian War Dead. 22 December 1942. Age 19. Daughter of Ebenezer Howe, The Royal Norfolk Regiment. Died at 81 St. Nicholas Road.

HUNN, Civilian, AGNES HANNAH, Civilian War Dead. 11 May 1943. Age 59. of 71 North Denes Road. Wife of Frederick Hunn. Died at 71 North Denes Road.

HUNN, Civilian, EILEEN, Civilian War Dead. 11 May 1943. Age 18. of 71 North Denes Road. Daughter of Frederick Hunn, and of Agnes Hannah Hunn. Died at 71 North Denes Road.

JAMES, Civilian, ALBERT, Civilian War Dead. 14 July 1941. Age 15. of 76 Exmouth Road. Son of Ethel Harriett and of the late R. James. Died at 14 St. Luke's Terrace.

JAMES, Civilian, ETHEL HARRIETT, Civilian War Dead. 14 July 1941. Age 50. of 76 Exmouth Road. Daughter of Mr. and Mrs. Varley, of 78 Northgate Street, Newton; widow of R. James. Died at 14 St. Luke's Terrace, Cobholm.

JOHNSON, Civilian, WILLIAM CHARLES, Civilian War Dead. 5 February 1941. Age 70. of 59 Palgrave Road. Died at 59 Palgrave Road.

KEABLE, Civilian, ARTHUR THOMAS, Civilian War Dead. 11 July 1940. Age 60. of 68 Wolseley Road, Southtown. Died at 68 Wolseley Road.

LACEY, Civilian, JAMES RICHARD, Civilian War Dead. 14 July 1941. Age 60. of 109 Wolseley Road, Southtown. Died at Anson Road, Southtown.

LEECH, Civilian, HARRY BENJAMIN, Civilian War Dead. 7 July 1941. Age 14. of 5 Frederick Road. Son of Erasmus Leech, and of Matilda Elizabeth Leech. Died at 5 Frederick Road.

LEECH, Civilian, MATILDA ELIZABETH, Civilian War Dead. 7 July 1941. Age 48. W.V.S.; of 5 Frederick Road. Wife of Erasmus Leech. Died at 5 Frederick Road.

LIMMER, Civilian, FREDERICK, Civilian War Dead. 10 April 1941. Age 55. of 138 Bells Road, Gorleston. Husband of Florence Harriett Limmer. Died at 138 Bells Road.

LIMMER, Civilian, FLORENCE HARRIETT, Civilian War Dead. 10 April 1941. Age 58. of 138 Bells Road, Gorleston. Wife of Frederick Limmer. Died at 138 Bells Road.

LINGARD, Civilian, CHARLES THOMAS, Civilian War Dead. 12 July 1942. Age 53. Firewatcher. Husband of Ellen Amanda Lingard, of 25 Paget Road. Died at Eastern Counties Omnibus Co., Wellington Road.

LITTLEWOOD, Civilian, ADELAIDE, Civilian War Dead. 21 November 1940. Age 51. of 78 Churchill Road. Wife of Percy John Littlewood. Died at 78 Churchill Road.

LOVE, Civilian, WILLIAM GEORGE, Civilian War Dead. 7 May 1943. Age 38. Air Raid Warden; of 45 High Mill Road, Southtown. Died at Olive Road.

MADDEYS, Civilian, EDWARD WILLIAM, Civilian War Dead. 25 January 1941. Age 13. Sea Cadet; of 12 Row 129. Son of Mr. and Mrs. E. J. Maddeys. Injured at South Quay; died same day at General Hospital.

MAGNUS, Civilian, PATRICIA MARY, Civilian War Dead. 7 July 1941. Age 34. A.R.P. Telephonist; of 7 Whittleton Place, Northgate Street. Daughter of John Cussock O'Brien and Gertrude Agnes O'Brien; wife of Arthur

Leonard Magnus. Died at 7 Whittleton Place.

MASTERSON, Civilian, EDWARD JAMES, Civilian War Dead. 7 May 1943. Age 48. of 2 Laughing Image Corner. Son of the late Alfred Charles Masterson. Died at coffee stall, Vauxhall Station.

MATTHEWS, Civilian, ALICE MARY, Civilian War Dead. 9 July 1941. Age 63. of 97 High Street, Gorleston. Widow of Jasper Matthews. Died at 20 Beccles Road.

McDONALD, Civilian, ETHELBERT, Civilian War Dead. 25 January 1941. Age 47. Son of Harriet Mary McDonald, of 10 Row 104. Died at South Quay.

McSTEEN, Civilian, PHYLLIS IRENE, Civilian War Dead. 9 May 1941. Age 26. of 26 Gatacre Road. Daughter of the late Mr. and Mrs. R. Symonds; wife of William McSteen. Died at 26 Gatacre Road.

MERRISON, Civilian, ETHEL JOAN, Civilian War Dead. 11 April 1941. Age 12. Daughter of Clarissa H. Merrison, of 14 Higham Place, St. Nicholas Road. Died at George Street Shelter.

MERRISON, Civilian, GLADYS NOREEN, Civilian War Dead. 22 December 1942. Age 22. of 14 Higham Place, St. Nicholas Road. Daughter of Mr. and Mrs. H. Conway, of 21 Croft Street, Bangor, Co. Down, Northern Ireland; wife of L.A.C. Joseph Frederick Merrison, R.A.F. (killed in same incident). Died at 14 Higham Place.

MOORE, Civilian, EDNA ALEXANDRA, Civilian War Dead. 22 December 1942. Age 28. Widow of William Arthur Moore. Died at 5 Isaac Buildings, Middle Market Road.

MOORE, Civilian, MYNA, Civilian War Dead. 16 February 1941. Age 70. of 42 Suffolk Road, Southtown. Daughter of the late Mr. and Mrs. W. Flaxman, of Cemetery Road, Bradwell; widow of F. Moore. Died at 42 Suffolk Road.

MOORE, Civilian, WILLIAM ALFRED, Civilian War Dead. 22 December 1942. Age 2. Son of Edna Alexandra and of the late William Arthur Moore. Died at 5 Isaac Buildings, Middle Market Road.

MOUGHTON, Civilian, WILLIAM JAMES GEORGE, Civilian War Dead. 22 February 1947. of 5 Albert Square. Husband of R. A. Moughton. Died at Great Yarmouth.

NEWMAN, Civilian, DORIS MAUD, Civilian War Dead. 7 May 1943. Age 30. F.A.P. member. Daughter of Mr. and Mrs. C. Newman, of Albion House, Fuller's Hill, at F.A.P., Northgate School.

NICHOLLS, Civilian, OWEN BASIL, Civilian War Dead. 7 May 1943. Age 16. of 34 Stanley Road. Son of Mrs. D. Nicholls. Injured at Vauxhall Station; died same day at General Hospital.

NOBBS, Civilian, WALTER GEORGE, Civilian War Dead. 11 April 1941. Age 81. of 15 Row 41, George Street. Son of James and Naomi Nobbs, of Smallburgh, Northwich; husband of the late Maria Anna Nobbs. Died at 15 Row 41, George Street.

NORTON, Civilian, BRIAN, Civilian War Dead. 8 April 1941. Age 2. of 26 Row 142. Son of A.B. T. B. Norton, R.N.R., and of Rose May Norton. Died at Row 142.

NORTON, Civilian, ROSE MAY, Civilian War Dead. 8 April 1941. Age 21. of 26 Row 142. Wife of A.B. T. B. Norton, R.N.R. (killed in same incident). Died at Row 142.

NOY, Civilian, EMMA, Civilian War Dead. 9 May 1941. Age 75. W.V.S.; of 25 Gatacre Road, Southtown. Wife of John Noy. Died at 25 Gatacre Road.

NOY, Civilian, EMMA MAY, Civilian War Dead. 9 May 1941. Age 31. W.V.S.; of 25 Gatacre Road, Southtown. Wife of Leonard Noy (H.M. Forces). Died at 25 Gatacre Road.

NOY, Civilian, JOHN, Civilian War Dead. 9 May 1941. Age 71. Home Guard; of 25 Gatacre Road, Southtown. Husband of Emma Noy. Died at 25 Gatacre Road.

O'BRIEN, Civilian, GERTRUDE AGNES, Civilian War Dead. 7 July 1941. Age 59. of 7 Whittleton Place, Northgate Street. Wife of John Cussock O'Brien. Died at 7 Whittleton Place.

O'BRIEN, Civilian, JOHN CUSSOCK, Civilian War Dead. 7 July 1941. Age 58. Special Constable; of 7 Whittleton Place, Northgate Street. Husband of Gertrude Agnes O'Brien. Died at 7 Whittleton Place.

PARMENTER, Civilian, CECIL, Civilian War Dead. 18 February 1942. Age 30. Special Constable. Husband of Olive Parmenter, of Maxwell, Gloucester Avenue, Gorleston. Died at 39 Northgate Street.

PARNELL, Civilian, ADELAIDE EMMA, Civilian War Dead. 18 February 1942. Age 45. of 39 Northgate Street. Daughter of J. and A. Patteson, of Commodore Road, Oulton Broad, Lowestoft, Suffolk; wife of William John Parnell. Died at 39 Northgate Street.

PARNELL, Civilian, JOHN ANTONY, Civilian War Dead. 18 February 1942. Age 12. of 39 Northgate Street. Son of William John and Adelaide Emma Parnell. Died at 39 Northgate Street.

PARNELL, Civilian, WILLIAM JOHN, Civilian War Dead. 18 February 1942. Age 41. Air Raid Warden; of 39 Northgate Street. Son of W. T. and A. M. Parnell, of 19 Love Road, Lowestoft, Suffolk; husband of Adelaide Emma Parnell. Died at 39 Northgate Street.

PERRY, Civilian, PHOEBE ANN, Civilian War Dead. 8 April 1941. Age 72. of 27 Row 142. Wife of William James Perry. Died at Row 142, Middlegate Street.

PERRY, Civilian, WILLIAM JAMES, Civilian War Dead. 8 April 1941. Age 73. of 27 Row 142. Husband of Phoebe Ann Perry. Died at Row 142, Middlegate Street.

PITCHERS, Civilian, JEAN EDIS, Civilian War Dead. 11 April 1941. Age 7. of 59 North Quay. Daughter of Harold Thomas William Pitchers, Merchant Navy, and of Nora Edis Eliza Pitchers. Died at North Quay Shelter.

PITCHERS, Civilian, MARGARET EILEEN, Civilian War Dead. 11 April 1941. Aged 2 months; of 59 North Quay. Daughter of Harold Thomas William Pitchers, Merchant Navy, and of Nora Edis Eliza Pitchers. Died at North Quay Shelter.

PITCHERS, Civilian, NORA EDIS ELIZA, Civilian War Dead. 11 April 1941. Age 27. of 59 North Quay. Wife of Harold Thomas William Pitchers, Merchant Navy. Died at North Quay Shelter.

PITCHERS, Civilian, PATRICIA ANN, Civilian War Dead. 11 April 1941. Age 2. of 59 North Quay. Daughter of Harold Thomas William Pitchers, Merchant Navy, and of Nora Edis Eliza Pitchers. Died at North Quay Shelter.

PITT, Civilian, THOMAS JAMES, Civilian War Dead. 8 April 1941. Age 60. of 13 Row 141. Died at 13 Row 141.

PLATT, Civilian, PHYLLIS IRENE, Civilian War Dead. 18 April 1941. Age 18. of 22 Elsie Road, Southtown. Daughter of M. E. Platt, of 1 Coronation Road, Cobholm, and of the late Richard Platt. Died at 22 Elsie Road.

PORTER, Civilian, CAROLINE CATHERINE,

Civilian War Dead. 9 May 1941. Age 62. of 10 Steam Mill Lane, Southtown. Widow of George Albert Porter. Died at Saw Mill Lane Shelter.

POWLEY, Civilian, ALAN, Civilian War Dead. 11 May 1943. Age 42. of 26 Beresford Road. Husband of Hilda Elizabeth Powley. Injured at Great Yarmouth; died same day at General Hospital.

PRIME, Civilian, EVELYN MAY, Civilian War Dead. 18 April 1941. Age 23. of 21 Elsie Road, Southtown. Daughter of Mr. Frederick David Wright, and of Edith Florence Wright; wife of Donald Prime. Died at 21 Elsie Road.

RANSOME, Civilian, FRED, Civilian War Dead. 8 April 1941. Age 51. of 41 Collingwood Road. Son of Richenda Ransome, of 32 St. Leonard's Road, Thorpe Hamlet, Norwich; husband of Maud Lucy Ransome. Died at 41 Collingwood Road.

RANSOME, Civilian, MAUD LUCY, Civilian War Dead. 8 April 1941. Age 50. of 41 Collingwood Road. Daughter of Lucy Blazeby, of Clematis Cottage, Blofield, Norwich; wife of Fred Ransome. Died at 41 Collingwood Road.

RICHARDS, Civilian, HAROLD CONRAD RICHARD, Civilian War Dead. 11 July 1940. Age 27. of 12 Row 122, King Street. Son of Mr. and Mrs. A. Richards, of 48 Peggotty Road; husband of Olive May Richards. Died at Wolseley Road, Southtown.

RICHES, Civilian, ALICE MARY, Civilian War Dead. 12 May 1943. Age 49. of Station Road, Ormesby. Widow of Arthur Isaac Riches. Died at General Hospital.

RICHES, Civilian, OLIVE KATHLEEN, Civilian War Dead. 7 May 1943. Age 29. F.A.P. member. Wife of Jack William Riches, of 70 Sturdee Avenue, Newtown. Died at Northgate School First Aid Post.

RISING, Civilian, VIOLET, Civilian War Dead. 10 September 1940. Age 39. of 74 Harbord Crescent. Daughter of John A. Harris, of 70 Mill Road, Southtown; wife of Samuel G. Rising. Died at 74 Harbord Crescent.

ROBERTS, Civilian, ALFRED DENNIS, Civilian War Dead. 2 February 1941. Age 17. Son of Robert William and Florence May Roberts, of 21 Louise Road. Injured 1 February 1941, at Dyson and Son's Workshop; died at General Hospital.

ROGERS, Civilian, HARRIET MATILDA, Civilian War Dead. 18 April 1941. Age 64. of 26 Elsie Road, Southtown. Wife of Robert William Rogers. Died at 26 Elsie Road.

ROGERS, Civilian, JUNE, Civilian War Dead. 18 April 1941. Age 7. Daughter of Mr. and Mrs. J. A. Rogers, of 61 Mill Road, Southtown. Died at 26 Elsie Road, Southtown.

ROGERS, Civilian, ROBERT WILLIAM, Civilian War Dead. 18 April 1941. Age 73. of 26 Elsie Road, Southtown. Husband of Harriet Matilda Rogers. Died at 26 Elsie Road.

ROWLAND, Civilian, IVY, Civilian War Dead. 11 April 1941. Age 34. of 3 Row 47. Wife of Pte. James Rowland, Royal Army Ordnance Corps (killed in same incident and buried with her). Died at 3 Row 47.

RUDD, Civilian, HARRY WILLIAM, Civilian War Dead. 18 April 1941. Age 47. Constable, Police War Reserve; of 63 York Road. Died at 23 Elsie Road, Southtown.

SADLER, Civilian, RHODA ALICE, Civilian War Dead. 12 June 1941. Age 24. of 1 Lowestoft Road, Gorleston. Daughter of Edward William and Rose Ellen Boyce; wife of Pte. Herbert Sadler, The Devonshire Regiment. Died at 1 Lowestoft Road.

SARJEANT, Civilian, MARY JANE, Civilian War Dead. 5 February 1941. Age 82. of 181 Palgrave Road. Wife of William Arthur Sarjeant. Died at 181 Palgrave Road.

SARJEANT, Civilian, WILLIAM ARTHUR, Civilian War Dead. 5 February 1941. Age 83. of 181 Palgrave Road. Son of the late Arthur Sarjeant, F.R.C.S., of Stratford-sub-Castle, Salisbury, Wiltshire; husband of Mary Jane Sarjeant. Died at 181 Palgrave Road.

SEARLES, Civilian, WILLIAM ROBERT, Civilian War Dead. 9 July 1941. Age 53. of 13 Row 96. Husband of A. C. Searles. Died at 13 Row 96.

SEWELL, Civilian, ALICE EVELYN, Civilian War Dead. 10 September 1940. Age 32. of 78 Harbord Crescent. Wife of H. J. Sewell. Died at 78 Harbord Crescent.

SHREEVE, Civilian, ALICE, Civilian War Dead. 18 February 1942. Age 65. of 38 Northgate Street. Wife of Thomas V. Shreeve. Died at 38 Northgate Street.

SMITH, Civilian, HENRY HERBERT, Civilian War Dead. 7 May 1943. Age 62. of 132 Havelock Road. Died at Market Place.

SMITH, Civilian, STANLEY ARCHER, Civilian War Dead. 7 July 1941. Age 37. Air Raid Warden; of 6 Whittleton Place, Northgate Street. Son of W. H. K. Smith, of 5 Bulmans Nursery, Northgate Street; husband of Victoria Ellen Elizabeth Smith, W.R.N.S. (killed in same incident). Died at 6 Whittleton Place.

SMOWTON, Civilian, PERCY JAMES, Civilian War Dead. 8 April 1941. Age 59. Special Constable; of 86 Nelson Road Central. Son of Mr. and Mrs. I. Smowton, of the same address. Died at Seagull Garage, Queen's Road.

SPARHAM, Civilian, CHARLES LEONARD, Civilian War Dead. 31 January 1947. Age 52. Fireman, N.F.S. Husband of Daisy Caroline Sparham, of 59 Alderson Road. Died at 59 Alderson Road, as the result of an illness contracted while on duty.

SPENCER, Civilian, ALBERT EDWARD, Civilian War Dead. 9 April 1941. Age 42. of 2 Alexandra Cottages, Nelson Road, Gorleston. Son of Mary Spencer, of 66 Blackwall Reach, Gorleston, and of the late William Everard Spencer; husband of Myrtle Hannah Spencer. Died at 2 Alexandra Cottages.

STOLWORTHY, Civilian, CHARLOTTE, Civilian War Dead. 11 May 1943. Age 29. of 26 Seymour Avenue. Daughter of Florence Read, of 37 Blackfriars Road; wife of L/Cpl. Leonard Wilfred Stolworthy, Royal Army Service Corps. Died at 26 Seymour Avenue.

STONE, Civilian, ALICE GERTRUDE, Civilian War Dead. 7 July 1941. Age 51. of 210 Northgate Street. Wife of Herbert Stone. Died at 210 Northgate Street.

STONE, Civilian, HERBERT, Civilian War Dead. 7 July 1941. Age 60. of 210 Northgate Street. Husband of Alice Gertrude Stone. Died at 210 Northgate Street.

STONE, Civilian, RICHARD JOHN, Civilian War Dead. 7 July 1941. Age 18. of 210 Northgate Street. Son of Herbert and Alice Gertrude Stone. Died at 210 Northgate Street.

SYMONDS, Civilian, ELIZA, Civilian War Dead. 9 May 1941. Age 65. of 26 Gatacre Road. Wife of Robert Symonds. Died at 26 Gatacre Road.

TERRELL, Civilian, ROSA ALICE, Civilian War Dead. 12 July 1942. Age 48. Daughter of the late Mr. and Mrs. R. Batley, of St. Peter's Road; wife of William Henry Terrell, of 59 St. Peter's Road. Injured at Eastern Counties Bus Station; died same day at General Hospital.

THACKER, Civilian, FREDERICK, Civilian War Dead. 25 June 1942. Age 76. of 69 Blackfriars Road. Husband of Mary Ann Thacker. Died at 9 Row 108.

THACKER, Civilian, MARY ANN, Civilian War Dead. 25 June 1942. Age 76. of 69 Blackfriars Road. Wife of Frederick Thacker. Died at 9 Row 108.

TOOLEY, Civilian, WILLIAM, Civilian War Dead. 7 May 1943. Age 65. of The Wherry, Widgeon. Son of the late Willam and Matilda Tooley. Died at coffee stall, Vauxhall Station.

TURNER, Civilian, RAYMOND, Civilian War Dead. 9 April 1941. Age 7. of 83 Blackfriars Road. Son of Rowena Jane Turner. Died at 83 Blackfriars Road.

TURNER, Civilian, ROWENA JANE, Civilian War Dead. 9 April 1941. Age 45. of 83 Blackfriars Road. Died at 83 Blackfriars Road.

WATSON, Civilian, CHARLES WILLIAM, Civilian War Dead. 9 April 1941. Age 37. of 18 Lower Cliff Road, Gorleston. Son of George and Edith Jane Watson; husband of Olive Emily Watson. Died at 18 Lower Cliff Road.

WELLS, Civilian, KENNETH, Civilian War Dead. 20 February 1941. Age 12. of 46 Southgates Road. Son of Mr. and Mrs. Basil Edward Wells. Injured 18 February 1941, at 46 Southgates Road; died at General Hospital.

WESTGATE, Civilian, ARTHUR, Civilian War Dead. 18 February 1942. Age 3. of 5 Nursery Place, Northgate Street. Son of Mr. A. J. Westgate. Died at 5 Nursery Place.

WESTGATE, Civilian, ROSE MARY, Civilian War Dead. 18 February 1942. Age 26. Daughter of Mr. and Mrs. R. Westgate, of 10 Townwall Road, Maygrove Estate. Died at 5 Nursery Place, Northgate Street.

WHITTAKER, Civilian, JOHN SAMUEL, Civilian War Dead. 29 July 1942. Age 78. Husband of Emma M. Whittaker, of Fern Cottage, Dyke Lane, Acle. Died at 49 Salisbury Road.

WILLSMORE, Civilian, FREDERICK GEORGE, Civilian War Dead. 8 April 1941. Age 38. Special Constable; of 13 South Beach Parade. Son of Emma Jane Willsmore, of 38 Lisle Road, Colchester, Essex, and of the late T. W. Willsmore; husband of Maud Florence Willsmore. Died at Seagull Garage, Queen's Road.

WILSON, Civilian, CLARISSA JESSIE MARGARET, Civilian War Dead. 11 April 1941. Age 23. of 59 North Quay. Daughter of Clarissa H. Merrison, of 14 Higham Place, St. Nicholas Road; wife of Gnr. Robert Wilson, R.A. Died at George Street Shelter.

WILSON, Civilian, DOROTHY EVELYN ROSE, Civilian War Dead. 7 May 1943. Age 40. F.A.P. member; of 96 Albion Road. Wife of W.O. Robert William Wilson, R.A.F. Died at Northgate School F.A.P.

WILSON, Civilian, MARGARET, Civilian War Dead. 11 April 1941. Aged 2 months; of 59 North Quay. Daughter of Gnr. Robert Wilson, R.A., and of Clarissa Jessie Margaret Wilson. Died at George Street Shelter.

WISEMAN, Civilian, FREDERICK THOMAS GEORGE, Civilian War Dead. 25 June 1942. Age 17. Home Guard; of 7 Row 108, South Quay. Son of Mr. and Mrs. T. Wiseman. Died at 7 Row 108.

WOOLTON, Civilian, GEORGE THOMAS, Civilian War Dead. 8 April 1941. Age 60. of 2 Row 143, Middlegate Street. Son of Mrs. M. A. Woolton. Died at 2 Row 143.

WRAGG, Civilian, JENNIFER JANE, Civilian War Dead. 11 May 1943. Age 4. of 25 Hawkins Avenue. Daughter of Thomas Bowers Nichols Wragg (H.M. Forces) and Lilian Maud Wragg. Died at General Hospital.

WRIGHT, Civilian, ETHEL EMILY, Civilian War Dead. 7 May 1943. Age 53. of 11 Swirles Buildings, North Market Road. Died at Vauxhall Station.

WRIGHT, Civilian, EDITH FLORENCE, Civilian War Dead. 18 April 1941. Age 53. of 21 Elsie Road, Southtown. Wife of Frederick David Wright. Died at 21 Elsie Road.

WRIGHT, Civilian, JAMES GEORGE, Civilian War Dead. 18 April 1941. Age 18. Home Guard; of 21 Elsie Road, Southtown. Son of Frederick David Wright, and of Edith Florence Wright. Died at 21 Elsie Road.

YARHAM, Civilian, DORIS MAY, Civilian War Dead. 11 May 1943. Age 11. of 28 Seymour Avenue. Daughter of Leonard Robert Yarham, and of Violet Edith Yarham. Died at 28 Seymour Avenue.

YARHAM, Civilian, VIOLET EDITH, Civilian War Dead. 11 May 1943. Age 46. of 28 Seymour Avenue. Wife of Leonard Robert Yarham. Died at 28 Seymour Avenue.

KING'S LYNN, MUNICIPAL BOROUGH, Norfolk, Civilian War Dead

ADAMS, Civilian, EVA MAY, Civilian War Dead. 12 June 1942. Age 44. W.V.S.; of 131 Austin Street. Wife of Leonard William Adams. Died at Eagle Hotel, Norfolk Street.

ADAMS, Civilian, ERNEST VICTOR, Civilian War Dead. 12 June 1942. Age 54. Husband of A. L. Adams, of 2 Kirby Street. Died at Norfolk Street.

ADAMS, Civilian, LEONARD WILLIAM, Civilian War Dead. 12 June 1942. Age 46. of 131 Austin Street. Son of Mrs. W. Adams, of Rose Cottage, Extons Place, and of the late W. Adams; husband of Eva May Adams. Died at Eagle Hotel, Norfolk Street.

ADAMS, Civilian, WILLIAM THOMAS, Civilian War Dead. 12 June 1942. Age 19. F.A.P. member. Son of A. L. Adams, of 2 Kirby Street, and of Ernest Victor Adams. Died at Norfolk Street.

BAKER, Civilian, GLADYS LOUVAIN, Civilian War Dead. 12 June 1942. Age 27. Daughter of Alfred and Emma Wenn, of 18 Graham Street; wife of Sidney Baker, of 38 Burkitt Street. Died at Norfolk Street.

BALLS, Civilian, ALICE MAUD MARY, Civilian War Dead. 10 November 1941. Age 62. of 2 Loke Road. Daughter of Mr. and Mrs. T. Peak, of 74 Tennyson Avenue; wife of George William Balls. Died at Loke Road.

BALLS, Civilian, GEORGE WILLIAM, Civilian War Dead. 10 November 1941. Age 63. of 2 Loke Road. Son of John and Fanny Balls, of 1 Lansdowne Street; husband of Alice Maud Mary Balls. Died at Loke Road.

BEANEY, Civilian, NELLIE MAY, Civilian War Dead. 20 November 1940. Age 46. of 48 South Street. Wife of Walter Beaney. Died at 48 South Street.

BEANEY, Civilian, RAYMOND, Civilian War Dead. 20 November 1940. Age 11. of 48 South Street. Son of Walter and Nellie May Beaney. Died at 48 South Street.

BEANEY, Civilian, WALTER, Civilian War Dead. 20 November 1940. Age 54. of 48 South Street. Husband of Nellie May Beaney. Died at 48 South Street.

BECKETT, Civilian, FREDERICK JAMES, Civilian War Dead. 20 November 1940. Age 33. Fireman, A.F.S.; of 44 South Street. Husband of Violet Grace Beckett. Died at 44 South Street.

BECKETT, Civilian, VIOLET GRACE, Civilian War Dead. 20 November 1940. Age 33. of 44 South Street. Daughter of F. C. and B. Sparrow, of 23 Field Lane, Gaywood; wife of Frederick James Beckett. Died at 44 South Street.

BOUCH, Civilian, FLORENCE REBECCA, Civilian War Dead. 20 November 1940. Age 68. of 16 Wood Street. Daughter of Mr. C. J. Bouch. Died at 16 Wood Street.

BOWEN, Civilian, MARGARET ANNIE, Civilian War Dead. 12 June 1941. Age 54. of 15 Whitefriars Terrace. Wife of William James Bowen. Died at 15 Whitefriars Terrace.

BOWEN, Civilian, WILLIAM JAMES, Civilian War Dead. 12 June 1941. Age 56. of 15 Whitefriars Terrace. Husband of Margaret Annie Bowen. Died at 15 Whitefriars Terrace.

BRITTAIN, Civilian, DONALD EDMOND, Civilian War Dead. 12 June 1941. Age 8. Son of Ernest Brittain, of 33 London Road, and of Leath Grace Brittain. Died at 4 Boal Street.

BRITTAIN, Civilian, DERRICK JOHN, Civilian War Dead. 12 June 1941. Age 8. Son of Ernest Brittain, of 33 London Road, and of Leath Grace Brittain. Died at 4 Boal Street.

BRITTAIN, Civilian, LEATH GRACE, Civilian War Dead. 12 June 1941. Age 42. Wife of Ernest Brittain, of 33 London Road. Died at 4 Boal Street.

CASTLETON, Civilian, GLADYS EVELYN, Civilian War Dead. 10 November 1941. Age 16. of Victoria Hotel, Estuary Road. Daughter of James R. F., and Margaret S. Castleton. Died at Victoria Hotel.

CURTIS, Civilian, EMMA, Civilian War Dead. 12 June 1942. Age 50. of 8 Johnson Square. Wife of Frederick Barnaby Curtis. Died at Norfolk Street.

CURTIS, Civilian, FREDERICK BARNABY, Civilian War Dead. 12 June 1942. Age 49. of 8 Johnson Square. Husband of Emma Curtis. Died at Norfolk Street.

DAVIS, Civilian, WILLIAM, Civilian War Dead. 12 June 1942. Age 66. of 12 Albert Avenue. Husband of the late Margaret Hano Davis. Died at Eagle Hotel, Norfolk Street.

DAWSON, Civilian, PETER NORIS, Civilian War Dead. 12 June 1941. Age 16. of 13 Whitefriars Terrace. Son of Mr. and Mrs. Sydney Charles Dawson. Died at 13 Whitefriars Terrace.

DRAYTON, Civilian, SARAH ANN, Civilian War Dead. 20 November 1940. Age 93. of 15 Wood Street. Widow of J. Drayton. Died at 15 Wood Street.

DREW, Civilian, CHARLOTTE, Civilian War Dead. 12 June 1942. Age 63. of 9 North Place North Street. Widow of James William Drew. Died at Norfolk Street.

ELVIN, Civilian, ANNA, Civilian War Dead. 13 November 1940. Age 78. Widow of J. R. Elvin. Died at 1 St. John's Terrace.

EMERSON, Civilian, JOHN WALTER, Civilian War Dead. 12 June 1941. Age 26. at 12 Whitefriars Terrace.

EMERSON, Civilian, MARGARET, Civilian War Dead. 12 June 1941. Age 59. Wife of John Emerson. Died at 12 Whitefriars Terrace.

FAULKNER, Civilian, ANNE ELIZABETH, Civilian War Dead. 12 June 1941. Age 71. of 14 Whitefriars Terrace. Daughter of Mr. and Mrs. Joseph Faulkner, of 18 London Road. Died at 14 Whitefriars Terrace.

FRANKLIN, Civilian, FLORENCE DAISY, Civilian War Dead. 12 June 1942. Age 49. of 24 Albert Street. Wife of M. J. Franklin. Died at Norfolk Street.

GIBBS, Civilian, ANN SUSAN, Civilian War Dead. 12 June 1942. Age 63. Wife of Cecil Marston Gibbs, of 11 Gaywood Road. Died at Norfolk Street.

GRIFFIN, Civilian, MILDRED MAY, Civilian War Dead. 13 November 1940. Age 59. Wife of W. Griffin, of 23 Melbourne Street. Died at Regent Street.

HOWARD, Civilian, WALTER, Civilian War Dead. 12 June 1941. Age 66. at 3 Boal Street.

JECKELLS, Civilian, WILFRED GEORGE, Civilian War Dead. 12 June 1942. Age 30. Leading Fireman, N.F.S. Husband of Mrs. Jeckells, of 43 Vancouver Avenue. Died at Norfolk Street.

JOHNSON, Civilian, SARAH, Civilian War Dead. 12 June 1942. Age 46. Wife of James Samuel Johnson, of 31 Lansdowne Street. Died at Norfolk Street.

JONES, Civilian, HERBERT WILLIAM, Civilian War Dead. 12 June 1942. Age 32. Chief Officer, Merchant Navy. Son of Ethel M. Jones, of 1 Burstock Road, Putney, London. Died at Norfolk Street.

KING, Civilian, KATHLEEN ELIZABETH, Civilian War Dead. 12 June 1942. Age 49. of 111 Norfolk Street. Wife of Ralph Evershed King. Died at 111 Norfolk Street.

KING, Civilian, RALPH EVERSHED, Civilian War Dead. 12 June 1942. Age 49. Fire Guard; of 111 Norfolk Street. Husband of Kathleen Elizabeth King. Died at 111 Norfolk Street.

McKENZIE, Civilian, JAMES, Civilian War Dead. 12 June 1942. Age 51. Fire Guard. Husband of D. E. McKenzie, of 1 Winfarthing Avenue. Died at Norfolk Street.

MOORE, Civilian, KATE, Civilian War Dead. 13 November 1940. Age 53. at 1 St. John's Terrace.

MOORE, Civilian, SARAH JANE, Civilian War Dead. 13 November 1940. Age 80. at 1 St. John's Terrace.

PADDY, Civilian, IVY EVELINE, Civilian War Dead. 12 June 1942. Age 26. Wife of Thomas William Paddy, of 14 Cresswell Street. Died at Norfolk Street.

PARR, Civilian, HARRY, Civilian War Dead. 24 July 1942. Age 67. Husband of Eliza Parr, of near The Fox, Burwell, Cambridgeshire. Died at King's Lynn Docks.

RICHES, Civilian, WILLIAM EDMONDS, Civilian War Dead. 12 June 1942. Age 50. Fire Guard. Son of the late William Riches, of Hospital Walk; husband of Florence Harriet Riches, of 11 Sidney Street. Died at Norfolk Street.

ROLFE, Civilian, PELHAM GEORGE, Civilian War Dead. 19 March 1945. Age 15. A.T.C. Son of Frank Frederick Rolfe, of Wanda, West Row, Bury St. Edmunds, Suffolk. Injured 17 March 1945, on way to King's Lynn; died at West Norfolk and King's Lynn Hospital.

SCULPHER, Civilian, STANLEY AUGUSTUS, Civilian War Dead. 12 June 1942. Age 36. F.A.P. member. Son of James and Margaret Sculpher, of 4 Jubilee Road, Clenchwarton; husband of Eugenie Emily Sculpher, of Mon Abri, Jubilee Road, Clenchwarton. Died at Eagle Hotel, Norfolk Street.

SEAMAN, Civilian, ALBERT, Civilian War Dead. 12 June 1942. Age 44. of 4 Johnson Square, Albert Street. Husband of Edith Mary Seaman. Died at Eagle Hotel, Norfolk Street.

SEAMAN, Civilian, EDITH MARY, Civilian War Dead. 12 June 1942. Age 44. of 4 Johnson Square, Albert Street. Daughter of the late Mr. and Mrs. Lift; wife of Albert Seaman. Died at Eagle Hotel, Norfolk Street.

SHARPIN, Civilian, ERNEST, Civilian War Dead. 12 June 1941. Age 31. Son of Florence, and of the late Thomas Sharpin. Died at 3 Boal Street.

SHARPIN, Civilian, EDNA MAY, Civilian War Dead. 12 June 1941. Age 28. of 38 Portland Place, Wisbech Road. Wife of Pte. Alfred Sharpin, The Royal Norfolk Regiment. Died at 3 Boal Street.

SHARPIN, Civilian, FLORENCE, Civilian War Dead. 12 June 1941. Age 64. Widow of Thomas Sharpin. Died at 3 Boal Street.

STRINGER, Civilian, BRENDA EILEEN, Civilian War Dead. 12 June 1941. Age 5. of 11 Whitefriars Terrace. Daughter of Albert Edward and Ethel G. Stringer. Died at 11 Whitefriars Terrace.

STRINGER, Civilian, MARIE, Civilian War Dead. 12 June 1941. Age 8. of 11 Whitefriars Terrace. Daughter of Albert Edward and Ethel G. Stringer. Died at 11 Whitefriars Terrace.

TAYLOR, Civilian, PRISCILLA, Civilian War Dead. 12 June 1942. Age 47. Daughter of Priscilla Chilvers, of 38 Burkitt Street, and of the late Noah Chilvers; wife of R. Taylor, of 39 Whincop Street. Died at Eagle Hotel, Norfolk Street.

THURLOW, Civilian, ARTHUR, Civilian War Dead. 12 June 1941. Age 65. of 1 Boal Street. Died at 1 Boal Street.

WALLER, Civilian, FREDERICK, Civilian War Dead. 12 June 1942. Age 44. of 8 Littleport Terrace. Husband of Violet Ethel Waller. Died at Eagle Hotel, Norfolk Street.

WALLER, Civilian, VIOLET ETHEL, Civilian War Dead. 12 June 1942. Age 51. W.V.S.; of 8 Littleport Terrace. Wife of Frederick Waller. Died at Eagle Hotel, Norfolk Street.

WATLING, Civilian, EDWARD, Civilian War Dead. 12 June 1942. Age 36. of 65 Austin Street. Husband of Freda Ellen Watling. Died at Eagle Hotel, Norfolk Street.

WATLING, Civilian, FREDA ELLEN, Civilian War Dead. 12 June 1942. Age 27. of 65 Austin Street. Daughter of Mr. and Mrs. F. Sharp, of 404 Foxhall Road, Ipswich, Suffolk; wife of Edward Watling. Died at Eagle Hotel, Norfolk Street.

LODDON, RURAL DISTRICT, Norfolk, Civilian War Dead

SEELY, Civilian, LUCY ESTHER, Civilian War Dead. 7 October 1943. Age 43. Wife of Frank Henry Seely, of Stubbs Green. Died at Stubbs Green.

SOANES, Civilian, BRYANT ROYAL, Civilian War Dead. 7 October 1943. Age 34. Husband of B. E. Soanes, of 10 Council Houses, Langley. Died at School Lane, Langley.

MITFORD AND LAUN-DITCH, RURAL DISTRICT, Norfolk, Civilian War Dead

GEORGE, Civilian, JOSEPH FRANCIS ROBBINS, Civilian War Dead. 30 November 1942. Age 28. Home Guard. Son of William and Muriel George, of Abbey Farm, Wendling, East Dereham. Died at Wendling.

KERRY, Civilian, AGNES MARY, Civilian War Dead. 29 April 1942. Age 50. Wife of John Kerry, of 13 Hackford Road, Hardingham. Died at Hardingham.

NORWICH, COUNTY BOROUGH, Norfolk, Civilian War Dead

ALDEN, Civilian, MAY BLANCHE, Civilian War Dead. 29 April 1942. Age 60. of 4 Home Street, Heigham Street. Wdow of Isaac John Alden. Died at Raynham Street.

ALDOUS, Civilian, CHARLES, Civilian War Dead. 28 April 1942. Age 74. of 43 Cherry Street. Died at The Lodge, Bowthorpe Road.

AMES, Civilian, DAISY, Civilian War Dead. 27 April 1942. Age 50. of 3 Bixfields Buildings, Rupert Street. Daughter of Ellen and of the late Thomas Ames. Died at 3 Bixfields Buildings.

AMES, Civilian, ELLEN, Civilian War Dead. 27 April 1942. Age 81. of 3 Bixfields Buildings, Rupert Street. Daughter of the late Mr. and Mrs. Fisher; widow of Thomas Ames. Died at 3 Bixfields Buildings.

APPLEGATE, Civilian, BERYL, Civilian War Dead. 6 September 1940. Age 12. of 14 Council Houses, Somerton Road, Martham. Daughter of Charles and P. M. Applegate. Injured 4 September 1940, at 14 Council Houses, Somerton Road; died at Norfolk and Norwich Hospital.

ASHFIELD, Civilian, ALFRED, Civilian War Dead. 22 February 1944. Age 57. Son of Mr. and Mrs. E. Ashfield, of Morleg, Wymondham; husband of J. Ashfield, of 65 Norwich Road, Scottow. Injured at Scottow; died same day at Norfolk and Norwich Hospital.

AUSTIN, Civilian, EPHRAIM, Civilian War Dead. 7 May 1942. Age 84. Husband of the late Frances Elizabeth Austin. Died of shock as a result of the April bombing, at The Lodge, Bowthorpe Road.

BACK, Civilian, HILDA MARY, Civilian War Dead. 29 April 1942. Age 54. F.A.P. member. Daughter of E. H. Back, of 5A Earlham Road, and of the late Revd. Arthur James Back. Died at 5A Earlham Road.

BACON, Civilian, CHARLES HENRY, Civilian War Dead. 9 July 1940. Age 36. of 40 Pilling Park Road, Plumstead. Died at Boulton and Paul's Works.

BALAAM, Civilian, MAUD PAMELA, Civilian War Dead. 9 July 1940. Age 40. Daughter of Edith Balaam, of 7 St. John's Terrace, Ashbourne Street, and of the late Walter Balaam. Died at Carrow Hill.

BALES, Civilian, WILLIAM GEORGE, Civilian War Dead. 1 August 1940. Age 32. of 22 Chapel Street. Son of Mrs. A. Bales, of 12 Henderson Road; husband of A. Bales. Died at Boulton and Paul's Works.

BARBER, Civilian, ALFRED GEOFFREY, Civilian War Dead. 28 April 1942. Age 32. of 55 Livingstone Street. Son of Henry and Eliza Emma Barber. Injured at 55 Livingstone Street; died same day at The Lodge, Bowthorpe Road.

BARBER, Civilian, ELIZA EMMA, Civilian War Dead. 30 April 1942. Age 64. of 55 Livingstone Street. Wife of Henry Barber. Died at 55 Livingstone Street.

BARBER, Civilian, HENRY, Civilian War Dead. 30 April 1942. Age 67. of 55 Livingstone Street. Husband of Eliza Emma Barber. Died at 55 Livingstone Street.

BARKWAY, Civilian, CAROLINE MARY ANN, Civilian War Dead. 1 May 1942. Age 89. of 143 Rosary Road. Widow of Charles Barkway. Injured 29 April 1942, at 143 Rosary Road; died at Thorpe Hamlet First Aid Post.

BELDING, Civilian, KENNETH GEORGE, Civilian War Dead. 5 September 1942. Age 25. Son of Mr. and Mrs. Belding, of 11 St. David's Place, Park Road, Hendon, Middlesex; husband of Vera Belding, of 187 Essex Street. Died at Frazer's Joinery Works.

BELL, Civilian, LEONARD PERCY, Civilian War Dead. 1 August 1940. Age 45. Husband of May Lucy Bell, of 56 Cardiff Road. Died at Goods Yard, Thorpe Station.

BETTS, Civilian, CLARE, Civilian War Dead. 27 April 1942. Age 63. of 8 Helena Road. Husband of Nellie Betts. Died at 8 Helena Road.

BETTS, Civilian, NELLIE, Civilian War Dead. 27 April 1942. Age 63. of 8 Helena Road. Wife of Clare Betts. Died at 8 Helena Road.

BLOGG, Civilian, GLADYS VIOLET, Civilian War Dead. 28 April 1942. Age 47. of 47 Elm Grove Lane. Daughter of the late Alexander and Hannah Rudling; wife of Sidney Albert Blogg. Died at 47 Elm Grove Lane.

BLOGG, Civilian, SIDNEY ALBERT, Civilian War Dead. 28 April 1942. Age 48. of 47 Elm Grove Lane. Son of the late Arthur Blogg; husband of Gladys Violet Blogg. Died at 47 Elm Grove Lane.

BLOMFIELD, Civilian, LAURA, Civilian War Dead. 27 June 1942. Age 84. of 16 Cotman Road. Daughter of the late Mr. and Mrs. James Warner, of White House, Scarning; widow of Edward Mills Blomfield. Died at 16 Cotman Road.

BOWDEN, Civilian, WILLIAM THOMAS, Civilian War Dead. 29 April 1942. Age 49. Son of Peter Thomas Bowden, of 8 Banksome Road; husband of Rosina Victoria Bowden, of the same address. Died at 121A Newmarket Road.

BOWERS, Civilian, MORRIS, Civilian War Dead. 28 April 1942. Age 84. of The Lodge, Bowthorpe Road. Husband of the late Betsy Bishop Bowers. Died at The Lodge, Bowthorpe Road.

BRACEY, Civilian, ARTHUR CYRIL, Civilian War Dead. 1 August 1940. Age 24. Son of A. A. and E. F. Bracey, of 25 Leonard Street, St. Augustine's; husband of D. E. Bracey, of 9 Caston Road, Thorpe-next-Norwich. Died at Boulton and Paul's Works.

BRAMBLE, Civilian, GWENDOLINE MARGARET, Civilian War Dead. 30 July 1940. Age 3. of 6 Victoria Terrace, Horns Lane. Daughter of Gnr. Harold John Bramble, R.A., and of Phyllis Mildred Bramble. Died at 6 Victoria Terrace.

BRAMBLE, Civilian, JILL JOCELYN, Civilian War Dead. 30 July 1940. Aged 17 months; of 6 Victoria Terrace, Horns Lane. Daughter of Gnr. Harold John Bramble, R. A., and of Phyllis Mildred Bramble. Died at 6 Victoria Terrace.

BRAMBLE, Civilian, PETER JOHN, Civilian War Dead. 30 July 1940. Age 5. of 6 Victoria Terrace, Horns Lane. Son of Gnr. Harold John Bramble, R.A., and of Phyllis Mildred Bramble. Injured at 6 Victoria Terrace; died same day at Norfolk and Norwich Hospital.

BRAMBLE, Civilian, PHYLLIS MILDRED, Civilian War Dead. 30 July 1940. Age 26. of 6 Victoria Terrace, Horns Lane. Daughter of Frederick Arthur and Margaret Elizabeth Blomfield, of 2 Wales Square, Prince of Wales Road; wife of Gnr. Harold John Bramble, R.A. Injured 30 July 1940, at 6 Victoria Terrace; died same day at

Norfolk and Norwich Hospital.

BRIDGES, Civilian, EDITH VIOLET, Civilian War Dead. 30 July 1940. Age 34. of 1 Lorne Place, Argyle Street. Wife of A. E. Bridges. Died at 1 Lorne Place.

BRIGHT, Civilian, THOMAS VICTOR, Civilian War Dead. 27 June 1942. Age 55. Air Raid Warden. Son of Ellen Bright, of Cambridge, and of the late William Bright; husband of Mabel Annie Hayward Bright, of 53 Mill Hill Road. Died at Maternity Home, Heigham Grove.

BRIGHTON, Civilian, BESSIE ALICE, Civilian War Dead. 28 April 1942. Age 36. of 71 Belvoir Street. Wife of Cpl. George Patrick Brighton, R.A.F. Died at 71 Belvoir Street.

BRIGHTON, Civilian, DOROTHY ALICE, Civilian War Dead. 29 April 1942. Age 32. of 16 Ethel Road, Thorpe. Daughter of Mr. and Mrs. J. T. Day, of Ethel Cottage, Whapload, Lowestoft, Suffolk; wife of Herbert (Howard) Brighton. Died at Ethel Road Shelter.

BRIGHTON, Civilian, ENID SHEILA, Civilian War Dead. 28 April 1942. Age 3. of 71 Belvoir Street. Daughter of Cpl. George Patrick Brighton, R.A.F., and of Bessie Alice Brighton. Died at 71 Belvoir Street.

BRIGHTON, Civilian, HERBERT HOWARD, Civilian War Dead. 29 April 1942. Age 35. Home Guard; of 16 Ethel Road, Thorpe. Son of Mr. and Mrs. L. H. Brighton, of 9 Beatrice Road, Thorpe; husband of Dorothy Alice Brighton. Died at Ethel Road Shelter.

BRIGHTON, Civilian, PETER GEORGE, Civilian War Dead. 28 April 1942. Age 11. of 71 Belvoir Street. Son of Cpl. George Patrick Brighton, R.A.F., and of Bessie Alice Brighton. Died at 71 Belvoir Street.

BRITCHER, Civilian, EDWARD JOHN, Civilian War Dead. 7 May 1941. Age 15. of 47 Cadge Close. Son of Edward Joseph and Ethel Maud Britcher. Died at 47 Cadge Close.

BRITCHER, Civilian, EDWARD JOSEPH, Civilian War Dead. 7 May 1941. Age 41. of 47 Cadge Close. Husband of Ethel Maud Britcher. Died at 47 Cadge Close.

BRITCHER, Civilian, ETHEL MAUD, Civilian War Dead. 8 May 1941. Age 37. of 47 Cadge Close. Wife of Edward Joseph Britcher. Injured 7 May 1941, at 47 Cadge Close; died at Norfolk and Norwich Hospital.

BRITCHER, Civilian, IRENE VIOLET, Civilian War Dead. 7 May 1941. Age 10. of 47 Cadge Close. Daughter of Edward Joseph and Ethel Maud Britcher. Died at 47 Cadge Close.

BRITCHER, Civilian, LEONARD CYRIL, Civilian War Dead. 7 May 1941. Age 13. of 47 Cadge Close. Son of Edward Joseph and Ethel Maud Britcher. Died at 47 Cadge Close.

BROOKS, Civilian, CHARLES ERNEST, Civilian War Dead. 9 July 1940. Age 39. Husband of Elsie May Brooks, of 11 Prospect Road. Died at Boulton and Paul's Works.

BROWN, Civilian, HILDA MARY, Civilian War Dead. 1 August 1940. Age 41. Wife of Joseph Brown, of 103 Barrett Road, Lakenham. Died at Iron Works.

BRUFF, Civilian, WILLIAM BERTRAM, Civilian War Dead. 2 August 1942. Age 54. of 28 York Street. Son of the late Benjamin and Henrietta Bruff. Died at Gunton Sons and Dyball's premises, St. George Street.

BRUNNING, Civilian, ROSA EDITH, Civilian War Dead. 2 December 1940. Age 31. of 47 St. John Street. Daughter of E. G. Freeman; wife of Cpl. William Bullock Brunning, R.A.F. (killed in same incident). Died at 47 St. John Street.

BURR, Civilian, BERTIE WILLIAM, Civilian War Dead. 28 April 1942. Age 51. Firewatcher. Husband of May Burr, of 122 Gipsy Lane. Injured at Oak Street; died same day at Norfolk and Norwich Hospital.

BURRELL, Civilian, MAUD ETHEL, Civilian War Dead. 12 July 1940. Age 37. Daughter of Mr. and Mrs. W. Burrell, of 21 Mansfield Lane. Injured 9 July 1940, at Norwich; died at Norfolk and Norwich Hospital.

BURTON, Civilian, CLARA, Civilian War Dead. 29 April 1942. Age 54. of 46 Alexandra Road. Wife of Ernest John Burton. Died at 46 Alexandra Road.

BURTON, Civilian, DAISLEY CHARLES MONTAGUE, Civilian War Dead. 19 August 1940. Age 30. Son of Charles and Mabel Burton, of 10 Rodgate, Marsham; husband of Ethel Marion Burton, of Matlaske, Erpingham. Injured at Scottow Aerodrome; died same day at Norfolk and Norwich Hospital.

BURTON, Civilian, ERNEST JOHN, Civilian War Dead. 29 April 1942. Age 56. of 46 Alexandra Road. Husband of Clara Burton. Died at 46 Alexandra Road.

BURTON, Civilian, JOHN ERNEST FRANK, Civilian War Dead. 29 April 1942. Age 19. of 46 Alexandra Road. Son of Ernest John and Clara Burton. Died at 46 Alexandra Road.

BURTON, Civilian, SYBIL CONSTANCE, Civilian War Dead. 29 April 1942. Age 13. of 46 Alexandra Road. Daughter of Ernest John and Clara Burton. Died at 46 Alexandra Road.

BUSH, Civilian, ANTHONY DAVID, Civilian War Dead. 30 April 1942. Age 4. Son of Charles Robert and Gladys Mary Bush. Died at The Lodge Bowthorpe Road.

BUSSEY, Civilian, SAM, Civilian War Dead. 28 April 1942. Age 39. Senior Company Officer, N.F.S. Son of James and Alice Bussey, of 5 Chapel Lane, Shaw, Lancashire; husband of Norah Mary Bussey, of 4 Flat, Fire Station, Bethel Street. Died at Oak Street.

BUTCHER, Civilian, ARTHUR, Civilian War Dead. 27 April 1942. Age 62. of 2 Bixfields Buildings, Rupert Street. Husband of Beatrice Louisa Butcher. Died at 2 Bixfields Buildings.

BUTCHER, Civilian, BEATRICE LOUISA, Civilian War Dead. 27 April 1942. Age 62. of 2 Bixfields Buildings, Rupert Street. Wife of Arthur Butcher. Died at 2 Bixfields Buildings.

BUTLER, Civilian, GEORGE WALTER, Civilian War Dead. 28 April 1942. Age 44. A.R.P. Rescue Service. Son of Walter Butler, of 12 Barker Street, and of the late Emma Butler; husband of Una Mary Butler, of 21 Civic Gardens. Injured at Oak Street; died same day at 21 Civic Gardens.

BUXTON, Civilian, CHRISTOPHER LAST, Civilian War Dead. 28 April 1942. Age 33. Son of John and Alice Buxton, of Red House, Botesdale, Bury St. Edmunds, Suffolk; husband of Gladys May Buxton, of 4 Council Houses, Thurston, Bury St. Edmunds. Died at 22 Northumberland Street.

CAREY, Civilian, VIOLET MARY, Civilian War Dead. 27 April 1942. Age 70. of 79 Northcote Road. Died at 79 Northcote Road.

CAREY, Civilian, WALTER ROBERT, Civilian War Dead. 27 April 1942. Age 70. of 79 Northcote Road. Died at 79 Northcote Road.

CARR, Civilian, CAROLINE MARY, Civilian War Dead. 29 April 1942. Age 85. of Elvina, Clabon Close, Wall Road. Widow of George Walter Carr. Died at Clabon Close.

CARR, Civilian, ELLEN KATHLEEN, Civilian War Dead. 1 August 1940. Age 17. Daughter of

Arthur James and Emily Rosetta Carr, of 32 Argyle Street. Died at Boulton and Paul's Works.

CARTER, Civilian, META VIOLET, Civilian War Dead. 28 April 1942. Age 41. of 142 Drayton Road. Daughter of Mr. and Mrs. N. J. Lean, of 1 Waterloo Terrace, Truro, Cornwall; wife of Lt. G. F. Carter, Pioneer Corps. Injured 27 April 1942, at 142 Drayton Road; died at Wardens' Post, Drayton Road.

CATCHPOLE, Civilian, SIDNEY MAURICE, Civilian War Dead. 27 April 1942. Age 12. of 23 Bacon Road. Son of G. Catchpole, and of William Thomas Catchpole. Died at 23 Bacon Road.

CATCHPOLE, Civilian, WILLIAM THOMAS, Civilian War Dead. 27 April 1942. Age 47. of 23 Bacon Road. Husband of G. Catchpole. Died at 23 Bacon Road.

CLAPHAM, Civilian, BARBARA, Civilian War Dead. 28 April 1942. Age 17. of 7 Globe Row, Globe Street. Daughter of Ronald Clapham. Died at 7 Globe Row.

CLAPHAM, Civilian, DAPHNE, Civilian War Dead. 28 April 1942. Age 14. of 7 Globe Row, Globe Street. Daughter of Ronald Clapham. Died at 7 Globe Row.

CLARKE, Civilian, ADA ELIZA, Civilian War Dead. 27 April 1942. Age 70. at 12 Bixfields Buildings, Rupert Street.

CLARKE, Civilian, JAMES, Civilian War Dead. 30 April 1942. Age 55. Husband of Fernande Louise Aline Clarke, of 9 Main Street, Dundrum, Dublin, Irish Republic. Injured 29 April 1942; died at Norwich.

CLAXTON, Civilian, CECIL, Civilian War Dead. 3 August 1940. Age 56. of 7 Victoria Terrace, Horns Lane. Husband of Gertrude Claxton. Injured 30 July 1940, at 7 Victoria Terrace; died at Norfolk and Norwich Hospital.

CLAXTON, Civilian, GERTRUDE, Civilian War Dead. 30 July 1940. Age 56. of 7 Victoria Terrace, Horns Lane. Wife of Cecil Claxton. Died at 7 Victoria Terrace.

CLENDINNING, Civilian, BLANCHE AGNES, Civilian War Dead. 27 April 1942. Age 51. of 44 Southwell Road. Daughter of James and Elizabeth Florence Jolly; widow of Lieut. Cdr. Robert Veitch Clendinning, R.N. Died at 44 Southwell Road.

COATES, Civilian, CHARLES HENRY, Civilian War Dead. 10 June 1945. Age 33. of 2 Wright's Yard, Muspole Street. Died at The Lodge, Bowthorpe Road.

CODLING, Civilian, LILY ELEANOR, Civilian War Dead. 29 April 1942. Age 44. Daughter of Mr. S. Smith, of 58 Heigham Street; wife of William Codling. Died at 185 Nelson Street.

COPLAND, Civilian, HARRY CHARLES, Civilian War Dead. 2 August 1942. Age 40. Son of Sidney Charles and Henrietta Copland, of 61 Bakers Road; husband of Florence Copland, of 120 Drayton Road. Died at Drayton Road.

CORNWELL, Civilian, MARY ANN, Civilian War Dead. 29 April 1941. Age 67. Widow of A. Cornwell. Died at City Road.

COUZENS, Civilian, PEGGY MURIEL, Civilian War Dead. 1 August 1940. Age 17. Daughter of W. S. and H. R. Couzens, of 4 George Borrow Road. Died at Boulton and Paul's Works.

CRISP, Civilian, JOHN ARTHUR, Civilian War Dead. 28 April 1942. Aged 4 months. Son of Mr. and Mrs. Arthur Crisp, of 34 Sewell Road. Died at 21 Rye Avenue.

CULYER, Civilian, FREDERICK, Civilian War Dead. 29 April 1942. Age 56. of 14 Livingstone Street. Died at Edinburgh Road.

CURSON, Civilian, GORDON ARTHUR, Civilian War Dead. 12 May 1942. Age 35. Son of John Roberts Curson, of 30 Greyhound Opening. Injured 29 April 1942, at Greyhound Opening; died at Isolation Hospital.

DANIELS, Civilian, ROBERT, Civilian War Dead. 10 July 1940. Age 30. Son of the late George and Sarah Daniels; husband of Kathleen Mabel Daniels, of 30 Bell Road. Injured 9 July 1940, at Boulton and Paul's Works; died at Norfolk and Norwich Hospital.

DAVISON, Civilian, JAMES WILLIAM, Civilian War Dead. 27 April 1942. Age 50. A.R.P. Rescue Service. Husband of Ethel Maud Davison, of 71 Hotblack Road. Died at Corporation Depot, Westwick Street.

DEBBAGE, Civilian, WILLIAM GEORGE, Civilian War Dead. 1 August 1940. Age 56. Husband of Ada Florence Debbage, of 7 Heigham Grove. Died at Boulton and Paul's Works.

DELAMERE, Civilian, JOSEPH ROBERT, Civilian War Dead. 27 April 1942. Age 46. Son of Helena Delamere, of 59 Rathgar Avenue, Rathgar, Dublin, Irish Republic, and of the late Robert Delamere; husband of Mary Pauline Delamere, of Wooddown, The Downs, Mullingar, Co. Westmeath, Irish Republic. Died at 23 Bacon Road.

DIXON, Civilian, ISOBEL JEAN, Civilian War Dead. 27 April 1942. Age 4. of 39 Patteson Road. Daughter of Frank F. Dixon, and of Laura May Dixon. Died at 39 Patteson Road.

DIXON, Civilian, LAURA MAY, Civilian War Dead. 27 April 1942. Age 36. of 39 Patteson Road. Wife of Frank F. Dixon. Died at 39 Patteson Road.

DOE, Civilian, CHARLES MONTAGUE, Civilian War Dead. 28 April 1942. Age 63. at The Lodge, Bowthorpe Road.

DORE, Civilian, ADA, Civilian War Dead. 28 April 1942. Age 72. of 140 Essex Street. Wife of John Edward Dore. Died at 140 Essex Street.

DRACASS, Civilian, GEORGE WILLIAM, Civilian War Dead. 27 April 1942. Age 64. Son of Leslie Dracass, of 7 Bakers Road; husband of Emma S. Dracass, of 25 Alma Terrace. Died at 182 Waterloo Road.

DYE, Civilian, HARRY LEONARD, Civilian War Dead. 9 July 1940. Age 35. Husband of Annie Lilian Dye, of 28 Berners Street, Aylshaln Road. Injured 9 July 1940, at Barnards Ltd.; died same day at Norfolk and Norwich Hospital.

EAGLETON, Civilian, JOSEPH, Civilian War Dead. 28 April 1942. Age 81. of 2 Quayside. Died at The Lodge, Bowthorpe Road.

EASTO, Civilian, LILIAN MAY, Civilian War Dead. 29 April 1942. Age 47. of 67 Palgrave Road, Great Yarmouth. Daughter of the late John and Ellen Jane Easto. Died at 75 Earlham Road.

EATHERLEY, Civilian, EDNA DORIS, Civilian War Dead. 27 April 1942. Age 18. of 33 Bacon Road. Daughter of Raymond Lionel and Hilda Ellen Smith; wife of Sgt. Kenneth Eatherley, R.A.F. Died at 33 Bacon Road.

EDRICH, Civilian, CATHERINE EVE, Civilian War Dead. 29 April 1942. Age 79. of 4 Hill House Road. Daughter of the late George and Sophia Winifred Morris, of Prince of Wales Road; widow of Robert Shepherd Edrich. Died at 4 Hill House Road.

EMMS, Civilian, CHARLES PERCY, Civilian War Dead. 28 April 1942. Age 65. of 55 Shipstone Road. Died at The Lodge, Bowthorpe Road.

EVERETT, Civilian, ETHEL MAUD, Civilian War Dead. 30 July 1940. Age 60. of 15 Victoria Terrace, Horns Lane. Daughter of the late Richard Elijah and Ann Everett, of 14 Victoria Terrace. Died at 15 Victoria Terrace.

EVERETT, Civilian, RICHARD CONNELL, Civilian War Dead. 30 July 1940. Age 66. of 15 Victoria Terrace, Horns Lane. Son of the late Richard Elijah and Ann Everett, of 14 Victoria Terrace; husband of the late Hebe Everett. Died at 15 Victoria Terrace.

FAULKNER, Civilian, MARY ELLEN, Civilian War Dead. 28 April 1942. Age 61. of 19 Rupert Street. Daughter of the late George and Rebecca Tuttle; widow of Ernest Faulkner. Injured at 19 Rupert Street; died same day at Norfolk and Norwich Hospital.

FEEK, Civilian, DENNIS HERBERT, Civilian War Dead. 1 August 1940. Age 15. Son of Mr. and Mrs. Herbert Henry Feek, of 130 Aylsham Road. Died at Boulton and Paul's Works.

FLOOD, Civilian, HARRIET, Civilian War Dead. 19 March 1943. Age 50. of 99 Pottergate. Died at 99 Pottergate.

FORDER, Civilian, DOROTHY MAUD, Civilian War Dead. 28 April 1942. Age 34. of 60 Elizabeth Fry Road, Earlham Estate. Daughter of Edward Rouse, of 2 Nursery Terrace, Great Yarmouth, and of the late Agnes Rouse; wife of Gnr. Walter Charles Forder, R.A. Injured 27 April 1942, at 60 Elizabeth Fry Road; died at Norfolk and Norwich Hospital.

FORDER, Civilian, JEAN MARY, Civilian War Dead. 28 April 1942. Age 7. of 60 Elizabeth Fry Road, Earlham Estate. Daughter of Gnr. Walter Charles Forder, R.A., and of Dorothy Maud Forder. Injured 27 April 1942, at 60 Elizabeth Fry Road; died at Norfolk and Norwich Hospital.

FOX, Civilian, FLORENCE ELIZABETH, Civilian War Dead. 28 April 1942. Age 45. of 73 Belvoir Street. Wife of Reginald Aubrey Fox. Injured at 73 Belvoir Street; died same day at The Lodge, Bowthorpe Road.

FOX, Civilian, JOYCE KATHLEEN, Civilian War Dead. 28 April 1942. Age 15. of 73 Belvoir Street. Daughter of Reginald Aubrey Fox, and of Florence Elizabeth Fox. Injured at 73 Belvoir Street; died same day at The Lodge, Bowthorpe Road.

FRANKLIN, Civilian, WILLIAM ROBERT, Civilian War Dead. 28 April 1942. Age 83. of 82 Nelson Street. Died at The Lodge, Bowthorpe Road.

FREEMAN, Civilian, ALICE ELIZABETH, Civilian War Dead. 2 December 1940. Age 59. of 47 St. John Street. Wife of E. J. Freeman. Died at 47 St. John Street.

FREEMAN, Civilian, CHARLES GEORGE, Civilian War Dead. 9 July 1940. Age 44. Husband of Edith Mary Freeman, of 102 Woodcock Road. Died at Thorpe Station Yard.

FREEMAN, Civilian, LUCRETIA LYDIA, Civilian War Dead. 28 April 1942. Age 72. of 25 Rupert Street. Died at 25 Rupert Street.

FULLER, Civilian, ALBERT EDWARD, Civilian War Dead. 27 April 1942. Age 57. of 6 Little Arms Street. Husband of Sarah Agnes Fuller. Died at 6 Little Arms Street.

FULLER, Civilian, SARAH AGNES, Civilian War Dead. 27 April 1942. Age 60. of 6 Little Arms Street. Wife of Albert Edward Fuller. Died at 6 Little Arms Street.

GAFFNEY, Civilian, LAURENCE, Civilian War Dead. 30 April 1942. Age 47. of Courtlough, Balbriggan, Co. Dublin, Irish Republic. Son of the late Laurence and Mary Gaffney. Died at 55 Livingstone Street.

GALEY, Civilian, JESSIE MARIA, Civilian War Dead. 28 April 1942. Age 70. of 25 Rupert Street. Daughter of the late Thomas Edward and Maria Galey, of Rutland Street. Died at 25 Rupert Street.

GAMBLE, Civilian, WINIFRED MAY, Civilian War Dead. 30 April 1942. Age 36. of 58 Ella Road. Daughter of William and Jane Hagg, of 6 Chalk Hill Road; wife of Pte. Leonard William Gamble, The Royal Norfolk Regiment. Injured 29 April 1942, at 58 Ella Road; died at Norfolk and Norwich Hospital.

GARNER, Civilian, FREDERICK, Civilian War Dead. 28 April 1942. Age 50. of 25 Esdelle Street. Died at Oak Street.

GAZE, Civilian, FLORENCE ELIZABETH, Civilian War Dead. 28 April 1942. Age 59. of 19 Rupert Street. Wife of William Wesley Gaze. Died at 19 Rupert Street.

GEOGHEGAN, Civilian, EINRI DAN, Civilian War Dead. 30 April 1942. Age 28. Son of Joseph H. Geoghegan, of Ballinsteen, Dundrum, Co. Dublin, Irish Republic. Died at 55 Livingstone Street.

GODDARD, Civilian, JOAN MIRIAM, Civilian War Dead. 28 April 1942. Age 21. of 39 Patterson Road. Wife of Cpl. Victor Charles Goddard, R.A.F. Died at Norfolk and Norwich Hospital.

GOODE, Civilian, HARRY, Civilian War Dead. 28 April 1942. Age 82. at The Lodge, Bowthorpe Road.

GOREHAM, Civilian, WALTER, Civilian War Dead. 27 April 1942. Age 46. of 43 Patteson Road. Died at 43 Patteson Road.

GRAY, Civilian, CHARLES EDWARD STAMP, Civilian War Dead. 29 April 1942. Age 36. Son of the late Frederick and Edith Gray; husband of Lilian Gray, of 13 Dickens Drive, Laindon, Essex. Died at 49 Buxton Road.

GREAVES, Civilian, LILY, Civilian War Dead. 1 August 1940. Age 58. of 10 Dakin Road. Widow of Robert Greaves. Died at Boulton and Paul's Works.

GREEN, Civilian, FRANK ROBERT, Civilian War Dead. 28 April 1942. Age 48. Son of Mr. and Mrs. R. Green, of 87 Eade Road; husband of H. M. Green, of 37 Palmer Road. Died at 69 Valpy Avenue.

HAMMOND, Civilian, HELEN MAIDA, Civilian War Dead. 2 December 1940. Age 50. Daughter of E. and H. Hammond, of 98 Spencer Street. Died at 228 King Street.

HANSELL, Civilian, CHARLOTTE PHOEBE, Civilian War Dead. 28 April 1942. Age 55 of 27 Orchard Street. Daughter of Mrs. S. Chapman, of 71 Knowsley Road; widow of William Russell Hnsell. Injured at 27 Orchard Street; died same day at Norfolk and Norwich Hospital.

HARBACH, Civilian, WILLIAM HENRY, Civilian War Dead. 27 April 1942. Age 47. Home Guard. Son of Joseph and Sarah Ann Harbach, of Lilac Lane, Cradley, Worcestershire; husband of Olive Irene Harbach, of 17 Elm Grove Lane. Died at Norwich.

HAWES, Civilian, JESSIE DOUGLAS, Civilian War Dead. 29 April 1942. Age 24. of 75 Earlham Road. Daughter of Edwin Jones, of 2 James Street, Lincoln, and of the late Jessie Douglas Jones; wife of L/Sjt. Cyril James Hawes, R.A. Died at 75 Earlham Road.

HAYHOE, Civilian, BENJAMIN, Civilian War Dead. 28 April 1942. Age 52. Firewatcher; of 7 Clifton Street. Husband of Clara E. Hayhoe. Died at Northumberland Street Shelter.

HEWITT, Civilian, EMILY MARIA, Civilian War Dead. 27 April 1942. Age 80. of 6 Bixfields Buildings, Rupert Street. Widow of John Hewitt. Died at 4 Bixfields Buildings.

HEWITT, Civilian, LYDIA MAY, Civilian War Dead. 29 April 1942. Age 48. of 13 Ethel Road. Wife of Ashley Walter Hewitt. Died at Ethel Road.

HIGH, Civilian, DAISY MAUD, Civilian War Dead. 18 February 1941. Age 36. of 46 Vauxhall Street. Daughter of Ernest E. and Emily S. Horne, of 11 Waldeck Road; wife of John Walter High. Died at 46 Vauxhall Street.

HIGH, Civilian, JOHN WALTER, Civilian War Dead. 18 February 1941. Age 36. SJ.A.B.; of 46 Vauxhall Street. Son of John and Christianna High, of 27 Bartholomew Street; husband of Daisy Maud High. Died at 46 Vauxhall Street.

HILL, Civilian, FREDERICK JOSEPH, Civilian War Dead. 28 June 1942. Age 72. Of Cinder Ovens Row. Died at The Lodge, Bowthorpe Road.

HOLLAND, Civilian, ANNE, Civilian War Dead. 27 April 1942. Age 78. of 45 Patteson Road. Widow of Clement Holland. Died at 45 Patteson Road.

HOLLAND, Civilian, PATRICK, Civilian War Dead. 27 April 1942. Age 45. of St. Patrick's, Gorse Avenue, Reepham Road. Son of Anne and of the late Clement Holland. Died at 45 Patteson Road.

HOPWOOD, Civilian, CHARLES JOSEPH, Civilian War Dead. 2 April 1941. Age 50. Husband of B. M. Hopwood, of 32 Spencer Street. Died at Thorpe Station Goods Yard.

HOULT, Civilian, BERTIE, Civilian War Dead. 9 July 1940. Age 55. Son of Frederick John Hoult, J.P., of Gresham House, Ethel Road; husband of Kathleen Hoult, of 12 Ethel Road. Injured at L.N.E.R., Thorpe Station; died same day at Norfolk and Norwich Hospital.

HOUSE, Civilian, VIOLET MAY, Civilian War Dead. 4 February 1941. Age 34. of 91 Plumstead Road. Wife of Jesse Henry House. Died at 91 Plumstead Road.

HOWES, Civilian, HERBERT ROBERT, Civilian War Dead. 1 August 1940. Age 47. Husband of Elizabeth Frances Howes, of 30 Ella Road. Died at Thorpe Station Goods Yard.

HOWETT, Civilian, CHARLES, Civilian War Dead. 28 April 1942. Age 76. of 24 Bowthorpe Road. Husband of Thirza Howett. Died at 24 Bowthorpe Road.

HOWLETT, Civilian, GEORGE, Civilian War Dead. 6 May 1941. Age 83. of 30 Bury Street. Husband of Emma Maud Howlett. Injured at 30 Bury Street, died same day at Norfolk and Norwich Hospital.

HOWLETT, Civilian, HANNAH, Civilian War Dead. 2 December 1940. Age 31. of 43 St. John Street. Wife of F. J. Howlett. Died at 47 St. John Street.

HUBBARD, Civilian, THOMAS, Civilian War Dead. 27 April 1942. Age 52. Home Guard; of 35 St. Martin's Road. Son of Thomas Hubbard, of 175 Sprowston Road; husband of G. M. Hubbard. Died at St. Martin's Road.

HUNT, Civilian, EDITH, Civilian War Dead. 29 April 1942. Age 70. of 32 Helena Road. Wife of Ernest Albert Hunt. Died at 32 Helena Road.

HUNT, Civilian, ELLA, Civilian War Dead. 30 April 1942. Age 59. of 52 Winter Road. Daughter of the late Mr. and Mrs. A. F. Hunt. Died at 52 Winter Road.

HUNT, Civilian, ERNEST ALBERT, Civilian War Dead. 29 April 1942. Age 67. of 32 Helena Road. Husband of Edith Hunt. Died at 32 Helena Road.

JACOB, Civilian, ALICE, Civilian War Dead. 27 April 1942. Age 78. Daughter of the late Robert and Susanna Jacob, of Holt. Died at 73 Adelaide Street.

JARVIS, Civilian, BERIS MABEL, Civilian War Dead. 27 April 1942. Age 25. of 41 Patteson Road. Daughter of Frederick William and May Martha Jarvis. Died at 41 Patteson Road.

JARVIS, Civilian, DOROTHY EDITH MAY, Civilian War Dead. 27 April 1942. Age 27. of 41 Patteson Road. Daughter of Frederick William and May Martha Jarvis. Died at 41 Patteson Road.

JARVIS, Civilian, FREDERICK WILLIAM, Civilian War Dead. 27 April 1942. Age 60. of 41 Patteson Road. Son of Richard and Mary Ann Elizabeth Jarvis, of Briningham; husband of May Martha Jarvis. Died at 41 Patteson Road.

JARVIS, Civilian, MAY MARTHA, Civilian War Dead. 27 April 1942. Age 56. of 41 Patteson Road. Daughter of Mr. and Mrs. Alfred Lambert, of Wickmere; wife of Frederick William Jarvis. Died at 41 Patteson Road.

JEFFRIES, Civilian, AGNES NOEL, Civilian War Dead. 18 February 1941. Age 26. Wife of H. J. Jeffries. Died at 47 Vauxhall Street.

JOHNSON, Civilian, AUDREY MAY, Civilian War Dead. 28 April 1942. Age 17. of 49 Elm Grove Lane. Daughter of Mr. and Mrs. Frederic Charles Johnson. Died at 49 Elm Grove Lane.

JOHNSON, Civilian, DORIS ELSIE MABEL, Civilian War Dead. 30 July 1940. Age 13. of 14 Victoria Terrace, Horns Lane. Daughter of George and Mabel Matilda Johnson. Died at 14 Victoria Terrace.

JOHNSON, Civilian, GEORGE, Civilian War Dead. 30 July 1940. Age 47. of 14 Victoria Terrace, Horns Lane. Husband of Mabel Matilda Johnson. Died at 14 Victoria Terrace.

JOHNSON, Civilian, MABEL MATILDA, Civilian War Dead. 30 July 1940. Age 47. of 14 Victoria Terrace, Horns Lane. Wife of George Johnson. Died at 14 Victoria Terrace.

JOLLY, Civilian, ELIZABETH FLORENCE, Civilian War Dead. 27 April 1942. Age 79. of 44 Southwell Road. Daughter of Lawrence and Eliza Neal; wife of James Jolly. Died at 44 Southwell Road.

JOLLY, Civilian, FLORENCE MAY, Civilian War Dead. 27 April 1942. Age 53. of 44 Southwell Road. Daughter of James and Elizabeth Florence Jolly. Died at 44 Southwell Road.

JOLLY, Civilian, JAMES, Civilian War Dead. 27 April 1942. Age 78. of 44 Southwell Road. Son of John and Charlotte Jolly; husband of Elizabeth Florence Jolly. Died at 44 Southwell Road.

JONES, Civilian, BRIAN MAURICE, Civilian War Dead. 14 January 1945. Age 11. Son of Henry Sidney and Iris Ivy Jones, of 16 Marshall Road, Mile Cross Estate. Died at Norwich.

JOPP, Civilian, ETHEL ADA, Civilian War Dead. 28 April 1942. Age 28. of 6 St. Mary's Road. Daughter of Charles and Lydia Seaman, of 4 Oak Lane, Catton Grove; widow of Sjt. Walter Henry Jopp, R.A. Died at 6 St. Mary's Road.

KEELEY, Civilian, ELLEN ELIZABETH, Civilian War Dead. 28 April 1942. Age 64. of 132 Millers Lane, St. Clement's Hill, New Catton. Wife of Henry Keeley. Died at 132 Millers Lane.

KEELEY, Civilian, HENRY, Civilian War Dead. 28 April 1942. Age 72. of 132 Millers Lane, St. Clement's Hill, New Catton. Husband of Ellen Elizabeth Keeley. Died at 132 Millers Lane.

KEMP, Civilian, MARY ELIZABETH, Civilian War Dead. 14 January 1945. Age 5. Daughter of Walter Frederick and Phyllis Kathleen Kemp, of 14 Spynke Road, Mile Cross. Died at 14 Spynke Road.

KENT, Civilian, ROBERT, Civilian War Dead. 27 April 1942. Age 67. Freeman of the City of Norwich; Fireman, A.F.S. Son of the late R. and Emma Maria Kent, of Priory Yard, Little Bill Close; husband of Martha Emily Kent, of 19 Appleyard Crescent, Mile Cross. Died at Edwards and Holmes Factory, Drayton Road.

KETT, Civilian, FREDERICK JOHN, Civilian War Dead. 28 April 1942. Age 68. Husband of Alice E. Kett, of 117 Ketts Hill. Died at 117 Ketts Hill.

KIDDELL, Civilian, HERBERT PERCY, Civilian War Dead. 9 July 1940. Age 44. of 209 Gertrude Road. Died at Boulton and Paul's Works.

KING, Civilian, DORIS MAY, Civilian War Dead. 28 April 1942. Age 16. of 62 Chapel Field Road. Daughter of Joseph Edward King. Died at Chapel Field Gardens.

KING, Civilian, HONOR LILIAN, Civilian War Dead. 28 April 1942. Age 14. of 62 Chapel Field Road. Daughter of Joseph Edward King. Died at Chapel Field Gardens.

KNIGHTS, Civilian, BEATRICE, Civilian War Dead. 29 April 1942. Age 62. of 35 Alexandra Road. Daughter of the late Frederick and Harriett Knights, of 15 Heigham Street. Died at 28 Alexandra Road.

KNIGHTS, Civilian, JOAN KATHLEEN, Civilian War Dead. 5 September 1942. Age 15. Daughter of Benjamin Rayner Knights, and Hilda Knights, of 61 Rackham Road. Died at Batson and Webster's Shoe Factory, Fishergate.

LAFFLING, Civilian, STANLEY DOUGLAS, Civilian War Dead. 9 July 1940. Age 23. Son of Albert Laffling, of 3 Gipping Cottages, Bramford, Ipswich, Suffolk, and of the late Emily Laffling; husband of E. May Laffling, of 253 Dereham Road. Died at Thorpe Station Engine Sheds.

LAKE, Civilian, ANN, Civilian War Dead. 27 April 1942. Age 63. of 81 Northcote Road. Wife of Thomas Arthur Lake. Died at 81 Northcote Road.

LAKE, Civilian, THOMAS ARTHUR, Civilian War Dead. 27 April 1942. Age 65. of 81 Northcote Road. Husband of Ann Lake. Died at 81 Northcote Road.

LAKEY, Civilian, THOMAS JOHN, Civilian War Dead. 29 April 1942. Age 25. Son of Thomas William and Myra Ruth Lakey, of Whissonsett, East Dereham. Died at 9 Ethel Road.

LAMB, Civilian, CECIL GEORGE, Civilian War Dead. 27 April 1942. Age 49. Firewatcher. Son of the late Mr. T. Lamb; husband of Hilda Lamb, of 3 Bowers Avenue. Died at Corporation Depot, Westwick Street.

LEMMON, Civilian, ALICE MILDRED, Civilian War Dead. 27 April 1942. Age 31. of 11 Northumberland Street. Daughter of Mr. and Mrs. G. Browne, of 128 Portland Street; wife of Frederick Charles Lemmon. Died at 11 Northumberland Street.

LEMMON, Civilian, YVONNE MARION, Civilian War Dead. 27 April 1942. Age 7. of 11 Northumberland Street. Daughter of Frederick Charles Lemmon, and of Alice Mildred Lemmon. Died at 11 Northumberland Street.

LESTER, Civilian, HETTY SELINA, Civilian War Dead. 27 June 1942. Age 70. at 16 Cotman Road.

LIGGATT, Civilian, DAVID, Civilian War Dead. 3 August 1941. Patrol Officer, Smethwick A.F.S. Died at Norwich.

LINCOLN, Civilian, JEREMIAH, Civilian War Dead. 28 April 1942. Age 63. Husband of Annie Lincoln, of 7 Wiggs Passage, Distillery Street. Died at The Lodge, Bowthorpe Road.

LOCKWOOD, Civilian, BERYL KATHLEEN, Civilian War Dead. 28 April 1942. Age 11. of 65 Rosebery Road. Daughter of Alfred George Lockwood, and of Hilda May Lockwood. Died at 65 Rosebery Road.

LOCKWOOD, Civilian, HILDA MAY, Civilian War Dead. 28 April 1942. Age 37. of 65 Rosebery Road. Daughter of Mrs. E. Reeve (formerly Fenn), and of the late E. Fenn; wife of Alfred George Lockwood. Died at 65 Rosebery Road.

LOCKWOOD, Civilian, JACK REGINALD, Civilian War Dead. 28 April 1942. Age 7. of 65 Rosebery Road. Son of Alfred George Lockwood, and of Hilda May Lockwood. Died at 65 Rosebery Road.

LOCKWOOD, Civilian, MARGARET WINIFRED, Civilian War Dead. 28 April 1942. Aged 3 months; of 65 Rosebery Road. Daughter of Alfred George Lockwood, and of Hilda May Lockwood. Died at 65 Rosebery Road.

LORD, Civilian, WILLIAM BENJAMIN, Civilian War Dead. 9 July 1940. Age 50. Husband of Harriet Lord, of 106 Bowthorpe Road. Injured at L.N.E.R., Thorpe Station; died same day at Norfolk and Norwich Hospital.

LOVETT, Civilian, KATE BRADFIELD, Civilian War Dead. 10 July 1940. Age 60. of Grange Cottage, Salhouse Road, Rackheath. Wife of Arthur James Lovett. Injured 9 July 1940, at Grange Cottage, Salhouse Road; died at Norfolk and Norwich Hospital.

MACE, Civilian, RONALD, Civilian War Dead. 19 May 1943. Fireman, N.F.S. Husband of Lucy Mace, of 86 Knowsley Road. Died at Norwich.

MAKIN, Civilian, ELLEN AGNES, Civilian War Dead. 18 February 1941. Age 27. Wife of Edward Thomas Makin. Died at 47 Vauxhall Street.

MAKIN, Civilian, EDWARD THOMAS, Civilian War Dead. 18 February 1941. Age 31. Husband of Ellen Agnes Makin. Died at 47 Vauxhall Street.

MANN, Civilian, GEORGE, Civilian War Dead. 27 June 1942. Age 89. at 41 Spitalfields.

McMILLAN, Civilian, JOHN HENRY, Civilian War Dead. 9 July 1940. Age 60. of 235 Littleton Road, Lower Kersal, Salford, Lancashire. Husband of Miriam McMillan. Injured at Boulton and Paul's Works; died same day at Norfolk and Norwich Hospital.

MEDLER, Civilian, BARBARA BEATRICE MARY, Civilian War Dead. 1 August 1940. Age 25. Daughter of Bernard Joseph and Beatrice Lucy Gurney, of 22 George Borrow Road, Earlham; wife of Stanley C. Medler. Died at Boulton and Paul's Works.

MEEK, Civilian, WILLIAM HENRY ROBERT, Civilian War Dead. 7 May 1942. Age 82. of 11 Midland Street. Died at The Lodge, Bowthorpe Road.

MIDDLETON, Civilian, LILIAN UNA, Civilian War Dead. 30 April 1942. Age 61. of 7 Trafford Road. Daughter of the late Mr. and Mrs. Thomas Middleton. Died at 7 Trafford Road.

MILLER, Civilian, JEAN AUDREY, Civilian War Dead. 28 April 1942. Age 8. Daughter of :Bertie James Miller, of 155 Olney Road, Walworth, London, and of Maud Helen Miller.

Injured 27 April 1942, at 81 Northcote Road; died at Norfolk and Norwich Hospital.

MILLER, Civilian, MAUD HELEN, Civilian War Dead. 27 April 1942. Age 39. Daughter of Thomas Arthur and Ann Lake; wife of Bertie James Miller, of 155 Olney Road, Walworth, London. Died at 81 Northcote Road.

MILLER, Civilian, SHEILA ANN, Civilian War Dead. 27 April 1942. Age 5. Daughter of Bertie James Miller, of 155 Olney Road, Walworth, London, and of Maud Helen Miller. Died at 81 Northcote Road.

MINISTER, Civilian, FLORENCE HANNAH, Civilian War Dead. 2 May 1942. Age 44. of 15 Northumberland Street. Wife of Sto. Edmund George Minister, R.N. Injured 27 April 1942, at 15 Northumberland Street; died at Norfolk and Norwich Hospital.

MINISTER, Civilian, VALERIE, Civilian War Dead. 27 April 1942. Age 3. of 15 Northumberland Street. Daughter of Sto. Edmund George Minister, R.N., and of Florence Hannah Minister. Died at 15 Northumberland Street.

MINTER, Civilian, MAY BEATRICE, Civilian War Dead. 28 April 1942. Age 48. of 117 Philadelphia Lane. Wife of Christopher Minter. Died at 113 Philadelphia Lane.

MONAGHAN, Civilian, SARAH, Civilian War Dead. 27 April 1942. Age 52. of 45 Patteson Road. Daughter of Anne and of the late Clement Holland; wife of John Monaghan. Died at 45 Patteson Road.

MOORE, Civilian, LILY AGNES, Civilian War Dead. 28 April 1942. Age 47. of 55 Union Street. Wife of Bertie James Moore. Died at Norfolk and Norwich Hospital.

MOORE, Civilian, SABINA ELIZABETH, Civilian War Dead. 29 April 1942. Age 60. of 46 Alexandra Road. Widow of Herbert Sidney Moore. Died at 46 Alexandra Road.

MUIRHEAD, Civilian, NEVILLE RICHARD GORDON, Civilian War Dead. 27 June 1942. Age 18. Son of J. Walter and Laura Muirhead, of Barjuli, Assam, India. Died at 36 Bracondale.

NASH, Civilian, AUDREY ELEANOR, Civilian War Dead. 27 April 1942. Age 49. of 52 Southwell Road. Daughter of Eleanor Seely, and of the late Herbert Thomas Seely, wife of Arthur James Nash. Died at 52 Southwell Road.

NASH, Civilian, ARTHUR JAMES, Civilian War Dead. 27 April 1942. Age 41. of 52 Southwell Road. Son of Charlotte Nash husband of Audrey Eleanor Nash. Died at 52 Southwell Road.

NEVE, Civilian, AGNES JULIA, Civilian War Dead. 29 April 1942. Age 85. Widow of William Neve. Died at 29 Alexandra Road.

NEWBY, Civilian, BARBARA OLIVE, Civilian War Dead. 27 April 1942. Age 8. of Walnut Tree Shades, Old Post Office, Castle Street. Daughter of Walter Newby, and of Hilda Newby. Died at 54 Patteson Road.

NEWBY, Civilian, HILDA, Civilian War Dead. 27 April 1942. Age 45. of Walnut Tree Shades, Old Post Office, Castle Street. Daughter of E. H. and Kate John, of 45 St. Barnabas Court, Midland Street, wife of Walter Newby. Died at 54 Patteson Road.

NEWMAN, Civilian, LEAH ALICE, Civilian War Dead. 30 July 1940. Age 56. of 5 Victoria Terrace, Horns Lane. Daughter of William and Sarah Hardy, of Coslany Street; wife of Robert Henry Newman. Died at 5 Victoria Terrace.

NEWMAN, Civilian, ROBERT HENRY, Civilian War Dead. 30 July 1940. Age 58. of 5 Victoria Terrace, Horns Lane. Son of Charles and Harriet Newman, of Waterloo Road;

husband of Leah Alice Newman. Died at 5 Victoria Terrace.

NINHAM, Civilian, MARTHA, Civilian War Dead. 27 April 1942. Age 73. of 2 William Street. Widow of Frederic Ninham. Died at 2 William Street.

O'TOOLE, Civilian, JOHN, Civilian War Dead. 27 April 1942. Age 25. Son of Elizabeth O'Toole, of 13 Convent Road, Wicklow, Irish Republic. Died at 23 Bacon Road.

PAGE, Civilian, ANNE, Civilian War Dead. 28 April 1942. Age 81. of 6 Globe Row, Globe Street. Widow of William Walter Page. Died at 6 Globe Row.

PALMER, Civilian, CECIL CHARLES HENRY, Civilian War Dead. 27 April 1942. Age 45. Fire-watcher of 12 Clarke Road. Son of Emily Palmer, of 246 Silver Road, and of the late Charles Henry Palmer; husband of the late Ethel Bessie Palmer. Died at Edwards and Holmes' Factory, Drayton Road.

PALMER, Civilian, ERNEST WILLIAM, Civilian War Dead. 27 April 1942. Age 65. of 48 Southwell Road. Husband of Mary Ann Palmer. Died at 48 Southwell Road.

PALMER, Civilian, MARY ANN, Civilian War Dead. 27 April 1942. Age 65. of 48 Southwell Road. Wife of Ernest William Palmer. Died at 48 Southwell Road.

PARKE, Civilian, ANNIE BLANCHE, Civilian War Dead. 27 April 1942. Age 77. Wife of George Robert Parke. Died at 42 Southwell Road.

PARKE, Civilian, GEORGE ROBERT, Civilian War Dead. 27 April 1942. Age 71. Husband of Annie Blanche Parke. Died at 42 Southwell Road.

PARKE, Civilian, HILDA LOUISA, Civilian War Dead. 27 April 1942. Age 37. Daughter of George Robert and Annie Blanche Parke. Died at 42 Southwell Road.

PARKER, Civilian, HAROLD GEORGE ROWING, Civilian War Dead. 1 August 1940. Age 32. of Glencoe, Marlborough Road, Oulton Broad, Lowestoft, Suffolk. Son of Mr. and Mrs. George Edgar Rowing Parker. Died at Boulton and Paul's Works.

PARKER, Civilian, RICHARD ALBERT, Civilian War Dead. 9 July 1940. Age 37. Son of Mr. W. Parker, of 8 Belsize Road; husband of Ivy M. Parker, of 5 Samuel Road. Injured at Thorpe Station Engine Sheds; died same day at Norfolk and Norwich Hospital.

PAYNE, Civilian, GEORGE ARTHUR, Civilian War Dead. 9 July 1940. Age 37. Husband of R. Payne, of 79 Bull Close Road. Died at Thorpe Station Engine Sheds.

PEARCE, Civilian, JAMES, Civilian War Dead. 28 April 1942. Age 53. Husband of Dora Angelina Pearce, of 24 Jubilee Avenue, East Dereham. Died at 22 Northumberland Street.

PEARCE, Civilian, RUSSELL LEONARD, Civilian War Dead. 25 March 1942. Fireman, N.F.S. Husband of B. M. Pearce, of 17 Newton Street, Ipswich, Suffolk. Died at Norwich.

PEDERSON, Civilian, ANDERS HAAGEN, Civilian War Dead. 29 April 1942. Age 56. Danish Subject; of 11 Brancaster Lane, Purley, Surrey. Husband of Dagmar Pederson. Died at Hippodrome, St. Giles Street.

PEDERSON, Civilian, DAGMAR, Civilian War Dead. 29 April 1942. Age 53. Danish Subject; of 11 Brancaster Lane, Purley, Surrey. Daughter of Mrs. Sanger, of Burstow Lodge, Purley, Surrey, and of the late John Sanger; wife of Anders Haagen Pederson. Died at Hippodrome, St. Giles Street.

PENNYMORE, Civilian, ARTHUR JOHN, Civilian War Dead. 2 December 1940. Age 55. of 70 Bracondale. Died at Bracondale.

PITCHFORD, Civilian, GERTRUDE IRENE, Civilian War Dead. 29 April 1942. Age 27. Wife of Harold Leslie Pitchford. in caravan, at Hippodrome, St. Giles Street.

PITCHFORD, Civilian, HAROLD LESLIE, Civilian War Dead. 29 April 1942. Age 44. Husband of Gertrude Irene Pitchford. in caravan, at Hippodrome, St. Giles Street.

PLAYFORD, Civilian, BERTHA ROSE, Civilian War Dead. 9 July 1940. Age 19. Daughter of Mrs. R. H. Playford, of 27 Copeman Street, Pottergate, and of the late J. Playford. Injured at Carrow Hill; died same day at Norfolk and Norwich Hospital.

PLUMMER, Civilian, REBECCA, Civilian War Dead. 27 April 1942. Age 65. of 7 Bixfields Buildings, Rupert Street. Died at 7 Bixfields Buildings.

POSTLE, Civilian, EMILY, Civilian War Dead. 29 April 1942. Age 90. of Unthank Road. Daughter of the late George and Sophia Winifred Morris; widow of William Postle. Died at 4 Hill House Road.

POTTER, Civilian, BRIAN ROYAL, Civilian War Dead. 28 April 1942. Age 10. of 6 St. Mary's Road. Son of A.C.2 Royal Potter, R.A.F., and Lilian Potter. Died at 6 St. Mary's Road.

POTTER, Civilian, LILIAN, Civilian War Dead. 28 April 1942. Age 30. of 6 St. Mary's Road. Daughter of Charles and Lydia Seaman, of 4 Oak Lane, Catton Grove; wife of A.C.2 Royal Potter, R.A.F. (killed in same incident). Died at 6 St. Mary's Road.

POTTER, Civilian, NOVA, Civilian War Dead. 28 April 1942. Age 3. of 6 St. Mary's Road. Daughter of A.C.2 Royal Potter, R.A.F., and Lilian Potter. Died at 6 St. Mary's Road.

PREST, Civilian, EVELYN BESSIE, Civilian War Dead. 28 April 1942. Age 45. of 59 Nelson Street, Dereham Road. Daughter of Martha and of the late Edward Prest. Injured at 59 Nelson Street; died same day at Norfolk and Norwich Hospital.

PREST, Civilian, MARTHA, Civilian War Dead. 28 April 1942. Age 76. of 59 Nelson Street. Widow of Edward Prest. Injured at 59 Nelson Street; died same day at Norfolk and Norwich Hospital.

RABY, Civilian, ELLEN, Civilian War Dead. 1 August 1940. Age 63. Wife of S. Raby, of 114 Shorncliffe Avenue, Drayton Road. Died at Boulton and Paul's Works.

RABY, Civilian, WILLIAM, Civilian War Dead. 1 May 1942. Age 73. Husband of Rosina Rebecca Raby, of 97 Goldwell Road, Hall Road. Injured 27 April 1942, at 97 Goldwell Road; died at Norfolk and Norwich Hospital.

RAVEN, Civilian, CYRIL ROBERT, Civilian War Dead. 28 April 1942. Age 41. Son of Mr. R. G. Raven, of 27 Quebec Road. Died at 49 St. Leonard's Road.

RAVEN, Civilian, GLADYS PATRICIA, Civilian War Dead. 28 April 1942. Age 17. Daughter of Cyril Robert Raven. Died at 49 St. Leonard's Road.

RAVEN, Civilian, ZENA MARY, Civilian War Dead. 28 April 1942. Age 15. Daughter of Cyril Robert Raven. Died at 49 St. Leonard's Road.

READ, Civilian, ALFRED ERNEST, Civilian War Dead. 27 April 1942. Age 39. Husband of Winifred Read. Died at 87 The Avenue.

READ, Civilian, ALBERT SAMUEL, Civilian War Dead. 6 February 1943. Age 35. Fireman, N.F.S. Husband of Evelyn Alice Read, of 103 Bury Street, Unthank Road. Died at Lads' Club.

READ, Civilian, CLIFFORD ROBERT, Civilian War Dead. 28 June 1942. Age 77. of 55 Hall Road. Son of Ransom and Louisa Read, of 16 Hereford Street, Bethnal Green, London. Injured 27 June 1942, at 55 Hall Road; died at The Lodge, Bowthorpe Road.

RISEBOROUGH, Civilian, WILLIAM GREEN, Civilian War Dead. 27 April 1942. Age 65. Of 362 Dereham Road. Husband of Mary Ann Riseborough. Died at 362 Dereham Road.

RIX, Civilian, JAMES, Civilian War Dead. 28 April 1942. Age 67. of 29 Rose Yard. Died at The Lodge, Bowthorpe Road.

ROBINSON, Civilian, FLORENCE MAY, Civilian War Dead. 30 April 1942. Age 19. Daughter of Minnie Emily Robinson, of 218 Heigham Street, and of Samuel John Robinson. Died at Heigham Street.

ROBINSON, Civilian, SAMUEL JOHN, Civilian War Dead. 30 April 1942. Age 52. Husband of Minnie Emily Robinson, of 218 Heigham Street. Injured at Heigham Street; died same day at The Lodge, Bowthorpe Road.

RUDRAM, Civilian, FREDERICK ALBERT, Civilian War Dead. 5 September 1942. Age 27. Son of Albert Mark and Ellen Rudram, of 40 Muriel Road; husband of Ruby Violet Rudram, of 2 Boundary Avenue, Mile Cross. Died at Frazer's Joinery Works.

SAMPSON, Civilian, GLADYS ROSE, Civilian War Dead. 10 July 1940. Age 18. of 29 Gloucester Street. Daughter of Mr. E. J. Sampson. Injured 9 July 1940 , at Carrow Hill; died at Norfolk and Norwich Hospital.

SANDELL, Civilian, ARTHUR ROBERT, Civilian War Dead. 29 April 1941. Age 48. Husband of Grace Frances Sandell, of 244 King Street. Died at Oat Mills, Carrow Works.

SAUNDERS, Civilian, MURIEL LOUISA ELIZABETH, Civilian War Dead. 27 April 1942. Age 24. of 10 Stafford Street. Wife of Cpl. Leslie P. W. Saunders, R.A.F. Died at 10 Helena Road.

SAVORY, Civilian, FLORENCE MAY, Civilian War Dead. 29 April 1942. Age 16. Daughter of L.A.C. A. W. Savory, R.A.F., and G. M. Savory, of 9 Shorncliffe Avenue, Junction Road. Died at 26 Dakin Road.

SCOTT, Civilian, EMILY CONSTANCE, Civilian War Dead. 28 April 1942. Age 54. Widow of John Scott. Died at 45 Elm Grove Lane.

SCOTT, Civilian, THOMAS, Civilian War Dead. 27 June 1942. Age 50. Husband of F. A. Scott. Died at 6 Vincent Road.

SEAGER, Civilian, ARTHUR GEORGE, Civilian War Dead. 18 February 1941. Age 73. of 41 Walpole Street, Vauxhall Street. Died at 41 Walpole Street.

SEAGER, Civilian, RICHARD LEECH, Civilian War Dead. 18 February 1941. Age 15. of 41 Walpole Street, Vauxhall Street. Son of Gladys Maud Smith. Died at 41 Walpole Street.

SELF, Civilian, WILLIAM, Civilian War Dead. 27 April 1942. Age 51. Firewatcher. Husband of Ethel Amelia Self, of 86 Philadelphia Lane. Died at Edwards and Holmes' Factory, Drayton Road.

SEWELL, Civilian, JAMES FREDERICK, Civilian War Dead. 27 April 1942. Age 48. A.R.P.; Firewatcher. Son of the late James and Agnes Sewell, of New Street, Holt; husband of Florence Edith Sewell, of 27 Harlington Avenue, Reepham Road. Died at Corporation Depot, Westwick Street.

SEWTER, Civilian, CARLOS ANTHONY,

Civilian War Dead. 12 July 1940. Age 46. Son of the late Edward and Amelia Sewter, of Mill Farm, Lyng; husband of Rose Sewter, of Little Melton. Injured 9 July 1940, at Boulton and Paul's Works; died at Norfolk and Norwich Hospital.

SHELDON, Civilian, SARAH ANNE, Civilian War Dead. 29 April 1942. Age 72. Wife of Alfred Ernest Sheldon, of 202 Nelson Street, Dereham Road. Died at 202 Nelson Street.

SHRIMPLIN, Civilian, BENJAMIN, Civilian War Dead. 27 June 1942. Age 75. of 39 Spitalfields. Died at Norfolk and Norwich Hospital.

SILOM, Civilian, ERNEST ROBERT, Civilian War Dead. 9 July 1940. Age 58. Husband of Alice Silom, of 41 North Walsham Road, Old Catton. Died at Thorpe Station Yard.

SKINNER, Civilian, HANNAH ELIZABETH, Civilian War Dead. 28 April 1942. Age 70. of 33 Albany Road. Daughter of the late Joseph and Betsy Emery, of Chatteris, Cambridgeshire; widow of Abraham Skinner. Died at 33 Albany Road.

SMITH, Civilian, ALBERT EDWARD HEYHOE, Civilian War Dead. 28 April 1942. Age 51. of 1 Rye Avenue. Died at Norwich.

SMITH, Civilian, ALBERT GEORGE, Civilian War Dead. 30 April 1942. Age 50. Air Raid Warden. Son of W. and R. Smith, of 34 Wymer Street, Heigham Road; husband of Kathleen Smith, of 56 Alexandra Road. Injured 29 April 1942, at 56 Aexandra Road; died at The Lodge, Bowthorpe Road.

SMITH, Civilian, ALICE KATE, Civilian War Dead. 27 April 1942. Age 68. of 23 Helena Road. Daughter of the late Robert George and Ellen Maria Hill; wife of Alfred Smith. Died at 33 Bacon Road.

SMITH, Civilian, EDITH MAY, Civilian War Dead. 27 June 1942. Age 30. of 4 Vincent Road. Daughter of Mr. and Mrs. Percy Goreham, of 99 Portland Street; wife of Harry George Smith. Died at 6 Vincent Road.

SMITH, Civilian, EMILY MARY, Civilian War Dead. 29 April 1942. Age 51. Daughter of William Burnham, of 201 Nelson Street, and of the late Sarah Burnham; wife of Albert Mark Smith, of 14 Raynham Street. Died at Raynham Street Shelter.

SMITH, Civilian, GEORGE GAMMON, Civilian War Dead. 5 September 1942. Age 43. Special Constable. Son of Frederick and Mary Jane Smith, of 10 Charles Street; husband of May Elsie Smith, of 75 Patteson Road. Died at Batson and Webster's Factory, Fishergate.

SMITH, Civilian, GRAHAM GOREHAM, Civilian War Dead. 27 June 1942. Aged 6 months; of 4 Vincent Road. Son of Harry George and Edith May Smith. Died at 6 Vincent Road.

SMITH, Civilian, HORACE, Civilian War Dead. 27 April 1942. Age 41. Air Raid Warden. Son of William and Martha Smith, of 8 Winchcombe Road, Newbury, Berkshire; husband of Florence Mary Smith, of 3 Fairstead Road, Sprowston. near Gate House, Dereham Road.

SMITH, Civilian, HILDA ELLEN, Civilian War Dead. 27 April 1942. Age 43. Firewatcher of 33 Bacon Road. Daughter of Alfred Smith, and of Alice Kate Smith; wife of Raymond Lionel Smith. Died at 33 Bacon Road.

SMITH, Civilian, HARRY GEORGE, Civilian War Dead. 27 June 1942. Age 34. of 4 Vincent Road. Son of E. R. Smith, of 4 Belsize Road, and of the late Ben Smith; husband of Edith May Smith. Died at 6 Vincent Road.

SMITH, Civilian, HERBERT RICHARD, Civilian War Dead. 6 May 1941. Age 55.

Freeman of the City of Norwich; of 28 Bury Street. Son of Mrs. Smith, of 28 Sunny Hills, Lakenham; husband of Maud Agnes Smith. Injured at 28 Bury Street; died same day at Norfolk and Norwich Hospital.

SMITH, Civilian, MAUD AGNES, Civilian War Dead. 6 May 1941. Age 51. of 28 Bury Street. Daughter of Mr. and Mrs. Smith, of Carrow Road; wife of Herbert Richard Smith. Injured at 28 Bury Street; died same day at Norfolk and Norwich Hospital.

SMITH, Civilian, MALCOLM GOREHAM, Civilian War Dead. 27 June 1942. Age 5. of 4 Vincent Road. Son of Harry George and Edith May Smith. Died at 6 Vincent Road.

SMITH, Civilian, RAYMOND LIONEL, Civilian War Dead. 27 April 1942. Age 53. Firewatcher; of 33 Bacon Road. Son of Mrs. B. E. Smith, of 36 Grosvenor Road; husband of Hilda Ellen Smith. Died at 33 Bacon Road.

SMITH, Civilian, WALTER GEORGE, Civilian War Dead. 9 July 1940. Age 23. Son of W. J. and F. E. Smith, of 114 Vincent Road. Died at Boulton and Paul's Works.

SPINKS, Civilian, BETTY ALEXANDRA, Civilian War Dead. 27 April 1942. Age 25. of 48 Southwell Road. Daughter of Ernest William and Mary Ann Palmer; wife of Harry Samuel Spinks. Died at 48 Southwell Road.

SPINKS, Civilian, CATHERINE MARY, Civilian War Dead. 27 April 1942. Aged 13 months; of 48 Southwell Road. Daughter of Harry Samuel Spinks, and of Betty Alexandra Spinks. Died at 48 Southwell Road.

SPRUCE, Civilian, LILIAN MABEL, Civilian War Dead. 9 May 1942. Age 32. of Octagon Farm, Bixley. Daughter of Mrs. F. Hewitt, of Mill Haven, Woodton, Bungay, Suffolk; wife of Hubert Marston Spruce. Died at The Lodge, Bowthorpe Road.

SQUIRE, Civilian, MARY, Civilian War Dead. 2 August 1942. Aged 1 week. Daughter of Bdr. Frank Squire, R.A., and Edith Florence Squire, of 6 Walpole Road, Great Yarmouth. Died at Sunnyside Nursing Home, Drayton Road.

STANNARD, Civilian, NELLIE ELIZABETH, Civilian War Dead. 1 May 1942. Age 60. of 21 Rowington Road. Wife of Donald Henry Stannard. Injured 30 April 1942, at 21 Rowington Road; died at Norfolk and Norwich Hospital.

STARLING, Civilian, ELIZA, Civilian War Dead. 7 May 1942. Age 62. of 20 Traverse Street. Wife of Sidney John Starling. Injured 27 April 1942, at 20 Traverse Street; died at The Lodge, Bowthorpe Road.

STARLING, Civilian, HILDA, Civilian War Dead. 28 April 1942. Age 41. of 20 Traverse Street. Daughter of Sidney John Starling, and of Eliza Starling. Injured 27 April 1942, at 20 Traverse Street; died at The Lodge, Bowthorpe Road.

STEVENS, Civilian, ROY, Civilian War Dead. 29 April 1942. Age 20. Air Raid Warden. Son of Mr. F. F. Stevens, of 12 Parr Road. Died at Mile Cross Road.

STRIKE, Civilian, ARTHUR SAMUEL, Civilian War Dead. 9 July 1940. Age 23. Son of Elizabeth Rant (formerly Strike), of 23 Clarkson Road. Died at Boulton and Paul's Works.

STROWGER, Civilian, GEORGE, Civilian War Dead. 9 July 1940. Age 27. Husband of May Eleanor Strowger, of 33 Horning Close, North Earlham. Died at Boulton and Paul's Works.

SUTTON, Civilian, DOUGLAS LEONARD, Civilian War Dead Link. (and others); see SMALLBURGH R.D. list.

SUTTON, Civilian, DOROTHY ROSALINE, Civilian War Dead. 26 April 1941. Age 31. of The Gideons, Horning, Wroxham. Wife of Henry Sutton. Injured at The Gideons, Horning; died same day at Norfolk and Norwich Hospital.

THIRTLE, Civilian, HERBERT RICHARD, Civilian War Dead Link. see BLOFIELD AND FLEGG list.

THIRTLE, Civilian, ROSE ALICE, Civilian War Dead. 27 June 1942. Age 58. of The Green, Little Plumstead, Blofield and Flegg. Daughter of Mr. and Mrs. C. High, of Great Plumstead; wife of Herbert Richard Thirtle. Injured at The Green, Little Plumstead; died same day at Norfolk and Norwich Hospital.

TIDD, Civilian, NOAH, Civilian War Dead. 30 April 1942. Age 53. Husband of L. M. Tidd, of 10 Bath House Yard, Oak Street. Died at Old Palace Road.

TIMPSON, Civilian, MARY ANN, Civilian War Dead. 18 February 1941. Age 70. at 49 Vauxhall Street.

TOOLE, Civilian, STEPHEN, Civilian War Dead. 5 September 1942. Age 39. Fireman, N.F.S. Son of Margaret Toole, of 187 Gertrude Road, Sprowston Road; husband of Elizabeth S. Toole, of 92 Plumstead Road East, Thorpe. Died at Frazer's Joinery Works.

TURNER, Civilian, ARTHUR, Civilian War Dead. 28 April 1942. Age 41. of 1 Read's Buildings, Globe Street. Son of William and Harriett Turner, of 151 Essex Street; husband of Edith Blanche Turner. Died at 1 Read's Buildings.

TURNER, Civilian, CLARA MAY, Civilian War Dead. 28 April 1942. Age 51. of 3 Globe Row, Globe Street. Wife of Frederick Thomas Turner. Died at 3 Globe Row.

TURNER, Civilian, FREDERICK THOMAS, Civilian War Dead. 28 April 1942. Age 54. of 3 Globe Row, Globe Street. Husband of Clara May Turner. Died at 3 Globe Row.

TUTTLE, Civilian, ALICE REBECCA, Civilian War Dead. 28 April 1942. Age 70. of 19 Rupert Street. Daughter of the late George and Rebecca Tuttle. Died at 19 Rupert Street.

UPTON, Civilian, BESSIE GLADYS, Civilian War Dead. 9 July 1940. Age 36. Daughter of Mrs. E. H. Upton, of 40 Lewis Street, Lakenham, and of the late S. Upton. Died at Carrow Hill.

URQUHART, Civilian, JOHN MACINTOSH, Civilian War Dead. 28 April 1942. Age 73. of 90 Rosebery Road. Died at The Lodge, Bowthorpe Road.

UTTING, Civilian, BERTRAM EDWARD, Civilian War Dead. 29 April 1942. Age 41. of 39 Midland Street. Son of Brian E. Utting, of West Farm, Attleborough; husband of Beatrice Utting. Died at Greyhound Opening.

VINCENT, Civilian, GERTRUDE, Civilian War Dead. 28 April 1942. Age 53. Wife of A. J. Vincent, of Avenue House, Wroxham. Died at 72 Millers Lane.

WALKER, Civilian, HENRY PLANE, Civilian War Dead. 28 April 1942. Age 64. Son of John H. P. Walker, of 129 Spencer Street; husband of Annie Elizabeth Plane Walker, of the same address. Died at 129 Spencer Street.

WALLACE, Civilian, ARTHUR, Civilian War Dead. 27 April 1942. Age 29. of 10 Helena Road. Son of Albert Edward Arthur Henry and Louisa Wallace. Died at 10 Helena Road.

WALLACE, Civilian, ALBERT EDWARD ARTHUR HENRY, Civilian War Dead. 27 April 1942. Age 65. of 10 Helena Road. Husband of Louisa Wallace. Died at 10 Helena Road.

WALLACE, Civilian, LOUISA, Civilian War Dead. 27 April 1942. Age 50. of 10 Helena Road. Wife of Albert Edward Arthur Henry Wallace. Died at 10 Helena Road.

WALLER, Civilian, ARTHUR PEACH, Civilian War Dead. 4 February 1941. Age 75. of 93 Plumstead Road. Husband of R. Waller. Died at 93 Plumstead Road.

WARD, Civilian, CONSTANCE MABEL, Civilian War Dead. 28 April 1942. Age 42. of 69 Valpy Avenue. Daughter of Mabel Adams, of 5 Ashford Street; widow of Robert Ward. Died at 69 Valpy Avenue.

WARD, Civilian, JOAN EVELYN, Civilian War Dead. 28 April 1942. Age 10. of 69 Valpy Avenue. Daughter of Constance Mabel and of the late Robert Ward. Died at 69 Valpy Avenue.

WARD, Civilian, OLIVE MAY, Civilian War Dead. 28 April 1942. Age 20. of 69 Valpy Avenue. Daughter of Constance Mabel and of the late Robert Ward. Died at 69 Valpy Avenue.

WARD, Civilian, RICHARD, Civilian War Dead. 28 April 1942. Age 18. of 69 Valpy Avenue. Son of Constance Mabel and of the late Robert Ward. Died at 69 Valpy Avenue.

WARNES, Civilian, EILEEN GERTRUDE, Civilian War Dead. 11 December 1940. Age 18. Daughter of John Henry and Kate Eliza Warnes, of 258 King Street. Died at 10 The Vale, Carrow Hill.

WATERS, Civilian, AGNES ELIZABETH, Civilian War Dead. 30 April 1942. Age 54. of 78 Helena Road. Wife of Albert Edmund Waters. Died at 76 Helena Road.

WATERS, Civilian, BRENDA LAVINIA, Civilian War Dead. 30 April 1942. Age 17. of 78 Helena Road. Daughter of Albert Edmund Waters, and of Agnes Elizabeth Waters. Died at 76 Helena Road.

WATERS, Civilian, EDWARD ALAN, Civilian War Dead. 30 April 1942. Age 15. of 78 Helena Road. Son of Albert Edmund Waters, and of Agnes Elizabeth Waters. Died at 76 Helena Road.

WATERS, Civilian, SYBIL HILDA, Civilian War Dead. 30 April 1942. Age 19. A.R.P. Ambulance Attendant; of 78 Helena Road. Daughter of Albert Edmund Waters, and of Agnes Elizabeth Waters. Died at 76 Helena Road.

WATSON, Civilian, REGINALD LESLIE, Civilian War Dead. 5 September 1942. Age 28. Home Guard. Husband of Dora Eleanor Watson, of 163 Sprowston Road. Died at Frazer's Joinery Works.

WEBB, Civilian, GERTRUDE ELIZABETH, Civilian War Dead. 27 April 1942. Age 62. of 5 Bixfields Buildings, Rupert Street. Daughter of the late Joshua Webb. Died at 5 Bixfields Buildings.

WELLS, Civilian, MAY REDGRAVE, Civilian War Dead. 29 April 1942. Age 66. at 5A Earlham Road.

WHALL, Civilian, GEORGE, Civilian War Dead. 28 April 1942. Age 56. of 67 Rosebery Road. Husband of Gertrude Whall. Died at 67 Rosebery Road.

WHALL, Civilian, GERTRUDE, Civilian War Dead. 28 April 1942. Age 54. of 67 Rosebery Road. Wife of George Whall. Died at 67 Rosebery Road.

WHITE, Civilian, BESSIE LOUISA, Civilian War Dead. 27 April 1942. Age 38. of 10 Little Arms Street. Daughter of the late Mr. and Mrs. H. G. Thrower; wife of Donald Wilfred White. Died at 10 Little Arms Street.

WHITE, Civilian, DONALD WILFRED, Civilian War Dead. 27 April 1942. Age 38. of 10 Little Arms Street. Son of Mrs. A. W. White, of 78 College Road, and of the late W. White; husband of Bessie Louisa White. Died at 10 Little Arms Street.

WILBY, Civilian, ARTHUR, Civilian War Dead. 27 June 1942. Age 3. Constable, Police War Reserve; of 55 Junction Road. Son of Elizabeth Wilby, of 44 Magdalen Close, and of the late Charles Wilby; husband of Kate Maud Wilby. Injured at St. Mark's Church; died same day at Norfolk and Norwich Hospital.

WILBY, Civilian, KATE, Civilian War Dead. 28 April 1942. Age 69. of 88 Nicholas Street. Daughter of the late Henry Wilby. Injured at 88 Nicholas Street; died same day at Norfolk and Norwich Hospital.

WILLIAMSON, Civilian, EMMA, Civilian War Dead. 29 April 1942. Age 73. of 11 Bixfields Buildings, Rupert Street. Widow of George Williamson. Injured 27 April 1942, at 11 Bixfields Buildings; died at Norfolk and Norwich Hospital.

WITHERICK, Civilian, EMMA SARAH ANN, Civilian War Dead. 28 April 1942. Age 74. Widow of Frank Witherick. Died at 18 Rose Valley.

WOOD, Civilian, ALICE ELVINA, Civilian War Dead. 28 April 1942. Age 56. of 146 Drayton Road. Wife of Arthur Frederick Wood. Injured 27 April 1942, at 146 Drayton Road; died at Wardens' Post, Drayton Road.

WOODROW, Civilian, LEONARD CHARLES, Civilian War Dead. 28 April 1942. Age 34. Son of William and Sarah Woodrow, of 75 Leicester Street; husband of Kathleen Woodrow, of 43 Junction Road. in ambulance at Oak Street.

WRIGHT, Civilian, FREDERICK, Civilian War Dead. 9 July 1940. Age 16. Son of Mrs. E. Wright, of 21 Hunter Road. Died at Boulton and Paul's Works.

WRIGHT, Civilian, HELEN, Civilian War Dead. 29 April 1942. Age 78. of 1 Ella Road, Thorpe Hamlet. Widow of Robert William Wright. Died at 1 Ella Road.

WRIGHT, Civilian, REGINALD EDWARD, Civilian War Dead. 27 April 1942. Age 11. of 11 Little Arms Street. Son of A.C.1 Reginald William Wright, R.A.F. Died at 6 Little Arms Street.

YALLOP, Civilian, ERNEST EDWARD, Civilian War Dead. 28 April 1942. Age 64. of 5 Quayside. Died at The Lodge, Bowthorpe Road.

YALLOP, Civilian, JAMES, Civilian War Dead. 28 April 1942. Age 69. of 125 Ber Street. Died at The Lodge, Bowthorpe Road.

YALLOP, Civilian, PATRICIA ANN, Civilian War Dead. 28 October 1940. Aged 7 weeks; of 6 Cross Street, Bungay, Suffolk. Daughter of Percy Charles and Florence Emily Yallop. Injured at 6 Cross Street; died same day at Norfolk and Norwich Hospital.

SHERINGHAM, URBAN DISTRICT, Norfolk, Civilian War Dead

ABBS, Civilian, CLARA, Civilian War Dead. 22 September 1940. Age 61. of Vale Lodge, Cromer Road. Widow of Thomas Mark Abbs. Died at Beal's Corner, Cromer Road.

BOUGHEN, Civilian, DAVID LESLIE, Civilian War Dead. 27 July 1942. Aged 5 months. Son of Sjt. L. Boughen, Royal Corps of Signals, and of Peggy Boughen. Died at 1 Scarborough Villas, Beeston Road.

BOUGHEN, Civilian, PEGGY, Civilian War Dead. 27 July 1942. Age 22. Daughter of W. H. Farrow, of 1 Garden Road, and of Emma Comfort Farrow; wife of Sjt. L. Boughen, Royal Corps of Signals. Died at 1 Scarborough Villas, Beeston Road.

FARROW, Civilian, EMMA COMFORT, Civilian War Dead. 27 July 1942. Age 54. Wife of W. H. Farrow, of 1 Garden Road. Died at 1 Scarborough Villas, Beeston Road.

HANNAH, Civilian, CHRISTINE ANN, Civilian War Dead. 27 July 1942. Age 4. of Ivydene, Priory Road. Daughter of Elsie Mary Hannah. Died at Ivydene, Priory Road.

HANNAH, Civilian, ELSIE MARY, Civilian War Dead. 27 July 1942. Age 39. of Ivydene, Priory Road. Daughter of M. A. E. Hannah, of Denleigh, New Road, and of William James Hannah. Died at Ivydene, Priory Road.

HANNAH, Civilian, WILLIAM JAMES, Civilian War Dead. 27 July 1942. Age 69. Husband of M. A. E. Hannah, of Denleigh, New Road. Died at Ivydene, Priory Road.

MARTINS, Civilian, BRENDA HANNAH, Civilian War Dead. 27 July 1942. Age 19. Daughter of Hannah Sophia and of the late J. B. Martins. Died at Glen Cairn, Priory Road.

MARTINS, Civilian, HANNAH SOPHIA, Civilian War Dead. 27 July 1942. Age 58. Widow of J. B. Martins. Died at Glen Cairn, Priory Road.

MARTINS, Civilian, PHYLLIS LOUISA, Civilian War Dead. 27 July 1942. Age 28. Daughter of Hannah Sophia and of the late J. B. Martins. Died at Glen Cairn, Priory Road.

RUSHMER, Civilian, MARGARET ANN, Civilian War Dead. 19 January 1942. Age 73. of Hainton House, Cremer Street. Wife of Robert Rushmer. Died at Hainton House.

SMITH, Civilian, CONSTANCE EMMA, Civilian War Dead. 19 January 1942. Age 52. of Fujiyama, Cremer Street. Daughter of Mr. and Mrs. S. W. Barnard, of 16 The Common, Hanworth, Norwich; wife of Frederick John Smith. Died at Fujiyama, Cremer Street.

SMITH, Civilian, CONSTANCE MARGARET, Civilian War Dead. 19 January 1942. Age 19. A.R.P. Telephonist; of Fujiyama, Cremer Street. Daughter of Frederick John and Constance Emma Smith. Died at Fujiyama, Cremer Street.

SMITH, Civilian, FREDERICK JOHN, Civilian War Dead. 19 January 1942. Age 64. of Fujiyama, Cremer Street. Son of the late Mr. and Mrs. C. Smith, of Buxton Lamas; husband of Constance Emma Smith. Died at Fujiyama, Cremer Street.

SMITH, Civilian, WILLIAM FRANCIS, Civilian War Dead. 8 March 1942. Age 62. Husband of Ellen Smith, of The Street, Bodham, Holt. Died at The Street, Bodham.

SMALLBURGH, RURAL DISTRICT, Norfolk, Civilian War Dead

ALMOND, Civilian, PATRICIA, Civilian War Dead. 26 April 1941. Age 20. of White Gates, Horning. Died at Horning.

BELL, Civilian, THOMAS HENRY, Civilian War Dead. 26 April 1941. Age 24. Son of Alfred Beaupre Bell, and Ada Sarah Bell, of Pine Corner, High Road, Drayton. Died at the Ferry Inn, Horning.

BLOMFIELD, Civilian, NELLIE, Civilian War Dead. 26 April 1941. Age 26. of The Pyramids, Horning. Daughter of Mr. and Mrs. H. C. Blomfield, of 184 Harrowden Road, Wheatley,

Doncaster, Yorkshire. Died at the Ferry Inn, Horning.

CRISP, Civilian, FREDERICK, Civilian War Dead. 26 April 1941. Age 60. A.F.S. Husband of Marion I. Crisp, of Ruthven, Cabbell Road, Cromer. Died at Horning.

HAWKER, Civilian, ALFRED, Civilian War Dead. 4 May 1941. Merchant Navy. Died at Lessingham.

LARKMAN, Civilian, RUSSELL CHARLES, Civilian War Dead. 26 April 1941. Age 27. Royal Observer Corps. Son of Mr. and Mrs. Edward F. Larkman, of 168 Aylsham Road, Norwich. Died at Horning.

LEJEUNE, Civilian, JOSEPH GILLIAN CLEMENT, Civilian War Dead. 26 April 1941. Age 49. Belgium Subject. Husband of Theodora Gladys Lejeune, of Dykeside, Horning. Died at Horning.

MEEK, Civilian, KINGSLEY LEGGETT, Civilian War Dead. 26 April 1941. Age 20. of Sycamore Farm, Hoveton, St. John. Son of Lt.-Col. and Mrs. S. A. Meek, of Bermuda. Died at Horning.

MIDDLETON, Civilian, GEORGE, Civilian War Dead. 19 August 1940. Age 32. Son of Harriet Middleton, of White Horse Street, Wymondham, and of the late Harry Middleton. Died at Scottow Aerodrome.

POWELL, Civilian, ETHEL KATE, Civilian War Dead. 27 February 1941. Age 55. Daughter of Mr. and Mrs. W. W. Bell, of 31 Northgate Street, Great Yarmouth; wife of Arthur Frederick Powell, of The Stores, Ludham. Died at Ludham.

RHODES, Civilian, ABRAHAM LINCOLN, Civilian War Dead. 26 April 1941. Age 66. of The Pyramids, Horning. Husband of A. L. Rhodes. Died at the Ferry Inn, Horning.

RIX, Civilian, SIDNEY ALEXANDER, Civilian War Dead. 19 August 1940. Age 55. Son of Robert and Martha Rix, of 19 Salford Street, Heigham; husband of Maud Rix, of Fairviews, Shorthorne Road, Stratton Strawless. Died at Scottow Aerodrome.

STONE, Civilian, LAWRENCE WILFRED, Civilian War Dead. 19 August 1940. Age 3. Husband of Laura A. M. Stone, of Church Cottages, Horstead. Died at Scottow Aerodrome.

SUTTON, Civilian, DOUGLAS LEONARD, Civilian War Dead. 26 April 1941. Age 27. of Shadingfield Lodge, Marine Parade, Great Yarmouth. Son of Henry Sutton. Died at The Gideons, Horning.

SUTTON, Civilian, DOROTHY ROSALINE, Civilian War Dead Link. see NORWICH list.

SUTTON, Civilian, HENRY, Civilian War Dead. 26 April 1941. Age 35. of The Gideons, Horning. Son of Henry Sutton; husband of Dorothy Rosaline Sutton. Died at The Gideons, Horning.

SUTTON, Civilian, HENRY, Civilian War Dead. 26 April 1941. Age 60. of Shadingfield Lodge, Marine Parade, Great Yarmouth. Died at The Gideons, Horning.

THIRST, Civilian, JEAN EDITH GERTRUDE, Civilian War Dead. 31 October 1940. Age 20. of Jesmond, St. John's Road, Stalham. Daughter of Percy Thirst. Died at Stalham High Street Bakery.

THIRST, Civilian, PERCY, Civilian War Dead. 31 October 1940. Age 56. of Jesmond, St. John's Road, Stalham. Son of the late James Thirst. Died at Stalham High Street Bakery.

WATSON, Civilian, DOUGLAS, Civilian War Dead. 26 April 1941. Age 56. Special Constable. Son of Henry and Margaret Watson, of Earlham Road, Norwich; husband of Gladys Knox Watson, of The Croft, Horning. Died at the Ferry Inn, Horning.

ST. FAITH'S AND AYLSHAM, RURAL DISTRICT, Norfolk, Civilian War Dead

ACTON, Civilian, JAMES GREENWOOD, Civilian War Dead. 7 May 1942. Age 76. of 53 The Avenues, Norwich. Injured 27 April 1942, at 53 The Avenues; died at St. Michael's Buildings, Aylsham.

BELL, Civilian, HARRIETT, Civilian War Dead. 3 May 1942. Age 64. of 421 Dereham Road, Norwich. Daughter of Mr. and Mrs. T. Chaplin, of Garvestone, widow of William Bell. Injured 27 April 1942, at 421 Dereham Road; died at Hellesdon Hospital.

BLOOMFIELD, Civilian, EDITH ADA, Civilian War Dead. 25 March 1941. Age 58. of 77 Lancaster Road, Great Yarmouth. Died at Emergency Hospital, Drayton.

BUCK, Civilian, CHARLES STEPHEN, Civilian War Dead. 9 May 1942. Age 67. of 2 Boundary Road, Hellesdon. Son of the late Stephen and Ann Buck. Died at 2 Boundary Road.

BURRELL, Civilian, JOHN WILLIAM, Civilian War Dead. 4 May 1942. Age 85. of 23 Paddock Street, Norwich. Husband of the late Emily Burrell. Injured at The Lodge, Bowthorpe Road, Norwich; died at St. Michael's Buildings, Aylsham.

ELVIN, Civilian, FREDERICK, Civilian War Dead. 9 July 1940. Age 32. Son of Jack Elvin; husband of Violet May Elvin, of 5 Cadge Close, Earlham Estate, Norwich. Died at Barnards Works, Salhouse Road, Sprowston.

GIBSON, Civilian, THOMAS, Civilian War Dead. 26 February 1941. Age 76. of The Heath, Hevingham. Died at The Heath.

KANTUREK, Civilian, OTTO W., Civilian War Dead. 26 June 1941. Age 42. Czechoslovak Citizen. Husband of Edith Maria Lucia Beatrix Kanturek, of 79 Charlbert Court, St. John's Wood, London. Died at Cawston.

SAYER, Civilian, ALBERT ERNEST, Civilian War Dead. 9 July 1940. Age 53. of 35 St. Peter's Street, Norwich. Died at Barnards Works, Salhouse Road, Sprowston.

SHREEVE, Civilian, ARTHUR LEONARD, Civilian War Dead. 9 July 1940. Age 30. Home Guard. Son of Alice M. Shreeve, of 53 Wymer Street, Norwich, and of the late John Spanton Shreeve. Died at Barnards Works, Salhouse Road, Sprowston.

SMITH, Civilian, ETHEL, Civilian War Dead. 21 September 1944. Age 69. of Rothbury, Hastings Avenue, Reepham Road, Hellesdon. Widow of George Arthur Smith. Died at Rothbury, Hastings Avenue.

STANER, Civilian, CLARA MAUDE, Civilian War Dead. 27 October 1940. Age 72. of The Rectory Cottage, Lamas. Died at The Rectory Cottage.

WALSINGHAM, RURAL DISTRICT, Norfolk, Civilian War Dead

ENGLISH, Civilian, JOSHUA, Civilian War Dead. 2 August 1942. Age 50. Husband of A. F. English, of 6 Grove Road, Melton Constable. Died at Railway Yards, Melton Constable.

NURSE, Civilian, GEORGE RUSSELL, Civilian War Dead. 2 May 1942. Age 21. Husband of Joyce Elsie Nurse, of 3 Hall Lane, Wiveton. Died at Langham Aerodrome.

Not forgotten: the graves of Daphne and Barbara Clapham, who lost their lives in the Baedeker Blitz and are buried in the Garden of Remembrance, Earlham Cemetery.

Appendix 2
German Aircraft Losses and Crew Burials
in Norfolk 1939-1945
The author would like to express his thanks to Robert J. Collis
for his generous assistance with this appendix.

21 October 1939
Heinkel He115B from 1/Küstenfliergruppe 406
Crashed into the sea 5 miles east of Spurn Head, Yorkshire after combat
with Hurricanes of No. 46 Squadron 1.00pm.

All crew killed.
Burials
Oblt. Zur See H. Schlicht
Lt. F. Meyer
Uffz. B. Wessels

All three bodies washed ashore between Mundesley and Happisburgh.
Their full honours burial was conducted in St Mary's Church and buried
in Happisburgh churchyard on 2 November 1939. The bodies were
exhumed after the war and rebuired at the Soldatenfriedhof German War
Cemetery at Cannock Chase.

6 December 1939
Heinkel He115 float plane (2081) from 3/Küstenfliergruppe
(Maritime Group) 506
Externally carrying the then new magnetic mines the Heinkel is thought
to have collided with Chain Home radiolocation mast at West Beckham
(The German loss-report attributed it to "icing or thunderstorm"), aircraft
narrowly missed Sheringham gas holder finally crashing onto the West
Beach, Sheringham at 3.15am. An engine from this Heinkel is still on the
sea bed in about 20 ft of water and is marked by a small buoy. Had this
aircraft crashed above the high water mark it would have been the first
enemy aircraft to crash on British soil in the Second World War.

All crew killed.
Burials:
Oberfw. Emil Rödel (29) was buried in an
unused corner of the Great Bircham
churchyard with full military honours on 9
December 1939. The coffin was draped in
2 swastika flags and there was a large
wreath inscribed, 'A tribute to a gallant
airman from the officers, NCO's and
airmen of the RAF'. Three Volleys were
fired, and the last post sounded.
Oblt. Zue See W. Wodtke and Oberfw. K.
Ullman were washed ashore later in the
month and were given full military
funerals at Sheringham. After the war the
remains of these latter two airmen were
exhumed after the war and rebuired at the
Soldatenfriedhof German War Cemetery at
Cannock Chase.

Grave of Oberfw. Emil Rödel, Great Bircham Cemetery

When British experts examined the
Heinkel, it was found to have self-sealing
fuel tanks. The British scientists had been
working for several years to perfect a
rubber material to line fuel tanks, so that in the event of a puncture by a
bullet the aircraft would not leak fuel and catch fire. It is said that the
capture of this aircraft enabled them to solve the problems and save many
British lives.

9 June 1940
Heinkel He 111H-4 (8747) from StabII/KG4
Shot down by Flt. Lt. R M B Duke-Woolley in a Blenheim of No. 23
Squadron and forced to ditch just off shore at The Hood, Cley next the
Sea at 12.50 am

Crew taken prisoner.
Major D. Frhr von Massenbach (Gruppenkommandeur), Oblt. U. Jordon,
Oberfw. M. Leimer, Fw K. Allenberger captured. Aircraft 5J+DM slipped
into the sea.

This aircraft was the first enemy machine shot down by a night-fighter

*Heinkel He 111H-4 (8747) from StabII/KG4 ditched just off shore at
The Hood, Cley next the Sea on 9 June 1940.*

over Britain during the Second World War and the crew (one wounded)
were the first Prisoners of War to be taken in Norfolk. The wreck remained
off shore until 1969 when it was blown up on the orders of Trinity House
as it was considered a hazard to navigation.

30 July 1940
Junker Ju88 from 2(F)/122 engaged on reconnaissance of shipping off
the east coast of England suffered sudden engine failure. Ditched in the
sea 30 miles off Happisburgh at 9.00am.

Crew taken prisoner.
Crew scrambled into their dinghy. Lt. H-J Rabbow and Uffz. J. Kehres
were unhurt. Uffz. G. Lemm and Gefr. R. Reimer were both injured. All
were eventually rescued on 3 August by a fishing boat and brought ashore
at Great Yarmouth. Aircraft F6-BK was lost.

21 August 1940
Dornier Do.17Z-3 from 2/KG2 was shot down by Blue Section of No.242
Squadron (Flt.-Lt. G. Powell-Sheddon, Sub-Lieut. R E Gardner, and Pilot
Officer J B Latta) during sortie over Norfolk. Attempted a forced landing
but overshot and ploughed into a wood and exploded at Conifer Hill,
Starston at 11.52pm.

Crew: 1 killed, 2 wounded.
Lieut H. Ermecke was killed. Uffz. G-D Wulf, Uffz. H. Herman and War
Correspondent Sonderführer Lt. Kurst Rasche (of Lw. Kr. Ber. Komp.
Mot.3) bailed out and were captured severely wounded. Aircraft U5+FK
was a write off. This was the only German aircraft shot down on land in
Norfolk during the Battle of Britain.

21 August 1940
Dornier Do.17Z-3 from 6/KG3 was engaged by Spitfires of Red Section
611 Squadron (RAF Digby) during sortie off the east coast of England.
Both engines severely damaged in attacks by pilot officers Watkins, J. W.
Lund and M. P. Brown. Crashed in the sea off Scolt Head, Brancaster
Roads at 12.40pm.

All crew killed.
The body of second observer Erich Kotulla, was recovered from the sea
at Brancaster and was buried at Holy Trinity churchyard at West Runton.
The bodies of Pilot Oberfw. Wilhelm Stolle and Observer Hellmut Krüger
were washed ashore at Brancaster and removed to Catton churchyard,
near Norwich for burial.

The air gunner, Heinrich Kascher (27) (In early reports this officer was
mistakenly identified as Uffz. W. Siegmund.) was also washed ashore at
Brancaster on 23 August and was buried at St Mary's churchyard, Great
Bircham on 29 August 1940.

Junkers Ju88A-5 (8180) of 1/KG30 ditched at Sparrow Gap, Weybourne at 3.30am, 3 May 1941

After the War, the bodies of Kotulla, Stolle and Krüger were were reburied at the Soldatenfriedhof German War Cemetery at Cannock Chase, Staffordshire.

22 January 1941
Operations confined to coastal activities
Junkers Ju88-5 (0578) was believed shot down off Great Yarmouth by three Hurricanes of 242 Squadron at 3.10pm. Aircraft V4-HT lost.

Crew: Missing
Lt. W. Lademann
Uffz. E. Plasa
Uffz. G. Reber
Gefr. E. Fink

26 January 1941
Several attacks were made on single ships and convoys off the East Coast. Junkers Ju88A-5 (0634) from 8/KG30 attacked HM Trawler *Galvani* hit by LMG Fire from the Trawler and crashed through masts and rigging. Landed on marsh at Somerton Holmes, Great Yarmouth 9.05am. The cockpit and centre section of this aircraft were destroyed by fire after the crew fired it following the crash-landing.

Crew taken prisoner:
Crew dragged their dinghy towards the coast but surrendered upon being confronted by two unarmed local residents. Fw. W. Guttmann, Uffz. J. Schmalze, Uffz. S. Gaber and Uffz. F. Martin taken prisoner. Aircraft 4D+LS burnt out.

18 February 1941
Heinkel He 111H-3 (3349) from 4/KG 3 was completely lost and had already jettisoned bombs when it flew over RAF Watton at 100ft and was hit by LMG fire and then in the wings by three PAC (Parachute and Cable rocket apparatus) weapons from RAF Watton, two of which partly tore through the wing spars. The Heinkel crash-landed and ended up across a drainage culvert at Waterend Farm, Ovington at 7.55am. The two men who captured the crew and prevented them firing the aircraft were mentioned in the *London Gazette*. Aircraft A1+CM wrecked.

Crew taken prisoner:
Fw. H. Busch
Oberlt. E. Langguth
Uffz. W. Schmoll
Gefr. K. Kammermeier (Slightly Wounded)
Heinrich Busch, pilot of the downed He 111 had a lucky escape; a bullet from the LMG fire tore the shoulder of his flying suit before grazing Kummermeir's face and exiting through the top of the fuselage. In Canada, Busch was involved in the murder of a fellow German PoW who had anti-Nazi convictions. He was tried by an Allied War Crimes Court and executed.

7 March 1941
Dornier Do17Z-2 (3391) of 2/KG3 ditched in the sea off Gorleston at 7.35 am after a sortie over the Thames Estuary. Hit by Bofors and LMG fire at 700ft, possibly from Royal Berkshire Regimentt based in area of Cliff Hotel, Gorleston but the 'kill' was credited to the Hopton AA battery. Aircraft caught fire in fuselage, ditched in sea opposite the wreck of the *White Swan*. The pilot managed to swim ashore, radio operator tried to follow but drowned in breakers, two remaining crew members were picked up by RN launch from Gorleston Harbour as Prisoners of War. Aircraft 5K+MK sank in the sea.

Killed:
Fw. W. Ophoff

Taken prisoner:
Oblt. E. Kunst
Oberfw. H. Vendland
Uffz. H. Ockinghaus

10 March 1941
Junkers Ju88C-2 (0343) on intruder sortie aircraft suffered engine failure and made a belly landing at Hay Green, Terrington St Clement at 11.30pm. Aircraft R4+CH captured damaged and transported to Farnborough. The was a real prize for the RAF as it was the first time a complete Ju 88 night-fighter with a 'solid' nose containing cannon and MG had fallen into British hands in one piece.

Crew taken prisoner:
Oblt. K. Hermann
Uffz. E. Bottner
Fw. W. Rüppel

3 May 1941
Junkers Ju88A-5 (8180) of 1/KG30 claimed by Pilot Officer Guy A. Edmison and Sergeant A G Beale of No.151 Squadron in a Defiant but during interrogation by ADI(K) the crew stated they had engine failure while crossing in over the Lincolnshire coast in AA fire, turned South, jettisoned their bombs over The Wash, were unable to maintain height and ditched offshore at Sparrow Gap, Weybourne at 3.30am. The observer, Major Seeburg, was 53 years old and was the unit admin officer, making his first operational flight. Aircraft 4D+BH captured damaged.

Crew taken prisoner:
Major W. Seeburg
Fw. E. Geiger
Fw. H. Laser
Fw. R. Altmayer

3 May 1941

Heinkel He 111H-4 (3235) of 3/KG53 was shot down by Pilot Officer Bodien and Sergeant Wrampling in a Defiant of No.151 Squadron. Aircraft made forced landing ending up across a lane at Eastmoor Farm at Sharrington at 1.04am and was fired by the crew. Aircraft A1+LL destroyed.

Killed:
Gefr. B. Kauhardt

Taken prisoner:
Lt. A. Plank von Bachfelden
Gefr. B. Reynat
Uffz. W. Richter
It later emerged Kauhardt apparently had a paranoid fear of RAF night-fighters; it is ironic then, that he was shot through the heart by a bullet from a night-fighter he probably never saw. The three survivors trecked off and were captured at Salthouse.

4 May 1941

Junkers JU88A-5 (4269) of 3/KG77 suffered engine failure and made a forced landing at Welney Wash, near Downham Market at 4.00am. Three of the crew baled out over March but the pilot crash-landed with an engine on fire. He emptied his sidearm into the burning Junkers to try and accelerate its destruction but he was disarmed and the fire extinguished by members of the 2nd Battalion, Norfolk Home Guard. Aircraft 3Z+CL was captured in a damaged state.

Crew taken prisoner:
Lt. J. Wreschnick
Uffr. F. Podlech
Uffz. R. Siekmann
Gefr. H. Pix

The grave of Uffz. Josef Simon, Earlham Cemetery, Norwich

5 May 1941

Junkers JU88A-5 (6027) of Stab II/KG 77 A W/T message from this aircraft which was picked up by the 'Y' Service indicated the crew were experiencing engine trouble and were short of fuel on a sortie to Belfast. Attempting a forced landing at Waxham at 4.12 am but aircraft hit a sand dune. The survivors were all seriously injured.

Killed:
Uffz. Josef Simon (22), was buried in Earlham Cemetery, Norwich
Taken prisoner:
Lt. K. Obenhack
Gefr. H. Rose
Uffz. W von Mohrendorf

11 May 1941

Junkers JU88A-5 (7170) of 4/KG1. The briefed target was RAF Sutton Bridge, base of 56 OTU training Hurricane pilots but this aircraft was shot down while making a low level attack on RAF Watton, hitting a tree and crashing at Rectory Farm. Aircraft V4+DM completely destroyed.

Killed:
Lt. F. Bäumel
Uffz. H. Simon
Oberfw. H. Ausserfeld

Taken prisoner:
Uffz. M. König (injured)
Two Ju 88s were claimed over the sea by pilots of 257 Sqn from Coltishall the same night; Sqn Ldr Tuck claimed one at a point 15 miles NE of Gt Yarmouth at 0014 hours, while Flt Lt Blatchford claimed one 10 miles NE of Happisburgh at 0017 hours.

26 May 1941

Junkers Ju88A-4 (0738) of 1/Küsten-fliegergruppe 506 crashed into the sea off the Norfolk coast in unknown circumstances.

Killed, but bodies never recovered:
Oberlt. J. Löhr

The grave of Uffz. Heinz Biesterfeld, Great Bircham.

Oberlt. F. Pohl
Obergefr. W. Nimwegen

Washed Ashore:
The body of Uffz. Heinz Biesterfeld was washed ashore on 29 June 1941 and buried at Great Bircham 4 July 1941.

21-22 March 1941 (night)

Junkers Ju88 of 7/KG6, a presumed 'kill' of a night fighter crashed into the sea and was lost off the Norfolk/Suffolk coast.

Killed:
Oberlt R. Knödler (Staffelkapitän)
Uffz. G. Harzheim

Killed, but body never recovered:
Oberfw. G. Becker

Fw. R. Trabant was found dead in emergency dingy in the North Sea on March 23 1941

14 June 1941 (night)

Junkers Ju88C-4 (0550) from 4/NJG2 was shot down by Squadron Leader H P Pleasance DFC and Sergeant B. Bent in Beaufighter of No.25 Squadron. Crashed at Eyetrap Plantation, Narford at 12.30am. Aircraft R4+DM destroyed.

Killed:
Gefr. J. Reisinger (who baled out but was killed when his parachute failed)

Injured:
Uffz. R. Hoffmann

Baled out and taken prisoner:
Fw. P. Mayer

14 June 1941 (night)

Junkers Ju88C-4 (0335) from 4/NJG2 shot down by Pilot Officers D W Thompson and Pilot Officer L D Britain in Beaufighter R2157 of No.25 Squadron RAF. Crashed on the mud flats 2 miles out from the sea bank at Wingland Marsh near King's Lynn at 1.00am. (Aircraft R4+AM destroyed)

Killed:
Uffz. H. Bähner (Body never found)
Fw. H. Schultz (Killed when the aircraft crashed. Buried in the Church-yard at Sutton Bridge, Lincolnshire)
Uffz. Jakob Ried (25) (Bailed out but his parachute failed and he was killed. His body was not recovered until 7th July 1941 and was buried at Great Bircham on 9th July 1941.)

15 September 1941

Junkers JU88A-5 (5247) from 2/Küstenfligergruppe 606 was seen attacking a convoy 15 miles off Lowestoft when it was shot down by Squadron Leader F J Soper in a Hurricane from No.257 Squadron. The Junkers crashed into the sea off Happisburgh at 7.00pm, the crew were picked up by a trawler and landed at Lowestoft as Prisoners of War, two required hospital treatment. Aircraft 7T+LK sank in the sea.

Crew picked up by trawler and taken prisoner:
Oberlt. H. Von Heyder
Oberfw. K. Ützen
Gefr. H. Lessmeister (injured)
Sonderführer W. W. Kelch (injured)

26 December 1941

Junkers JU88 (1442) from 3/Küstenfligergruppe 506 crashed into the sea off Winterton at 5.30pm during a mine laying mission. The exact cause of the crash is unknown. Aircraft S4+DL sank in the sea.

Killed:
Oberlt. W. Gospodarek

Missing:
Lt. Zur See H. Deters
Uffz. H. Holzapfel
Uffz. V. Eschke

2 February 1942

Dornier Do217E-2 (1101) from 6/KG40 was shot down by Pilot Officer

J. Henderson in a Spitfire from No.19 Squadron. Crashed into the sea two miles north-east of the Happisburgh Lightship at 1.47pm. Aircraft F8+GP lost.

Killed:
Oberlt. E. Eckert

Died:
Oberfw. G. Borkowski baled out and was picked up alive at 2.10pm but died later of exposure. (Buried at North Coates)

Missing:
Uffz. F. Geisler
Fw. E. Schütt

24 February 1941

A Dornier Do217E-4 (1166) from StabIII/KG2 was believed to be shot down by Spitfires from No. 266 Squadron while approaching Convoy FS 34. Crashed into the sea off Cromer at 6.15pm. Aircraft U5+AD lost.

Killed:
Lt. E. Jasper

Missing:
Obergefr. F. Stumpp
Fw. F. Helzmann
Obergefr. R. Raulin

22 August 1941

Heinkel He 111H-5 (4081) from 8/KG40 was shot down into the sea NW of Wells-next-Sea at 22.05hrs by Wing Comdr J. "Cats Eyes" Cunningham DSO, DFC & Bar and Pilot Officer C.F. Rawnsley DFC, DFM & Bar in a Beaufighter of No 604 Squadron. Aircraft F8+BS sank in the sea.

Missing:
Gefr. G.Dohmen
Gefr. H.Hädrich
Obergefr. K.Dändel

The body of Gefr. Rudolf Faath (20) was washed ashore at Burnham Overy on 31 Aug 1941 and he was buried at Great Bircham on 5 September 1941. The bodies of the other 3 crew members were never found.

4 March 1942

Junker Ju88A-4 (1384) from Erpro/KG30 was on an anti-shipping operation when it was hit by Anti-Aircraft fire near Great Yarmouth and crashed off Mundesley at 4.20pm. Aircraft 4D+DA sank in the sea.

Killed:
Fw. Oskar Haug (31)
Uffz. Richard Prohaska (24)
Fw. Hans Trökes (27) (Body was washed up on 2nd May 1942)
All three recovered aircrew were buried in Scottow cemetery.

Missing:
Uffz. W. Dick

The grave of Fw. Oskar Haug, Scottow Cemetery

9 May 1942

Dornier Do217E-4 (5375) from 1/KG2 hit a balloon cable at 3,500 ft over Lakenham dived to a low altitude and was shot down by LAA guns from the Stoke Holy Cross (Poringland) Chain Home site, crashing on a field at West Green Farm, West Poringland at 1.20am. Aircraft U5+EH disintegrated.

Killed.
Oberlt. W. Böllert
Oberfw.R. Bucksch
Uffz. M. Speuser
Uffz. A. Otterbach
All crew share a communal grave in Norwich Cemetery, Earlham. A memorial service was

The original headstone marking the communal grave of the crew of Dornier Do217E-4 (5375), Earlham Cemetery

held at the crew grave in 1986 at the request of the widow of the pilot, and the CWGC subsequently added more details to the headstone, which up until then had carried only the initials and surnames of the four crew.

15 May 1942

Dornier Do217E-4 (1190) from 4/KG40 was shot down by Spitfire Mk 5bs of No.610 Squadron crashing into the sea off Happisburgh at 6.00pm. Aircraft F8+LM sank in the sea.

Killed
Oberfw. M. Kalisch
Obergefr. R. Stein
(Both bodies recovered from the sea)

Missing:
Oberfw. F. Wimmer
Obergefr. H-G. Westermann

16 May 1942

Two Dornier Do217s from 3/KG2 believed shot down into the sea by Spitfires from No.412 Squadron while over a convoy off Great Yarmouth.

30 July 1942 (night)

Dornier Do217E-4 (1213) from 6/KG2 was shot down by Flying Officer Raybould and Flight Sergeant Mullaley in a Beaufighter from 68 Squadron. Crashed on Salthouse Marshes at 2.00am. Aircraft U5+DP destroyed.

Killed:
Oberlt. F. Dörflinger
Uffz. E. Ohnesorge (22) (His body was washed ashore on 30th July 1942 and was buried in Scottow Cemetery)
Oberfw. J. Ziegaus

Baled out and taken prisoner:
Gefr. H. Skryczak
It is believed that two of the crew were either blown to pieces or burned up in the wreckage and have no known graves.The aircraft was en route for Derby with containers of the (then) new B2.2 explosive incendiary bomb (a standard B1E1 IB with a round-nosed, steel-cased explosive charge at the front). The crash was in a coastal minefield, and in addition to this, the bombs on board were detonating in the fire. The wreckage was still alight 16 hours after the crash, hence the 'missing' crewmen.

30 July 1942 (Night)

Junkers Ju88A-4 (3810) from 9/KG26 was returning from a raid on Birmingham and at 50ft was hit in the tail by AA fire from Caister. Crashed into the sea one mile off Hemsby at 2.30am. 3 crew paddled ashore in their dinghy; another swam ashore some distance away. Aircraft 1T+KT sank in the sea.

Crew taken prisoner:
Oberfhr. G. Knobel
Obergefr. E. Schiborr
Obergefr. U. Calaminus
Obergefr.H. Gronau

23 August 1942 (Night)

Dornier Do 217E-4 (4267) from 2/KG2 was shot down by Squadron Leader W. J. Alington and Flying Officer D B Keith in a Beaufighter of No.25 Squadron. The Beaufighter responsible was fired on by another Beaufighter. The pilot said in his combat report: "...his shooting was as bad as his aircraft recognition and he missed." The Dornier crashed at Walton Wood, East Walton at 11.25pm. Aircraft U5+CK disintegrated.

Killed:
Oberfw. R. Bodenhagen
Hptmn. R. Hellmann (Staffelkapitän)
Oberfw. G. Rockstroh
Oberfw. T. Römelt

17 September 1942

Dornier Do217E-4 (4265) from 7/KG2 was shot down by Flight Lieutenant H. E. Bodien DFC and Sergeant G. B. Brooker in a Mosquito MkII of No.151 Squadron during an attack on King's Lynn (This was the last "Baedeker" raid against an East Anglian target). Crashed at Church Farm, Fring at 9.55pm. Aircraft U5+UR disintegrated.

Crew baled out and taken prisoner:
Fw. F. Elias

Gefr. G. Buchner
Uffz. F. Leibrecht
Gefr. W. Berg

19 October 1942

Ju88D-1 (1342) from 3(F)/33 shot down by Flight Lieutenant W D Winward and Pilot Officer C. K. Wood in a Beaufighter of No.68 Squadron. Crashed into the sea 20 miles North of Cromer. Aircraft 8H+KL sank in the sea.

Missing:
Oberlt. H. Dürr
Uffz. A. Schäfer
Uffz. J. Wahl

Washed Ashore:
Body of Lt. Wolfgang Lauth (19) was washed ashore at Cromer on 17 November 1942 and was buried at Scottow.

The grave of Lt. Wolfgang Lauth, Scottow Cemetery.

18 March 1943 (Night)

Dornier 217 was intercepted by Flying Officer D. Williams and Pilot Officer D. Walton in a Mosquito MkII of 410 Squadron. The Mosquito pursued the Do 217 as it dived through cloud to escape them, the night-fighter pulled out at low-level (800 ft) and the enemy aircraft did not and before the crew opened fire it crashed on marshes near Terrington St. Clement at 11.10pm.

Exactly which aircraft came down that night is open to debate. Two Do 217s went missing on this night, the target for both was Norwich. AI2(g) gives location as "Over a sandbank in the River Ouse, 2 miles N of King's Lynn". To date neither bodies, wreckage or equipment bearing identifications by way of markings or Werk-Nr have not been found to identify this aircraft.

7 May 1943

Focke-Wulf FW190A-5 (52526) from 7/SKG10. Some witnesses claim this aircraft hit either (a) a telegraph pole, (b) a net-drying rail, or (c) the roof of a cottage. It was also claimed by a Bofors gun crew. The Focke-Wulf came down the sea 200 yards off Newport Cliffs near its target of Great Yarmouth at 7.15am. The pilot's body came ashore on 9 May 1943 and he was originally buried at Caister. Aircraft Yellow A+ sank.

Killed:
Oberlt. W. Freudenreich

6-7 November 1943

Dornier Do 217K-1 Werk-Nr.4509 from KG.2. The aircraft had a full load of AB500/1 IB containers and 50 kg phosphorous IBs on board and was en route for Norwich. It was ripped in half by a direct AA hit over Beccles at midnight on 6-7 November and crashed at Winston Hall Farm, Gillingham. The main part exploded and burned, setting fire to a barn. One crewman was lost in the explosion/fire. Two others were too low for their parachutes to open. Aircraft U5 + GT was destroyed by fire and explosion.

Killed:
Lt. G. Wulfhorst
Gefr. W. Geyer
Obergefr. N. Komp

Taken prisoner:
Uffz Alwin Kork, who was captured and ended up at Beccles Police Station.

22 April 1944 (Night)

Messerschmitt Me 410A-1 (420458) was shot down by return fire from the 389th Bomb Group B-24 it had attacked. Crashed at Hall Farm, Ashby St Marys at 10.10pm. Aircraft 9K+HP was totally destroyed.

Killed:
Lt. K. Krüger
Fw. M. Reichardt

A rare survival – a data plate from the Weybourne Junkers Ju88A-5.

Appendix 3
Air Raids, Flying bomb (V1) and
Rocket (V2) attacks on Norfolk 1940-1945

<table>
<tr><td colspan="2" align="center">KEY</td></tr>
<tr><td>HE</td><td>High Explosive</td></tr>
<tr><td>IB</td><td>Incendiary Bomb</td></tr>
<tr><td>HE/IB</td><td>High Explosive Incendiary Bomb</td></tr>
<tr><td>MG</td><td>Machine Gunned</td></tr>
<tr><td>PM</td><td>Parachute Mine</td></tr>
<tr><td>'G' Mine</td><td>This mine had no parachute and if it did not explode on impact, buried itself deeply in the ground becoming a dangerous UXB</td></tr>
<tr><td>SD.1</td><td>Fragmentation Bomb (length 6.7 inches)</td></tr>
<tr><td>SD.2</td><td>Butterfly Bomb</td></tr>
<tr><td>SD.10</td><td>Fragmentation Bomb (length 21.6 inches)</td></tr>
<tr><td>Phos.</td><td>Phosphor Bomb (Smoke)</td></tr>
<tr><td>Oil</td><td>Oil Bomb</td></tr>
<tr><td>Flying Bomb</td><td>V1</td></tr>
<tr><td>Rocket</td><td>V2</td></tr>
</table>

*Where no number appears next to abbreviation,
the number of bombs of that type dropped was not recorded*

25 May 1940
Aylsham	1 HE
Burgh St Peter	1 HE
Langley with Hardley	1 HE
Raveningham	2 HE
Raynham	13 HE

2 June 1940
Strumpshaw	2 HE

6 June 1940
Bircham	200 IB
Hainford	1 HE
North Tuddenham	8 HE

7 June 1940
East Rudham	14 HE
Foulden	15 HE
Needham	6 HE
North Tuddenham	6 HE

18 June 1940
Bressingham	18 HE
Pentney	11 HE
Methwold	4 HE

19 June 1940
East Rudham	5 HE
Narford	16 HE
West Dereham	7 HE

21 June 1940
Pulham St Mary	24 HE

22 June 1940
East Rudham	14 HE
Felmingham	11 HE
Flordon	2 HE
Long Stratton	2 HE
Martham	1 HE
Rockland St Mary	1 HE
Strumpshaw	1 HE
Somerton	6 HE
Swanton Abbot	12 HE
Worstead	2 HE

Wymondham	12 HE

24 June 1940
Attleborough	2 HE	
Caston	2 HE	
East Rudham		57 IB
Runton	5 HE	
Stokesby with Herringby	1 HE	
Tattersett	4 HE	3 IB

25 June 1940
Grimston	4 HE

26 June 1940
Stiffkey	6 IB
Syderstone	58 IB

28 June 1940
North Lopham	2 HE	
Surlingham	9 HE	60 IB

3 July 1940
Fulmodeston	10 HE

7 July 1940
East Rudham	4 HE

9 July 1940
Ashmanhaugh	1 HE	
Norwich	14 HE	
Pulham St Mary	2 HE	
Sprowston	36 HE	3 IB

10 July 1940
Cockley Cley	9 HE
East Rudham	16 HE
Marham	20 HE
Pulham St Mary	20 HE
Weybourne	12 HE

11 July 1940
Acle	6 HE
Cromer	11 HE
Great Yarmouth	7 HE
Martham	4 HE

19 July 1940
Norwich	7 HE
Sprowston	7 HE

20 July 1940
Aylsham	1 IB

23 July 1940
Pulham St Mary	16 HE

24 July 1940
Great Yarmouth	6 HE

25 July 1940
Scarning	20 HE

30 July 1940
Norwich	20 HE

Norwich Bus Station, as illustrated in the German Military Objektbilder Ost-Anglia.

The wreckage at Norwich Bus Station after the air raid of 30 July 1940.

1 August 1940

Norwich	4 HE

10 August 1940

Framingham Earl	1 HE
Hethersett	15 HE
Norwich	4 HE

11 August 1940

Cromer	2 HE

12 August 1940

Brumstead	4 HE	
Burnham Market	10 HE	
Denver	3 HE	
Ingham	1 HE	100 IB
Upwell	1 HE	

14 August 1940

Bressingham	4 HE
Walpole St Peter	1 HE

15 August 1940

Aslacton	3 IB
Fleggburgh	6 IB
Hemsby	2 HE
Kenninghall	3 IB
Potter Heigham	3 HE

18 August 1940

Aylsham	7 IB	
Bracon Ash	3 IB	
Bressingham	4 IB	
Brettenham	9 HE	
Cranwich	19 HE	IB
Denton	4 HE	
Diss	2 IB	
Forncett	4 IB	
Needham	15 IB	
Northrepps	4 IB	
Pulham St Mary	8 HE	
Scottow	3 HE	
Winfarthing	2 HE	

19 August 1940

Scottow	10 HE
Southery	4 IB

20 August 1940

Alby with Thwaite	3 IB	
Great Yarmouth	20 HE	10 IB
Halvergate	60 IB	
Hethersett	2 HE	
Horsford	1 IB	
Norwich	7 IB	
Whitlingham	5 IB	

21 August 1940

Banham	5 IB
Bircham	4 HE
Carlton Rode	2 IB
Catton	7 HE
Cranwich	2 HE
Horning	2 HE
Hoveton	2 HE
Matlaske	10 HE
Pulham St Mary	17 HE
St Faiths	2 HE
Snetterton	4 IB
Sprowston	2 IB
Thorpe	12 HE
Watton	13 HE
West Caister	3 IB
Wickmere	9 HE

23 August 1940

Gayton	10 HE	1 Oil.	100 IB
Gt. Massingham	50 IB		

24 August 1940

Banham	200 IB

Binham	1 HE
Bunwell	2 Oil
Carlton Rode	2 Oil
Great Yarmouth & Gorleston	20 HE
Gunthorpe	6 HE

25 August 1940

Barton Turf	100 IB	
Edgefield	3 HE	
Fransham	3 HE	
Gt. Ryburgh	18 HE	50 IB
Hockwold	2 IB	
Itteringham	4 HE	
Potter Heigham	1 IB	
Saxlingham	1 IB	
Tunstead	10 HE	
West Caister	2 IB	
Wood Norton	6 HE	

26 August 1940

Docking	2 HE
East Bradenham	96 IB
Feltwell	2 IB
Foulsham	3 HE
Great Ellingham	12 IB
Guist	2 HE
Ovington	25 IB
Saham Toney	182 IB

An ARP Demolition Squad at work on the unsafe gable ends of F. & G. Smith's Maltings at Great Ryburgh, set on fire by incendiary bombs dropped during the air raid of 26 August 1940.

27 August 1940

Cantley	1 IB
Field Dalling	3 IB
Dereham	1 IB
Hempnall	1 IB
Kenninghall	1 HE
Newton Flotman	40 IB
Norwich	2 IB
Saxlingham	150 IB
Topcroft	2 IB
West Caister	1 IB
Weston Longville	1 IB

28 August 1940

Barsham	2 HE
Calthorpe	3 HE
Gresham	70 IB
Gt. Massingham	4 IB
Gunthorpe	1 HE
Hickling	5 HE
Holkham	1 Oil
Starston	4 IB
Terrington St John	7 HE
Walpole St Peter	100 IB

29 August 1940

Rockland St Mary	1 IB

30 August 1940

New Buckenham	3 IB

31 August 1940

Barnham Broom	7 HE	
Beechamwell	2 HE	
Beeston St Andrew	4 HE	
Cockley Cley	30 IB	
Colby	13 IB	
Downham West	2 Oil	1 IB
Hardingham	6 HE	
Hilborough	2 HE	
Hilgay	100 IB	
Hingham	4 HE	
Kimberley	5 HE	
Lessingham	6 IB	
Marham	3 IB	
Marlingford	4 HE	
Mundham	6 IB	
Neatishead	50 IB	
Narborough	13 HE	
Ovington	2 HE	
Pudding Norton	50 IB	
Nordelph	2 Oil	
Rackheath	8 HE	
Riddlesworth	1 IB	
Runhall	5 HE	
Ryston	4 HE	
Sprowston	16 HE	
Stow Bardolph	1 HE	
Terrington St Clement	19 HE	
Tottenhill	2 Oil	7 HE
West Dereham	7 HE	100 IB
West Winch	110 IB	
Wormegay	4 Oil	
Wroxham	8 IB	

1 September 1940

Bagthorpe	5 HE
North Creake	2 HE
Yaxham	21 IB

3 September 1940

Blofield	1 HE

4 September 1940

Martham	9 HE	
Old Buckenham	7 HE	
Somerton	9 HE	
Wicklewood	3 HE	4 IB

5 September 1940

Potter Heigham	5 HE
Somerton	5 HE

6 September 1940

Brancaster	1 IB	
Cawston	9 HE	200 IB
Docking	6 IB	
Haddiscoe	2 HE	
Heckingham	2 HE	
Norton Subcourse	4 HE	20 IB
Roughton	5 IB	
Stow Bardolph	250 IB	

7 September 1940

Alburgh	1 IB
Costessey	4 IB
Drayton	1 IB
Hethersett	2 IB
Horsford	1 IB
Marshland St James	62 IB
Thetford	6 IB
Wicklewood	5 IB

8 September 1940

Alburgh	1 IB
Burnham Market	7 HE
Harleston	4 IB
Hindringham	8 IB

Ketteringham	2 IB
Langham	12 IB
Starston	2 IB
Thetford	IB
Wymondham	3 IB

9 September 1940

Hevingham	7 HE
Honingham	4 IB

10 September 1940

Dickleburgh	2 IB
Great Yarmouth	8 HE
Kirstead	11 HE
Langham	6 HE

The wreckage of Harbord Crescent, Great Yarmouth after the air raid of 10 September 1940. Two people were killed and three were injured here.

14 September 1940

Great Yarmouth	5 HE 1 Oil
Winfarthing	5 IB

15 September 1940

Burnham Market	3 IB
Deopham	2 IB
Docking	5 HE
East Tuddenham	1 HE
East Winch	10 IB
Felthorpe	3 IB
Flitcham	10 IB
Grimston	1 HE
Hingham	4 IB
Marham	IB
North Pickenham	2 HE 5 IB
Oxborough	1 IB
Snettisham	3 IB
Wicklewood	2 IB

16 September 1940

Ashill	1 HE
Dersingham	2 HE
Feltwell	1 HE
Hockwold	5 HE
Morningthorpe	1 HE
Oulton	2 HE
Sall	3 HE
South Pickenham	15 HE
Southrepps	11 HE

17 September 1940

Edgefield	10 IB

18 September 1940

Long Stratton	1 IB

19 September 1940

Docking	2 HE 1 Oil
Great Yarmouth	6 HE (landed in sea off Britannia Pier)
Norwich	2 HE 2 IB

20 September 1940

Bunwell	3 IB
Clenchwarton	4 HE
Winfarthing	2 IB
Wymondham	1 HE

21 September 1940

Cawston	12 IB
Sall	2 IB

22 September 1940

Bircham	5 HE 1 IB
Docking	9 IB
Dunton	3 IB
East Rudham	6 IB
Fring	7 IB
Harpley	1 IB
Hillington	4 IB
Houghton	7 IB
Methwold	1 HE 20 IB
Sheringham	4 HE
Terrington St Clement	7 HE
West Rudham	6 IB

Wrecked houses, Cromer Road, Sheringham after the first raid on the town during the Second World War, Sunday 22 September 1940. Mrs Clara Abbs (61) was killed at Beal's Corner, fifteen others were injured, six of them seriously.

23 September 1940

Feltwell	3 HE
Hilborough	9 HE 1 Oil. 6 IB
Ketteringham	1 HE
Roydon	1 HE
Wells- next-the-Sea	1 HE

24 September 1940

Feltwell	13 HE
Houghton	14 HE
West Rudham	2 HE

26 August 1940

West Bradenham	6 HE

31 August 1940

West Bradenham	1 HE

26 September 1940

Ashwellthorpe	1 IB

30 September 1940

Gissing	1 HE
Hilborough	4 HE 40 IB

1 October 1940

Docking	6 IB
Thornham	5 IB

4 October 1940

Great Yarmouth	1 HE (fell in sea off Wellington Pier)

5 October 1940

Great Yarmouth	2 HE
Old Buckenham	1 HE 4 Oil.
Sheringham	1 HE

6 October 1940

Bedingham	5 HE
Beighton	4 HE
Burlingham	3 HE
South Walsham	1 HE
Topcroft	7 HE

7 October 1940

King's Lynn	4 HE

The crater left beside Gaywood Church, King's Lynn after the air raid of 7 October 1940

8 October 1940

Harling	5 HE
Newton Flotman	4 HE
Snettisham	7 HE
Sturston	5 HE

9 October 1940

North Wootton	7 HE

10 October 1940

Blakeney	IB
Field Dalling	4 HE
Holt	2 IB
Letheringsett	1 HE
North Wootton	7 HE
Salthouse	1 IB
South Lopham	3 IB

11 October 1940

Great Yarmouth	12 HE

14 October 1940

Banham	11 HE
Harling	3 HE

15 October 1940

Swaffham	3 HE 1 Oil.

16 October 1940

Harling	10 HE 4 IB

New Buckenham	3 IB
North Lopham	3 IB
Old Buckenham	3 IB
Roudham	2 IB
Shropham	1 IB
South Lopham	6 IB
Snetterton	3 IB

17 October 1940

Loddon	4 HE

19 October 1940

Rollesby	3 HE

20 October 1940

Docking	1 PM
Emneth	7 HE
Stoke Ferry	2 HE

21 October 1940

Freethorpe	4 HE

23 October 1940

Heydon	2 HE
North Tuddenham	1 HE

25 October 1940

Rougham	5 IB	
Stanhoe	2 IB	
Welney	4 HE	IB

27 October 1940

Buxton Lamas	2 HE	
Cockley Cley	2 HE	2 IB
Fakenham	15 IB	
Feltwell	6 HE	
Gateley	3 HE	
Great Dunham	1 HE	
Gt. Massingham	21 HE	8 IB
Guist	13 HE	
Harpley	3 HE	
Hillington	6 IB	
Marham	4 HE	
Norwich	3 HE	
Raynham	100 HE	
St Faiths	6 HE	
Shelton	19 HE	
South Creake	1 HE	7 IB
Sprowston	20 HE	
Stratton Strawless	3 HE	
Syderstone	10 HE	
Thetford	12 HE	
Thorpe	7 HE	
Walcott	18 HE	
Weasenham All Saints	9 HE	
West Rudham	16 HE	
Worstead	2 HE	

28 October 1940

Buxton Lamas	5 HE
Ditchingham	1 HE
Methwold	2 HE
Snetterton	1 HE
Terrington St Clement	21 HE
Tunstead	5 HE

29 October 1940

Beetley	7 HE	100 IB
Carbrooke	10 HE	
Feltwell	29 HE	
Fincham	20 HE	
Helhoughton	14 HE	
Matlaske	28 HE	
Methwold	13 HE	
Reepham	1 IB	
Scoulton	9 HE	
Shipdam	2 HE	
Shouldham	20 HE	IB
Stow Bedon	2 HE	
Swannington	1 IB	

West Rudham	34 HE
Wretham	9 HE

30 October 1940

Colkirk	1 HE
Dereham	10 IB
Diss	1 IB
Reepham	1 IB
Strumpshaw	1 IB
Swannington	1 IB
Swanton Morley	9 IB
Swanton Novers	3 IB
Wretton	3 IB
Wymondham	1 IB

31 October 1940

Aylsham	7 HE	100 IB
Dereham	2 HE	
Fulmodeston	19 HE	
Great Yarmouth	4 HE	
Hickling	2 HE	
Ingham	3 HE	
St Faiths	16 HE	
Stalham	3 HE	
Sutton	9 HE	
Tottenhill	1 HE	

1 November 1940

Banham	1 IB	
Colby	12 HE	
Dunton	10 IB	
Filby	4 IB	
Fleggburgh	1 IB	
Garveston	12 IB	
Great Melton	6 IB	
Marsham	3 HE	2 IB
Norwich	4 IB	
Old Buckenham	1 IB	
Ormesby St Michael	2 IB	
Langham	3 IB	
South Pickenham	2 HE	3 IB
South Walsham	1 IB	
Southacre	1 HE	
Tattersett	3 HE	
Thorpe Market	1 HE	2 IB

2 November 1940

Hickling	7 HE
Lessingham	4 HE
West Caister	2 HE

5 November 1940

Great Yarmouth	1 HE
Sheringham	2 HE
South Lynn	MG
Swanton Morley	10 HE
West Beckham	6 HE
Weston Longville	2 HE

6 November 1940

Docking	2 HE

7 November 1940

Aylsham	18 HE
Cromer	2 HE
Potter Heigham	5 IB
Scottow	3 HE

8 November 1940

Buxton Lamas	4 HE
Marham	20 HE
Wymondham	19 HE

9 November 1940

Bacton	2 HE	
Buxton Lamas	10 HE	
Freethorpe	1 HE	
Frettenham	8 HE	
King's Lynn	2 HE	MG
Pentney	1 HE	

Tharston	2 HE	1 Oil

10 November 1940

Cranworth	1 HE
Great Yarmouth	1 HE
Hainford	1 HE
Thorpe	12 IB
Yaxham	4 HE

11 November 1940

Fransham	8 HE
Hilborough	8 HE
Norwich	26 HE
Rocklands	5 HE

13 November 1940

Garboldisham	20 HE

14 November 1940

Ashill	7 IB
Attleborough	2 HE
Carbrooke	2 IB
Swaffham	1 IB
Watton	4 IB

15 November 1940

Garveston	1 HE

16 November 1940

Docking	10 HE
Hockwold	7 HE
Stow Bedon	2 PM

17 November 1940

Brancaster	10 HE	
Cromer	5 HE	IB
Gillingham	1 IB	
South Walsham	1 HE	
Titchwell	5 HE	
Trunch	4 HE	

18 November 1940

Ashwellthorpe	1 HE
Broome	1 HE
Cantley	1 IB
Chedgrave	4 IB
Deopham	5 HE
Wymondham	2 HE

19 November 1940

Downham Market	3 HE	
Filby	4 HE	
Ingham	7 HE	10 IB
King's Lynn	19 HE	
New Buckenham	2 PM	
Nordelph	2 PM	
Stalham	8 HE	
Stow Bardolph	2 HE	
Wiggenhall		
St Mary Magdalen	9 HE	
Wimbotsham	8 HE	
Wymondham	1 HE	

20 November 1940

Flitcham	3 HE	
Hilgay	5 HE	
King's Lynn	8 HE	
Necton	43 IB	
Sandringham	1 HE	
Southery	2 HE	
Sporle	9 HE	2 PM

21 November 1940

Downham Market	5 HE
Downham West	11 HE
Great Dunham	2 PM
Great Yarmouth	12 HE
Shipdam	2 PM
Stow Bardolph	2 HE

26 November 1940
Ashmanhaugh	1 HE	
Norwich	26 HE	

27 November 1940
Thurning	20 HE

28 November 1940
Middleton	1 Oil.

29 November 1940
Trimingham	3 IB

2 December 1940
Bressingham	1 HE
Norwich	19 HE

4 December 1940
Southrepps	2 HE	50 IB

6 December 1940
Northrepps	2 HE

7 December 1940
Great Yarmouth	4 HE

8 December 1940
Rougham	30 IB

11 December 1940
Catfield	18 IB
Field Dalling	3 IB
Kelling	1 IB
Mautby	5 IB
Norwich	4 HE
Salhouse	5 IB
Tattersett	5 HE
West Caister	4 IB
Wymondham	5 HE

12 December 1940
Acle	4 HE
Docking	8 IB
Gt. Massingham	5 HE
Ringstead	1 IB
Scole	7 HE
Sculthorpe	7 HE

16 December 1940
Cromer	3 IB
Great Yarmouth	1 HE
Leziate	5 HE
Norwich	4 HE

17 December 1940
Gresham	3 IB

19 December 1940
Bixley	1 HE	41 IB
Reedham	1 HE	

20 December 1940
Beeston with Bittering	1 HE	1 PM

21 December 1940
Costessey	4 PM
Holkham	3 IB
Kempston	1 PM
King's Lynn	5 IB
North Runcton	5 IB
Norwich	2 HE
Upton with Fishley	2 HE
Wissington (Northwold)	2 PM

23 December 1940
Dereham	2 HE
Runton	2 HE
Sandringham	9 IB
Sheringham	2 HE

30 December 1940
Attleborough	6 HE	IB
Diss	1 IB	
Eccles (nr Norwich)	2 HE	

4 January 1941
Bawburgh	5 IB
Easton	2 IB
Elsing	4 IB
Lyng	7 IB
Watton	2 HE 1 Oil.

5 January 1941
Norwich	16 HE

6 January 1941
Bircham	15 HE
Docking	10 HE
Swaffham	10 HE
Wymondham	MG

7 January 1941
Feltwell	8 HE

9 January 1941
Great Yarmouth	14 HE

10 January 1941
Leziate	6 HE

15 January 1941
Roughton	9 HE
Walcott	2 HE
Westwick	2 HE

16 January 1941
Feltwell	11 HE	
Grimston	MG	
Hockwold	1 HE	50 IB
Marham	10 HE	
Thetford	2 HE	
Trowse	3 HE	

18 January 1941
Feltwell	13 HE	50 IB
Gt. Massingham	20 HE	
Hockwold	MG	
Watton	6 HE	

20 January 1941
Sandringham	2 HE

21 January 1941
Feltwell	9 HE
Heacham	2 HE
Swaffham	10 HE
Trunch	3 HE

22 January 1941
Mautby	8 HE
Shotesham	4 HE

23 January 1941
Burgh St Peter	1 HE
Great Yarmouth	4 HE
Halvergate	10 HE
West Caister	10 HE

25 January 1941
Great Yarmouth	10 HE (2 HE also fell at the Harbour's Mouth)

30 January 1941
Harleston	MG
Kenninghall	MG

31 January 1941
Marham	10 HE

1 February 1941
Attleborough	2 HE
Baconsthorpe	9 HE
Carlton Rode	MG
Great Yarmouth	24 HE
Hanworth	MG
Hunstanton	MG
Shropham	2 HE
Snetterton	2 HE
Wretham	2 HE

2 February 1941
Wymondham	10 HE

3 February 1941
Feltwell	9 HE
Harleston	MG
Southery	1 HE
Wretham	15 HE

4 February 1941
Boughton	6 HE	
Dereham	7 IB	
Feltwell	6 HE	IB
Filby	2 IB	
Norwich	21 HE	
Sheringham	10 IB	
Sporle	17 IB	
Tivetshall St Margaret	2 HE	

5 February 1941
Blakeney	2 IB
Great Yarmouth	10 HE
Horsey	3 HE
West Caister	6 HE

9 February 1941
Blakeney	2 IB
Gt. Massingham	1 HE
Mundford	36 IB
Oxborough	1 HE
South Creake	1 HE

10 February 1941
Aylsham	12 HE	20 IB
Paston	2 HE	
Weeting	6 HE	12 IB
Wroxham	4 HE	

11 February 1941
Field Dalling	100 IB
Langham	100 IB
North Walsham	2 HE

13 February 1941
Colkirk	20 HE	15 IB
Great Yarmouth	8 HE	MG
Kettlestone	3 HE	
Kimberley	3 HE	
Little Snoring	2 HE	12 IB
North Elmham	115 IB	
West Winch	60 IB	
Wighton	5 HE	

14 February 1941
Bacton	2 HE		
Bawdeswell	5 HE		
Beeston St Andrew	1 HE		
Bircham	20 HE		
Blakeney	2 HE		
Catton	4 HE		
Cockley Cley	24 HE	50 IB	
Crostwick	20 IB		
Dereham	2 HE		
Fleggburgh	7 HE	59 IB	1 Oil
Frettenham	2 HE	1 Oil	
Great Yarmouth	4 HE		
Hemsby	6 HE		
Hunstanton	4 HE		
Kettlestone	5 HE	14 IB	1 Oil

King's Lynn	4 HE	
Morston	7 IB	
Nordelph	25 IB	
North Tuddenham	2 HE	
Terrington St Clement	47 HE	150 IB 1 Oil
South Pickenham	12 HE	

15 February 1941

Crostwick	1 Oil
Feltwell	11 HE

16 February 1941

Barton Bendish	1 HE	
Bircham	8 HE	30 IB
Bressingham	1 HE	
Burnham Market	1 HE	
Cawston	10 HE	
Cockley Cley	6 HE	
East Winch	MG	
Great Yarmouth & Gorleston	33 HE	
Hemsby	4 HE	
Hilborough	3 HE	
Horsey	3 HE	
Hunstanton	10 HE	
Marsham	1 HE	
North Lopham	32 IB	
Palling	2 HE	
Pulham St Mary	4 HE	
Raynham	15 HE	
Salthouse	4 HE	
South Pickenham	5 HE	
Weybourne	3 HE	
Worstead	14 HE	
Wretton	1 HE	

18 February 1941

Cobholm Marshes	100 IB	
Cockley Cley	7 HE	
Corpusty	1 HE	
Dereham	3 HE	
Dickleburgh	2 IB	
Ellingham	2 HE	
Fleggburgh	13 HE	
Great Yarmouth	28 HE	10 IB
Haddiscoe	8 HE	
Hockham	5 HE	
Houghton	2 HE	
Kettlestone	3 HE	
Mautby	3 HE	
North Tuddenham	6 HE	
Norwich	1 HE	
Pulham St Mary	4 HE	
Raynham	1 HE	
Salthouse	5 HE	
Scarning	2 HE	
Scole	5 HE	
Sheringham	2 HE	
South Pickenham	1 HE	
Stiffkey	2 HE	
Sustead	MG	
Swanton Morley	3 HE	
Terrington St Clement	9 HE	
Toft Monks	2HE	
Weston Longville	16 HE	
Wretham	3 HE	

20 February 1941

Fulmodeston	3 HE
Weston Longville	MG

21 February 1941

Briningham	MG
Gunthorpe	MG
Hainford	MG
Horstead with Stanninghall	MG
Lt. Witchingham	MG
Palling	MG
Reepham	MG

Sutton	MG
Wroxham	MG

24 February 1941

Kenninghall	1 HE	
Methwold	5 HE	2 Oil. 36 IB
Oxborough	3 IB	

25 February 1941

Bixley	5 HE	
Cockley Cley	6 HE	
Cringleford	4 HE	
Crostwick	16 HE	
Emneth	8 HE	20 IB
Felthorpe	1 HE	
Hellesdon	1 HE	
Kirby Bedon	5 HE	
Mattishall	20 HE	30 IB
Morningthorpe	1 HE	
Mulbarton	12 HE	25 IB
Reepham	5 HE	20 IB
Stoke Holy Cross	1 HE	
South Pickenham	16 HE	72 IB
Swainsthorpe	1 HE	
Themelthorpe	8 HE	
Wymondham	4 HE	

26 February 1941

Beechamwell	5 HE
Bircham	8 IB
Docking	8 HE
East Rudham	7 HE
Hemsby	3 HE
Hevingham	8 HE
Horstead with Stanninghall	2 HE
Marham	1 HE
Rackheath	6 HE
Reepham	3 HE
Syderstone	14 HE

27 February 1941

Bressingham	MG	
East Rudham	18 IB	
Great Yarmouth	17 HE	MG
Hoveton	MG	
Ludham	MG	
Martham	MG	
Norwich	3 HE	
Seething	2 HE	
Shelfanger	2 HE	
Sprowston	4 HE	
South Lopham	MG	
Swanton Morley	20 HE	
Tattersett	9 HE	
Wheatacre	8 HE	
Winfarthing	6 HE	

28 February 1941

Crostwick	10 HE
Frettenham	3 HE
Hainford	2 HE

1 March 1941

Beeston St Andrew	50 IB	
Blakeney	15 HE	
Blickling	7 HE	
East Beckham	3 HE	
Feltwell	1 HE	
Great Yarmouth	2 HE	
Hemsby	7 HE	
Itteringham	8 HE	8 IB
Reedham	4 HE	
Scoulton	3 HE	
Sedgeford	1 HE	
Sheringham	36 IB	
Swaffham	13 HE	33 IB
Thetford	1 HE	
West Caister	2 HE	
Winterton	20 HE	100 IB

2 March 1941

Hockham	9 HE

3 March 1941

Anmer	6 HE	36 IB
Bodham	7 HE	
Dunton	1 HE	
Feltwell	60 IB	
Hockwold	17 HE	
Kelling	7 HE	30 IB
Langham	12 HE	
Litcham	17 HE	30 IB
Morston	7 HE	
Great Yarmouth	30 IB	
Ormesby St Margaret with Scratby	16 HE	20 IB
Raynham	11 HE	20 IB
Winterton	20 IB	

4 March 1941

Great Yarmouth	2 HE	30 IB
Kettlestone	5 HE	

5 March 1941

Palling	2 HE

6 March 1941

Baconsthorpe	MG
Catfield	MG
Catton	5 HE
Edgefield	MG
Feltwell	21 HE
Great Yarmouth	11 HE MG
Halvergate	1 HE
Hempstead	MG
Horsford	3 HE
North Walsham	MG
Oulton	8 HE
Plumstead	MG
Reepham	MG
Sheringham	4 HE
West Beckham	MG
Weybourne	MG

7 March 1941

Feltwell	22 HE
Freethorpe	MG
Great Yarmouth	12 HE (all landed in sea off Britannia Pier)
Halvergate	MG
Hickling	2 HE
Norton Subcourse	MG
Raveningham	MG
Reedham	MG
South Runcton	3 HE
West Caister	6 HE
Winterton	4 HE

8 March 1941

Bircham	10 HE
Blofield	10 IB
East Walton	1 HE
Gooderstone	2 HE
Great Yarmouth	4 HE (4 more landed in the sea off Britannia Pier)
Mattishall	2 HE 28 IB

9 March 1941

Martham	2 HE
Sheringham	2 HE

11 March 1941

Blakeney	18 IB
Burnham Thorpe	6 IB
Cley-next-the-Sea	22 IB
Docking	200 IB
Heacham	2 HE
Kelling	2 HE
Salthouse	18 IB

12 March 1941

Great & Little	
Plumstead	MG
Scottow	20 IB
Skeyton	13 IB
Walsoken	5 IB

13 March 1941

King's Lynn	9 HE
Marham	6 HE
Wood Norton	3 HE

14 March 1941

Norwich	30 IB
Oulton	8 HE
Rackheath	25 IB
South Runcton	2 PM

15 March 1941

Great Yarmouth	4 HE 30 IB

16 March 1941

Cley-next-the-Sea	MG

18 March 1941

Great Yarmouth	8 HE
South Pickenham	8 HE

21 March 1941

Guestwick	2 HE
Stoke Holy Cross	10 HE

24 March 1941

Honingham	4 IB
Weston Longville	4 HE

25 March 1941

Great Yarmouth	2 HE

26 March 1941

Great Yarmouth	6 HE (8 more HE landed in sea off Harbour's Mouth)

27 March 1941

Hunstanton	MG

29 March 1941

Aylsham	MG
Brundall	MG
Burlingham	MG
Catfield	MG
Great Yarmouth	8 HE (landed in sea off North End of town)
	MG
North Walsham	MG
St Faiths	MG
Sprowston	MG

30 March 1941

Caistor St Edmund	4 HE
Norwich	3 HE

31 March 1941

Bergh Apton	1 IB
Fleggburgh	2 IB
Halvergate	4 HE
Happisburgh	3 HE
Hemsby	2 HE
Hevingham	1 HE
Horsey	30 HE IB
Langham	3 HE
Lessingham	5 HE
Marsham	1 HE
Mautby	3 HE
Northwold	5 HE
Norwich	2 HE
Old Buckenham	3 HE
Potter Heigham	2 PM

Spixworth	1 HE
Stow Bardolph	2 HE
West Caister	3 HE
Winterton	1000 IB
Woodbastwick	3 IB

1 April 1941

Gorleston	2 HE (landed in sea)

2 April 1941

Norwich	2 HE

3 April 1941

Gillingham	7 HE

4 April 1941

Burlingham	1 HE 200 IB
Freethorpe	1 HE
Great Yarmouth	2 HE (landed in sea off Harbour's Mouth) 500 IB
Halvergate	2 HE 2000 IB
Marham	10 HE
Mautby	387 IB
Langley with Hardley	6 HE 100 IB
Stokesby with Herringby	1 HE
Strumpshaw	2 HE 200 IB
West Caister	2 HE 50 IB

5 April 1941

Loddon	8 HE
Wretham	11 HE

7 April 1941

Hemsby	500 IB
Ketteringham	1 HE
Martham	1 HE
Runton	2000 IB
Shropham	1 HE
Tibenham	1 HE

8 April 1941

Great Yarmouth & Gorleston	8 HE 4000 IB 4 PM
Mattishall	16 IB
Norwich	6 IB
St Faiths	6 HE
Swanton Morley	14 IB

9 April 1941

East Tuddenham	1 HE
Great Yarmouth	10 HE
Halvergate	3 HE 100 IB
Hockering	1 IB
Honingham	5 HE
Weston Longville	2 HE

10 April 1941

East Ruston	9 IB
Great Yarmouth & Gorleston	18 HE
Haddiscoe	3 HE
Mautby	13 HE
North Walsham	12 IB
Raynham	7 HE IB
Sheringham	8 HE
Shipdam	4 HE
Trunch	30 IB

11 April 1941

Blo Norton	1 HE
Burlingham	2 HE
Cromer	4 HE
Field Dalling	7 HE
Garboldisham	4 HE
Great Yarmouth	4 HE
Langham	7 HE 500 IB

16 April 1941

Great Yarmouth	10 HE 50 IB 2 PM
Halvergate	1 PM
Holme next the Sea	2 HE
Itteringham	4 HE
Ludham	1 HE
Newton Flotman	1 HE
Ormesby St Margaret with Scratby	2 HE
Thorpe	8 HE
West Caister	400 IB
Weston Longville	56 IB
Woodbastwick	3 HE

17 April 1941

Gorleston	8 HE
Langham	60 HE
Sedgeford	8 HE 10 IB

18 April 1941

Great Yarmouth	8 HE
Hemsby	36 IB
Ormesby St Margaret with Scratby	2 HE

21 April 1941

Ashby St Mary	8 HE 200 IB
Halvergate	100s IB
Hellington	2 HE
Holverstone	7 HE
Langham	4 HE
North Elmham	14 HE 14 IB
Pulham St Mary	1 HE
Reedham	4 IB
Ringstead	5 HE 1 IB
Tharston	100 IB

23 April 1941

Great Yarmouth & Gorleston	20 HE
Langham	5 HE
Morston	3 HE

24 April 1941

Gateley	4 HE
Great Yarmouth	4 HE

25 April 1941

Cockley Cley	10 HE
Gt. Massingham	8 HE

26 April 1941

Beighton	10 HE
Blofield	4 HE
Cantley	2 HE
Cockley Cley	4 HE
East Winch	1 HE 6 IB
Haddiscoe	11 HE
Halvergate	8 HE 200 IB
Horning	5 HE
Horstead with Stanninghall	8 HE 14 IB
Marham	13 HE IB
South Pickenham	4 HE
Woodbastwick	10 HE

27 April 1941

Ashby with Oby	1 HE
Bergh Apton	1 HE
Hempstead	12 IB
Holme next the Sea	2 HE
Melton Constable	20 IB
Old Hunstanton	2 IB
Stoke Holy Cross	1 HE
West Beckham	8 HE 30 IB

28 April 1941

Great Yarmouth	5 HE

29 April 1941

Banham	3 HE

Gorleston	3 HE	
Great Melton	17 HE	
Norwich	16 HE	130 approx.

2 May 1941

Broome	8 HE	
Ditchingham	6 HE	
Flitcham	5 HE	6 IB
Hillington	3 HE	IB
Rollesby	4 HE	

3 May 1941

Booton	8 HE	
Dereham	7 IB	
Eccles (nr Norwich)	2 HE	
Garveston	3 IB	
Great Yarmouth	8 HE	
Halvergate	8 HE	
Hoe	2 IB	
Mattishall	5 IB	
Stiffkey	5 HE	
Wighton	10 HE	50 IB
Wretham	6 IB	

4 May 1941

Buxton Lamas	8 HE	
Hickling	3 HE	
West Lynn	IBs	
Mattishall	4 IB	
Salthouse	2 HE	
Scottow	2 HE	

5 May 1941

Beeston St Andrew	5 HE	12 IB
Gorleston	1 HE	
Great Massingham	6 HE	
Great Yarmouth	6 HE	
Methwold	3 HE	
Raynham	8 HE	
Scottow	3 HE	
Thetford	8 HE	
Weasenham All Saints	4 HE	

6 May 1941

Bircham	4 H	13 IB
Brandeston	2 HE	
Happisburgh	4 HE	
King's Lynn	8 HE	100 IB approx
Norwich	4 HE	30 IB approx
North Runcton	72 IB	

7 May 1941

Barsham	5 HE	
Great Massingham	2 HE	IB
Norwich	22 HE	
Thornage	2 HE	8 IB
West Caister	20 HE	

8 May 1941

Antingham	2 HE	
Fakenham	9 HE	
Gissing	4 Oil	
Great Yarmouth	22 HE	
Halvergate	6 HE	
Little Snoring	300 IB	
Ormesby St Margaret with Scratby	2 HE	
Swaffham	4 HE	36 IB
Witton	10 HE	

9 May 1941

Great Yarmouth	18 HE	
Ormesby St Margaret with Scratby	4 HE	
Raynham	10 HE	IB
Rockland St Mary	4 HE	
Watton	8 HE	
Weasenham All Saints	1 HE	

10 May 1941

Norwich	4 HE	
Swaffham	10 HE	50 IB
Tunstead	4 HE	

11 May 1941

Bircham	8 HE	
Burston	2 HE	
Feltwell	10 HE	
Pulham St Mary	3 HE	
Shelfanger	3 HE	
Swanton Morley	5 HE	3 IB

12 May 1941

Acle	2 HE	
Barton Bendish	19 HE	IB
Brinton	3 HE	
East Rudham	6 HE	
East Tuddenham	40 IB	
Erpingham	1 HE	
Fincham	MG	
Fulmodeston	20 IB	
Great Yarmouth	38 HE	
Hilborough	14 HE	
Hindolveston	1 HE	
Hockering	39 IB	
Horning	4 HE	
Hickling	100 IB	
Little Barningham	4 HE	
Marham	31 HE	
Narborough	4 HE	40 IB
North Wootton	1 HE	
Pulham St Mary	2 HE	100 IB
Raynham	11 HE	IB
Reedham	4 HE	
Sandringham	3 HE	
South Creake	1 HE	
Sporle	120 IB	
Stibbard	15 HE	
Terrington St Clement	13 HE	24 IB
Weston Longville	148 IB	
Wickmere	1 HE	

13 May 1941

Brumstead	4 HE	
Dilham	4 HE	
Gorleston	4 HE	
Hunstanton	8 HE	
Martham	1 HE	
Matlaske	200 IB	
Potter Heigham	2 HE	

14 May 1941

Gorleston	1 HE	
Great Yarmouth	7 HE (landed in the sea)	
North Walsham	2 IB	
Norwich	MG	
Sprowston	6 HE	

16 May 1941

Clenchwarton	12 HE	
Docking	7 HE	
Great Yarmouth	4 HE (Landed in sea off South End)	
Harleston	5 HE	100 IB
Holkham	8 HE	4 IB
Palling	40 IB	
Suffield	2 HE	

17 May 1941

Ingham	20 IB	
Lessingham	50 IB	
Norwich	2 HE	
Poringland	1 HE	
Runton	8 HE	
Tattersett	2 HE	
Weasenham St Peter	10 HE	

18 May 1941

Mautby	1 HE	
Thorpe Market	1 HE	

20 May 1941

Carbrooke	4 HE

24 May 1941

Brooke	3 HE
Great Yarmouth	4 HE (4 more HE landed in the sea)
Hainford	MG
Hevingham	MG
Holverstone	1 HE
Weybourne	4 HE

26 May 1941

Barton Turf	3 HE	3 IB
Dickleburgh	1 HE	

29 May 1941

Salthouse	1 HE

5 June 1941

Great Yarmouth	1 HE
Walpole St Andrew	8 HE
West Caister	2 HE
Winterton	8 HE

12 June 1941

Diss	6 HE	
Great Yarmouth	3 HE	MG
King's Lynn	6 HEs	
Snettisham	8 HE	

Royal Engineers Bomb Disposal team after the defusal and removal of a 4,000 pounder that was dropped on Frederick Road, Gorleston during the air raid of 12 June 1941.

13 June 1941

Docking	10 HE
Swaffham	8 HE
Wells- next-the-Sea	3 HE
Wighton	3 HE

14 June 1941

Shropham	5 HE
Warham	3 HE
Wormegay	1 HE

15 June 1941

Gorleston	7 HE

17 June 1941

Great Yarmouth	6 HE
Holkham	7 HE
Holt	2 PM
Lt. Melton	8 HE
Repps with Bastwick	5 HE
Stiffkey	2 PM

18 June 1941

North Tuddenham	7 HE
Wighton	8 HE

19 June 1941

Caister on Sea	8 HE	
West Caister	8 HE	110 IB

20 June 1941

East Tuddenham	4 HE

21 June 1941

Blakeney	50 IB
Cley-next-the-Sea	8 HE
Mattishall	4 HE
Terrington St Clement	5 HE

23 June 1941

Caister on Sea	28 HE 500 IB
Great Yarmouth	200 IB

24 June 1941

Great Yarmouth & Gorleston	42 HE 200 IB
Haddiscoe	17 HE
Honing	6 HE
Mundesley	1 HE
Thurlton	12 HE

25 June 1941

Buxton Lamas	4 HE
Foxley	3 HE

29 June 1941

Dereham	5 HE
Skeyton	5 HE

1 July 1941

Felbrigg	5 IB
Happisburgh	4 IB
Ingham	6 IB
Roughton	1 IB

2 July 1941

Gorleston	8 HE (in sea off Gorleston Pier)

5 July 1941

Cranwich	20 IB
Great Yarmouth & Gorleston	16 HE
Halvergate	4 HE
Wiggenhall St Mary the Virgin	9 HE

7 July 1941

Great Yarmouth	13 HE
Stiffkey	3 HE
Witton	4 HE

8 July 1941

Marham	8 HE

9 July 1941

Brancaster	3 HE	5 IB
Caister on Sea	4 HE	
Choseley	3 HE	
Cockley Cley	3 HE	
Docking	2 HE	10 IB
Great Yarmouth	80 HE 1000 IB Propaganda Leaflets	
Halvergate	1 HE	
Sheringham	8 HE	
Wighton	8 HE	

11 July 1941

East Rudham	9 HE
Great Yarmouth & Gorleston	11 HE
Hemblington	2 HE
Horsey	8 HE

13 July 1941

Hainford	7 HE

One of the propaganda leaflet dropped on Great Yarmouth during the air raid of 9 July 1941

14 July 1941

Great Yarmouth	4 HE

17 July 1941

Bacton	8 HE	
Halvergate	12 HE	
Houghton	9 HE	30 IB
Palling	5 HE	

18 July 1941

Halvergate	4 HE	
South Pickenham	9 HE	30 IB
Wretham	9 HE	

19 July 1941

Wretham	10 HE

21 July 1941

Docking	6 HE	6 IB
Great Yarmouth	4 HE (a further 4 HE landed in the sea)	
Swanton Novers	2 HE	
Tivetshall St Mary	8 HE	
Wendling	7 HE	16 IB

22 July 1941

Reedham	10 HE

23 July 1941

Alby with Thwaite	8 HE
Great Yarmouth	12 HE
Wighton	5 HE

24 July 1941

Brettenham	8 HE
Kelling	8 HE

25 July 1941

Great Yarmouth	4 HE (landed in the sea)
Horstead with Stanninghall	10 HE

26 July 1941

Caister on Sea	8 HE	
Frettenham	4 HE	3 IB
Hillington	2 HE	
Horstead with		

Stanninghall	3 HE
Swaffham	5 HE
Walsoken	2 HE

28 July 1941

Great Yarmouth	8 HE

30 July 1941

Hevingham	12 HE
Norwich	1 HE
Salhouse	1 HE
Weeting	5 HE

31 July 1941

Raynham	3 HE

1 August 1941

Halvergate	6 HE
Mattishall	10 HE

2 August 1941

Honingham	3 HE
Ketteringham	1 HE
Southrepps	4 HE
Swannington	1 HE

3 August 1941

Hemblington	1 HE
Surlingham	1 IB

6 August 1941

Kirby Cane	8 HE
Long Stratton	10 HE

7 August 1941

Great Yarmouth	8 HE (landed in the sea)
Hickling	4 HE
Potter Heigham	6 HE

8 August 1941

Baconsthorpe	7 HE
Great Yarmouth	6 HE (a further 4 HE landed in the sea)
Norwich	8 HE
Wretham	10 HE

9 August 1941

Brettenham	11 HE
Brumstead	4 HE
Caister on Sea	4 HE
Cromer	10 HE

12 August 1941

Burnham Norton	2 HE

13 August 1941

Docking	4 HE
Downham West	3 HE
Somerton	4 HE
Caister on Sea	2 HE

14 August 1941

Gorleston	2 HE (landed in sea)

15 August 1941

Caister on Sea	7 HE
Feltwell	5 HE IB
Great Yarmouth	4 HE (landed in sea north of the Borough)
Happisburgh	8 HE
Swanton Novers	11 IB

16 August 1941

Great Yarmouth	6 HE (landed in sea north of the Borough)
Scottow	1 HE
Sloley	9 HE
Stiffkey	6 HE

17 August 1941
Gorleston   2 HE (landed in sea off
               Gorleston Pier)
Stamford   8 HE
Wretham   6 HE   28 IB

18 August 1941
Wells- next-the-Sea   16 SD.2

19 August 1941
Great Yarmouth   10 HE

20 August 1941
Cockley Cley   4 HE   IB
Felbrigg   80 SD.2
Scottow   4 HE
Worstead   4 HE

21 August 1941
Wood Dalling   8 HE

22 August 1941
Bridgham   5 HE   20 IB
Great Yarmouth   6 HE (landed in the sea
               but sank a ship)
Tilney All Saints   4 HE
Wiggenhall St Mary
   the Virgin   1 HE

24 August 1941
Caister on Sea   2 HE
Terrington St Clement   10 HE

25 August 1941
Skeyton   10 HE   IB

26 August 1941
Hindolveston   3 HE   72 IB

27 August 1941
Wroxham   3 HE   2 IB

28 August 1941
Marham   9 HE   IB
St Faiths   6 HE

29 August 1941
Blakeney   5 IB
Feltwell   13 HE 72 IB

1 September 1941
Shouldham   9 HE

2 September 1941
Caister on Sea   6 HE

3 September 1941
Warham   10 HE

7 September 1941
Downham Market   6 HE   30 IB
Foulsham   50 SD.2
Great Yarmouth   4 HE
Letheringsett   2 HE
Ludham   2 HE

8 September 1941
Aldborough   10 HE
Barton Bendish   12 IB
Beechamwell   7 HE   IB
Brettenham   1 HE
Fring   4 IB

9 September 1941
Foulsham   8 HE

11 September 1941
Ormesby St Margaret
   with Scratby   4 HE

12 September 1941
Choseley   2 HE
Coltishall   5 HE

16 September 1941
Dereham   6 HE
North Tuddenham   4 HE
Sall   6 HE

17 September 1941
Clenchwarton   10 HE

18 September 1941
Barton Turf   2 HE
Brumstead   1 HE

21 September 1941
Great Yarmouth   8 HE   50 IB
Guist   10 HE

22 September 1941
Wramplingham   1 HE
Wymondham   2 HE

25 September 1941
Gorleston   4 HE (landed in the
               sea)
Halvergate   1 HE

30 September 1941
Docking   10 HE   12 IB

2 October 1941
Sedgeford   6 HE   63 IB

3 October 1941
Great Yarmouth   8 HE (landed in the sea
               off the South Denes)
Potter Heigham   8 HE

11 October 1941
Great Yarmouth   4 HE
Shelton   10 HE

13 October 1941
Fring   3 HE
Great Yarmouth   4 HE (landed in the sea
               off the South Denes)
Weybourne   40 SD.2
Witton   7 HE   6 IB

14 October 1941
Walcott   6 HE

16 October 1941
Gorleston   1 HE   1PM
Great Yarmouth   4 HE
Halvergate   2 HE
Happisburgh   5 HE
Hemsby   2 HE
Langham   4 HE
Lessingham   4 HE
Palling   2 HE

18 October 1941
Caister on Sea   6 HE
Great Yarmouth   2 HE

19 October 1941
Great Yarmouth   4 HE

22 October 1941
Northwold   4 HE

25 October 1941
Carleton St Peter   2 HE
Strumpshaw   1 HE

26 October 1941
Hickling   4 HE

30 October 1941
Great Yarmouth   7 HE
Reedham   3 HE

31 October 1941
Great Yarmouth   12 HE (landed in sea
               off the South Denes)

1 November 1941
Great Yarmouth   4 HE (landed in the
               sea)

2 November 1941
Great Yarmouth   12 HE (landed in the
               sea)
Repps with Bastwick   4 HE

6 November 1941
Halvergate   3 HE
Repps with Bastwick   4 HE

7 November 1941
Felbrigg   1 HE

10 November 1941
King's Lynn   4 HE
Northrepps   4 HE

15 November 1941
Wroxham   4 HE

17 November 1941
Great Yarmouth   4 HE (landed in the sea
               off the Harbour's
               Mouth)

18 November 1941
Caister on Sea   3 HE
Great Yarmouth   1 HE

24 November 1941
Winterton   1 HE

18 December 1941
Happisburgh   2 HE

21 December 1941
Honing   8 HE

10 January 1942
Honing   4 HE

19 January 1942
Halvergate   4 HE
Sheringham   2 HE

20 January 1942
Halvergate   1 HE

21 January 1942
Great Yarmouth   2 HE

22 January 1942
Hemsby   4 HE

31 January 1942
Raveningham   4 HE
Sidestrand   2 HE

5 February 1942
Great Yarmouth   4 HE (landed in the
               sea)

6 February 1942
Hoveton   2 HE
Potter Heigham   4 HE
Wroxham   3 HE

7 April 1942
North Wootton   4 HE

8 February 1942
St Faiths   1 HE

18 February 1942
Great Yarmouth   4 HE

19 February 1942
West Bradenham   50 IB

27 February 1942
East Ruston   4 HE

8 March 1942
Brinton   2 PM
Great Yarmouth   2 PM
Kelling   3 HE
Salthouse   4 HE

7 April 1942
Burnham Norton   4 HE
Terrington St Clement 6 HE

'Baedeker Blitz' on Norwich
27/28 April 1942
29/30 April 1942
1 May 1942
9 May 1942   in total - 322 HE
                       approx   1000s IB

*Searching the ruins on Rupert Street after the
'Baedeker Blitz' on Norwich, April 1942*

27 April 1942
Costessey   3 HE   IB
Catton   510 IB

28 April 1942
Gimingham   MG
Hellesdon   5 HE

29 April 1942
Costessey   4 HE
Cringleford   3 HE
Drayton   2 HE
Horsford   16 HE
Sheringham   MG
Spixworth   1 HE
Taverham   1 HE   IB

1 May 1942
Cromer   1 HE
Roughton   2 HE

9 May 1942
Bixley   3 HE
Caistor St Edmund   30 HE 1000s IB 2 PM
Cawston   3 HE
Colney   4 IB
Framingham Earl   4 HE
Haveringland   4 HE
Hanworth   4 HE
Happisburgh   30 IB

Heckingham   1 HE
Hellesdon   3 HE
Hoveton   3 HE
Kirby Bedon   5 HE
Marlingford   4 HE
Poringland   30 HE IB   2PM
Postwick   6 HE
Runhall   4 HE
Salhouse   4 HE
Shotesham   2 HE
Stoke Holy Cross   62 HE 1000s IB
Swainsthorpe   7 HE
Swardeston   1 HE
Thorpe   4 PM
Woodbastwick   1 HE
Wroxham   4 HE

28 May 1942
Caister on Sea   4 HE
Great Yarmouth   4 HE

29 May 1942
Bramerton   2 HE
Cley-next-the-Sea   4 HE
North Walsham   4 HE

30 May 1942
Barton Bendish   20 IB
Beechamwell   150 IB
Caister on Sea   4 HE
Great Yarmouth   7 HE
Guist   2 HE
Marham   130 IB
Mautby   3 HE   1 'G' Mine
Trimingham   4 HE

9 June 1942
Ashwellthorpe   1 HE

10 June 1942
Caister on Sea   4 HE
Great Yarmouth
 & Gorleston   16 HE

*Rescue workers picking over the debris of the
Eagle Hotel, King's Lynn after the worst raid
on the town during the war Friday 12 June
1942. A total of 42 local people and
servicemen were killed. Acting Sergeant
Francis Faulkner of the Royal Artillery was
awarded the George Medal for his devotion
to duty in the rescue efforts during and after
the raid.*

12 June 1942
Bacton   4 HE
King's Lynn   4 HE
Mattishall   MG
Scarning   MG
Sporle   MG
Wiggenhall
 St Mary Magdalen   MG

18 June 1942
Feltwell   5 HE

25 June 1942
Broome   187 IB
Ditchingham   102 IB
Great Yarmouth   8 HE   1500 IB
Sedgeford   243 IB
Terrington St Clement 600 IB
Thwaite St Mary   141 IB
Wiggenhall
 St Mary Magdalen   266 IB

*Surveying the damage caused by incendiary
bombs to the ancient St Nicholas Church,
Great Yarmouth during the raid of 25 June
1942.*

27 June 1942
Beighton   12 IB
Costessey   IB
Great & Little
 Plumstead   4 HE   IB
Hellesdon   3 HE   150 IB
Horstead with
 Stanninghall   71 IB
Norwich   33 HE 15-20,000 IBs
                              approx
Sprowston   4 HE
Surlingham   100s IB
Thorpe   1000 IB
Trowse   3 HE
Weston Longville   350 IB
Witton   500 IB

30 June 1942
Aslacton   4 HE
Billingford   2 HE
Crimplesham   12 HE   IB
Fleggburgh   4 HE
King's Lynn   MG   100s IB
North Runcton   60 IB
Overstrand   100s IB
Tilney All Saints   100s IB
Weston Longville   5 HE
West Dereham   4 HE   IB

4 July 1942
Great Yarmouth   1 HE
Halvergate   1 HE

10 July 1942
Hemsby   4 HE

12 July 1942
Great Yarmouth   4 HE

15 July 1942
Wretham   8 HE

22 July 1942
Cromer   4 HE
Mundesley   4 HE
Overstrand   4 HE
Sheringham   360 IB

23 July 1942
Choseley   250 IB
Scottow   100 IB

Clearing up on Church Street, Cromer the morning after the air raid of 22 July 1942.

24 July 1942

Bracon Ash	3 HE
Great Yarmouth	4 HE
King's Lynn	3HE 500 IBs
Ringstead	4 HE 500 IB

27 July 1942

Brockdish	MG
Docking	4 HE
Pulham St Mary	4 HE
Sheringham	4 HE
Southrepps	4 HE
Wretham	IB

28 July 1942

Mileham	12 Phos.
Norwich	1 HE 240 IB

29 July 1942

Great Yarmouth	4 HE

30 July 1942

Brancaster	700 IB
Guist	97 IB
Heydon	54 IB
Rocklands	500 IB
Shropham	2 HE 50 IB
Warham	9 HE 250 IB
Worstead	9 HE 1000 IB

31 July 1942

Sloley	31 July 1942

2 August 1942

Bintree	MG
Melton Constable	4 HE
Norwich	6 HE 3000 IB approx 2000 HE/IB approx
Spixworth	4 HE 240 IB
Sprowston	IB
Trowse	IB

3 August 1942

East Carlton	10 HE 500 IB
Edgefield	MG
Foulsham	MG
Gt. Ryburgh	4 HE
Haddiscoe	4 HE
Hempstead	300 IB
North Wootton	MG

6 August 1942

Gt. Snoring	4 HE

7 August 1942

Feltwell	60 IB
Hockwold	IB
Wacton	360 IB

11 August 1942

Feltwell	4 HE 8 Phos. 115 SD.2

13 August 1942

Gt. & Lt. Plumstead	1000 IB

Kirby Bedon	1000 IB
Norwich	4 HE 270 IB approx
St Faiths	100s IB
Sprowston	100s IB
Thorpe	100s IB

15 August 1942

Caister on Sea	4 HE
Hainford	2 HE

16 August 1942

Tunstead	2 HE IB

18 August 1942

Burnham Overy	2 HE
Felbrigg	150 IB
Fulmodeston	4 HE 1000s IB
Hindolveston	120 IB
Langham	300 IB
Little Snoring	4 HE
Runton	200 IB
Sparham	IBs

22 August 1942

Great Yarmouth	4 HE

23 August 1942

Costessey	360 IB
Marlingford	200 IB
Wells- next-the-Sea	2 HE 250 IB

5 September 1942

Norwich	4 HE

17 September 1942

East Ruston	7 HE/IB
King's Lynn	37 HE/IB
North Runcton	12 HE/IB
South Wootton	2 HE 7 HE/IB
West Bradenham	14 HE IB

30 September 1942

Haddiscoe	4 HE

7 October 1942

Mautby	4 HE

8 October 1942

North Wootton	2 HE

17 October 1942

King's Lynn	4 HE IB

19 October 1942

Attleborough	MG
Cromer	2 HE
Foulsham	MG
Great Yarmouth	4 HE
Norwich	8 HE
Shelton	4 HE
Sheringham	2 HE
Winterton	3 HE
Worstead	MG
Wretham	MG

21 October 1942

Briston	2 HE
Great Yarmouth	4 HE (landed in sea off the North End) 6 IB (Fire Pot Type)
Stody	8 Phos.

5 December 1942

Bacton	MG
Norwich	1HE
Sprowston	4 HE

12 December 1942

Great Yarmouth	2 HE (landed in sea off Britannia Pier)

22 December 1942

Filby	MG
Great Yarmouth	2 HE 10 Phos.

31 December 1942

North Walsham	8 HE

1 January 1943

Catfield	MG
Neatishead	MG
Norwich	10 HE
Salhouse	MG
Sprowston	MG
Sutton	MG
Wroxham	MG

11 January 1943

Caister on Sea	MG
Great Yarmouth	MG
Halvergate	10 HE
Seething	4 HE

5 March 1943

Hardingham	7 HE

6 March 1943

Hempstead	2 HE 1 'G' Mine

9 March 1943

Martham	1 HE

10 March 1943

South Walsham	1 HE

13 March 1943

Sprowston	8 HE/IB

18 March 1943

Bedingham	250 IB
Beetley	5 HE 240IB Phos. 4
Brisley	3 HE IB
Catton	14 HE/IB
Cawston	4 PM
Colkirk	500 IB
Colney	100 IB 1 HE/IB 2PM
Costessey	120 IB
Cringleford	1 HE/IB
East Bradenham	7 HE/IB
Elsing	3 HE 115 SD.2
Great Yarmouth	6 HE 240 IB 4 PM
Hainford	7 HE/IB
Hales	480 IB 7 HE/IB
Halvergate	2 PM
Heckingham	2 PM
Hempnall	1 HE
Hemsby	1 PM
Hethersett	360 IB 4 HE/IB
Hingham	12 Phos.
Kettlestone	2 HE
Kirby Cane	1 PM
Langley with Hardley	3 HE
Loddon	3 HE
Mulbarton	360 IB 4 HE/IB
Norwich	67 HE 8 Phos.
Ormesby St Margaret with Scratby	6 HE IB 5 HE/IB
Ormesby St Michael	240 IB
Oulton	2 PM
Pudding Norton	4 HE/IB
Raveningham	7 HE/IB
Raynham	12 HE/IB
St Faiths	1 HE
Stoke Holy Cross	2 PM
Seething	3 HE 480 IB
Skeyton	400 IB
Tharston	1 HE
Toft Monks	720 IB
Topcroft	IB
Woodton	2 HE 120 IB
Wymondham	16 HE 120 IB 1 Oil.

	1 Phos. 2 PM

28 March 1943

Acle	4 HE/IB
Cantley	240 IB 20 HE/IB 2 PM
Claxton	2 PM
East Ruston	8 HE
Freethorpe	4 HE IB
Gorleston	4 IB (Fire Pot Type)
Haddiscoe	6 HE 360 IB
Halvergate	120 IB
Heckingham	4 HE/IB
Holverstone	4 HE
Kirby Bedon	2 PM
Mundham	240 IB
Norton Subcourse	120 IB 25 HE/IB
Rackheath	IB
Raveningham	30 HE/IB 3PM
Saxlingham	7 HE
Sisland	10 HE/IB
Somerton	2 HE 2 HE/IB
Sprowston	11 HE
Stalham	120 IB
Stokesby with Herringby	11 HE
Strumpshaw	1 PM
Swardeston	36 IB
Thurton	240 IB
Toft Monks	3 HE
Winterton	2 HE IB
Yelverton	11 HE

24 April 1943

Cromer	4 HE/IB 480 IB

5 May 1943

Attlebridge	3 HE
Aylsham	2 PM
Barford	40 HE 2 Phos.
Barnham Broom	16 HE
Bawburgh	10 HE
Colney	120 IB
Coltishall	7 HE
Costessey	2 PM
Croxton	1 PM
East Tuddenham	24 HE 4 HE/IB 2 PM
Easton	9 HE
Gt. Melton	13 HE 300 IB 11 HE/IB
Gt. Walsingham	8 HE
Hellesdon	1 HE 1 HE/IB
Hempstead	2 HE
Honingham	1 HE 2 PM
Horsford	2 PM
Kimberley	19 HE 240 IB 4 PM
Marlingford	IB 6 HE/IB 4 Phos.
Mattishall	2 PM
Mundesley	4 HE/IB 1 PM
Norwich	27 HE 500IB 18 Phos.
Reepham	16 HE 240 IB 5 Phos. 1 PM
Ringland	28 HE
Runhall	16 HE 5 PM
Salthouse	2 HE
Sheringham	8 HE/IB
Shropham	2 PM
Sidestrand	7 HE 2 PM
Southrepps	7 HE
Suffield	4 HE
Swanton Abbot	2 HE
Taverham	2 PM
Themelthorpe	1 PM
Trimingham	IB
Trunch	1 PM
Weybourne	4 HE 4 HE/IB
Wramplingham	19 HE IB
Wymondham	1 HE
Yaxham	1 PM

7 May 1943

Great Yarmouth	8 HE
Hemsby	6 HE
Winterton	6 HE

8 May 1943

Paston	8 HE 1 PM

11 May 1943

Caister on Sea	1 HE MG
Filby	MG
Great Yarmouth	14 HE
Hemsby	1 HE
Mautby	MG
Ormesby St Margaret with Scratby	2 HE
Ormesby St Michael	MG
Winterton	1 HE MG

18 May 1943

Swainsthorpe	2 PM

7 June 1943

Martham	IB

6 July 1943

Horsey	MG
Potter Heigham	MG

7 July 1943

Hickling	MG

14 July 1943

Wretham	2 HE

24 July 1943

Choseley	2 PM

11 August 1943

Caston	115 SD.2
Cranwich	SD.2
Didlington	SD.2
Griston	SD.2
Ickburgh	SD.2
Merton	1 HE 2 HE/IB
Methwold	3 HE
Northwold	92 SD.2
Stow Bedon	SD. 2
Thompson	SD.2

17 August 1943

Wells- next-the-Sea	4 HE 92 SD.2

18 August 1943

Burnham Market	8 HE
East Rudham	7 HE

23 August 1943

Dereham	3 HE
Downham Market	1 HE 115 SD.2
Ellingham	1 HE
Geldeston	23 SD.2
North Tuddenham	2 HE
Raveningham	2 HE 23 SD.2
Scottow	46 SD.2
Shipdam	3 HE 69 SD.2
Westwick	115 SD.2

24 August 1943

Scottow	3 HE
Sheringham	2 HE 69 SD.2

1 September 1943

Halvergate	3 HE

8 September 1943

East Winch	1 HE
Kirstead	1 HE
Palling	1 HE

23 September 1943

Raveningham	3 HE 115 SD.2

28 September 1943

Langley with Hardley	2 HE
Palling	1 HE
Scottow	69 SD.2
Winterton	13 HE

29 September 1943

Freethorpe	12 HE

3 October 1943

Acle	2 HE 138 SD.2

4 October 1943

Dereham	92 SD.2
Happisburgh	2 HE SD.2
Lessingham	115 SD.2
Thetford	3 SD.2

Beware the SD.2 Anti-Personnel 'Butterfly' Bomb!

7 October 1943

Acle	4 HE
Alpington	IB
Ashwellthorpe	1 HE
Belaugh	4 HE 560 IB
Bixley	6 HE
Blofield	620 IB
Broome	2 HE
Burlingham	8 HE 560 IB
Cantley	700 IB 8 Phos.
Carlton Rode	2 HE 2 Phos.
Chedgrave	2 HE 1080 IB 2 Phos.
Claxton	3 HE 1340 IB 4 HE/IB
East Ruston	3 HE 3 Phos.
Ellingham	3 HE
Fleggburgh	420 IB
Halvergate	2 HE 1 Phos.
Heckingham	3 HE
Hellington	280 IB
Holverstone	620 IB
Ketteringham	140 IB
Kirstead	1 HE
Langley with Hardley	24 HE 3060 IB 7 Phos.
Loddon	12 HE
Mundham	23 HE
Norwich	4 HE
Repps with Bastwick	IB
Rockland St Mary	2 HE
Shotesham	140 IB
Stokesby with Herringby	140 IB 1 Phos.
Strumpshaw	8 HE 900 IB 4 Phos.
Surlingham	420 IB

23 October 1943
Gorleston   240 IB
Halvergate   6 HE
Ludham   13 HE   2 HE/IB

24 October 1943
Gillingham   1 HE
Toft Monks   13 HE

6 November 1943
Gillingham   1 HE   420 IB
Heckingham   900 IB
Loddon   1 HE
Norwich   4 HE   500 IB approx
Toft Monks   140 IB

19 February 1944
Haddiscoe   200 IB

14 March 1944
Fransham   280 IB

19 March 1944
Attleborough   640 IB
Gresham   2 HE
Kettlestone   280 IB
Kirstead   1 HE
Weston Longville   1920 IB
Wiveton   1280 IB

21 March 1944
Seething   MG

31 March 1944
Brockdish   2 HE

12 April 1944
Binham   MG
Kirstead   6 HE
Mundesley   MG

19 April 1944
Hempstead   640 IB
Hockwold   5 HE

21 April 1944
Shipdam   34 SD. 10

22 April 1944
Langley with Hardley 2 HE
Loddon   MG
Rackheath   5 HE

27 April 1944
Cranworth   34 SD.10

1 June 1944
Deopham   8 HE
Great Yarmouth   4 HE (landed on fore-
                       shore of the South
                       Denes)
Hethersett   8 HE

13 June 1944
Cley-next-the-Sea   8 HE

28 June 1944
Seething   4 HE

10 July 1944
Ovington   1 Flying Bomb

31 July 1944
Whinburgh   1 Flying Bomb

24 September 1944
Mulbarton   1 Flying Bomb

26 September 1944
Ranworth   1 Rocket

27 September 1944
Beighton   1 Rocket
Horsford   1 Rocket
Kirby Bedon   1 Rocket

29 September 1944
Hemsby   1 Rocket
Horstead with
  Stanninghall   1 Rocket
Whitlingham   1 Rocket

30 September 1944
Halvergate (Tunstall) 1 Rocket

1 October 1944
Bedingham   1 Rocket

3 October 1944
Beeston St Lawrence 1 Rocket
Denton   1 Rocket
Great Witchingham   1 Rocket
Hellesdon   1 Rocket
Hopton   1 Rocket

4 October 1944
Crostwick   1 Rocket
Rockland St Mary   1 Rocket
Spixworth   1 Rocket

5 October 1944
Acle   1 Rocket
Ashmanhaugh   1 Rocket
Little Plumstead   1 Rocket
Surlingham   1 Rocket
Taverham   1 Rocket

6 October 1944
Shotesham All Saints 1 Rocket

9 October 1944
Brooke   1 Rocket
Langley   1 Rocket

10 October 1944
Bramerton   1 Rocket

11 October 1944
Haddiscoe   1 Rocket
Rockland St Mary   1 Rocket

12 October 1944
Ingworth   1 Rocket

13 October 1944
Fransham   1 Flying Bomb
Little Cressingham   1 Flying Bomb

19 October 1944
Thurton   1 Flying Bomb
Thwaite St Mary   1 Flying Bomb

30 October 1944
Hellesdon   1 Rocket

31 October 1944
Gt. Witchingham   1 Rocket

4 November 1944
Stow Bedon   1 Flying Bomb

26 October 1944
Runhall   1 Rocket

10 November 1944
Wymondham   1 Flying Bomb

18 December 1944
Ickburgh   1 Flying Bomb

3 January 1945
Deopham   1 Flying Bomb
Topcroft   1 Flying Bomb
Sutton   1 Flying Bomb

3 March 1945
Raveningham   1 Rocket

4 March 1945
Cringleford   MG
Fulmodeston   34 SD.10 (Fragmenta-
                       tion Bomb)
Hemsby   MG
Lexham   MG
Little Cressingham   2 HE

17 March 1945
Buxton Lamas   34 SD.10
Dereham   MG
Marsham   MG
Newton with
  Castle Acre   MG
Tilney St Lawrence   MG
Tunstead   34 SD.10

20 March 1945
Langham   224 SD.1   17 SD.10
Sustead   MG
Swanton Morley   34 SD.10
Thornage   MG
Wendling   34 SD.10

Appendix 4
The Nominal Roll of Members of Auxiliary Units in the County of Norfolk

Auxiliary Unit Group Commanders and Assistant Commanders

No. 2 Region

(Number two region spread from Yorkshire, Co. Durham, Lincolnshire, Norfolk and Cambridgeshire)

Capt C H Buxton, Norwich
Capt R W Eades, Norwich
Captain Walter G Gentle MC, Brandon (Norfolk and Suffolk Borders Patrol)
Capt J L Hardy DSO MC, Rougham
Capt H W R Mitchell, Kirby Bedon, Norfolk
Capt E J Robinson, King's Lynn
Lieut A G Able, Aylsham
Lieut L. N. Brock, Walsingham
Lieut D C Cary, East Dereham
Lieut Eric G Field, Brandon (Norfolk and Suffolk Borders Patrol – 10 Group)
Lieut P N Neave, North Walsham
Lieut M Newings, King's Lynn
Lieut G F Rutterford, Brancaster
Lieut R R Stanton, Dersingham
Lieut R F St. B. Wayne, East Dereham
Lieut W W Ward, Fritton, Great Yarmouth
Lieut H Wharton, Mautby

Group No. 1 (Norwich)
HQ
Capt. C H Buxton (Group Commander)
Sjt. J. Page

No. 1 Patrol (Earlham Hall)
Sjt C G Haines
Cpl S A Haines
Pte R G Bailey
Pte F Brown
Pte B C Claxton
Pte J G Fish
Pte J E Walker

No. 2 Patrol
Sjt F G Matthews
Cpl H F Lambert
Pte T R Foulger
Pte D P Cozens
Pte R V Creed

No. 3 Patrol (Rackheath)
Sjt R L Wright
Cpl J D Thorne
Pte H P Bowman
Pte E R Higgs
Pte J E Smith
Pte J A Ridgway
Pte F Taylor

Group No. 2 (Kirby Bedon)
HQ
Captain H R W Mitchell (Group Commander)

No. 1 Patrol
Sjt W. Eke
Cpl E A Reeve
Pte A Browne
Pte H J Cracknell
Pte R J Ewles
Pte B J Rix

No. 2 Patrol
Sjt A W Dickerson
Cpl H W Lynes
Pte G R Allen
Pte R B Allen
Pte G A E Newman
Pte J E Sayer

No. 3 Patrol
Sjt F J Brewington
Cpl. S H J Saxton
Pte W H Alderton
Pte W E Symonds
Pte T W Trett

No. 4 Patrol (Fundenhall)
Sjt H E Bothway
Cpl P Myhill
Pte E Dring
Pte J Gamble
Pte L Lawn
Pte J Moore
Pte D G Warman

Group No. 3 (North Walsham & Aylsham)
HQ
Lieut P N Neave (Group Commander)
Lieut A G Able (Assistant Group Commander)
Sjt A. Barritt

No.1 Patrol
Sjt J H Dye
Pte T G Bailey
Pte A J Clark
Pte D J Lee

No. 2 Patrol
Sjt H J West
Cpl W S Seaman
Pte R H Bix
Pte A E Roper
Pte D R Thaxter
Pte L A Youngs

No. 3 Patrol
Sjt A E High
Pte F Andrews
Pte W K Emery
Pte E R Hazelwood

No. 4 Patrol (Baconsthorpe)
Sjt J G Seaman
Cpl H G Smith
Pte D L Dalglish
Pte A A Newstead
Pte J F Rix

No. 5 Patrol
Sjt F Kidman
Cpl F N Tofts
Pte T J Bell
Pte W C Hannant
Pte A W Hicks

No. 6 Patrol (Thorpe Market)
Sjt A Scott
Cpl J P Everett
Pte M Cremer
Pte L A Daniels
Pte G H Wostenholme

Group No.4 (Norwich)
HQ
Capt R W Eades (Group Commander)

No. 1 Patrol
Sjt G M Deane
Cpl H B Sands
Pte A H Dawson
Pte P J Harmer
Pte W W Love
Pte J E Owles

No. 2 Patrol
Sjt B W Cox
Cpl P G Jolly
Pte C W Bush
Pte H Harvey
Pte E A Kirk
Pte S E Storey

No. 3 Patrol (Hoveton)
Sjt J R Howes
Cpl B C Durrant
Pte V B Allen
Pte W S Collinge
Pte J G Nash
Pte C J Colchester

Group No. 5 (Mautby)
HQ
Lieut H Wharton MM (Group Commander)
Sjt G V Bowles

No .1 Patrol
Sjt G H Mixer
Pte J L Chapman
Pte R G Chapman
Pte H F Edwards
Pte R Moore
Pte O G Tovell
Pte H P E Neave

No. 2 Patrol
Sjt G H Wain
Pte E J Nichols
Pte L J Tungate
Pte A J K Wooltorton
Pte S C Locke

No. 3 Patrol
Sjt E J Starkings
Cpl W J Gould
Pte B L Evans
Pte L F Smith
Pte G J Starkings
Pte J W White

Group No. 6 (Brancaster)
HQ
Lieut G F Rutterford (Group Commander)
Sjt F E T Robinson

No. 1 Patrol
Sjt B C Griffin
Cpl H R Payne
Pte W R Dix
Pte W Palmer
Pte J T Payne
Pte D L Raven

No. 2 Patrol (Holkham)
Sjt E H Thompson
Cpl A J Wroth
Pte R J C Green
Pte E A Wroth
Pte L Wroth
Pte W H Wroth

No. 3 Patrol
Sjt G E Bix
Pte W A Havers (Junior)
Pte L Hewitt

Group No. 7 (Dersingham & Sandringham)
HQ
Lieut. R. R. Stanton (Group Commander)
Sjt. J. Young
Sjt W. Newstead

No. 1 Patrol
Sjt G R Carter
J V Betts
W E Claxton
A H C Hazle
D W Jarvis
G R Winner
D V Smith

No. 2 Patrol
Sjt F J Burton
Pte L H Batterbee
Pte F Goff
Pte R R Griggs
Pte W H Riches
Pte C W Todd

No. 3 Patrol
Sjt W G Cunningham
Cpl W C Walden
Pte R E Codman
Pte W H Cross
Pte J Futter
Pte E Parsons
Pte A F Doggett

Group No. 8 (Rougham)
HQ
Captain J L Hardy DSO, MC
  (Group Commander)
Lieut. M. Newnes
  (Assistant Group Commander)

No. 1 Patrol
Sjt H J Haggas
Pte E W Causton
Pte R W Eggleton
Pte G R Grief
Pte R W Pennell
Pte H E Shackcloth
Pte F P Welham

No. 2 Patrol (Narford)
Sjt G F Attwood
Cpl D Sneezum
Pte R R Bennett
Pte R J Mallett
Pte W Welham

No. 3 Patrol
Sjt A G Sykes
Pte T W Bedford
Pte D S Crawford
Pte D G H Neville
Pte A R Wilson

No. 4 Patrol
Sjt T W Garner

Sjt L S C Warren
Pte E V Drew
Pte A Hudson
Pte A E Marsters
Pte J R C W Marsters
Pte C F Robin

No. 5 Patrol
Sjt H C Spreckley
Cpl F W Walker
Pte E W Baker
Pte A E Brown
Pte W J Ely
Pte R P Libbey
Pte E de G Seaman

Group No. 9 (Fritton, Great Yarmouth)
HQ
Lieut. W. W. Ward (Group Commander)
Sjt E. W. Longfield

No 1 Patrol
Sjt R R Leech
Cpl S C Fuller
Pte R J Botwright
Pte D T Colebrook
Pte W J T Dolder
Pte S Porter
Pte B G Rudd

No. 2 Patrol
Sjt G. H. Blyth
Cpl J. C. White
Pte S C Howlett
Pte W H Meadows
Pte H F Watson

No. 3 Patrol
Sjt H M Salmon
Cpl F D H Ellis
Pte F Fletcher
Pte A G Gooch

Group No. 10 (East Dereham & Brandon)
HQ
Captain W G Gentle MC (Group Commander)
Lieut. R F St. B Wayne
  (Assistant Group Commander)
Lieut. D C Carey
  (Assistant Group Commander)
Lieut. E G Field
Sjt C E Holmes

No. 1 Patrol
Sjt H E Parfitt
Cpl M H Thompson
Pte R C Beck
Pte J Goram
Pte F H Ottoway
Pte E W Pratt
Pte B P Walpole

No. 2 Patrol
Sjt B Warnes
Cpl C J Williams
Pte G Brown
Pte R Fuller
Pte H Gates
Pte D F Gilder
Pte E C Huggins

No. 3 Patrol
Sjt P R Field
Cpl S W Baker
Pte R D Budde
Pte A L Drewery
Pte G A Eagle

Pte D Smith
Pte G H Holden

No. 4 Patrol
Sjt F A Crowther
Cpl H W Crocker
Pte G Palfrey
Pte A E Rolph
Pte S W Rolph
Pte H W Smith
Pte R H T Young

No. 5 Patrol
Sjt W T Cooper
Cpl A Maggs
Pte R. Bartlett
Pte J A M Enefer
Pte E A A Hicks
Pte R C Rolph
Pte A E Starling

Group No. 11 (Walsingham)
HQ
Captain E J Robinson
Lieut L N Brock (Group Commander)
Sjt J E Taylor

No. 1 Patrol
Sjt R L Wells
Cpl E W Beckham
Pte G M Frary
Pte E P Geary

No. 2 Patrol (Thursford)
Sjt A Cargill
Cpl B H Flint
Pte A Bailey
Pte C T Colman
Pte E W C Davies
Pte H C Lewis

No. 3 Patrol (Blakeney)
Sjt H Harcourt
Cpl G W Cubitt
Pte J E Betts
Pte A R Holman
Pte E Parsons
Pte P G Harcourt

No. 4 Patrol (Cley)
Sjt J A Barnard
Cpl W R Bishop
Pte W J Fuller
Pte H A W Hart
Pte B P Ramm

No 5 Patrol
Sjt G Savory
Cpl J C Thistleton-Smith
Pte J D Burgis
Pte C Cornwall
Pte A E Newstead

*Please note: There were undoubtedly more
genuine members Auxiliary Units who served in
the county than those who appear on this roll
but this list is compiled exclusively from the 202
Battalions GHQ Reserve Nominal Roll
September 1942 - December 1944 deposited by
the War Office in the National Archives (WO
199/3389) with the addition only of known
locations for the Group Areas or Patrols shown
in brackets.*

Select Bibliography and Sources

Banger, Joan *Norwich at War* (Albion 1982)

Bird, Christopher, *Silent Sentinels* (Lark's Press 1992)

Bowman, Martin *Fields of Little America* (Patrick 1988)

Bowyer, Michael J. F. *Air Raid! The Enemy Offensive Against East Anglia* (Patrick Stephens 1986)

Bowyer, Michael J. F. *Action Stations: Wartime military airfields of East Anglia 1939-1945* (Stephens 1979)

Box, Charles G. *Great Yarmouth Front Line Town* (c1945)

Brettingham, Laurie *Even When the Sparrows are Walking* (Librario 2001)

Brooks, Peter *Coastal Towns at War* (Poppyland 1988)

Brown, R. Douglas *East Anglia 1939* (Dalton 1980)

Brown, R. Douglas *East Anglia 1940* (Dalton 1981)

Brown, R. Douglas *East Anglia 1941* (Dalton 1986)

Brown, R. Douglas *East Anglia 1942* (Dalton 1988)

Brown, R. Douglas *East Anglia 1943* (Dalton 1990)

Brown, R. Douglas *East Anglia 1944* (Dalton 1992)

Brown, R. Douglas *East Anglia 1945* (Dalton 1994)

Carrodus, Charles F. (ed.) *A Norfolk Village in Wartime* (1946)

Collier, Basil *The Battle of the V-Weapons 1944-45* (Elmfield 1964)

Falconer, Jonathan *Bomber Command Handbook 1939-1945* (Sutton 1998)

Fleming, Peter *Invasion 1940* (Hart-Davis 1957)

Freeland, Lt Col I H, DSO *A History of 7th Battalion, The Royal Norfolk Regiment in World War II (July 1940-August 1944)* (Privately Published for the Battalion 1946)

Freeman, Roger A. *Airfields of the Eighth: Then and Now* (After the Battle 2001)

Freeman, Roger A. *The Mighty Eighth* (Arms & Armour 1989)

Grant, Ian & Maddren, Nicholas *The Countryside at War* (Jupiter 1975)

Graves, Charles *The Home Guard of Britain* (Hutchinson 1943)

Hoare, Adrian *Standing Up to Hitler* (Reeve 1997)

Kemp, Lieut-Commander P K, RN, *History of The Royal Norfolk Regiment 1919-1951* (Norwich 1953)

Kent, Peter *Fortifications of East Anglia* (Dalton 1988)

LeGrice, Edward Charles *Norwich, The Ordeal of 1942* (Soman Wherry 1945)

Longmate, Norman, *Island Fortress: The Defence of Britain 1603-1945* (London 1991)

Mottram, R.H. *Assault Upon Norwich* (Soman Wherry 1945)

Osborne, Mike *20th Century Defences in Britain: Norfolk* (Concrete 2008)

Overill, Tony *Crash Boats of Gorleston* (Woodfield 2005)

Ramsey, Winston G. (ed.) *The Blitz Then and Now September 1939 – September 1940* (After the Battle 1987)

Ramsey, Winston G. (ed.) *The Blitz Then and Now September 1940 – May 1941* (After the Battle 1988)

Ramsey, Winston G. (ed.) *The Blitz Then and Now May 1941 – May1945* (After the Battle 1987)=[

Reymond, John *D-Day Fortitude South* (KCC Arts & Libraries 1994)

Richards, Denis *RAF Bomber Command in the Second World War* (Hodder 1994)

Snelling, Joan *A Land Girl's War* (Old Pond 2004)

Storey, Neil *A Norfolk Century* (Sutton 1999)

Storey, Neil *Norfolk at War* (Sutton 1995)

Storey, Neil *The Home Guard* (Shire 2009)

Storey, Neil *The Pride of Norfolk – A History of the Territorials* (Halsgrove 2009)

Storey, Neil *The Royal Norfolk Regiment* (Sutton 1997)

Swain, George *Norwich Under Fire* (Jarrold 1945)

Tillett, Iris *The Cinderella Army* (Tillett 1988)

Tooke, Colin & Scarles, David *Great Yarmouth at War* (Poppyland 1989)

Veriod, Brian S. *A History of the Norwich City Fire Brigade* (Veriod 1986)

Walker, Peter M. *Norfolk Military Airfields* (Walker 1997)

Warwicker, John *Churchill's Underground Army* (Frontline 2008)

Warwicker, John *With Britain in Mortal Danger* (Cerberus 2002)

Way, Chris *Glenn Miller in Britain* (After the Battle 1996))

Wills, Henry *Pillboxes, A Study of UK Defences 1940* (Leo Cooper 1985)

Wilson, Ray *Red Alert – Lynn* (Panda 1985)

Wood, Derek *Attack Warning Red* (Carmichael 1992)

For Remembrance: A DVD to record for perpetuity the Memorials to the Fallen, Rolls of Honour and Those Who Served Their Country from North Walsham & District and The Paston School in The Great War 1914-1918 and The Second World War 1939-1945. Director: Neil Storey (Griffon Area Partnership 2008)

Newspapers & Magazines

ARP Journal for King's Lynn and District

Britannia Magazine

Diss Express

Dereham & Fakenham Times

East Anglian Magazine

Eastern Daily Press

Eastern Evening News

Family Tree

Firefighters Bulletin

Home & Country

Lynn News

Militaria Collector

Norfolk Chronicle

Norfolk Fair

Norwich Mercury

Norwich Warden's Post

Picture Post

The Gresham

The Illustrated

The Land Girl

The Times

Yarmouth Mercury

Documents in The National Archives

WO 166/329

WO 166/464

WO 166/468

WO 166/625

WO 192/67

WO 199/23

WO 199/29

WO 199/85

WO 199/544

WO199/626

WO 199/1779

WO 199/2500

WO199/3389

Websites

http://www.2ndair.org.uk/2admemlib/

http://www.100thbg.com/

http://www.cwgc.org/debt_of_honour.asp

http://www.roll-of-honour.com/

http://www.naval-history.net/xDKWW2-4101-26RNHome.htm

http://www.gorlestonhistory.org.uk/wwii.html

http://www.bbc.co.uk/ww2peopleswar/

The Defence of Britian Project Database

http://ads.ahds.ac.uk/catalogue/collections/blurbs/324.cfm

The Norfolk Section of *Britannia & Castle* online maintained by Major J L Raybould TD http://www.norfolkbc.fsnet.co.uk/index_2.htm

Documents in the Norfolk Record Office

Norfolk Civil Defence War Diary C/ARP 2/1-59